Inside Alpha

Explorations in Evangelism

STUDIES IN EVANGELICAL HISTORY AND THOUGHT

STUDIES IN EVANGELICAL HISTORY AND THOUGHT

Inside Alpha

Explorations in Evangelism

James Heard

Foreword by Andrew Walker

WIPF & STOCK · Eugene, Oregon

Wipf and Stock Publishers
199 W 8th Ave, Suite 3
Eugene, OR 97401

Inside Alpha
Explorations in Evangelism
By Heard, James and Walker, Andrew
Copyright©2009 Paternoster
ISBN 13: 978-1-60899-450-2
Publication date 2/18/2010
Previously published by Paternoster, 2009

This Edition published by Wipf and Stock Publishers
by arrangement with Paternoster

STUDIES IN EVANGELICAL HISTORY AND THOUGHT

Series Preface

The Evangelical movement has been marked by its union of four emphases: on the Bible, on the cross of Christ, on conversion as the entry to the Christian life and on the responsibility of the believer to be active. The present series is designed to publish scholarly studies of any aspect of this movement in Britain or overseas. Its volumes include social analysis as well as exploration of Evangelical ideas. The books in the series consider aspects of the movement shaped by the Evangelical Revival of the eighteenth century, when the impetus to mission began to turn the popular Protestantism of the British Isles and North America into a global phenomenon. The series aims to reap some of the rich harvest of academic research about those who, over the centuries, have believed that they had a gospel to tell to the nations.

Series Editors

Dedicated to Clare

Contents

Foreword

The Alpha Course is undoubtedly the most successful evangelistic tool to come out of the United Kingdom in decades. A process approach to mission with a crisis theology of conversion is an explosive combination; when you throw-in a charismatic firecracker – the controversial Holy Spirit weekend – one can see why this spiritual dynamite has taken the world by storm – the cordite still lingering in the air.

Alpha, however, may be spiritual nitro-glycerin, but it comes in a safety bottle. This may sound like sanitised spirituality for the middle classes, but I don't mean that: I mean that Alpha is a product – in the form of a seminar programme or focus group – and quality control of this product is a key feature of its success. The Revd Nicky Gumbel, now the incumbent vicar at Holy Trinity Brompton, has been the driving force behind Alpha, and his professional presentations and attention to detail are designed to ensure that Alpha is not so much uniform as consistent.

Inevitably given the success and the urbane style of Alpha it has come in for criticisms of many kinds, some of which are beyond the limits of rational discussion. 'Bayith Ministries', for example, an online religious watchdog, thinks that Alpha is imbued with the spirit of Emerson's New Thought Metaphysics passed on through the Faith Movement of Kenneth Hagin *et al*; Hindu mysticism and New Age are also supposedly rampant in the headquarters of Alphadom. By contrast, Stephen Hunt's *Alpha Enterprise* (2004) was a less jaundiced but methodologically limited sociological study. I participated in what was in effect the pilot study, *Anyone For Alpha?* (2001), which I thought tried hard to be balanced and was an honest attempt to make sense of it all. The main study, however, was disappointing: it was sociologically light and less neutral in tone, and, as quantitative studies often do, told us what we already knew – namely that most seekers on Alpha Courses were either lapsed Christians, committed Christians who wanted a shot in the arm, or at the very least had some Christian background. The unchurched, so to speak, those people who have lived their life in the shadow of secularisation, were very few and far between.

In the light of all this, James Heard's monograph is like manna from heaven. It is the first in-depth qualitative sociological account to appear, but it's much more than that: this is a multi-disciplinary study that contains a substantial theological critique in addition to the empathetic ethnography. *Inside Alpha: Explorations in Evangelism*, while it stands on its own, is also recognisable as being in the tradition of scholarship established at the Centre for Theology Religion and Culture at King's College, London, where James Heard studied for his doctorate. The Centre specialises in the application of Christian theology and the social sciences to help us interpret religious phenomena in contemporary society and to have an impact on leadership and training in churches. It is especially pleasing to see James Heard in print with Paternoster which has so extensively and clearly published a substantial number of monographs and collections reflecting the work of CTRC.[1]

The present book benefits from three essential features of Heard's account of Alpha. First, it is an inside account. A former member of Holy Trinity Brompton, then a student at King's and an ordinand at Ridley Hall, Cambridge, James Heard knows Alpha from the inside out. Second, he puts this experience to good use in his chosen sociological method of investigation – participant observation; he was able to adopt the role of helper which he could do in good faith as a committed Christian and as one who was familiar with Alpha. Attaching himself to six Alpha groups over a two-year time period he emerged with an ethnographic study that is well written, deeply textured and reflective. The third, and perhaps the crucial benefit, Heard brings to this study is that he uses a particular theological frame as the hermeneutic, which unpacks for him both the paucity and the abundance of the Alpha approach to mission and Church initiation.

It has to be said that these three benefits of the study can be stood on their head and be seen as cause for legitimate criticism. One could argue that an insider turned outsider (a turncoat some might say) is bound to present a jaundiced view. James Heard is not guilty of this hypothetical accusation, however, and his measured criticisms are without vitriol and sarcasm. Indeed, while the nub of the critique of Heard's ethnography is that Alpha falls between two stools – catechesis and evangelism – he also offers specific examples of ways in which Alpha could be improved. Take the small groups: the group leaders are not always theologically well read and are not sufficiently mature or experienced enough to deal with really awkward questions. Genuine de-churched seekers – those with no Christian background at all – are not in fact free to be as free as they thought they could be in their questioning. For many in this category the small groups are as far as they will go in the Alpha process

---

[1] See, for example, J. H. S. Steven, *Worship in the Spirit: Charismatic Worship in the Church of England* (2002), A. Walker and K. Aune, *On Revival: A Critical Examination* (2003), D. MacLaren, *Mission Implausible: Restoring Credibility to the Church* (2004), P. Ward, *Selling Worship* (2005), R. Warner, *Reinventing English Evangelicalism, 1996–2001: A Theological and Sociological Study* (2007), A. Walker and L. Bretherton, *Remembering our Future: Explorations in Deep Church* (2007).

and they drop out. This is an area where Nicky Gumbel could tighten-up and, alert as he is to weaknesses in the programme, he probably will.

James Heard, with a personal history of Pentecostalism and Charismatic Renewal, has moved further away from his roots and closer to the Anglican *via media* (with a distinctive though faint aroma of Affirming Catholicism). This, of course, colours the study, and raises questions of objectivity and bias, but by the same token it also deepens it. From Heard's perspective of what is known as 'deep church', he and Nicky Gumbel may no longer be on the same dining table together or reading from the same menu, but they are still on speaking terms. In fact, I suspect that James Heard is getting some of his criticisms answered for him already by the vicar of Holy Trinity: some think HTB is a 'one trick pony' – Alpha, Alpha, and then more Alpha – but they will have to take into account that it has also created a truly ecumenical centre of excellence in theology which stands in its own right as St Paul's Theological Centre and as a constituent college of the training centre for London Diocesan ordinands, St Mellitus College. The Archbishop of Canterbury and the Lord Bishop of London have spoken there. Perhaps the invitation could be extended to James Heard. If they should ask him I feel sure that he would be more than happy to sign copies of this outstanding book.

Professor Andrew Walker
King's College, London
June 2009

Acknowledgements

I would like to extend my sincere thanks to all those who have helped me throughout this exacting task. I am indebted to the community at Ridley Hall, whose company in worship, lectures and informal talks both over dinner and during fierce croquet matches, greatly alleviated the inevitable loneliness of doctoral research. I would particularly like to express my gratitude to Christopher Cocksworth and Paul Weston for their invaluable conversation and patient listening.

The success or otherwise of the participant observation represented in this work has always depended upon the degree of hospitality and welcome shown by the churches that I researched, and on the willingness of leaders, helpers and guests to be interviewed. In all of these areas I found them unstinting in the generosity of their help and co-operation.

Special thanks are due to the following: my supervisors Andrew Walker and Luke Bretherton. Andrew, for his gentle yet profound insight and for his guidance throughout the development of this research; Luke, for his careful reading, constructive criticism and encouragement; to my seminar group at King's College London's Centre for Theology, Religion and Culture; and to Brian Moore for his help in the final stages of editing.

I am further sincerely grateful for the financial support received from the Ministry Division of the Church of England, and the London Diocesan Fund, and to All Saints Fulham for allowing me the time and space with which to complete this thesis.

A study of this nature ineluctably involves a degree of struggle, as well as isolation from friends and family. But for the forbearance and support of my wife, Clare, in these periods of frustration – as well as her delight in my small moments of triumph – this work would not have been possible.

James Heard
London
September 2009

Introduction

What Alpha offers, and what is attracting thousands of people, is permission, rare in secular culture, to discuss the big questions – life and death and their meaning (Madeleine Bunting, *The Guardian*).[1]

In the context of haemorrhaging UK church attendance,[2] one course has been championed for being the most effective tool for 'turning back the tide'. That course is Alpha, a ten-week introduction to the basics of Christianity. Churches from across the denominational spectrum have enthusiastically seized upon the course, seeing it as the remedy for declining church attendance. Alpha has experienced exponential growth from merely five courses in 1993 to over 41,000 in 163 countries.[3] In purely numerical terms, Alpha is an outstanding success story. It is a course that has flourished despite, or perhaps because of, secularising forces.

1. Secularisation

Secularisation remains a contested thesis[4] and it is beyond the scope of this work to address adequately all the arguments involved. However, it is worth briefly highlighting the context in which the Alpha course has not only survived but flourished.

The 1960s and 1970s was a time where the 'classic' secularisation thesis, that modernisation entails decline in the public significance of religion,[5] was taken as axiomatic. It is a process which saw a reduction in church attendance, Christian belief, participation in Christian rites, Sunday School attendance and in candidates for the priesthood.[6] In sum, it was a time of the decline of the ecclesiastical institution in terms of its power and influence, and the decline of religious belief in the minds of individuals. However, this trend has been far from straightforward and predictable.[7] The confident pronouncement of the

---

[1] Cited in http://www.alphacourse.org.
[2] Brierley 2000.
[3] *Alpha News*, AI 2009.
[4] See Berger 1967, 1999, 2000, 2001; Brown 1982; Bruce 1996; Casanova 1994; Davie 1994, 1999; Davie, Heelas and Woodhead 2003; MacLaren 2003, 2004; Martin 1969; Stark and Bainbridge 1987; Wilson 1982; Woodhead 2001.
[5] MacLaren 2003.
[6] See Bruce 1996; 2003; Wilson 1982, 2003.
[7] What has been particularly unhelpful in the secularisation debate is in the way that the theory has been positioned in binary terms, as an either/or. That is, either Christian or

'death of God' during the 1960s, with the expectation that religion would soon follow, has been unexpectedly succeeded by resurrection. MacLaren writes:

> Although many of the major indices of religiosity continued to plummet at an alarming rate, in the past two decades it has become clear that there are other things going on besides decline: Europeans have not abandoned Christian beliefs in the way that was predicted; a huge majority of the British still call themselves Christian; across Europe, confidence in the church is rising; in cultural terms we are still a Christian continent; religion is increasingly on the public agenda; and, from some unexpected quarters, new forms of Christianity are rising from the ashes of the burnt-out churches of Europe.[8]

It seems a truism now to state that there is decreasing church attendance.[9] Conversely, Walker describes how the various religious indices indicate that religious belief remains remarkably high, despite a decline in religious attendance.[10] Percy writes: 'It seems that religion persists, but not necessarily in its traditional forms. Faith is mutating rather than disappearing.'[11] Indeed, in contrast to the 'classic' theory of secularisation, following the horrors of the so-called 9/11 and 7/7, and the rise of Islamic fundamentalism, together with other forms of fundamentalism, as well as the appearance of more than 20,000 New Religious Movements,[12] the actual role of religion has become *increasingly* rather than less significant.[13] There is rarely a day when religion does not feature in the media. This trend suggests a revision or refinement of the secularisation thesis rather than its abandonment.

Helen Cameron also points to a transformation of Christianity, rather than a decline, noting the alternative forms of Christian affiliation, such as para-church leisure and small face-to-face groups.[14] Within this context, argues Percy, there is the rise of Pentecostal–Charismatic Christianity, a religion of

---

secular. It is a dichotomy that artificially constrains and distorts our vision (Davie, Heelas and Woodhead 2003:3 and 8). Casanova (2003) argues that it is preferable to abandon entirely monolithic theories of religious decline and to look instead at the specificities of each particular case. Casonova (1994:211) views secularisation as referring to three different and unintegrated ideas: differentiation of the secular spheres from religious institutions and norms, decline of religious belief and practices, and the marginalisation of religion to a private sphere.

[8] MacLaren 2004:iix.

[9] Rather than seeing secularisation as referring to declining church attendance, secularisation can alternatively be viewed as a process of de-institutionalisation, a process that has also affected political parties and trade unions (Davie 1994, 1999; see also Berger 1999).

[10] Walker 1992:50-51; see also MacLaren 2004.

[11] Percy 2001:77.

[12] Beit-Hallahmi and Argyle 1997:130.

[13] See Woodhead 2001.

[14] Cameron 2003; see also Martin 1981:51; Berger 1999.

experience and affect.[15] Alpha is one of these 'new forms of Christianity' that have arisen and flourished in response to secularisation and within the context of the de-institutionalisation of religion in Europe. Nicky Gumbel, the originator of the current Alpha course, starts the course with a satirical quote from *Private Eye* about God leaving the Church of England and of church being boring.[16] Indeed, at the heart of Alpha it is not the institutional Church, but the small face-to-face group, where relationships are built and where there is an emphasis on an affective experiential dimension to the Christian faith.

Charismatic–Evangelicalism in general, and Alpha in particular, stands in a complex relationship to secularisation. Berger observes that religious communities have survived and even flourished to the degree that they have not tried to adapt themselves. He writes: '...religious movements with beliefs and practices dripping with reactionary supernaturalism...have widely succeeded'.[17] With significant stress on present day supernatural theology, Alpha can be viewed as a reaction against secularising forces. The course's success depends upon the extent to which it is able to construct a religious subculture. Such is the purpose of the Alpha small group. It is a means of building an alternative plausibility structure. So, Alpha's Charismatic–Evangelical theology has resisted secularisation. At the same time, it has made use of the processes of modernisation by availing itself of modern business and marketing techniques in a pragmatic attempt to win converts. As such, it has shown itself willing to use modern technology to mobilise revival. Commenting on Charismatics, Walker writes: '...its almost "show-biz" obsession with the big-name charismatic stars, and its reliance on management and commercial techniques, render it guilty of the old sectarian charge of worldliness'.[18] Alpha, with Evangelicalism generally, has in all sorts of ways thus been 'contaminated by the modern world'[19] and has shown itself willing to incorporate processes of modernisation.[20]

---

[15] Percy 2003.

[16] See Alpha introductory talk, 'Christianity: boring, untrue and irrelevant?'

[17] Berger 1999:4. See Percy (2001:54ff) for a positive assessment of forms of accommodation and adaptation to secularisation.

[18] Walker 1992:60.

[19] Taylor 1992:497; see also Martin 1981:44-45; Abraham 1989:Ch.9.

[20] See Ward's (1998) analysis of Alpha as fitting with late capitalism, assessed in Chapter 3, and MacLaren's (2004) description of Alpha as consumerist religion. MacLaren (2004:174-82) outlines the way 'consumer religion' draws upon consumer culture in general. For example, religious institutions produce the 'commodities' that are on offer, while their members consume them. Ward (2005) also describes how religious entrepreneurs and Evangelical businesses are engaged in 'selling worship', the title of his book.

2. Thesis Outline

This book has three aims. First, to compare and contrast the structural dimensions of Alpha, as set out by Alpha International (AI), with what happens 'on the ground'. Rather than relying solely on the official Alpha discourse, my focus was upon what Healy describes as a 'grounded ecclesiology'.[21] My objective has been to compare and contrast the 'proven and tested recipes'[22] of Alpha with my empirical data, which might suggest alternative views on the phenomena. The second objective has been to research conversion on Alpha, which is one of the primary aims of the course.[23] The third aim of this book complements the sociological investigation of Alpha by assessing its theological foundations.

In relation to the first aim, it is essential to provide an outline of the official Alpha discourse. In Chapter 1, the recent history of HTB and the rise of Alpha is related. The course's discipleship roots are noted, including its mutation into a course directed towards non-churchgoers. Chapter 2 is devoted to a description of Alpha *as it sees itself*, outlining the ethos and content of the course. Gumbel represents Alpha as being only part one of a two-year programme. As such, he has attempted to create a programme that combines mission and spiritual formation. The question that arose for my empirical work was to assess whether it adequately does both, or either. In Chapter 2, the attempt has also been made to situate Alpha both contextually and theologically, noting the various influences upon the course itself. In this chapter, I begin to 'draw some lines', highlighting some of the more contentious theological issues, ones that resurface in the empirical data (Chapters 5 and 6). A critique of Alpha's theology has been reserved for Chapter 7.

Chapter 3 is devoted to a review of the literature. What becomes apparent is the dearth of any substantial research on Alpha, with an almost complete lack of ethnographic research. It is a lack that this book will attempt to redress. In the methodology chapter (Chapter 4), the importance of participant observation is emphasised as a way of providing in-depth contextual data. As such, it is a method unrivalled for uncovering the relatively subtle and complex social processes involved in human interaction. The role that I took as a 'marginal insider' placed me in a unique position to research Alpha, giving me access to what Goffman described as 'back region' activities,[24] thus enabling a rich and detailed account of the course and its participants.

My empirical data is found in Chapters 5 and 6. Drawing from the official Alpha discourse set out in Chapter 2, the Alpha course as found in praxis is assessed in Chapter 5. To what extent was the Alpha recipe followed and where

---

[21] Healy 2000:169-85.
[22] Schutz 1962-1966.
[23] See Gumbel 2001g:110.
[24] Goffman 1990.

were the main areas of deviancy? What were the prior religious identities of the Alpha guests, and through what means did they join? What were the factors on the course that invited discerption, and to what extent were guests followed up after Alpha? In Chapter 6, theories in the sociology of conversion are taken into consideration to describe conversion on Alpha, which is the second aim of this book. To discuss this issue, I shall draw upon the work of Lewis Rambo[25] and Duncan MacLaren.[26] Rambo's five conversion types are related to Alpha, as is his process theory of conversion. MacLaren proposes a theory of the social construction of plausibility, and presents a theoretical model of conversion including three interweaving explanations: social–psychological explanations attempt to describe conversion in terms of human need; structural explanations locate the explanation primarily in changing social structures; and cognitive explanations describe it in terms of the perceived logic of the beliefs themselves. These are employed as a theoretical framework in helping to decipher conversion on Alpha.

Further, within the sociology of conversion there has been a fascination with the more 'deviant' or marginal conversions to New Religious Movements (hereafter NRM). Such conversions only account for one per cent of religious believers[27] and consequently this has led to a rather skewed perception of personal religious change. By focusing upon conversion within a mainstream religious group this book helps make a contribution to the sociology of conversion by redressing this imbalance.

Finally, in Chapter 7, some of the salient theological themes are enlarged upon that have arisen throughout this book. It is not sufficient to apply only sociological analysis to decipher Alpha. It is also essential to assess its theological foundations on its own terms.[28] This is given from the fiduciary framework of what has been called 'Deep Church'.[29] This is an ecumenical conversation that draws from the common historical tradition as reflected in, as Walker puts it, 'the scriptures, creeds and councils of the early church, and in the lives of the community of saints'.[30] This book particularly assesses how the Alpha programme fits within the liturgical process of the catechumenate and whether or not it is successful in its stated aims of combining mission and spiritual formation.

---

[25] Rambo 1993.

[26] MacLaren 2003; 2004.

[27] Beit-Hallahmi and Argyle 1997:8.

[28] On the dialectical relationship between sociology and theology, see Martin 1997. See also Healy 2000.

[29] Deep Church is a phrase coined by C. S. Lewis in *The Church Times* in 1952. The other term that Lewis used to describe this outlook was 'mere Christianity', a phrase commandeered from the Puritan divine Richard Baxter. See http://deepchurch.org.uk.

[30] Cited in Stackhouse 2004:xiii; see also Walker and Bretherton 2007.

3. Personal Identity

Before proceeding I shall 'declare my hand'. I began this research having worked at Holy Trinity Brompton (HTB) for five years. HTB is a large and prominent Charismatic–Evangelical Anglican church and the home of the Alpha course. My work at HTB was that of publications editor. This also involved managing the production of the Alpha videos. Following this period, I went to theological college between 2003 and 2006, to train for the Anglican priesthood. It was from there that I conducted my research on Alpha. I have subsequently been ordained and so this research spans my time at theological college and parish ministry in South West London. My personal identity is related in greater detail in Chapter 4, where the role that I took in my research as a 'marginal insider' is described. I write, then, neither as an agnostic outsider, nor as a 'subcultural spokesperson' for Alpha, but rather as a critical analyst from within the Christian tradition. Having been raised on revivalist campaigns, such as those of Billy Graham and Luis Palau (and other more exotic preachers), my motivation for conducting this book is a long-standing general interest in the spiritual journeys of people. How exactly is one to understand conversion? What is it to 'be Christian'? How does ambiguity and doubt fit within one's journey of faith? This was of personal interest because when I experienced doubt, my Evangelical tradition told me that it was either the result of sin in my life, or a Satanic attack. While at HTB, I found myself dissatisfied with the stark 'testimonies' that are often championed within the Evangelical tradition, and what I now consider to be a gnostic tendency of stressing a 'spiritual elite' form of Christianity.[31] Being a priest and thus a 'practitioner' of the Christian faith, the importance of this research is in discovering – through an engagement with Alpha – how people might appropriately be initiated into and discipled within the Christian faith in contemporary culture.

Including the pre-course training, Alpha spans approximately three months. I decided that to cover a broad spectrum of courses I would research six of them. I attended these courses in their entirety,[32] apart from holiday absence. In total, this included fifty-two Alpha sessions and fifty-one post course interviews. Thus, the central part of the originality of this research lies in its empirical work. Further, the value of this work is not in its being *extensive*, but in its being extremely *intensive*. It is the first comprehensive qualitative study of social science to evaluate Alpha.[33]

---

[31] See Lee 1986.
[32] However, as reported in Chapter 5, one course ended after five weeks due to lack of guests.
[33] While Hunt (2004) includes some qualitative research, his primary focus has been quantitative (see Chapter 4 for a critique).

Chapter 1

The Genesis of Alpha

1. Holy Trinity Brompton

Before embarking upon a history of the Alpha course, it is appropriate here to take a broader look at Holy Trinity Brompton, the church where it all began.[1]

The church, consecrated on 6 June 1829, is located close to the world-famous Harrod's department store, surrounded by museums and expensive flats and houses, and hidden behind the Roman Catholic Brompton Oratory. Until the 1960s, HTB could be described as a traditional Anglican Church. It had two Sunday services: an eight o'clock communion service and an eleven o'clock 1662 sung matins with a robed choir. However, beneath the surface, there were Holy Spirit 'rumblings'. During an interregnum (1969-70), the curate in charge, Nicholas Rivett-Carnac, held 'secret' monthly meetings where Jean Darnell and Colin Urquhart came to speak on the Holy Spirit. After the interregnum came John Morris (1969-1975). He was followed by Raymond Turvey (1976-1980), who invited Sandy Millar to be the curate, specifically because he wanted Millar to introduce Charismatic Renewal.

Originally from a Scottish Presbyterian background, Millar had previously practised as a barrister in London for ten years. It was during this time that his then fiancée, Annette, took him to the Metropolitan Tabernacle where Pentecostal leader David du Plessis spoke.[2] At the end of the meeting, du Plessis invited people to come to the front to be prayed for to be filled with the Spirit. Millar describes this experience:

> I couldn't wait to get to the front…David encouraged us simply to ask and gave us the promise of Jesus that if we asked we would receive. I was happy to dare to believe that…I didn't start to pray in tongues at that time, but I wasn't worried. I went home to my room…and I simply knelt down on my bed and started trying to tell God how much I loved him. I was overwhelmed by that sense of love and I

---

[1] In this chapter I have given references, where possible, although some of the material I have gleaned through a process rather like osmosis, having worked at HTB for five years (see Chapter 4).

[2] For the significance of du Plessis in Charismatic Renewal in the UK, see Hocken (1997:Ch.8).

started, 'Oh Lord, I really praise you, I really bless you, I really love you.' But I
felt that was inadequate so I started again, 'Lord I really really bless you...' At
that moment I seemed to hear a voice in my head saying, 'What you need is
another language, isn't it?' 'That's exactly what I need' I thought. And I found
myself starting to pray in a language that I didn't know – praying in the Spirit,
praying in tongues. And on and off I have never stopped...and what a blessing it
has been.[3]

In 1976, after training for ordination at Cranmer Hall, Durham, Millar joined
HTB as curate. He held a weekly Bible-study group which provided an
opportunity to 'experiment' with spiritual gifts.

In 1980, John Collins became the next vicar at HTB. Collins had previously
been at St Mark's, Gillingham, one of the first places in the UK to experience
Charismatic Renewal under the influence of du Plessis.[4] In the 1960s, with the
emergence of Charismatic Christianity in Britain, leading Charismatics
included John Collins and David Watson, both of whom would become very
influential at HTB.[5] Collins's two curates at St Mark's were David McInnes
and David Watson. Watson moved to the Round Church, Cambridge, and from
there went in 1965 to St Michael le Belfrey, York. In 1981 he became friends
with John Wimber, the pastor of Anaheim Vineyard Church, who was to exert a
great influence on him. Wimber viewed this meeting as being fore-ordained by
God.[6] Watson's biographers, Saunders and Sansom, note the change in
Watson's view on healing, from his book, *I Believe in Evangelism* (1976),
where he was not really expecting miracles, to *Discipleship* (1981) where he
believed that 'signs and wonders were still available to those who believe'.[7]
Before Watson died,[8] he helped write and present an evangelistic video course
called *Jesus, Then and Now*.[9] This became one of the sources for the current
Alpha course.[10]

---

[3] Millar 2005:36-38.
[4] Buchanan 1998:14. St Mark's came to be regarded by many Anglicans as a model for
the integration of the charismatic and the (Evangelical) Anglican (Hocken 1997:96).
[5] Goodhew 2003. Watson was converted at a meeting in Cambridge in 1954 at which
John Collins preached (Porter 2003:4).
[6] Saunders and Sansom 1992:205.
[7] Saunders and Sansom 1992:209.
[8] Watson died on 18 February 1984, a few weeks before his fifty-first birthday (Porter
2003).
[9] Watson and Jenkins 1983.
[10] Gumbel described how many of Watson's illustrations actually came from John
Collins (cited in Portman 2003).

1.2 John Wimber

It was due to Watson that Wimber became very influential in the UK in the 1980s and early 1990s.[11] His laid-back, relaxed style endeared him to the Church of England. Wimber, a Californian, came from an independent Quaker background. His church had a Pentecostal-style experience in 1981, an event that launched what became known as Wimber's 'signs and wonders' ministry.[12] Wimber and his associated ministry was described as the 'Third Wave' by Peter Wagner, Wimber's teaching colleague at Fuller Theological Seminary.[13] The first wave was the Pentecostal movement at the beginning of the twentieth century, the second being the Charismatic Movement of the 1950s and early 1960s.[14] The 'third wave' modified the language of charismatic experience, moving away from 'baptism in the Spirit' to terms such as 'filled with the Spirit'. Such encounters were seen as steps in spiritual growth rather than being initiatory (see Chapter 2). Further, it was inclusive of those who did not speak in tongues. The filling of the Spirit was seen as something given to equip all Christians, and especially for personal evangelism. This had a pragmatic appeal for charismatics because it held out hope that evangelism and healing would be more effective if 'signs and wonders' accompanied them.[15]

The transition of HTB from a traditional Anglican church, perhaps with mild 'catholic tendencies', to a Charismatic–Evangelical church, was not without its tensions. And it was the combination of Sandy Millar, Nicky Lee, Nicky Gumbel and Ken Costa who pushed HTB towards renewal. The turning point came with Wimber's first visit to HTB in 1982. It was Watson who introduced Wimber to HTB. At the time, Watson had moved to Eaton Row, London, where he could be close to HTB and where he based what had become an international ministry.[16] John Collins asked Watson if he could recommend anyone to speak at HTB. Without hesitation, Watson suggested Wimber.[17]

Wimber arrived at HTB and gave a talk on healing to the home groups. Millar describes how he was shocked when Wimber announced that they were going to '*do* some healing'. Wimber gave a word of knowledge about a lady who was barren and invited her to come forward. It is worth quoting Millar's response:

---

[11] For a theological critique of Wimber and Vineyard, see Percy 1996.

[12] Steven 2002:25.

[13] Steven 2002:26.

[14] Andrew Walker (1983) describes this as the 'gentrification' of Pentecostalism, attracting as it did largely from the middle-classes. For a history of the Charismatic Movement see *Streams of Renewal* (Hocken 1997), *Worship in the Spirit* (Steven 2002:Ch.2), and *Apostolic Networks in Britain* (Kay 2007).

[15] Steven 2002:26-29.

[16] Saunders and Sansom 1992:221.

[17] Millar 2005:41.

Well I can remember still the sense of embarrassment and anxiety that I felt as he said that. First of all there were only about five or, at the most, six married women in the room and I knew, in so far as you can tell, that not one of them was trying to conceive. By which I mean they were all young couples with mortgages and things just getting going in life. But the second reason I was embarrassed was that we who live in a sophisticated church don't talk about these things…While all these things were going on in my mind, Sarah Wright, who was sitting two or three seats away from me, got to her feet and said, 'I think that must be me.'

I think that was the moment when our church began to grow up. Suddenly it became possible for a beautiful woman in a beautiful church in a beautiful setting to say, in front of all her friends, 'All is not well and I would love your help. Please pray for me.'

So she came to the front and John prayed very simply for her. And that model has stayed with us ever since.[18]

Perhaps the great attraction of Wimber to an upper-class conservative British gentleman like Millar, was the way in which Wimber modelled intense religious experience within a disciplined framework.[19] This is in contrast to some of the more outlandish and over-emotional Pentecostal characters, which no doubt would have put someone like Millar off. Wimber's visit had such an impact that the following year twenty-six people from HTB went out for the two-week Vineyard pastors' conference. This resulted in several subsequent visits to these conferences, which were to play a crucial role in the growth and direction of HTB. It is here where Millar, and others at HTB, imbibed the Vineyard values.[20] In the foreword to Millar's book, director of communications Mark Elsdon-Dew, describes how in California, Millar 'saw a new model of worship and ministry under the leadership of John Wimber which excited him like nothing he had seen before and which was to have a powerful impact upon his life'.[21]

1.3 'Church Growth Movement' Principles

Foundational among the Vineyard theology, which HTB absorbed, were intimacy with God and intimacy with one another. For Wimber, steeped in the Church Growth Movement of McGavran and Wagner, it is such values that ultimately lead to numerical church growth, and the founding of new churches, or church-plants. These plants were, 'by their very nature, expansive and agents of the same power that brought them to life'.[22]

---

[18] Millar 2005:42-43. A baby boy was born nine months later.
[19] See Wright 1995:72; Kay 2007:168-69.
[20] During this time, in 1985, Millar changed places with John Collins.
[21] Cited in Millar 2005:16.
[22] Percy 1996:105. HTB started planting churches in the mid-1980s (Lings and Perkins 2002) and hosted a conference on church planting in May 1991 (Steven 2002:30).

HTB's movement towards Charismatic Renewal and its absorption of the Vineyard ethos brought a shift in ecclesiology:[23] HTB gradually changed from being a parish church to a 'network church'.[24] This emphasis reflects the Homogeneous Unit Principle (HUP) of the Church Growth Movement. Using all the available empirical tools – including history, sociology, anthropology and so on – McGavran,[25] among others, conducted research that looked at factors that led to the church's numerical growth. From his observations in India, where the gospel spread across whole people groups, he suggests that the church should self-consciously choose to operate in clearly defined homogenous units. This is how the gospel travels most easily. Convinced that those without an explicit knowledge of Jesus were 'doomed to a Christless eternity',[26] the most important thing for the Church Growth Movement was to lead people to an individual relationship with Christ, even if that required catering to their imperfect predispositions. In a critique of this approach, Farnsley writes:

> Men and women could be led to Christ, but in ways that were most comfortable for them, which is to say, with other people most like themselves. So the homogeneity of churches – by race, class, education and other measures – was portrayed as beneficial towards the end of individual salvation, even if such prejudice was ultimately a necessary evil measured against God's ideal. Better that we be separate now that we might be together one day in God's eternal kingdom.[27]

Further studies by Church Growth advocates found that approximately eighty per cent of church members join a church through existing networks of contacts with church members. In other words, friendship is one of the keys to church growth. This was a significant factor in Alpha's growth, as we shall discover in Chapter 2 and 5. Observing the HUP, numerous reporters have noted the professional 'clientele' of HTB.[28] Jon Ronson describes his experience when he arrived at HTB for an Alpha course: 'Porsches and Aston Martins are parked up, and attractive young people, even some famous names, in casual wear and summer dresses are wandering up a tree-lined drive.'[29] There is a reason why a joke circulated around London churches about HTB in the 1990s: 'Why does it take two people from HTB to change a light bulb? One to make the Martinis and one to call for an electrician!' Apart from the recent arrival of several ex-

---

[23] Church Growth thinkers have a particular 'ecclesiology', which will be assessed in Chapter 7.

[24] See Clarke 1995; Cray 2004.

[25] McGavran 1955; 1970.

[26] McGavran 1970:9.

[27] Farnsley 2004:30.

[28] Gill 2001; Ronson 2000; Appleyard 2001; Atik 2001; Rose 2004.

[29] Ronson 2000.

offenders, HTB is full of London's professional middle and upper-middle classes. This simply reflects the make-up of its clergy, a high percentage of whom are Oxbridge educated. The upper middle class emphasis has a connection with the Stewards' Trust.[30] Set up to link with the Billy Graham crusades, its intentional missional strategy was to evangelise the 'cocktail party set'. These house parties, where leading Alpha figures participated as helpers, also became a major conduit for charismatic teaching.[31] Alpha, then, originated within a precise milieu where a particular strategy operated. Further, its methodological style – including 'supper parties' at HTB[32] and a basic meal on the Alpha course for people to share directly after work – attracted London's professionals.

Along with the HUP, there is another element to Church Growth ecclesiology. Hopewell reports that they advocate a mechanistic approach where the congregation works like a machine as it attempts to do the work of God, which is understood to be the converting of individuals and the numerical enlargement of congregations.[33] Mechanistic approaches operate according to rational principles. With the aims of conversion and church growth, the Church Growth Movement thus sought reliable formulas for gathering large numbers of persons into congregations.[34] As a machine, the congregation, by grasping these 'formulas' and adjusting practices accordingly, will grow. Since the 1980s, the Church Growth perspective has been supplemented by organisational studies. Both have a preoccupation with efficiency, focusing on the internal operations of congregations rather than on their relationship with a wider context.[35]

The technique most relentlessly employed is the annual report, prepared by almost every congregation, portraying the congregation as a machine whose work is detected by quantitative measurements and programme vectors. Data about money, membership and meetings make up most of the report of collective activity in the previous year. Statistics comparing the current year with the previous year are included to reveal the relatively greater efficiency of the parish mechanism. A satisfactory account, by mechanistic standards, reports the hum of increased funds and attendance expanded in programmes that themselves turn like dynamos.[36] As we shall see below, such a perspective would heavily influence both HTB and the expansion and running of Alpha. Stackhouse suggests that the Church Growth Movement principles have only

---

[30] See http://www.stewardstrust.org.uk, accessed 11 May 2007. These contrasted with the earlier and more conservative Iwerne Minster camps, or 'Bash camps', for children from top public schools (see Goodhew 2003).

[31] Interview on 6 July 2007 with a former leader of the Stewards' Trust.

[32] Clarke 1995.

[33] Hopewell 1988.

[34] Hopewell 1988:25; cf. Meadows 2007.

[35] Guest, Tusting and Woodhead 2004:5-6.

[36] Hopewell 1988:26.

been loosely incorporated in the UK, such as strong leadership, lively worship, homogeneity and the mobilising of the laity.[37] These principles became the defining marks of HTB. This encounter with Vineyard led HTB to a period where anything remotely Anglican was discarded. The robed choir went, as did the Anglican liturgy, and services became more informal. HTB included many of the marks of a revivalist movement, going through a Durkheimian 'effervescence' early phase. Mary Douglas describes this stage amongst revivalist movements:

> Emotions run high, formalism of all kinds is denounced, the favoured patterns of religious worship include trance or glossolalia, trembling, shaking or other expressions of incoherence and dissociation. Doctrinal differentiation is deplored. The movement is seen to be universal in potential membership.[38]

1.4 Toronto Blessing

Another source of influence for HTB was the 'Toronto Blessing', a term coined by the British media when the experience of the Toronto Airport Vineyard,[39] led by John Arnott, was brought to Britain by way of Eleanor ('Elli') Mumford.[40] Mark Stibbe (1995) suggested that this represented the 'fourth wave' of the Spirit.[41] Hilborn describes Tuesday 24 May 1994 as the pivotal day for the new movement in Britain.[42] When Elli prayed for everyone to be filled with the Holy Spirit at her husband's home, where Nicky and Pippa Gumbel were present, the characteristic 'Toronto' manifestations[43] took hold and a dramatic session continued uninterrupted through lunchtime. Nicky Gumbel returned to an HTB meeting late from this encounter, and when he closed the meeting in prayer, the same sort of manifestations happened to the HTB staff. When Sandy Millar returned from a meeting at the Evangelical Alliance, he found people still 'resting in the Spirit' past 5pm. Elli Mumford

---

[37] Stackhouse 2004:18.

[38] Douglas 2003:81.

[39] However, on 5 December 1995 Wimber withdrew support for the church because he saw them falling outside the Vineyard model, by which he meant that, according to the Vineyard understanding, manifestations do not need to be encouraged, highlighted, explained, defended or prayed for. Wimber also sensed the use of manipulation and crowd control at the Toronto church (Hilborn 2001:269 and 277-78).

[40] For an analysis of the Toronto Blessing, see Gumbel 1995; Porter and Richter 1995; Hilborn 2001; Scotland 2000; Steven 2002; Warner 2003; Kay 2007:Ch.16.

[41] Stibbe 1995.

[42] Hilborn 2001.

[43] The manifestations associated with the Toronto Blessing included falling to the ground and lying on the floor, shaking, trembling and jerking, laughing, weeping and wailing, apparent drunkenness and intense physical activity such as running on the spot and animal sounds (Steven 2002:33).

preached at HTB on the following Sunday and scenes similar to those earlier in the week took place.[44] Sandy Millar, Jeremy Jennings and Emmy Wilson flew to Toronto on 31 May 1994. A week later, on Sunday 5 June 1994, the 6.30pm service at HTB was completely full with 1,200 or so in attendance and with ministry continuing until after 10pm. In June and July, Millar and Bishop David Pytches organised meetings at HTB for clergy and church leaders keen to experience the 'blessing' in their own churches.[45] As the Blessing spread throughout the UK, parallels were drawn with the revivals of Jonathan Edwards, Charles Finney and John Wesley.[46]

Manifestations of 'drunkenness' experienced at HTB included Jeff Lucas, Vice-President of the Evangelical Alliance and his wife, who were 'intoxicated' to the point of being completely incapacitated and unable to drive home.[47] Richter notes that HTB had to reassure taxi drivers that their fares were 'not drunk as you suppose' and safe to have in their taxi.[48] By September, there were regularly queues of 500 to get into HTB's 6.30pm service. Mark Elsdon-Dew, Director of Communications at HTB, said, 'For years, at the end of services, we've been inviting the Holy Spirit to come – and he has – though not necessarily in a way that would be obvious! What's happening now is new in the sense that you can't miss it!' Elsdon-Dew suggested that the close relationship with Wimber meant that to some extent a way had already been smoothed for the reception of the Blessing, although Elsdon-Dew insisted that what happened at HTB was not to be referred to as the Toronto Blessing but a blessing of the Holy Spirit.[49] After the peak of the Toronto experience at HTB, during the summer and autumn of 1994, things eventually slowed down.[50] However, HTB continued to draw large numbers of people, and required five Sunday services to fit everyone in. And this was despite the 'planting', 'grafting' or 'replanting' of multiple churches throughout London.[51]

Opinion over the Toronto Blessing was mixed. Some felt it was a genuine time of refreshment, or even a new 'revival'.[52] HTB's (1994) newspaper carried the headline 'A Mighty wind from Toronto – The word "revival" is on everyone's lips'. Gumbel defined revival as 'bringing new life' in terms of

---

[44] Hilborn 2001:160.

[45] Steven 2002:33.

[46] Hilborn 2001.

[47] Scotland 2000:237.

[48] Richter 1995:25.

[49] Cited in Hilborn 2001:191 and 271.

[50] Hilborn 2001:216.

[51] See Lings and Perkins 2002.

[52] Previously, Paul Cain, one of the Kansas City Prophets, had prophesied in 1991 that revival would break out starting in London (see Steven 2002:32). When revival did not break out, Wimber suggested that revival came in stages, and that the earliest tokens of it were evident in the form of a deepening emphasis on signs and wonders (Hilborn 2001:141). For a critique of Cain see Wright 1995:115-19.

converts.[53] Others described the 'blessing' as mass hysteria[54] or an essentially cathartic experience, 'something like a cleansing spiritual enema'.[55] Scotland viewed the Toronto Blessing as 'a mixture of the Divine, the human and the psychologically-induced'.[56] Whatever was made of the Toronto Blessing, its effect on UK churches was startling. The estimate for the number of churches affected ranged between 4,000 and 5,500, and the natural question arose: 'Where do we go from here?'[57] Millar saw the next step as something involving a major influence on the world which he believed, though in its early days, was already happening.[58] Was Alpha to be the tool for this worldwide impact?

To bring this account up to date, in the summer of 2005 Sandy Millar handed the reigns of HTB over to Nicky Gumbel, and moved to St Mark's, Tollington Park, North London, where he was licensed as its priest-in-charge. In November 2005, Millar was appointed Assistant Bishop in the Church of Uganda, a role where he would act as a 'missionary bishopric' in the London Diocese using his wide experience as a church planter and growth practitioner.

Having traced some of the key events and influences on HTB, we next turn to Alpha. It is within the context of Charismatic Renewal, John Wimber and the Toronto Blessing, over a twenty year period, that the Alpha course arose and was developed. These influences will become clear in what is set out below, particularly in Chapter 2.

2. The Genesis of Alpha

To trace the beginnings of Alpha we must go back to 1976 when Sandy Millar's fellow curate was Charles Marnham. Marnham was approached by Tricia, an ordinary, churchgoing twenty-six-year-old, who had noticed a number of people with little church background starting to attend HTB. During a breakfast meeting with Marnham, Tricia spoke about her idea of a course, and talked about the content and the name. She said, 'The Book of Revelation says, I am the Alpha and Omega, the beginning and the end, so why don't we call it Alpha?'[59] The course that was subsequently designed was four weeks in length, and was held in Marnham's flat with eleven new Christians.[60] The structure that was created in this group became fundamental for Alpha: a meal, a talk and then a small group discussion. According to Marnham, the aim was to follow up people who had recently become Christians, although from the beginning it

---

[53] Gumbel 1995:81.
[54] See Steven 2002:34; Hilborn 2001.
[55] Percy 2005.
[56] Scotland 2000:249.
[57] Hilborn 2001:224-61.
[58] Cited in Hilborn 2001:226.
[59] Rose 2004.
[60] Gumbel 2001g:24.

began to attract non-Christians.[61]

The next curate, John Irvine, took on Alpha in 1981 and lengthened it to ten weeks. Under the advice of John Collins, Irvine added the weekend away with teaching on the Holy Spirit. Nicky Lee then ran Alpha from 1985 to 1990 and the course grew from 30 to 120 people.[62] Next came Eton and Cambridge-educated Nicky Gumbel. Both of Gumbel's parents were barristers. His father was from a secular Jewish background, and his mother was a nominal Christian. Although as a child Gumbel was baptised and confirmed and regularly went to chapel while at Eton, he considered that 'it had not meant much to me'.[63] He converted while at university in 1974. After university Gumbel moved to London, became a barrister and joined HTB. In 1982 Gumbel had an experience of the Holy Spirit during a meeting at HTB led by Wimber. He explains:

> I arrived late. I'd been in court that day, practising as a barrister, I arrived in my three-piece pinstriped suit, stiff white collar, looking very smart and very pompous!...[Wimber] spoke about healing. And then there were various words of knowledge. And he asked people to stand in response to the words of knowledge. I was still very cynical, but I was amazed! Again, people I knew stood in response to these words of knowledge!

Gumbel eventually asked someone from Wimber's team to pray for him:

> After he'd been praying for about thirty seconds I experienced something I had never experienced before in my life. I experienced, in a physical way – and I know it's not true for everybody, but for me at that moment it was like 10,000 volts of electricity. I experienced the power of God in a way I had never experienced it before. In fact it was so powerful, that after a bit I just couldn't take it any more...So eventually there was this shouting match going on between him and me! By this stage everybody else in the room had stopped praying, and they were just watching what was happening, right in the middle of the room! John Wimber had obviously had a lot of experience in this area, and he'd obviously had difficult people in his meetings before, because he said 'Oh, take that one out!' And literally they carried me out...And as I was being carried out, he said, 'God is giving to that man the ability to tell people about Jesus.'[64]

This seems to have been a definitive experience for Gumbel. In 1986 he finished his theological training at Wycliffe Hall, Oxford, and became curate at HTB. As noted above, in 1990, he took over Alpha from Nicky Lee and revised the course further, attempting to focus on those outside the church.

Upon receiving interest from other churches wanting to run Alpha, Ken

---

[61] Cited in Ireland 2000.
[62] Gumbel 2001g:24.
[63] Gumbel 2001e:67.
[64] Gumbel 2001d.

Costa, Vice Chairman of UBS Warburg, Church Warden of HTB and now Chairman of AI, suggested that HTB should host an Alpha conference. The first Alpha conference took place in 1993 with 1,000 delegates, and over 200 courses started as a result. Conferences became a regular feature of Alpha, with two per year held at HTB, and multiple conferences held throughout the world. 1993 was also the year in which Nicky Gumbel had his book, *Questions of Life* published by Kingsway publications. It soon became a best-seller and is the Alpha syllabus in book form. It has now sold over 750,000 copies and has been translated into 36 languages.[65] No doubt encouraged by the interest shown from other churches, the following year saw the production of the first set of Alpha videos. The first videos included reference to the Toronto Blessing in which Gumbel describes the impact that Elli Mumford had on HTB. Such references were removed when the Alpha talks were refilmed in 1997. Since then, the talks have been regularly refilmed in order to keep the videos up to date. However, there has been no major revision of the course since the beginning of the 1990s.

With Alpha rapidly expanding, HTB lacked the organisational structures to manage the growth. If Ken Costa was one of the entrepreneurial visionaries and financiers behind Alpha, Tricia Neill implemented the vision. Gumbel had head-hunted Neill when she was working at News International Exhibitions.[66] She joined HTB in 1993 as the Executive Director of Alpha. Neill effectively turned Alpha from a course run by a handful of churches into a global franchise. Alpha was 'rolled out' across Britain and throughout the world, with churches authorised to conduct courses using the Alpha name and Alpha's standardised operating methods. Churches were able to buy into the 'success package' from HTB, who then showed them how to use it. Ray Kroc was to McDonalds[67] what Tricia Neill is to Alpha.

Standardisation is essential to a franchisor's success as a method of distribution. Alpha, including the whole training surrounding the course, became a standardised prepackaged product. With this came the support structure expected from a franchisor: country offices and publishers (complete with contracts), regional advisers, websites and multiple resources. This not only revolutionised Alpha, but presented reciprocal demands and influences both on the way HTB functioned and on its very ecclesiology. Neill describes how she 'embarked on the systematic process of applying business principles to the running of HTB'.[68] The background to this was Neill's experience of reporting for work at HTB on her first day to find that no provision had been made for her arrival, despite their having had three months to prepare. She

---

[65] http://alphainternational.org/about, accessed 5 March 2007.
[66] Neill 2006:7-11.
[67] Rizter (1996:30-32) describes the way Kroc became the franchising agent of McDonalds, building it into an empire of franchises.
[68] Neill 2006:16.

writes: 'I had no office, no desk, no phone. I had nothing...Later on I remember thinking, "No other staff member's ever going to have that happen when they arrive so long as I am here".'[69] The staff at HTB soon became a highly motivated, efficient team, complete with job descriptions, line-managers and yearly appraisals. Alpha is now a medium sized business, with meetings producing minutes and decisions, and with church offices equipped with computers, photocopiers, the production of colour magazines and leaflets, and websites. HTB can afford to employ professional staff who have the skills to perform specific tasks: worship leaders, youth workers, conference, finance, publications, web design and fund-raising teams. All this contributes towards arriving at an efficient and professional bureaucratic mind-set. And, as with any business, streamlining came in November 2005 with fourteen redundancies.

One of the difficulties of a franchise is the potential loss of control. After hearing of 'deviant' Alpha courses, HTB introduced a copyright statement in 1997 in which it stated that in order to 'preserve confidence and quality control' substantive variations were not to be permitted.[70] Franchisees, unlike independent business owners, do not have the freedom to change the way that they run their businesses. They must carefully follow the standardised, and pre-tested, 'success' formula. As Freebury notes, similar to the coffee franchise Starbucks, Alpha now offers a diversified product. There is Daytime Alpha, Alpha for youth, Alpha for students, Alpha for prisons, Alpha for 'seniors', Express Alpha (for use in business contexts where time is limited), and so on. As with the Starbucks ethos, the core brand identity is retained (there is no change in the Alpha content) but it is packaged to suit different contexts.[71]

2.1 Nicky Gumbel

To what extent has Gumbel been a factor in the rise of Alpha? He has been the public face and spokesperson of Alpha since it became more widely available. With Costa and Neill, he has been the main driving force behind the course's expansion. Gumbel also embodies many of the characteristics of a Weberian charismatic leader,[72] and part of Alpha's success since he assumed leadership

---

[69] Neill 2006:11.

[70] Millar in Gumbel 2001g:207.

[71] Freebury 2004:43.

[72] At least in Gumbel's public persona, a role that he assumes both as a clergyman and as Alpha's spokesman. He is actually quite shy. Weber (1964:258-59) describes 'charisma' as a certain quality in an individual personality by virtue of which he is set apart from ordinary people and treated as endowed with supernatural, or at least specifically exceptional powers of qualities. These are not accessible to the ordinary person, but are regarded as being of divine origin. Weber made a basic distinction between *pure charisma*, which arises from the leader's behaviour, and *routinised charisma*, which stems from a formal or hereditary position that an individual occupies.

may be due to this. Hopewell describes the singular authority attributed by mechanists to leaders of growing churches.[73] The 'idealised vision'[74] of charismatic leaders lies in the belief that they are particularly attuned to God for world evangelism. As a public speaker, Gumbel builds sufficient prestige through his highly self-confident manner, by appearing an expert on evangelism. At the Alpha conferences and Strategy Days, Gumbel provides a strongly articulated and 'idealised vision': 'the re-evangelisation of this country and the transformation of our society'.[75] Such a vision, passionately argued for, has a head start over a sober presentation, where there is doubt, uncertainty and an acknowledgement of the possibility of error.[76] This is backed up by anecdotal evidence and statistical reports of the growth of Alpha around the world, thereby emphasising the 'high performance outcomes'[77] of the course.

A number of Alpha leaders have been attracted by Gumbel's charisma, as Todd Hunter, the former National Director at Alpha USA, makes clear:

> Nicky is, I believe, an apostle, in almost every sense of the word. I've never actually said that before, and it's kind of scary to do so, but that's what I really believe in my heart. He's a Paul for this generation, as Billy Graham was for the last.[78]

The journalist, Hilary Rose, noticed the extent of Gumbel's influence, describing how team members whom she interviewed mimicked exactly the same phrases as Gumbel in describing Alpha: 'it's all about friends introducing friends. It's really good fun. It's a low-pressure environment'.[79] In sum, part of Alpha's success can be attributed to Gumbel's charismatic leadership since he took over the reigns from Nicky Lee.

2.2 Marketing

Peter Berger wrote that as the public discourse of religion declines, people increasingly struggle to talk about it.[80] As a result religion has suffered a crisis of plausibility. Religious beliefs and practices can no longer be assumed, and

---

See also recent discussions of 'transformational leadership' (Bass and Steidlmeier 1999; Burns 1978; Conger 1999; Tourish and Pinnington 2002; Yukl 1999).

[73] Hopewell 1988:28.

[74] Awamleh and Gardner 1999:346.

[75] Gumbel 2005. HTB has since described their vision on an even greater scale: 'the re-evangelisation of the *world* and the transformation of society' (Neill 2006:16 emphasis added).

[76] Tourish and Pinnington 2002:159.

[77] Awamleh and Gardner 1999:367.

[78] Hunter 2004.

[79] Rose 2004.

[80] Berger 1967:137.

now have to be marketed. Branding has become a way for consumers to place trust in their choices.

Alpha has become well-known for its marketing, although Gumbel prefers to see this as part of evangelism.[81] It has recognised that in a world where high media standards are taken for granted, the gospel must be 'sold' or presented in a professional way. The range of Alpha products available and 'service support' offered is intended to make it an easy-to-follow recipe. The training conferences for church leaders, the training before Alpha starts for team members, the network of Alpha Advisers to provide local support, encouragement and general 'know-how', the videos, DVDs, manuals, books (the list goes on) and the quarterly publication of *Alpha News*[82] give people nationwide a strong sense of being part of a national programme and instils confidence in those wanting to start an evangelistic course for the first time. In 1997, a group of churches in Thanet advertised their Alpha courses in the local press using the caption, 'The Alpha Course – an opportunity to explore the meaning of life. Coming soon to a church near you.' Inspired by this, the following year HTB launched a national Alpha advertising campaign. AI has continued a yearly Alpha initiative since then, with additional stress on training and prayer meetings. The general awareness of Alpha has been traced by Alpha-sponsored MORI polls both before and after each Alpha initiative. The MORI research shows that between 2000 and 2002, awareness of Alpha as a Christian course nearly doubled, increasing from 9 per cent to 17 per cent of the UK population.[83] The most recent research showed that awareness of Alpha as a Christian course had reached 24 per cent.[84] In July 2001 Alpha received high media profile in the national reality television series, 'Alpha: will it change their lives?' This ten week programme, hosted by Sir David Frost, followed the lives of an Alpha small group. Despite the irregular timing of the series, the viewing figures for the programme levelled out at approximately one million.

This is religion coming out from the margins in to the public arena. Alpha has clearly acquired a recognised brand identity. As MacLaren suggests, consumer religion makes people sit up and take notice.[85] The social significance gained by virtue of this engagement at a national level also lends legitimacy to local expressions of Alpha. As Chapter 5 will reveal, although very few guests joined Alpha solely through non-personal (media) means, the national advertising, posters and website had a facilitating function for some guests. Jo

---

[81] Gumbel 2003c. For a critique of consumerism and marketing see Bartholomew and Moritz 2000. Storkey (2000:113) argues that advertising is backed by the institutionalisation of lying: 'Thousands of customers are coming back to BT each week.' But thousands are also leaving, and we hear less about them.

[82] In 2006, due to cutbacks, *Alpha News* production has been reduced to twice a year.

[83] http://alpha.org/runningacourse/tours/initiative/default.htm, accessed 5 March 2005.

[84] *Alpha News*, AI 2008.

[85] MacLaren 2003.

Ellen Grzyb, a psychotherapist, considers why she thinks Alpha has become so popular:

> If you think of how successful Nike has been in hitting the right market, I think Alpha has done the same thing. It's hit the right market in the same way, it's appealed to not a huge broad range of people but to a very targeted market, and its working.[86]

2.3 Funding Alpha

In 2001 Alpha International was established as a separate charity, with its own fund-raising and separate accounts. It is, however, still closely tied to HTB with most of Alpha's staff accommodated in HTB's new office on the Cromwell Road, opposite the Natural History Museum. Alpha is far from a being a self-sustaining business and its continuing solvency is due to the generosity of HTB itself and 'Alpha partners'.[87] In 2006 AI's income from sales, royalties and conferences was just under £1 million. However, in addition to this, it required over £3.8 million from HTB and AI partners to cover its costs.[88]

2.4 Alpha's Growth

The Alpha website[89] describes the course's 'astonishing growth, both in the United Kingdom and internationally' (see chart below). From just five courses running in the UK in 1992, to over 7,150 registered Alpha courses in the UK and 32,592 courses worldwide.[90]

AI's latest figures estimate that over eleven million people have now attended an Alpha course in 156 countries. How is it possible to account for such growth? Is it due to HTB's entrepreneurial skills and financial clout? Or is it because God has especially 'anointed' Alpha as a tool for evangelism? What are difficult to ignore are the events of the 1990s in the rise of Alpha. That is, the expected revival prophesied by Paul Cain in 1991,[91] and the Toronto Blessing in 1994. It is possible that the vast amount of energy that the Toronto Blessing released, and the high profile that HTB gained from being one of the main focuses of that phenomenon,[92] fuelled a desire for churches to evangelise and to use Alpha as the main tool.

---

[86] Grzyb 2004.

[87] HTB is now one of the wealthiest Anglican churches in the UK with an annual income in excess of £5 million (HTB Annual Review 2007).

[88] *Annual Review*, AI 2007.

[89] http://uk.alpha.org/runningacourse/facts_figures.html, accessed 5 March 2007.

[90] *Alpha News*, AI 2006:2.

[91] See Hilborn 2001:9-13.

[92] Scotland (2000:226) notes how HTB became affectionately known as the 'cathedral of the charismatics'.

Year	Number of registered Alpha courses worldwide	Estimated cumulative number of guests
1992	5	n/a
1993	200	4,600
1994	750	25,000
1995	2,500	100,000
1996	5,000	400,000
1997	6,500	800,000
1998	10,500	1.3 million
1999	14,200	2 million
2000	17,000	2.7 million
2001	19,800	3.8 million
2002	24,400	4.7 million
2003	27,000	5.7 million
2004	29,051	6.7 million
2005	31,167	8 million
2006	32,592	9.3 million
2007	35,092	10.8 million
2008	35,385	12.3 million

A number of critics of the Toronto Blessing emphasised that it was by the fruits that it would be judged. Andrew Walker asserted that for all the rhetoric there was no evidence of cultural change, and noticed how the Alpha course had 'replaced and conveniently eclipsed the Toronto phenomenon'.[93] Hunt describes the concurrent decline in the Toronto Blessing with the rise of Alpha, particularly in the timing of Alpha's first national initiative in 1998. He speculated that it could be interpreted as being a way of forcing the expected revival and fulfilling prophecy.[94]

There does seem to be a strong link between the 'blessing' and the rise of Alpha. And by including an experiential dimension on the Holy Spirit at the Alpha Weekend, the course was pitched perfectly for 4,000 to 5,500 estimated churches affected by the Toronto Blessing.[95] Gumbel (1995) himself makes this link explicit in his article in *The Impact of Toronto*.[96]

---

[93] Cited in Hilborn 2001:313; see also Scotland 2000:249-50.

[94] Hunt 2004:51-53.

[95] Rob Warner, Michael Green and Mark Stibbe note the move from Enlightenment rationalism to the post-modern experiential (Hilborn 2001), a theme also stressed by Wimber, and picked up by Alpha (Gumbel 2001g:36-37).

[96] Gumbel 1995. Since the heady days of the summer of 1994, Gumbel has become more circumspect in his views of 'the blessing'. In an interview with Ronson (2000) Gumbel commented, 'I don't talk about it now…It divides people. It splits churches. It is very controversial. But I'll tell you – I think the Toronto Blessing was a wonderful, wonderful thing.'

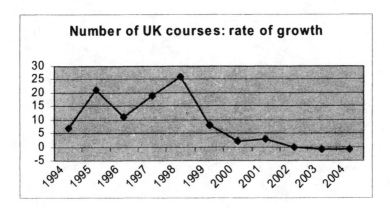

While Alpha has continued to grow worldwide, as Freebury's chart[97] above makes clear (in percentage), the take up of Alpha in the UK has most certainly peaked following the first Alpha initiative in 1998. Freebury bases this on the number of UK churches registering Alpha, given by AI.[98] Although Hunt has questioned the accuracy of the number of Alpha courses registered by AI,[99] it does provide a helpful impression of 'market saturation' in the UK, based upon HTB's own publicity. But to what extent does Alpha succeed in its aim of 're-evangelising Britain'? According to Brookes, compared with a yearly decline in church attendance of 78,000 (excluding deaths and transfers) the rate of conversion on Alpha is approximately 13,700 per year.[100] Despite Alpha's optimism, church attendance in Britain remains in freefall.

3. Summary

In this chapter, I have outlined both the recent history of HTB and the genesis of Alpha, and noted the salient influences upon the course. This has included Charismatic Renewal, John Wimber, the Church Growth Movement, and the Toronto Blessing. The energy that the 'blessing' released, combined with the high profile that HTB gained from its involvement, led many churches to adopt Alpha as the tool for revival.

Vital to Alpha's expansion was the entrepreneurial spirit and business acumen of Ken Costa and Tricia Neill, the charismatic leadership of Nicky Gumbel, and the generosity of HTB in terms of human resources and finance. I shall now turn to look in greater detail at the Alpha course itself.

---

[97] Freebury 2004:9.

[98] Freebury 2001:26.

[99] Hunt 2004.

[100] Brookes 2007:165-66. Brookes calculates these *approximate* figures from Brierley's 2005 research and by estimating a conversion rate of 15 per cent – half of whom, he suggests, are already churchgoers.

Chapter 2

An Outline of Alpha

Alpha International claims that Alpha's theology is that of basic Christianity; that it includes only those things upon which all Christians agree. As such, Alpha stands within the Evangelical tradition that views itself not as one tradition among many but 'as the custodian of pure New Testament faith'.[1] In this chapter, I shall describe Alpha *as it sees itself*, outlining the ethos and content of the course. How it relates to Alpha 'on the ground' will be assessed in Chapters 5 and 6. I shall also attempt to situate Alpha both contextually and theologically, noting the various influences upon the course itself. Without wishing to pre-empt my critique of Alpha's theology (see Chapter 7), I shall begin to 'draw some lines' here. In doing so, some of the more contentious theological issues will be highlighted, issues that shall resurface in the empirical data.

1. The Principles of Alpha

The evangelistic theory, or ethos, behind Alpha has been set out in *Telling Others*,[2] first published in 1994. It includes detailed advice on how to go about setting up a course and contains much of the material from the two-day conference, which Gumbel encourages all potential Alpha leaders to attend. At these conferences delegates can also *experience* the professional Alpha 'culture'. They are organised by two full-time staff members. Before conference delegates arrive, a team of approximately eight maintenance workers at HTB set up a marquee adjacent to the church. This is used for computerised registration, and later for lunch. The maintenance team also sets up the church, ensuring such things as chairs being lined up in neat rows. String is applied between the front and back chair as a means of ensuring this precision. Flowers are placed in the lavatories. At the pre-conference staff meeting, after enthusiastic praise for their prospective and expected hard work over the following two days, the AI/HTB team are instructed to smile and go out of their way to assist delegates.

On the actual day, delegates are welcomed by volunteers as they enter the church. Cloakroom facilities are offered in the crypt and run by HTB staff

---

[1] Cocksworth 1993:3.
[2] Gumbel 2001g.

members and volunteers. An extra bookshop to cover the increased demands of a conference is set up and overseen on a rota by more HTB staff. Coffee and biscuits are served by more volunteers. Professional HTB musicians lead the worship with words projected on a screen, operated by a trained staff member on computers backed up by a highly proficient IT team from HTB. During the conference, as well as numerous talks and seminars, there are times of intercessory prayer, worship and 'ministry time', where a team of HTB staff are available to pray for conference delegates. The organisational quality and the quantity of personnel involved in such a major operation is truly impressive.

Gumbel confesses that although he believes Alpha is a work of God, it is 'greatly marred by human error and frailty. There is much room for improvement and we try to listen carefully to constructive criticism'. Yet while modestly disclaiming Alpha's greatness, AI enthusiastically reports the effectiveness of the Alpha recipe both in growth statistics and in the multiple testimonies in its resources.

Gumbel outlines Alpha's basis on six New Testament (hereafter NT) principles, although he admits that these are *post hoc* justification for existing practice on Alpha. He notes, rather pragmatically: 'We found something that works and we've been trying to find out why it works'.[3] These principles are scattered with quotes and examples from across the Christian spectrum. In an example of ecumenical inclusivism Gumbel mentions, within one two-page spread, Anglicans, Lutherans, Methodists, Evangelicals, Roman Catholics, Salvation Army and United Reformed.[4] I shall now examine these six principles and where possible situate them historically and theologically, noting the main sources of influence.

1.1 Evangelism is Most Effective Through the Local Church

Conducting evangelism within the local church means that 'what you see is what you get'. In contrast to the Billy Graham-style 'crusades', which were held in large stadiums, Alpha earths evangelism in the church, conducted by the church community. This has the potential advantage of making possible the development and continuity of relationships. In the early 1990s this was revolutionary.[5] In an attempt to make the Christian faith 'accessible', HTB have reduced its services to such an extent that the Alpha course is not too dissimilar to its Sunday services. This drive to be relevant and accessible is similar to the aims and ethos of Willow Creek Community Church,[6] of which HTB is an associate member. Yet in contrast to Willow Creek, with its ethos of not

---

[3] Gumbel 2006.

[4] Gumbel 2001g:38-39.

[5] For other recent styles of evangelism, see Peace 1999:Part 3.

[6] See www.willowcreek.org. For a critique of such an approach see Abraham 2003:78-92, Earey and Headley 2002 and Morgenthaler 1995.

including worship in its 'services' aimed at enquirers, Alpha encourages the use of elements of worship from the start of the course. This includes prayer, singing, and times of 'prayer ministry'. Absent from this worship is any connection to the catholic liturgical tradition of the church, creeds, confession and absolution, images, rituals and symbols, and a minimalist presentation and practice of the dominical sacraments.

Because Alpha is conducted by a local church it means that the course mobilises, in rather militarily language, a whole army of evangelists. Gumbel notes that some people have said how exhausted they have become after running three Alpha courses a year, the amount he recommends for the course to maintain momentum.[7] His response is that different people in the church should be running the course, with leaders moving on and helpers becoming leaders and the guests becoming the helpers. Whether churches have enough people to run Alpha continually or have the backing of the minister and church itself, will obviously affect how the course is run. According to the instructions given in *Telling Others*, it takes an extensive team to conduct a course properly. It includes 'greeters', 'runners' (volunteers who escort guests arriving on the first week to their allocated small group), a treasurer, worship leader, an administrator and a 'task force' that deals with all of the practicalities arising during an Alpha session.[8]

Another advantage that Gumbel perceives in many local churches running Alpha is in its efficiency. Again, in contrast to one big evangelistic rally, Gumbel writes: 'The more checkouts, the more customers'.[9] With a stress on efficiency, his mechanistic ecclesiological framework is apparent here.[10] The logic is that it is more efficient to run multiple evangelism courses in contrast to just one big event. A charismatic speaker is not restricted to speaking at one event but, through modern technology, can be transmitted, via DVD, to multiple groups.

1.2 Evangelism is a Process

Alpha is a ten-week course involving a total of fifteen talks. It includes a weekend or day away and a celebration supper at the end. This, again, is in contrast to one-off evangelistic events, with its focus on sudden conversions. Alpha enables people to assimilate the Christian faith at their own pace, and for

---

[7] Gumbel 2001g:66.

[8] The specialisation of jobs is a key feature of McDonaldization (Ritzer 1996).

[9] Gumbel 2001d:33.

[10] See Hopewell 1988. In its drive for efficiency, Alpha's discourse is regularly full of mechanistic terms such as 'effectiveness', 'planning', 'networking', 'tools' and 'maximising'. Similar 'buzzwords' are used by popular business and life-style guru Stephen Covey (1989) in *The Seven Habits of Highly Effective People*.

trust to develop in relationships.[11] Gumbel sees Alpha as being a reversal of previous models of evangelism which expected people to come to faith, and then belong to a local church. On coming to Alpha, guests start to belong to a Christian community, so that 'belonging is coming *before* belief'.[12] According to AI, this makes integrating them into the local church easier. As I shall discuss in Chapter 7, this is similar to the early church's catechumenate, where Christian leaders assumed that people did not think their way into a new life, but rather lived their way into a new kind of thinking.[13] The importance of process for conversion has good empirical support. Later, in Chapter 6, the importance of social networks and relationships that form between a potential convert and a religious group, will be described in more detail. The significant point is that interpersonal involvement is the thing that leads a person gradually to accept the beliefs of those people he or she has come to trust. On Alpha, this resocialisation begins during the meal and the small groups, and develops over the duration of the course.

John Finney discovered that 31 per cent of the converts he researched said that their coming to faith was datable, whereas 69 per cent said that it was gradual. The average time taken was approximately four years.[14] Churches have recognised that people are in general reluctant to be persuaded to make an 'instant' decision for Christ. This is a move away from the past two hundred years or so of evangelism. Evangelicals have tended to replicate what they believe was St Paul's experience: a sudden, point-in-time transformation based upon an encounter with Jesus.[15] And if St Paul is taken as paradigmatic, it would seem natural to arrange evangelistic events that promote such stark encounters. John Wesley's experience of faith, in which he felt his heart 'strangely warmed', propelled his mass evangelism, and popularised the 'invitation' or altar call to a personal, life-changing decision to be a follower of

---

[11] Gumbel 2001g:33-55.

[12] Gumbel 2001d.

[13] Richard Rohr in Kreider 1999:22.

[14] Finney 1992:24-25; see also Jackson 2002:47.

[15] Michael Green writes, 'So far from [St Paul's conversion experience] being exceptional, I believe it is meant by St Luke to be normative for all Christians everywhere' (Green 1970:193). This itself is heavily contested, with many NT scholars insisting that it is inappropriate to speak of Paul as having experienced a 'conversion', if that means a 'change of religion'. Krister Stendahl (1977:7-23) plays down the role of a guilty conscience in conversion and argues that Paul experienced a 'calling', an assignment to a new task (see also E. P. Sanders 1977). Certainly, if one sees conversion as a change of religion, Stendahl is clearly correct. Paul did not change religions. 'Christianity' was still a sect within Judaism, not a new religion. By contrast, following F. F. Bruce's work, Seyoon Kim (1982) suggests that it is Paul's conversion experience that holds the key to Paul's theology. Attempting to hold these views together, contemporary scholarship has tended to view Paul's account as more accurately being a call/conversion (Wright 2003).

Jesus.[16] Others followed Wesley's pattern, including Charles Finney,[17] D. L. Moody,[18] Billy Sunday[19] and Billy Graham.[20] For example, Finney's 'new measures' included the use of 'anxious meetings' and an 'anxious seat' which were used 'so as to lead ['anxious sinners'] immediately to Christ'.[21] The context for such evangelism was 'nominal Christianity'. Evangelicalism, Hindmarsh notes, was a protest against the idea that adhering to Christian civil society as a nominal Christian was sufficient for salvation. While infant baptism, Christian nurture, catechesis and worship might be valuable in preparation, *no one* was a Christian until they had personally encountered God in Jesus Christ, personally repented and accepted God's gift of salvation through faith in Christ.[22] Further, the close alignment between Evangelicalism and the Enlightenment can be seen in its taking the modern concept of the person as an autonomous individual.[23] By doing so, Evangelicalism emphasised individual conversion and commitment, after which the individual might then join a church, with varying degrees of success.[24]

---

[16] Webber 2003:32.

[17] See William G. McLoughlin 1958; Charles Finney c1835.

[18] See John Pollock 1997 and David Bebbington 2005.

[19] See Lyle Dorsett 1991.

[20] See William G. McLoughlin 1960.

[21] Finney c1835:296. Finney notes that the church has always used something like the anxious seat. 'In the days of the apostles *baptism* answered this purpose. The Gospel was preached to the people, and then all those who were willing to be on the side of Christ were called on to be baptised. It held the precise place that the anxious seat does now, as a public manifestation of a determination to be a Christian' (Finney c1835:305).

[22] Hindmarsh 2002.

[23] Bebbington 1989.

[24] While Wesley's meetings included 'crisis conversions', his doctrine of entire sanctification, despite being controversial, gave a strong teleological sense to conversion. Webber (2003:32-33) notes how Wesley's revival crusades led to small groups for spiritual formation and discipleship. Wesley's biographer observed that, 'from the outset he realised the comparative futility of merely preaching to a miscellaneous crowd of people and leaving the matter there'. Wesley realised that 'individuals needed to be befriended, shepherded, instructed and encouraged, and hence arose the Societies which became the nuclei of the Methodist Church' (Doughty 1955:57). As Snow and Machalek (1983:263) point out, 'George Whitefield was content merely to preach and hope for the best. Wesley, however, declined to preach where it seemed impossible to consolidate his evangelical efforts.' Whitefield ultimately realised the genius of Wesley in this regard, admitting, towards the end of his life, 'My brother Wesley acted wisely. The souls that were awakened under his ministry he joined in class, and thus preserved the fruit of his labour. This I neglected, and my people are a rope of sand' (Doughty 1955:57). Wesley's groups would meet weekly with other like-minded people who would exercise a mutual accountability for their discipleship.

From Alpha's mutation from a discipleship course to aiming at both mission *and* spiritual formation, Alpha stumbled upon, and is perhaps a return to, the traditional means of communicating the faith in the Anglican tradition. For centuries this was understood as being more of a process. Ireland points out that the style of crusade evangelism exemplified by Billy Graham was a variation from the norm, at a time when most people had some form of Christian background.[25] Gumbel has recognised that people need time to explore new beliefs and to test their reality within the context of relationship. Undoubtedly, this explains some of its appeal. Gumbel takes the analogy of the birth of a child, which may be one event but part of a much longer process before and afterwards. He writes: 'We recognise that people need time to think, watch, listen, and to talk through their questions and difficulties. Each person is beginning [the Alpha course] at a different stage...the fact that Alpha is a process enables trust to develop'.[26] Alpha has wisely recognised (or perhaps arrived at the truism) that conversion is not just an individual decision – that it is also a social process. Despite the stress on process, most of Alpha's published testimonies refer to a datable event-type of conversion.[27] Ireland writes:

> The effort required to find and research these testimonies suggests that sudden, dramatic conversions from unbelief to committed discipleship are unusual rather than typical among those who attend Alpha – often it is a more untidy process.[28]

1.3 Evangelism Involves the Whole Person

This includes the mind, heart, conscience and will. While the Alpha course seeks to *persuade* people, Gumbel asserts: 'We try to avoid all forms of pressure.'[29] This is in contrast to the nineteenth century revivalist preachers who first made their 'audiences' terrified of going to hell, and then proceeded to instruct them on what they must do to be saved.[30] Such tactics are unlikely to attract many 'customers' today, but is there not an analogous, if less intense, pressure present within Alpha? Gumbel does not appeal to the horrors of hell, but he does suggest that, by appealing to the conscience, the aim during the

---

Billy Graham's crusades had varying levels of success. In his crusades in Glasgow (1956), Toronto and Seattle (1976), between 7, 11 and 15 per cent, respectively, of those who professed conversion had been incorporated into a church (Peace 1999:288-90).

[25] Ireland 2000:33. Ireland limits this to Graham's ministry, between 1954–84. I have argued above that this style of evangelism goes back considerably further.

[26] Gumbel 2001g:34-35.

[27] See §2.1.4 below and cf. Brian 2003:Ch.4.

[28] Ireland 2003:29.

[29] Gumbel 2001g:38.

[30] Argyle 1983; Zimbardo, Ebbesen and Maslach 1977.

course is to stress the sinfulness of guests before 'urging people to repent and turn to Christ'.[31] And while Gumbel emphasises the importance of avoiding pressure, are there not more subtle, implicit and unspoken group processes, what Janis calls 'group think',[32] involved within the group dynamics that could be said to be coercive? (see Chapter 5 and 6).

1.4 Models of Evangelism in the New Testament include Classical, Holistic and Power Evangelism

Gumbel's fourth NT principle of evangelism includes the three models of 'classical', 'holistic' and 'power evangelism'. These three types are also emphasised by the Church Growth Movement,[33] although, because they believe those 'without a personal relationship with Jesus Christ are doomed to a Christless eternity', they 'affirm the priority of [classical] evangelism over social ministries'.[34] First, classical evangelism means 'the proclamation of the unchanging message'.[35] This involves a process of inculturation, to ensure that the packaging is not a stumbling block. The problem for most people, Gumbel maintains, is not the message of the gospel, but the cultural packaging within which it comes. Such a statement might be contested. For example, St Paul seems to suggest that the message of Christ crucified is offensive, 'a stumbling-block to Jews and foolishness to Gentiles' (1 Cor. 1.23). Gumbel proposes that the right cultural package means making use of contemporary music rather than organ music. However, it is actually a very particular style of contemporary music. For example, it is not R&B, hip/hop, drum and bass, house, or gospel. Rather, the notion of contemporary for HTB, and for the Charismatic Movement in general, has tended to mean guitar and male-led 'soft rock'.[36] Some see this as a sort of Charismatic imperialism, an extension of a diluted form of Charismatic Christianity including those churches previously untouched by the renewal movement.[37]

Second, holistic evangelism includes social justice and relieving human need. Gumbel states: 'We attempt on Alpha to avoid the dangers of pietism by our teaching and example, believing that evangelism is fundamentally linked to social responsibility.'[38] Gumbel describes how 'Many, many of our young people now get involved in ['Grandma's'] Aids charity', which was started by

---

[31] Gumbel 2001g:37.

[32] Janis 1982.

[33] See Wagner 1992:D-47.

[34] McGavran 1970:9 and 23.

[35] Gumbel 2001g:38.

[36] Jeremy Begbie (1991:233) suggests that the style is largely Radio 2 'easy listening', with occasional forays into Radio 1.

[37] Brian 2003; Hunt 2004:54; Race 2004.

[38] Gumbel 2001g:39.

Alpha graduate Amanda Williams.[39] Social engagement has not been a part of
HTB or Alpha's DNA; rather, this emphasis is a recent appendage to Alpha in
response to criticism that the course has received.[40] HTB have also sought to
rectify this omission by starting an 'Urban School of Mission' and by
encouraging links with charities like Besom and The Regeneration Trust.[41] Its
work among ex-prison offenders has also steadily increased over the years.[42]

The difficulty with having a major emphasis on church growth, is that it
ultimately leads to a prioritising of 'classical' evangelism and church planting
over social action. William Abraham writes:

> Given the obvious significance of eternity over against time it will not be difficult
> to show that evangelism takes precedence over all else the church does. It ignores
> the primary horizon of the kingdom of God within which evangelism, social
> action, pastoral care and all else the church does must ultimately be set.[43]

Indeed, while on Alpha there is a *theory* of holistic evangelism, the actual
practice, compared with classical and power evangelism, has been relatively
underdeveloped. As with the Church Growth Movement, the priority is on
classical and power evangelism (see below). And in contrast to the perception
Gumbel gives on the number of people from Alpha joining the Grandma's
charity, a former leader of the charity told me that it was one of many charities
with links to HTB that found volunteers low in relation to their needs. The third
style of evangelism, power evangelism, will be discussed with the fifth NT
principle, to which I shall now turn.

1.5 Evangelism in the Power of the Holy Spirit is both Dynamic and Effective

Wimber's influence can be seen in the major emphasis given to power
evangelism and the fifth and sixth NT principle that undergirds Alpha.[44]
Gumbel notes that all theologians agree that Jesus's central theme in his
teaching was about the kingdom of God. However, there is a variety of
understandings of the kingdom. The two prominent streams in the nineteenth
and twentieth century included those who emphasised the future element of

---

[39] Gumbel 2001d.
[40] See Booker and Ireland 2003:26; Brookes 2007.
[41] For a full list, see the HTB website www.htb.org.uk. See also the AI published course,
'Simplicity, Love and Justice' (Odgers 2004).
[42] Without wishing to diminish the importance of this work, Race (2004) points out that
HTB's ex-offenders programme 'is a relatively young, inexperienced and small
organisation when compared to other agencies and organisations working in the prison
and after care of the ex-offender field'.
[43] Abraham 1989:85.
[44] Wimber's 2001; Gumbel 2001g:40-43.

Jesus's kingdom proclamations,[45] and others[46] who sought to explain away the future references. Wimber draws on the work of George Ladd[47] who holds a mediating position by teaching that the kingdom is an eschatological reality that is both present and future.[48] Wimber tends to stress the reign of God in the hearts and lives of people *now*. He holds to a 'dominion theology' where Christians possess 'kingdom authority' and thus power over sickness, demons, and nature, rather than viewing the kingdom as lying beyond the Church.[49] Percy describes how, for Wimber, while the 'kingdom of God' is not totally identified with the Church, he presents the Church as the agent of the kingdom of God, with kingdom authority and power. There is an inevitable feeling of over-realised eschatology in such approaches.[50]

The kingdom of God operating on Alpha derives from Wimber's account, with a particular stress on its supernatural elements: '...conversions, miraculous signs, healings, visions, tongues, prophecy, raising the dead and casting out evil spirits'.[51] These are taken as 'proof' of the power and truth of God. Those who are filled with the Holy Spirit will see the kingdom of God at work in the same way as the early church and they thus seek to replicate the kind of signs, wonders and experiences that might have occurred then. On Alpha, this is played out on the weekend/day away and on the healing session, discussed below. However, in contrast to the early church, there seems to be a disparity between the logic of Wimber's teaching on the kingdom of God and his ministry session. Warner writes:

> ...while the logic of power evangelism would suggest a ministry session out on the streets, the actual ministry times were specifically for delegates and intensely therapeutic, often dealing with such issues as rejection, addiction and low self-esteem.[52]

1.6 Effective Evangelism requires the Filling and Refilling of the Spirit

This sixth and final NT principle undergirding Alpha is similar to the fifth. All of the examples that Gumbel gives to legitimate this experience in *Telling Others* are Evangelicals, including John Wesley, George Whitefield, Charles Finney, D. L. Moody, R. A. Torrey and Billy Graham, although in the most recent edition of the book, Gumbel includes the Roman Catholic charismatic,

---

[45] Weiss 1971 and Schweitzer 1954.

[46] Dodd 1961.

[47] Wimber 2001:31-32; cf. Ladd 1980.

[48] The current debate is on how normative the eschatological character of the kingdom is for contemporary Christians (Gaffin 1991).

[49] See *We Believe in the Holy Spirit* Report 1991:46.

[50] Percy 1996:105.

[51] Gumbel 2001g:45.

[52] Warner 2003:229.

Father Raniero Cantalamessa. By quoting these people, Gumbel is attempting to provide legitimation for this pneumatic experience. But unless the reader has some knowledge of Evangelicalism, they will be unaware that all of them, bar the recent addition, are from the same 'club', namely, Evangelicals.

Those who have been filled with the Holy Spirit 'know that a radical change has occurred in their lives…This experience of God gives them the stimulus and power to invite their friends to the next Alpha'.[53] Here, the stress of the individual's experience of the Holy Spirit and being 'empowered' is linked to church growth, an emphasis also emphasised by the Church Growth Movement. According to this movement and to Alpha, the task of the church as a social body is, as Percy insists, to be a multiplying agent of God's power so that non-believers might experience for themselves the certainty of God.[54]

1.7 Summary

In this section I have provided an overview of the ethos underlying the Alpha course and Gumbel's six NT principles. As Gumbel admits, these are *post hoc* justification for existing practice on Alpha. The style of evangelism on Alpha contrasts with the previous two hundred years or so of mass evangelism: it places evangelism within the local church, primarily conducted by the laity; it recognises that communicating the Christian faith includes a process, a resocialisation, and that people need time to assimilate what they hear and discuss. I have suggested that this has similarities to the traditional Anglican way of communicating the faith and that the recent style of evangelism in large stadiums was an aberration from the norm. With that acknowledged, the vast majority of Alpha testimonies refer to a datable crisis–event, which usually occurs on the Alpha weekend. Although Gumbel describes three styles of evangelism – classical, holistic and power – the actual practice of holistic evangelism compared with the other two is relatively underdeveloped, although HTB has recently attempted to redress this lack. The last two principles are heavily influenced by John Wimber's power evangelism: the kingdom of God is primarily described in supernatural terms, with the expectation that this is normative for today's church and thus for Alpha.

I shall now turn to the structure of Alpha, looking in particular at its aim, then examining a typical Alpha session and the content of the course, and lastly its organisational ethos and post-Alpha follow up.

---

[53] Gumbel 2001g:50.
[54] Percy 1996:108.

2. The Structure of Alpha

Gumbel gives a mnemonic to describe Alpha.[55] 'A' is for 'anyone can come'. Gumbel outlines the very broad scope of Alpha:

- Alpha is for people who would not consider themselves Christian which, Gumbel suggests, constitutes 50 per cent of the UK population. This actually conflicts with the 2001 census, where 72 per cent of the population self-designated themselves Christian.[56]
- Those who are not churchgoers, which is 92.5 per cent of the population.
- Those who are new Christians.
- Those who want to brush up on the basics. It is a refresher course for mature Christians who have 'never known what it's like to have a personal relationship with Jesus'. Such terminology is common among Evangelicals and is the *sine qua non* of being Christian.
- Those new to the church.

Alpha is essentially an attempt to combine both mission and spiritual formation. This multi-pronged focus means that Alpha guests come from a huge range of backgrounds and with different and sometimes conflicting motivations for participating on a course. 'L' is for learning and laughter in which the key questions at the heart of the Christian faith are tackled.[57] John Finney suggests that such an approach resonates with contemporary culture: 'Approaches that can laugh at themselves and the world will be given a hearing. This does not mean that they should not deal with serious matters, but do so with a light touch in presenting them.'[58] 'P' is for pasta, where people are welcomed over food and where relationships are built. Gumbel quotes someone who described how there is 'something almost sacramental about the meal' because friendships are made and people start to relax and become much more open.[59] John Clarke, who used to attend HTB, suggests that it was these 'supper parties' that originally brought growth to the church. HTB had experienced spiritual renewal but there were few people becoming Christians. With many professional Londoners in their twenties used to socialising after work, within two or three years the evening service had grown from 200 people to 700.[60]

---

[55] Gumbel 2001g:61-75.

[56] See http://www.statistics.gov.uk/CCI/nugget.asp?ID=293&Pos=1&ColRank=2&Rank =224, accessed 9 February 2007.

[57] Gumbel 2001g:60.

[58] Finney 2000:147. See Rebecca Nye (Watts, Nye and Savage 2002:126) for the importance of *play* on Alpha as a way of building up and knocking down one's schemata.

[59] Gumbel 2004.

[60] Clarke 1995:8.

'H' is for helping one another. This is similar to the emphasis the catechumenate gives to an accompanied journey and is the role of a 'sponsor'.[61] 'A' is for ask anything. No question is considered too simple or too hostile.

The outline of an Alpha evening has not changed to any great extent from Marnham's original course. A typical evening session includes the below:

6.15pm	Leaders and helpers meet to pray.
7.00pm	Supper is served. The importance of no religious talk is stressed, so as to enable friendships to develop and to avoid any intensity.
7.40pm	Welcome. This is the time for notices, recommendation of books relating to the session's talk, and a joke is told.
7.50pm	Worship. Gumbel admits that this only works for larger courses of 25 people or over because there are then enough team members to sing. Guests often say how this was one of the hardest parts of the course but also, eventually, the most enjoyable part of the course. For mid-sized courses, Alpha has produced an audio-tape or CD with a songbook, which can be used 'karaoke' style.
8.00pm	Talk. Gumbel notes that it is best to have a 'live speaker' but advises that new courses start with the DVDs/videos. This is because there are many other things to organise when starting a course, and because a huge amount of effort has been put into the talks, with every sentence scrutinised. Each of Gumbel's talks lasts approximately forty-five minutes. According to Gumbel, 80 per cent of churches use the videos. Every guest should be given an Alpha manual free of charge.
8.50pm	Coffee
9.00pm	Small group discussion. This is considered the most important part of the evening and is discussed in more detail below.
9.45pm	Finish

2.1 The Alpha Content

The syllabus of Alpha is found in Gumbel's book, *Questions of Life*.[62] The titles of the talks are:

Introductory session	'Christianity: boring, untrue and irrelevant?'
Session 1	'Who is Jesus?'
Session 2	'Why did Jesus die?'

---

[61] See *On the Way* 1995:35; Kavanagh 1978:131; Johnson 1999:360; Webber 2001:118.
[62] Gumbel 2001e.

Session 3	'How can I be sure of my faith?'
Session 4	'Why and how should I read the Bible?'
Session 5	'Why and how do I pray?'
Session 6	'How does God guide us?'
Weekend talk 1	'Who is the Holy Spirit?'
Weekend talk 2	'What does the Holy Spirit do?'
Weekend talk 3	'How can I be filled with the Spirit?'
Weekend talk 4	'How can I make the most of the rest of my life?'
Session 7	'How can I resist evil?'
Session 8	'Why and how should we tell others?'
Session 9	'Does God heal today?'
Session 10	'What about the Church?'

As well as the continuity that has existed in the structure of Alpha since the early-1980s, its content has remained largely unchanged. Gumbel points out that because he did not invent the course, he feels a deference towards it and thus avoids tampering with it too much. He describes how, when he took on the leadership of the course in 1990, he slightly modified it to aim at non-churchgoing guests.[63] These changes included the re-ordering of some of the talks. 'Who is Jesus?' was moved from Week 4 to Week 1. 'How can I be sure of my faith?' was moved from Week 1 to Week 3. Each talk was 'tweaked' slightly to aim at non-churchgoers. The training of leaders was soon added. Following the first Alpha questionnaire in 1991, two people wrote: 'We only enjoyed the small groups when we were allowed to discuss.' As a result, the group dynamics changed from what was essentially a Bible study to a discussion time. The key thing that altered, suggests Gumbel, was allowing the guests to answer their own questions, and not to force them into arriving at particular conclusions. Further, when Gumbel took the reigns, there was a pre-Alpha course aimed at non-Christians called 'Enquirers'. This course included questions like 'Who is God?', 'Why does God allow suffering?', 'What about other religions?', 'Did the resurrection really happen?', 'Can we trust the Bible?' However, there were only six people on this course, compared with the hundreds of people joining Alpha. Gumbel thus decided to merge the two courses and placed the pre-Alpha material into a book, *Searching Issues*,[64] and for the small group to discuss. His rationale for this was that questions such as 'Why does God allow suffering?' were, to take a cricketing analogy, defensive strokes. In contrast, each of the talks on Alpha constitute 'attacking shots'.[65] This means, for the talks at least, that the agenda and the questions raised are

---

[63] Gumbel 2006.

[64] Gumbel 2001f.

[65] Gumbel 2006.

controlled by Alpha.[66] Such an approach is in contrast to the *Catechumenate Network*, which first attempts to listen to, and then address the issues that matter to people in the group.[67]

Alpha's main evangelistic thrust comes in the first few weeks. Up until Week 3, Gumbel goes for 'closure', with an opportunity for guests to say the 'sinner's prayer' at the Introductory Session, Session 2 and Session 3.[68] The aim of such a prayer is to procure a personal conversion. As the titles of the talks suggest, following the third week, Christian faith tends to be assumed. We shall now move on to outline the Alpha talks.

2.1.1 CHRISTIANITY: BORING, UNTRUE AND IRRELEVANT?

The Introductory Session acts as a link between one Alpha course and the next: it functions, first, as a celebration party at the end of the course and, second, as a way for guests to recruit family and/or friends to the course. At HTB, the supper (and course) itself is organised by a team of about five full-time employees, includes paid security parking attendants and many volunteers to help with registering the 600-plus guests. As guests enter the church itself, they are entertained by a jazz band on the 'stage', with subdued, colourful lighting to give an intimate 'bistro' atmosphere, and they wine and dine with other young and attractive professionals with food provided by professional caterers. It would be incredible if anyone were *not* to be impressed by such an evening. Such is the Alpha course at HTB. Gumbel gives an after dinner talk. He argues that Christianity, far from being boring, untrue and irrelevant, provides direction for a lost world, reality in a confused world and life in a dark world. The talk is packed with humorous anecdotes and quotes from writers and thinkers ranging from Leo Tolstoy to Bernard Levin. To illustrate what life is like as a Christian, Gumbel draws an analogy with a television set. He contrasts a television set without an aerial (life before becoming a Christian) with one that has an aerial (life as a Christian), where the picture becomes clear. To quote Gumbel's talk:

> And once someone has an *experience*, a relationship with God through Jesus Christ, it's like the aerial (emphasis added).

This experience is supposed to occur at the Alpha weekend, which will be examined in more detail later. We shall now move on to Alpha proper. As the titles make clear, Gumbel starts with Jesus. For the first two sessions, a distinctly modernist apologetic is used. This has been a general feature of

---

[66] Brookes (2007:97) suggests that Alpha, rather than encouraging dialogue, could be 'compared to a tennis match where the one player insists on serving in each game, rather than alternating!'

[67] See Richter and Francis 1998:153; Ball and Grundy 2000:87.

[68] See Gumbel 2001e:64-65. There is another opportunity for this at the Alpha Weekend, see below.

Evangelicalism. Since the eighteenth century, Evangelicals have not only attempted to defend the faith in a 'reasonable' way, but in a decidedly rationalist way.[69] The appeal is to the evidence of facts and to conclusions resulting from such facts. Percy summarises this classic technique in apologetics: caricaturing 'objections' to faith, or setting up 'straw men', then demolishing them.[70] Alpha's approach is very similar to that seen in Josh McDowell's forensic textbook *Evidence that Demands a Verdict* and Francis Schaeffer's *Escape from Reason*, with their exposition of the 'unchanging facts' of Christian faith.[71] Gumbel provides the 'logical proofs' for the Christian faith in the classic, deductive way: hypotheses are established, possible responses adduced before the proper Evangelical conclusion is drawn.

2.1.2 WHO IS JESUS?

In the first talk, Gumbel seeks to locate the foundations for belief based upon the historical existence and reliability of the Bible. There is a sort of biblical foundationalism noticeable in Gumbel's statement, 'How do we know that what [the biblical writers] wrote down has not been changed over the years? The answer is that we do know, very accurately *through the science of textual criticism*, what the New Testament writers wrote'.[72] By comparing the Bible to other ancient books whose authenticity is undenied, this provides external self-evident proof for the reliability of the Bible. Abraham describes how viewing the Bible as an epistemic criterion is a classical type of theological foundationalism, and is another version of inerrancy.[73] In contrast to Alpha's largely Reformed basis, this is one of the few moments in the course where a form of evidentialist apologetic is used.[74] From this point onwards, the

---

[69] Hilborn 1997:212; Noll 1994. For an overview of different styles of apologetics, see Cowan 2000 and Dulles 1999.

[70] Percy 1997.

[71] Although Schaeffer is generally *inductive* in his apologetic.

[72] Gumbel 2001e:24, emphasis added.

[73] Abraham 2002. Percy (1996:13) criticises this because it views revelation as being closed and complete rather than recognising that faith and knowledge are incomplete (1 Cor. 13.9).

[74] Another place where a similar apologetic arises is in Alpha's recommended reading list in which C. S. Lewis' *Mere Christianity* presents the moral argument for the existence of God. For a discussion on different styles of religious epistemology, see *Contemporary Perspectives on Religious Epistemology* (Geivett and Sweetman 1992). Foundationalism, the attempt to find fixed foundations, utterly indubitable truths, upon which further knowledge can be built, has come under serious attack. It is based upon an impossible quest for absolute truth where the demand for certainty and omniscience replaces God and generates a quest for what is humanly unrealisable. Colin Gunton (1992:459) writes: 'There are no certain and indubitable sets of concepts, no certain and agreed reports of sense experience.' Rather than reverting to a non-foundationalist epistemology (see Phillips 1998), where there is no intersubjective way by which

authority of the Bible is now assumed. Having, it is believed, established the reliability of the Bible, Gumbel goes on to use C. S. Lewis' 'trilemma' argument in an attempt to prove Jesus's divinity. The argument is expressed in this syllogism:

- Jesus was either a liar, a lunatic, or God.
- Jesus was neither a liar nor a lunatic.
- Therefore, Jesus is God.

This is far from a watertight argument. First, it is reliant on the view that the Bible is authoritative, an unlikely assumption for non-churchgoers. Second, the only possibilities offered apart from Jesus being God are the two extremes of either insanity or deliberate liar. A less radical alternative, for example, would be to suggest that Jesus was simply deluded. N. T. Wright, questions such an Enlightenment-based apologetic. The study of first-century Judaism and Christianity has moved on: picking a few phrases from John's Gospel and elsewhere, and claiming that Jesus was conscious of his divinity[75] is far too simplistic, and may well by implication buy in to similarly misleading and potentially docetic views of what 'divinity' might actually mean.[76]

Gumbel, perhaps assuming that guests have some church background, and thus a basic trinitarian framework, looks for evidence that Jesus is 'God the Son, the second Person of the Trinity'.[77] Alpha's history as a discipleship course at HTB underlies such assumptions. Although the doctrine of the Trinity is outlined in Gumbel's *Searching Issues*,[78] it does seem strange that the Alpha course itself, which specifically targets non-Christians, does not attempt to elaborate on the doctrine. In effect, group leaders are expected to elaborate on the Trinity if the subject comes up in discussion. The lack of an explicit trinitarian theology on Alpha has been heavily criticised.[79]

Lastly, Gumbel very briefly moves on to the resurrection and attempts to refute possible objections. Such scant attention given to the resurrection led one

---

truthfulness of beliefs may be assessed, Gunton argues that it is better to see the problem as not being the quest for foundations *per se*, but the form that the quest has taken from the Presocratic to the present day. There may be a quest for foundations but it is one engaged in by fallible, finite and fallen human beings (Gunton 1993).

[75] Gumbel 2001a:27.

[76] Wright 1996; 2000. Wright describes Jesus's self-understanding as characterised by vocation: 'As part of his human vocation, grasped in faith, sustained in prayer, tested in confrontation, agonised over in further prayer and doubt, and implemented in action, he believed he had to do and be, for Israel and the world, that which according to scripture only YHWH himself could do and be' (Wright 1996:653). With that said, suitably adapted, C. S. Lewis' argument might still be convincing to some people.

[77] Gumbel 2001e:27.

[78] Gumbel 2001f:99-113.

[79] See Booker and Ireland 2003:27; Freebury 2004:51; Percy 1997.

church in Ireland's research to create an alternative course to Alpha.[80]

2.1.3 WHY DID JESUS DIE?

While Gumbel points out that there are a variety of ways to understand the atonement, the main focus of the second talk is on the penal substitutionary theory of atonement. As sinners and 'cut off' from God, we 'deserve punishment'.[81] Gumbel writes,

> He came to earth, in the person of his Son Jesus, to die instead of us (2 Corinthians 5:21; Galatians 3:13)...This is [quoting John Stott] the 'self-substitution of God'.[82]

In the 1960s, this became one of the defining doctrines for Evangelicals. The Church in England was facing a sharp decline in religious practice and Evangelicals felt alarmed by the rising liberalism, along with such things as the publication of John Robinson's *Honest to God*,[83] Bultmann's de-mythologising of the Bible, and radical liberals such as Don Cupitt being ordained. Behind the Evangelicals was the guiding hand of John Stott, who was a sort of touchstone of Evangelical respectability.[84] Penal substitution became like a 'badge of honour'.[85] In *Knowing God*, Packer contended that a gospel without propitiation was no gospel at all.[86] John Collins and David Watson were part of this conservative Evangelical group in the sixties, although they were also at the forefront of the Charismatic Movement.[87] With such influences upon HTB, it is perhaps not surprising that Gumbel emphasises a Reformed atonement theology. And with Alpha's aim of securing conversions, this theory is, Gillett argues, based upon a pragmatic need to preach the gospel in a straightforward step-by-step way that leads to a response.[88]

More recently penal substitution has been self-contested in the debates between Evangelical 'spokesperson' Steve Chalke, who provocatively called the theory 'cosmic child abuse', and the Evangelical Alliance (EA).[89] Although others had previously challenged the theory, many saw Chalke's book as a

---

[80] Ireland 2003:24.

[81] Gumbel 2001e:42, 44.

[82] Gumbel 2001e:45.

[83] Robinson 1963.

[84] Hastings 2001:533. The other significant Evangelical voice was James Packer.

[85] Christopher Cocksworth, personal correspondence 19 July 2006.

[86] Packer 1973. See also John Stott's *The Cross of Christ* (1996). Percy (1996:169-70 n.12) makes reference to IVP/UCCF insistence on 'penal substitution' as the only way of understanding the atonement. Members are required to sign a 'statement of faith' in which other possible interpretations are denied.

[87] Goodhew 2003.

[88] Gillett 1993:73.

[89] Chalke 2003.

challenge to the very identity of Evangelicalism. The EA[90] responded to Chalke, calling into question whether one could still be a member of EA without signing up to the doctrine. The doctrine is also contended by churches running Alpha. When concerns were raised over what some clergy felt was an over-emphasis on an Evangelical substitutionary atonement,[91] Gumbel responded by saying that conservative Evangelical churches wanted *more* of an emphasis, and so viewed it as a sign to leave the talk unchanged. However, conservative Evangelicals have remained dissatisfied with the deficient emphasis on sin and repentance on Alpha, the lack of biblical exposition, and the course's charismatic emphasis. As a result, the preference for conservative Evangelical churches has become *Christianity Explored*, a course written by Rico Tice of All Soul's, Langham Place.[92]

2.1.4 HOW CAN I BE SURE OF MY FAITH?

The third talk stresses personal conversion. Christians can *know* they have a relationship with God based upon the 'word of God', the 'work of Jesus' and the 'witness of the Spirit', who 'brings an inner experience of God'.[93] Charles Taylor traces the roots of the 'inward turn'. He notes that the Reformers' rejection of mediation – the idea that the church could mediate the sacred – meant that everyone's personal commitment became essential. The root of this stress on the inward experience of God comes from Romantic expressivism, which arose in protest against the Enlightenment ideal of disengaged, instrumental reason.[94] It is also found in the religious revivals of the period, among Pietists and Methodists. The Pietist movement, which began in the late seventeenth century in Germany, turns away from the orthodox Protestant emphasis on doctrinal correctness and seeks to bring about a 'new birth', a conversion whose fruits will be a deep piety and holy life. It was a call for a passionate Christianity marked not only by right doctrine but also by a feeling of forgiveness.[95] The line from Alfred H. Ackley's hymn (1887-1960) expresses this well: 'You ask me how I know He lives? He lives within my heart.' This personal experiential conversion was one of the crucial moulding influences on Wesleyan Methodism. Although Count Zinzendorf and the German Pietists tended to be anti-rational in a way that Wesley was not, all these movements made conviction[96] and devotion more central than learning and theology. Taylor notes: 'This was their transposition of the Reformation

---

[90] See http://www.eauk.org/theology/headline_issues/atonement/atonement-statement. cfm, accessed 21 July 2006.

[91] Booker and Ireland 2003.

[92] Tice 2001. For a list of process evangelism courses, see Appendix 2.

[93] Gumbel 2001e:55-64.

[94] Taylor 1992:363.

[95] Webber 2003:32.

[96] This was understood as being 'struck' by the Holy Spirit.

demand of total personal commitment, but in the climate of the eighteenth century this fervour took the form of displays of strong emotion.'[97] Andrew Wright portrays the Romantic experimental–experience shift in Evangelical spirituality as characterised by 'subjective religious sensibility' and 'expressions of inner religious experience'.[98] This heart-oriented Christianity of the Pietists and revivalists has its modern successors in the Pentecostals[99] and now, via the Charismatic Movement, experienced on Alpha.

Personal conversion is bound up with another Evangelical doctrine: assurance. Bebbington notes, 'once you had experienced the *feeling* of forgiveness at conversion, how could you not know about it?'[100] Fanny J. Crosby's (1820-1915) hymn 'Blessed assurance' expresses the potential for all when they are born again. Bebbington notes the influence of the Enlightenment's empiricist philosophy on Wesley and Evangelicalism. While the rationalism of the Enlightenment led many to reject belief in God, Evangelicals included religious experience, as a sort of 'sixth sense', within the orbit of evidence. Evangelicals referred to true Christianity as 'experimental religion'.[101]

Gumbel describes how 'God wants us to be sure about our relationship with him'.[102] This is experienced on the Alpha weekend whereby one gains assurance, discussed below. Although both gradual and event type of conversions are described as legitimate ways of becoming a Christian,[103] the predominant model in the Alpha publicity are event type conversions, with dramatic stories particularly valued. For example, in Gumbel's talk, 'Principles of Alpha',[104] all eight of the quotes he uses from questionnaires refer to an experience on the Alpha weekend which gave guests assurance.

This talk ends with another opportunity to say the 'sinner's prayer'. From Week 4 onwards, the Alpha content presumes faith and thus functions more like a catechetical course, dealing with various aspects of discipleship and evangelism.

2.1.5 WHY AND HOW SHOULD I READ THE BIBLE?

Gumbel notes the range of the Bible's literary genre, including historical,

---

[97] Taylor 1992:302.

[98] Wright 1998:52-53.

[99] Howes 2001; Wilson 1970.

[100] Bebbington 1989:8 emphasis in original. See also Smith 1978:56; Packer 1986:101; Grudem 1994:803-806. Before the rise of Evangelicalism, assurance of personal salvation was a prominent feature of seventeenth century Puritanism, although it demanded hard work and was an exceptional possession rather than normative for Christians (see Gillett 1993:Ch.3).

[101] Bebbington 1989:57.

[102] Gumbel 2001e:55.

[103] Gumbel 2001e:54.

[104] Gumbel 2001d.

narrative and apocalyptic literature as well as prophecy, letters and poetry.[105] Gumbel views the Bible as a rulebook. He describes how 'Rules and regulations can in fact create freedom and increase enjoyment...[God] tells us what is "in" and what is "out"' and gives an analogy of a football game, the enjoyment of which depends upon having boundaries.[106] Alpha can again be seen as something located within the Reformed tradition, with the emphasis on *sola scriptura*, rather than, for example, on the Roman Catholic teaching authority.[107] Rather than viewing the Church as locus of interpretation under the leading of the Holy Spirit, the Reformer's attitude towards the Church tended to be one of criticism and suspicion.[108] *Sola scriptura* was interpreted in different ways. For Hooker, and in the official Anglican formularies, the stress was on what was necessary for salvation. Hooker viewed other things, such as church order, as 'accessory'; not necessary but prudent and edifying to follow.[109] In contrast, the Puritans tended to take the Bible as a body of prescriptive truths legislating for every aspect of Christian worship and discipline. If something could not be found directly in Scripture, it was rejected. While Gumbel affirms that the Bible is the Christian's 'supreme authority' and above church leaders, he is careful to describe the importance of giving weight to 'what church leaders and others say provided it does not conflict with the revealed word of God'.[110] I shall return to the issue of ecclesiology and authority in Chapter 7.

Also within Alpha's Reformed heritage, the view of the Bible on Alpha is largely an inerrant one, where the perspicuity, or clarity, of the Bible is assumed.[111] Such arguments rely on a view of the Bible that predates most modern 'critical' scholarship and assume that the four Gospels are at least *prima facie* reliable historical documents, representing eyewitnesses or those who were conversant with eyewitnesses. Many contemporary scholars take a

---

[105] Gumbel 2001e:72.

[106] Gumbel 2001e:75. See Hopewell's (1988:79-81) canonical category.

[107] In a heavy polemic of the Reformers, William Abraham (2002:472) notes the roots of this doctrine:

Driven by soteriological interests and obsessed with what they took to be a corruption of the life of the primitive and patristic church, the Reformers sought to reform and then to rebuild the church virtually from scratch. In doing so, they quickly adopted a thoroughly epistemic conception of the canon of Scripture. They turned to a doctrine of *sola scriptura* as the strategy for comprehensive reform.

See also O'Collins 1981:196-200.

[108] Abraham 2002:149.

[109] Avis 2002:46.

[110] Gumbel 2001e:73-74.

[111] Gumbel 2001e:70-73. However, in the Reformed tradition, one can believe the latter, without holding to the former. Wayne Grudem (1994:108) describes perspicuity of the Bible as 'being written in such a way that its teachings are able to be understood by all who will read it seeking God's help and being willing to follow it'.

more sceptical view of these documents, seeing them as largely created by the early church for liturgical and polemical purposes.[112] Gumbel avoids reference to the last 200 years of biblical scholarship in an attempt at communicating an evangelistic message. Neither is there any recognition of post-modern hermeneutics such as literary criticism, nor sociological approaches like feminist and liberation hermeneutics.[113] Presumably, this would be too advanced for a course whose aim is 'stripping the gospel down to its bare essentials'.[114] Gumbel's response to the historicity of the gospels is in an endnote, recommending R. T. France and N. T. Wright.[115]

Building on the assumption of biblical perspicuity, Gumbel suggests a particular hermeneutical approach for the Alpha guest, which involves three stages.[116] First, read the passage and ask what it says. Second, what did it mean to the original authors? Gumbel suggests 'notes' might help for this. And third, how does it apply to me? Authority is attached to the meaning which was fixed in the ancient past. Although there are more sophisticated versions of authorial intention,[117] such a view has come under attack from various directions.[118] Is there just one meaning in the text? And what about the interplay between the intention of the original author, the editors and the canonising body of believers?

Percy describes how many Evangelical groups find difficulty in distinguishing between the text and the interpreter. There might be a notional clarity about the difference but in practice the belief tends to be much more blurred.[119] This has implications for Alpha and Gumbel as the authoritative interpretation of the Bible. What is the place of tradition in the hermeneutical task? There is no recognition that we read the text within the context of wider society, with all the power structures and other issues involved in that. And no other approaches to reading the Bible, for example, *lectio divina*, are suggested.[120]

2.1.6 WHY AND HOW DO I PRAY?

In the talk on prayer, Gumbel again assumes a basic trinitarian grammar. He describes prayer as being to the Father, through the Son, and by the Spirit.[121]

---

[112] Borg 1994; Clines 1997; Hick 1993.

[113] See Klien, Blomberg and Hubbard 1993:427-57.

[114] Millar in Gumbel 2001g:22.

[115] R. T. France, *The Evidence for Jesus* (1986); N. T. Wright, *Jesus and the Victory of God* (1996).

[116] Gumbel 2001e:81.

[117] See Hirsch 1967; Vanhoozer 1998.

[118] Fish 1980; Kelsey 1975; Thiselton 1992.

[119] Percy 1996.

[120] See Houston 1996:96; Peterson 2006. For the Roman Catholic Church, catechesis should be 'an authentic introduction to *lectio divina*' (Pope Paul VI 1971 para 127).

[121] Gumbel 2001e:84-86.

The Christian prays so as to develop their relationship with God, to follow Jesus's example, because there are 'rewards for prayer' and because prayer changes both the Christian and particular situations. Unanswered prayer is a result of unconfessed sin, disobedience, wrong motivation, or because the request is not according to God's will. Although Gumbel states that there is no set way to pray, he does suggest a format for prayer: adoration, confession, thanksgiving and supplication. Then Gumbel gives a description of the Lord's Prayer. No other forms of prayer are mentioned or encouraged, for example, meditation, silence, or the Jesus Prayer.

2.1.7 How Does God Guide Us?

Gumbel assures Alpha participants in the talk on guidance that God has a good purpose for our lives, which we need to ask him about. One can receive God's guidance through the Bible; through the Holy Spirit; common sense; the counsel of saints, by which Gumbel means godly Christians rather than in a more catholic sense; and lastly, circumstantial signs, which can often include supernatural occurrences.

2.1.8 Alpha Holy Spirit Weekend

The Alpha day away or weekend is considered to be a crucial part of the course, and focuses on the Holy Spirit. In contrast to Alpha's minimalist theology of the Old Testament, Trinity, ecclesiology, sacraments, creation, and social justice, Alpha includes a major emphasis on the Holy Spirit. Gumbel considers a weekend as being far better than a day away, because during this time friendships are deepened much more easily, and barriers begin to come down as guests unwind in a relaxed environment.[122] Gumbel says that the weekend is played down so that guests do not think that what they experience on it is the be all and end all, but that they grow into the disciplines of the Christian life, that is, Bible reading, prayer, church involvement, sacraments and social action.[123]

A typical weekend, outlined below, includes a mixture of worship, talks and small group discussions, as well as a free afternoon and a 'revue' on Saturday evening.

Friday

6.30pm onward	Arrive
8.00–10pm	Supper
9.45pm	Worship and short introduction to the weekend.

Saturday

8.45am	Breakfast

---

[122] Gumbel 2001g:64.
[123] Gumbel 2004.

9.30am	Worship followed by Talk 1 'Who is the Holy Spirit?'
10.45am	Coffee
11.15pm	Talk 2 'What does the Holy Spirit do?'
12 noon	Small group discussion on the gifts of the Spirit.
1.00pm	Lunch followed by free afternoon.
4.00pm	Optional tea
5.00pm	Worship followed by Talk 3 'How can I be filled with the Spirit?' and 'ministry time'.
7.00pm	Supper
9.00pm	Revue. A variety of sketches and songs without anything distasteful, religious or nasty.

Sunday

9.00am	Breakfast
9.45am	Small group discussion about what the guests experienced or saw experienced the previous evening.
10.30am	Worship followed by Talk 4 'How can I make the most of the rest of my life?' Holy Communion and another 'ministry time'.
1pm	Lunch.

The overall aim of the weekend is for guests to be 'filled with the Spirit' and using charismatic gifts. Watling writes:

> Alpha aims to make Christianity emotionally relevant for individuals, *felt* as much as *learnt*. It encourages (and ideally involves) *embodiment* of Christian beliefs.[124]

While 'becoming a Christian' on Alpha involves the matrix of repentance, faith, receiving the Holy Spirit and baptism, the main stress of initiation is on an experience, a charismatic encounter with the Holy Spirit, which then brings assurance of salvation. This presents quite a complex and rich vision of conversion. For example, it contrasts with the 'four spiritual laws' espoused by Bill Bright.[125] Such a perspective resonates with Gumbel's (above) stress on the process involved on the course. It is an emphasis that could potentially be understood within the framework of deification.[126] Given Alpha's historical roots in Charismatic Renewal and the influence of John Wimber, of far greater influence than deification is the Pentecostal–Charismatic emphasis on a 'second blessing', 'baptism in the Spirit', or being 'filled with the Spirit'.[127] There have

---

[124] Watling 2005:93 emphasis in original.
[125] See www.campuscrusade.com, accessed 12 July 2006.
[126] See Hart 1997; Louth 2005; Ware 1997.
[127] See Hocken 1997:165-70; Kay 2004:83-87.

been major debates between the classical Pentecostal position that emphasises a distinct post-conversion second-blessing, a *donum superadditum*,[128] and the Charismatic Renewal stress that the Spirit is given at conversion, but can be continually experienced in post-conversion fillings.[129] The latter was what David Watson taught[130] and is what Gumbel describes below. The Charismatic Movement did not insist that glossolalia was a proof of baptism, they played down the initiatory emphasis implicit in the Pentecostal phrase, and, unlike the Pentecostals, did not have a period of 'deep heart-searching and persistent seeking', or 'tarrying' for the Spirit.[131]

Gumbel makes explicit reference to Wayne Grudem's theology and situates Alpha within the charismatic position.[132] Gumbel explains:

> We're not talking about a 'second blessing'. Please don't misunderstand anything that we're saying. What we're talking about is experiencing God as Trinity: Father, Son and Holy Spirit. And we believe that that experience should happen at conversion – and should *continue* in the life of the believer.[133]

In other words, baptism of the Spirit or, preferably, being 'filled with the Spirit',[134] happens at conversion, with the possibility of further 'growth experiences'.[135] Yet, having so positioned himself, Gumbel then seems to argue for a distinct post-conversion experience. He describes this in the talk, 'How can I be filled with the Spirit':

> We have at home a gas boiler, and it has a pilot light. The pilot light is on all the time. And that, if you like, is like a person who's a Christian: every Christian has the Holy Spirit living within them. But when the boiler fires, when the heat and the water go on, so to speak, the boiler goes *bbbrrrr*! Like that, *whoooosshh*! And then it starts firing on all cylinders, so to speak, if you'll forgive me mixing the

---

[128] See Menzies 1994.

[129] See Turner 1996a; 1996b. Notwithstanding the differences between the Pentecostal and Charismatic traditions, phenomenologically, there seems to be a common experience. As Hocken (1997:178) points out, the 'grace of baptism in the Spirit is the same among Pentecostals and Charismatics' while the difference was 'in the context of its reception and in the framework within which it is understood' (cf. Fiddes 1984:22-23).

[130] Saunders and Sansom 1992.

[131] Steven 2002:8-9.

[132] Grudem's 1994:763-87. See also Turner (1996a:158) who writes that the gift of the Spirit 'is granted in the complex of conversion–initiation...Both Paul and Luke anticipate a succession of further fresh experiences of the Spirit...'

[133] Gumbel 2001d.

[134] Gumbel tends to use 'filled with the Spirit' and 'baptism of the Spirit' as synonymous terms.

[135] Turner 1996a:166.

metaphors! And some Christians are pilot light Christians, and other Christians are *bbbrrrr* Christians! And Paul encourages us to be *bbbrrrr* Christians!

Gumbel goes on to describe 'baptism in the Spirit':

> Baptism with water is very important, but it is not enough. Jesus is the Spirit baptiser. The Greek word means 'to overwhelm', 'to immerse' or 'to plunge'. This is what should happen when we are baptised in the Spirit. We should be completely overwhelmed by, immersed in and plunged into the Spirit of God.[136]

While Gumbel does not view this experience of the Holy Spirit as being a one-off event, it does seem more in line with the classical Pentecostal notion of a two-stage, subsequent and separable experience.

Gumbel continues: 'The filling of the Spirit rarely happens imperceptibly, although the experience is different for everyone'.[137] The opportunity for this experience is on the weekend. There is the expectation that the Holy Spirit will come when asked, and that being filled with the Spirit will be immediate, clearly discernible and (potentially) will include speaking in tongues.[138] During the 'ministry time' at the weekend, participants are asked to stand, close their eyes and to hold out their hands in front of them if they would like to receive. Gumbel says a 'sinner's prayer', where guests are invited to become Christian. After the 'sinner's prayer' (the point of conversion) Gumbel suggests waiting for the Holy Spirit to come. Then worship songs begin and there is an opportunity, instigated by the worship leader and team members, to 'sing in tongues'. Other 'manifestations' of the Spirit are suggested including various feelings like 'glowing all over', 'liquid heat', or 'burning in my arms when I was not hot'.[139]

In the reports published by AI, the overwhelming majority describe a particular experience on the Alpha weekend, a 'Holy Spirit encounter', which provides assurance.[140] And despite Gumbel's stress that conversion can be a process, the normative experience is a crisis. Brian's analysis of thirty-six testimonies reported in seven successive editions of *Alpha News* noted that they all featured these sorts of dramatic experience.[141] He compared them to van Gennep's description of 'special acts' that mark transitions from one stage or group to another. Brian complains:

---

[136] Gumbel 2001e:123.

[137] Gumbel 2001e:145.

[138] Gumbel 2003a:14-17.

[139] Gumbel 2001e:146.

[140] Gillett (1993:62-63) suggests that the Charismatic Movement's emphasis on an experience of the Holy Spirit is re-owning the fullness of the Spirit's work of assurance that John Wesley emphasised but which had become a doctrine to be taught rather than an experience to be encouraged.

[141] Brian 2003:57-67.

The problem for the wider church, however, is that Gumbel equates these experiences with authentic Christianity. Those who have not had these experiences have a faith which is lacking.[142]

Despite Gumbel's distinction between pilot light Christians, and those 'firing on all cylinders', he insists that there are no first or second class Christians. This was not, however, the perception of Alpha guests, as I shall discuss in Chapter 5.[143] In some way, then, the experience of the Holy Spirit on the Alpha weekend is seen as being initiatory, and involves an affective element similar to John Wesley, where he felt his heart 'strangely warmed'.

For Roman Catholics, Orthodox and Anglicans, the two rites linked with the Holy Spirit are baptism and confirmation, or some kind of rite giving symbolic–sacramental expression to the sealing gift of the Holy Spirit. So, does Alpha teach about the sacraments? Gumbel answers, 'Yes...You won't find the teaching on the videos, because we do it in the context of a communion service'.[144] Because not everyone is in agreement about the sacraments, teaching on them is very limited owing to Alpha's ecumenical aims. It is important that denominational-particular teaching be added post-Alpha, otherwise there would be 'Baptist Alpha', 'Catholic Alpha', and so on. An informal communion service takes place on the Sunday morning of the weekend and is, Gumbel describes, 'the climax of the whole course'. Those who 'know and love Jesus Christ' are invited to receive communion,[145] in the fashion of the 'self-service' sacrament,[146] where people pass a loaf one to another. I shall discuss the rather unusual positioning of the Eucharist in the conversion–initiation matrix, in Chapter 7. The weekend ends with the talk 'How can I make the most of the rest of my life?' This is essentially a discipleship talk based upon Romans 12:1–2.

2.1.9 HOW CAN I RESIST EVIL?

The talk on evil is placed strategically because it is thought that, following the experience of the Holy Spirit at the weekend, guests will be attacked by the devil. 'As soon as we start to serve the Lord, [the Devil's] interest is aroused'.[147] Gumbel describes the aims and tactics of this personal devil: to

---

[142] Brian 2003:86.

[143] Philip Lee (1986:33, Ch.8) contends that the idea of a 'spiritual elite' who yearn for the kind of faith that is more intense and spiritual compared to 'ordinary Christians' is a form of gnosticism. Such an elitist attitude is highly divisive. The gnostics in the early church viewed themselves as Christians who *knew* what they believed and why. 'They were not content to be counted with nominal Christians, who simply attended public services but were too ignorant to speak meaningfully about their faith' (Lee 1986:162).

[144] Gumbel 2004.

[145] Gumbel 2001g:154.

[146] Martin 1981:51.

[147] Gumbel 2001e:159; cf. Wimber 2001:38.

destroy human beings, to stop them from becoming Christians and to raise doubts.[148] However, because 'we' are Christians, we belong to Christ and the kingdom of God, although not in its fullness. We must thus defend ourselves with the 'armour of God' (Eph. 6) and attack Satan through prayer and action (by which he means proclaiming the gospel, healing the sick and casting out demons).[149] The devil and his angels on Alpha are personal beings, cunning, powerful but evil.[150] As a result, spiritual warfare tends to be understood in terms of battling against a well-organised and trained army with great powers of detection and destruction[151] rather than, or perhaps also, recognising the social and institutional context of evil.[152] In Hopewell's categories, Alpha here reveals its charismatic world-view:

> [T]he charismatic narrative is a more frightening and thrilling place…The world in which the charismatic lives is fundamentally equivocal and dangerous, challenging the believer to seek its blessings amid the peril of evil forces and events. God's steady providence, however, accompanies the self who launches out toward God in an exciting romantic adventure.[153]

Although Gumbel rejects a dualist theology, that there exists 'two equal and opposite powers',[154] there is an implicit dualism on Alpha.[155] This can be seen in the chart below, taken from the Alpha manual (p.43).

Dominion of darkness	Kingdom of Light
Satan	Jesus
Sin	Forgiveness
Slavery to sin	Slaves of God (i.e. Freedom in Christ)
Death	Life
Destruction	Salvation

There is here the tendency, common in charismatic theology, to divide the world into God's kingdom of light and Satan's dominion of darkness, and of dissecting the world into 'us' and 'them'.

---

[148] Gumbel 2001e:158-64.

[149] Gumbel 2001e:166-70.

[150] Gumbel 2001e:158.

[151] Walker 1995:101.

[152] Walker 1987.

[153] Hopewell 1988:76.

[154] Gumbel 2001e:169.

[155] One critique of Alpha described the 'Manichean tendencies in the Alpha presentation, which can be contrasted with the Thomist understanding of evil as a distortion of the good' (Arguile 2002).

Walker notes that such theology is in danger of adopting and becoming entrapped and socialised into a paranoid universe.[156]

The next two talks are concerned with evangelism and mission. In 'Why and how should we tell others?' various means of evangelism are outlined, including 'presence,' 'persuasion', 'proclamation', 'power', all of which should be undergirded by prayer.[157] St Paul's 'testimony' (or rather Luke's version of it in Acts)[158] is suggested as a good way to tell others. Similar to Evangelical testimonies in general, it has a three-part structure comprising an early sinful life before the conversion, the conversion experience itself and changed lifestyle after the conversion. With the course reaching its final stages, the aim here is to encourage guests to invite others to the next Alpha course. Positively, these public acts of testifying serve as a ritual of welcome and inclusion and engage people on a very personal level.[159] Negatively, there is a tendency for a particular 'formula' to be used, with the result that people's conversion experiences end up being reformulated into a certain mould, to fit a preconceived (Evangelical) notion of how a 'true' conversion should be.[160] Alternatively, the type of person being interviewed will only be those who fit the prescribed interview formula. *Alpha News* choose particularly stark testimonies that emphasise the dramatic changes that characterise the testifier's life before and after conversion.

2.1.11 DOES GOD HEAL TODAY?

John Wimber is the inspiration of the talk 'Does God heal today?' with Wimber's first visit to HTB described in *Questions of Life*. Gumbel outlines the 'now' and 'not yet' of the kingdom of God, which is largely understood in supernatural terms. Although not everyone will be healed, Christians can regularly expect to heal, raise the dead and exorcise demons. This is one of the few moments on Alpha where Christian tradition is referred to. Examples from Irenaeus, Origen and Augustine are cited as proof that healings did not stop with the cessation of miracles beyond the apostolic age.[161] Gumbel's selective use, for example, of Augustine to build his case ignores the fact that Augustine was among the first to suggest that glossolalia had ceased.[162]

---

[156] Walker 1995:89. Walker (1995:88) instead suggests the patristic idea of a Christian world-view that is divided into the tripartite arenas of the divine, the natural, and the demonic, and in which the fallen and natural world includes the human will neither yet demonised nor yet redeemed.

[157] Gumbel 2001e:175-86.

[158] For the contrast between Luke and Paul's version see Gaventa 1986.

[159] Rambo 1993:158-59.

[160] See McKnight 2002.

[161] See Turner (1996a:286-302) on cessationism.

[162] See *Homilies on John*, VI:10 in Schaff 1995, c1888.

Following the talk, instead of a small group discussion, the groups pray for one another. This involves the use of spiritual gifts such as words of knowledge, gathered from team members during the prayer meeting before the Alpha session, which Gumbel gives at the end of his talk. The 'theology', 'model' and 'practice' of ministry is derived from Wimber and was imbibed by HTB through its visits to the Vineyard Conferences.

2.1.12 WHAT ABOUT THE CHURCH?

The primary way the Church is described is as a Christian family rather than being associated with the clergy, denomination or church buildings. Gumbel appeals to the NT for five analogies to describe the Church. The Church is the 'people of God'. Following Church Growth advocates, Gumbel outlines three types of gathering: celebration, congregation and cell. The Church is 'the family of God', which gives it its unity. Appeal is made to the *koinonia*[163] experienced between church denominations. 1 Corinthians is appealed to, which expresses the church as the 'body of Christ'. Wimber is again referred to, as is the Church Growth emphasis on 'every member ministry', in contrast to a view of Church that is either pulpit or altar-centred, and which is priest led. Next, the Church as a 'holy temple', and the priesthood of all believers is stressed. For Gumbel, priesthood is equated with being a 'leader'. Lastly, the church is described as being the 'bride of Christ'.[164]

Since the course became more ecumenical in focus, Gumbel has stripped back this talk to what is essentially a rather minimalist ecclesiology. A short description of both baptism and the Eucharist is outlined. Baptism is the visible 'mark' of being a member of a church, and 'signifies' cleansing from sin, rather than conferring or mediating God's grace sacramentally. For the Eucharist, the word 'represent' is used, thus avoiding controversies over what 'real presence' might mean. There is no discussion of an organising principle of Spirit and institution, church life and structure.[165] Other controversies are also avoided, such as no mention of women priests.[166]

2.1.13 SUMMARY

In this section, I have given an outline of Alpha's content. While Gumbel perceives the basics on Alpha as including those things upon which all

---

[163] This word, expressing the mystery of communion, has been particularly helpful ecumenically following its prominence at the Second Vatican Council (see Ratzinger 1992), although there are questions on whether the word has been given more weight than it is able to carry (WCC Report 1998).

[164] Gumbel 2001e:203-17.

[165] Bebbington (1989:244) comments that an anti-institutional bias has been a common characteristic among Charismatics.

[166] Although there are a number of women involved in various aspects of HTB's church life, and although several from HTB have been ordained, as yet, the church has not had a female curate.

Christians agree, a sort of pure gospel package taken straight from the NT, I have attempted to situate Alpha historically and theologically. This has included the use of an Enlightenment rationalist apologetic, and various influences from the Reformed and Evangelical–Charismatic tradition, with a particular indebtedness to John Wimber. Alpha's roots as a discipleship course were also noted, with an assumption that guests will have a basic understanding of NT books and trinitarian grammar. We next move on to a description of the practical structuring of the course and small group dynamics.

2.3 Preparation

Detailed advice is given on setting up an Alpha course. First, dates must be fixed well in advance. It is necessary to run Alpha at least nine times in a row before you know whether or not it will work. For the first three courses, mostly Christians attend the course. When the numbers on these three courses invariably drop, because most of the church members have done the course, churches lose heart and conclude that Alpha is not working. However, Gumbel would maintain, Alpha has not yet really begun. It is usually during the third course that non-churched guests start to come. To maintain a momentum, it is important 'to run *at least* three courses a year'.[167] This is based around academic terms rather than linked to the Church's liturgical year. Gumbel quotes Peter Brierley of Christian Research, in which 96 per cent of the churches running Alpha were getting people from outside of the church. Gumbel concludes that getting non-churchgoers is becoming less of a problem, commenting, 'I've never myself had an experience of being on a course where it's only Christians'.[168] This will be assessed in Chapter 5, but it is worth noting that Gumbel gets a rather skewed perception of Alpha small groups due to the fact, commonly known among staff at HTB, that he ensures his Alpha group are 'hand picked' to include an assortment of young, bright and high achieving non-churchgoers.

Second, the ideal venue is a home, but if a bigger venue is needed, it needs to be with a welcoming atmosphere. Third, the importance of advertising to the non-churched and those on the fringes. Alpha regularly uses the endorsement of celebrities in its publicity.[169] This is a common motif among Evangelicals and has been critiqued by Cheryl Forbes[170] and Martyn Percy.[171] Forbes writes:

> We like to know that famous and beautiful people are Christians; it makes us average Christians seem that much more important. But the ugly, the maimed, the

---

[167] Gumbel 2001g:66 emphasis in original.

[168] Gumbel 2004.

[169] On 'Christian celebrity power' see Bartholomew 2006.

[170] Forbes 1986.

[171] Percy 1996.

poor, the weak, the untalented?...who would buy our products without the right packaging?[172]

Next, careful advice is given about selecting and training a team, although Gumbel notes that twenty-six per cent of the churches that are running Alpha have not conducted any team training. And as a result 'small groups will almost certainly be a disaster'.[173] Alpha small groups are arranged so that when guests arrive, they are, first, preferably greeted by a 'normal' person.[174] Behind this statement is Gumbel's desire to construct what he perceives to be a positive image of the Christian faith. This is also seen in their approach to marketing, as its use of celebrities demonstrates. The guest is then given a name label and then put into a group with a balance of characters, social backgrounds, profession, and so on.[175] It is suggested that, if possible, one should find out as much as one can about guests before they arrive so as to put them into an appropriate group. Every guest is given an Alpha manual which provides the outline for each talk, provides space for notes, and gives a recommended reading list. This list ranges from popular novels to theological books 'for the advanced reader'. Alpha small group leaders are given a 'leader's manual', which covers the pre-Alpha training and provides questions for the discussion.

2.4 Small Groups

One of the most significant features of Alpha is the small group. An ideal small group has twelve people, with two leaders, two helpers and eight guests. Careful instruction is given to the leaders and helpers, with two training sessions before Alpha begins, covering 'pastoral care' and 'leading small groups', and the third session held before the Alpha weekend, covering 'ministry'. In 'Leading small groups', the leaders learn how to host an Alpha discussion. The overall goal here, along with the course as a whole, is to convert the guests, although such language as 'bring people into a relationship with Jesus Christ' is used.[176] There is another role within Alpha that has not yet been specifically acknowledged or defined by AI or others, namely, sponsors. Similar to the emphasis given on the catechumenate to an accompanied faith journey[177] sponsors are Christians who accompany a friend to a course, and informally support them outside the official Alpha context. Sponsors are enrolled as guests but they often assume the role of a helper but without any Alpha training.

---

[172] Forbes 1986:61.

[173] Gumbel 2004.

[174] Gumbel 2001g:174.

[175] Gumbel 2001g:171.

[176] Gumbel 2001g:110.

[177] See *On the Way* 1995:35; Kavanagh 1978:131; Johnson 1999:360; Webber 2001:118.

The small group has six aims: to facilitate discussion; to model Bible study; to pray together, although this must be done sensitively; to develop relationships; to minister to one another, which ideally means 'praying for each other, laying on hands and praying for healing'; and training others to lead.

The latest videos have a 'ball game' object lesson. The essential point of it is that the ball, or discussion, should be passed around to all of the people in the group rather than always returning to the group leader. Three styles of leadership have been identified by management theorists: autocratic, democratic and laissez faire.[178] Autocratic leaders retain as much power and decision-making authority as possible. They tend not to consult and *they* decide which group members can speak, when and how much. Democratic leaders take a shared, participatory approach to decision-making. Laissez faire leaders take a 'hands off', non-participatory approach, providing little or no direction in a group, so that they are free to determine goals and make decisions on their own. Research has found that the most effective style is democratic.[179] The democratic style tended to be more efficient and engendered an enhanced level of originality or creative thinking. In addition, there was more group-mindedness and friendliness.[180] In contrast, autocratic leadership can create hostility, aggression, and discontent that does not appear on the surface, and it can result in people leaving groups.[181] Alpha's aim is to engender a democratic style of leadership. This is significant in that, as Lewin discovered, greater change is produced when people are allowed to participate compared with when they are not.[182] There is an inherent pejorative value judgment in Lewin's typology that makes its use problematic. I shall, instead, use the following terms: directive, participatory and non-directive.

Very detailed advice is given on the environment, including ventilation, light and timing. Leaders are instructed to ask two basic questions: 'What do you think?' and 'What do you feel?' Leaders should be encouragers and good at listening. This is similar in some respects to the 'brainstorming' approach used by many industrial organisations where the basic rule is that ideas are expressed with no evaluation permitted and where any idea, no matter how absurd, is acceptable.[183] However, it is also dissimilar because if someone says something that is 'not correct', the leader should respond 'with a phrase like "How interesting", or "I have never heard that before".' The idea behind this is to include the rest of the group and to 'reach the right conclusion'.[184] It is easy to

---

[178] Lewin, Lippitt and White 1939; Lewin 1947; White and Lippitt 1968; Van Vugt et al. 2004.

[179] Lewin, Lippitt and White 1939; White and Lippitt 1968; Argyle 1983.

[180] White and Lippitt 1968:326-27.

[181] Van Vugt et al. 2004.

[182] Lewin 1958.

[183] Shaw 1961.

[184] Gumbel 2001g:111.

see how such advice is viewed by critics of Alpha as being prescriptive.[185]

The 'pastoral care' training session emphasises the importance of developing genuine friendship with guests. 'There must be no false pretence', with one-to-one care perhaps the most crucial aspect of Alpha.[186] Gumbel describes the main aim as being spiritual maturity (Col. 1.28-9), although he recognises that this will take longer than a ten-week course. The way to bring spiritual maturity is, first, to convert people, or 'lead [non-Christians] to Christ'.[187] Instruction for how to do this is given; leaders and helpers are encouraged to use the 'sinner's prayer' at the back of Gumbel's *Why Jesus?* booklet. Following conversion leaders are told to help guests with Bible reading and prayer. Gumbel sees these small groups as being ecclesial communities, as a part of the Church. However, this relationship is not described in any detail.

The advice given in 'leading small groups' is reiterated in pastoral care. Small groups must have an atmosphere of love and encouragement. Leaders must be good at listening and take a genuine interest in guests. This means not quickly correcting non-Christian views and avoiding arguments. Lastly, leaders are told that Alpha is hard work, to give it the same priority they would give to their jobs, but they can expect to be 'fuelled' or empowered by the Holy Spirit.[188]

2.5 After Alpha

Gumbel recognises that Alpha does not always convert people, and HTB's research found that approximately 30 per cent of Alpha guests had, for various reasons, dropped out.[189] Gumbel has therefore recognised the importance of integrating Alpha graduates into the life of the Christian community. Gumbel states:

Alpha is Term 1 in a two-year programme of adult Christian education.[190]

He has written four follow on courses with the aim of providing solid biblical roots for the Alpha 'graduate'. He views these courses as constituting an integral part of the ongoing spiritual formation of Alpha guests. They include *A Life Worth Living*,[191] which is a Bible study based upon the book of Philippians. *Searching Issues*[192] deals with the seven most commonly asked questions and

---

[185] Brian 2003; Drane 2007; Gill 2001; Ireland 2000; Meadows 2007; Percy 2001.

[186] Gumbel 2001g:89-90.

[187] Gumbel 2001g:92.

[188] Gumbel 2001g:93-97.

[189] Gumbel 2001g:92.

[190] Gumbel 2004.

[191] Gumbel 2001c.

[192] Gumbel 2001f.

the most difficult and controversial parts of the Alpha content. The seven subjects are suffering, other religions, sex before marriage, the New Age, homosexuality, science and Christianity, and the Trinity. This corroborates Hunt's research[193] and suggests that *Searching Issues* is, on the whole, presenting the relevant questions. *Challenging Lifestyle*[194] lasts for two terms and is a study on the Sermon of the Mount. Lastly, *The Heart of Revival*[195] is ten Bible studies based on the book of Isaiah.

3. Summary

In this chapter, I have attempted to describe Alpha as it sees itself. Alpha's basis on six New Testament principles was outlined, although as Gumbel admits, these are *post hoc* justification for existing practice. The practicalities of starting and running a course were also described. Alpha's primary aim is to convert guests, although Gumbel recognises that the longer term aim of 'spiritual maturity' or discipleship will take more than ten weeks. Hence Alpha represents only part one of a two-year programme. Gumbel has attempted to create a package that combines mission and spiritual formation. Its roots as a discipleship course were noted, with an assumption that guests know the basics of the Christian faith. The course starts with an apologetic thrust and with a push for 'closure', although Gumbel has left the more contentious issues for the small group discussion. From Week 3 onwards, the content is specifically catechetical rather than evangelistic.

I also attempted to situate Alpha contextually and theologically. By doing so, I have challenged Gumbel's assumption that Alpha only includes those things upon which all Christians agree. In his claim to be teaching basic NT Christianity, Gumbel is forced to draw from a very narrow range of sources and to be highly selective, for example, in his limited appeal to the Church Fathers. Cooper writes:

> History belies any attempt at defining an essence of Christianity...the development and enactment of Christian community is always culturally specific, influenced by – and, in turn, influencing – the concrete and material conditions of the society around it.[196]

Although Gumbel dislikes being described as Evangelical, the ethos and theology of the course is firmly within the Charismatic–Evangelical tradition, with a particular indebtedness to John Wimber and the Church Growth Movement. Particular doctrines, among others, within this tradition include a rationalist apologetic, penal substitution, *sola scriptura* and the perspicuity of

---

[193] Hunt 2004:135.
[194] Gumbel 2001a.
[195] Gumbel 2001b.
[196] Cooper 2001:360-61.

the Bible, a life changing encounter with the Holy Spirit which brings assurance of faith, and a minimalist ecclesiology.

Alpha's methodology and theology seems to be reasonably unproblematic for Charismatic–Evangelicals, judging by the sixteen pages of endorsements of Alpha in *Telling Others*.[197] However, those from other parts of the Church are less content, and it is to these that we turn to in the following chapter.

---

[197] Gumbel 2001g. These endorsements are almost entirely from leaders within the Charismatic–Evangelical tradition.

Chapter 3

Literature Review

A search of the internet will reveal links to thousands of articles relating to the Alpha course. Reaction tends to be polarised. Those who are opposed to the course have various criticisms based upon their churchmanship. For example, several conservative Evangelicals[1] rule out Alpha primarily because the course is not conservative Evangelical. For them, Alpha does not have enough focus on the Bible, God's holiness, sin, wrath and repentance, 'the lack of fire' for non-believers,[2] too much emphasis on the Holy Spirit, and excessive humour (which detracts from the seriousness of the gospel). This group also discounts Alpha both because of its ecumenical stance[3] and for its 'liberal' sources.[4] They conclude that Alpha is not biblical Christianity, not the 'true gospel', but rather a dangerous New Age version of it. As previously noted, from a more moderate conservative Evangelical perspective, Rico Tice has in response written *Christianity Explored*.[5]

In this chapter, I shall review six of the most significant assessments and researches of Alpha (see Appendix 1 for a fuller list). It will become apparent that there is a dearth of substantial research on Alpha, and an almost complete lack of qualitative research, a lack that this book will attempt to redress.

1. Martyn Percy

Martyn Percy, Principal of the Anglican theological college, Ripon College Cuddesdon, wrote a short journal article entitled 'Join-the-dots Christianity'.[6] Not having attended Alpha, Percy's critique was based upon the course's resources. He praised Alpha for not being 'hit and run' evangelism, that it was situated in local churches and that it included supportive literature to aid enquirers. He then raised various objections to the course. First, Alpha's weak

---

[1] Hand 1998; McDonald 1996; McDonald and Peterson 2001.

[2] McDonald and Peterson 2001.

[3] McDonald (1996:19) accuses it of Romanism, which she equates with Jehovah Witnesses and Moonies.

[4] Hand (1998:91) refers to Tillich and Moltmann, and to Mother Teresa who 'is accepted as a Christian despite evidence that she held no firm Christian convictions'.

[5] For an analysis, see Booker and Ireland 2003.

[6] Percy 1997; see also Percy 2001:179-89.

ecclesiology, seen in the way that it expects people to become Christians first and then to think about joining a church. Second, a question over *who* decides what constitutes the basics of Christianity. Third, Alpha's over-emphasis on the Holy Spirit. He objects to Alpha's presentation of an individualistic 'personal, therapeutic, home-counties' presentation of the Spirit, with little mention of the Spirit's work in creation, justice, peace, reconciliation and the wider church. Its 'sugar-coated, crude and narrow' version of the Christian faith is weak on sin, suffering, atonement, sacraments and sacrifice. Percy suggests that the basics should include the trinity, baptism, communion or community. While Percy admits the basic skeleton of the course provides a good template for churches to use and adapt, its weakness lies in its theological foundations. Alpha sets up its own caricatured objections to Christian faith and then offers answers to them. As a result, it is rather prescriptive; a package rather than a pilgrimage. Percy is correct about the style of apologetics used on Alpha, as we have seen in Chapter 2. Further, he comments that guests have little space to reflect on and vent their own concerns. This contrasts with the ideal dynamics of an Alpha small group, such groups being designed for that very purpose. However, as we shall discover in Chapter 5 (§4.4), the groups largely failed to achieve such open discussion.

Cambridge theologian, Markus Bockmuehl, responded to what he called Percy's 'spirited diatribe' on Alpha.[7] These old arguments relate to Evangelicalism in general – weak ecclesiology and trivialisation of the sacraments – and have a significant grain of truth in them. Nevertheless, Percy's 'shooting from the hip', he argues, often misses the target. Bockmuehl points to Percy's contradiction in his critique that Alpha offers an uncontextual Christianity, yet accuses it of relating to the 'home-counties context' and its 'middle-class outlook'. Bockmuehl is correct in noting the way that Percy locates HTB's particular context; after all, we are all situated within some *lebenswelt*. But Bockmuehl misses Percy's point that HTB's context, and the basics it includes, has been pre-packaged and copyrighted so that local adaptation in other contexts is 'illegal'.

Bockmuehl also questions Percy's unsubstantiated comments, for example, that most Alpha converts fail to become church members. Further, Percy's accusation of Evangelicalism's lack of social conscience ignores the tradition's long history of social engagement. What Bockmuehl finds most puzzling is Percy's distaste for Christian catechesis that is concerned with 'basics'. In particular, he notes Percy's fear that elementary Christianity 'keeps more issues out than it actually addresses' and that it should attempt to formulate 'answers' to certain basic questions. This, Bockmuehl argues, is not bad as pedagogical principles go, and at least it helps people to 'join (some of) the dots' of the faith rather than leaving them in the mire of half-Christian platitudes and neo-paganism. However, Bockmuehl again neglects an important aspect of Percy's

---

[7] Bockmuehl 1998.

argument, which is about authority. Simply put, who exactly chooses what basics constitute the Christian faith; why are certain basics selected and others omitted? This again relates to HTB's theology and context. Percy's concern does not seem to be associated with the idea of introducing people to the Christian faith, contra Bockmuehl, but with the particular sort of Christianity offered on Alpha.

2. Stephen Brian

Liberal Anglican priest, Stephen Brian, takes up Percy's point about Alpha's basics in his Ph.D thesis entitled, 'The Alpha Course: an analysis of its claim to offer an educational course on the meaning of life'.[8] His two main questions are: does Alpha provide an opportunity of exploring the meaning of life – as it promotes itself as doing in its publicity? His short answer to this is no, which leads to his next question: what is the function of Alpha's teaching? Brian's conclusion about this is that Alpha is primarily about the expansion of its own version of Christianity within the existing Church.

Brian's methodology includes content analysis of Alpha resources, eighty three semi-structured questionnaires and seventy three semi-structured interviews in a 'southern diocese' in England. Those interviewed comprised forty-one Alpha graduates, including two drop-outs, fourteen parochial clergy, two senior clergy, one academic (Pete Ward) and Nicky Gumbel. He also interviewed fourteen random individuals, most of whom had little or no contact with the church or with Alpha and who were asked what they would expect from any course offering 'an opportunity to explore the meaning of life'.

Brian raises the important question regarding what exactly Alpha is: is it essentially evangelistic, catechetical or educational? Brian notes that Alpha uses the language of education ('a course', 'exploring') yet it claims to be evangelistic, and also has a catechetical style.[9] Brian assesses it from an educational perspective. He critiques Alpha for misleading people in its advertising because it does not offer an opportunity to explore the meaning of life from a genuinely open educational perspective. The Alpha content, in contrast, is fixed and the non-negotiable 'truths' are promulgated in the name of orthodoxy. It is, Brian argues, promoted as an 'exploration', yet allows no room for exploration, deviation or criticism.[10] Brian's main conclusion is that Alpha is not really, 'An opportunity to explore the meaning of life'; rather, it is, 'An opportunity to explore the meaning of life from a Charismatic–Evangelical ethically conservative point of view' – while painting itself as normative Christianity. As a priest, Brian seemed concerned that those who attended Alpha and disliked the content would be put off Christianity because they

---

[8] Brian 2003.
[9] Brian 2003:11.
[10] Brian 2003:92.

would assume that Alpha teaches Christian orthodoxy. However, while AI may be disingenuous in not being more explicit about its theological moorings, it never claims, contra Brian, to be an open educational programme. The Alpha resources make this abundantly clear (see Chapter 2). Its use of terms such as 'explore' and 'meaning of life' are simply the 'hooking technique' it uses in its marketing campaigns.[11]

Further, the Alpha posters have consistently included the strap line, 'coming to a church near you', thus disclosing its Christian identity. In short, Brian's main thesis question – to assess Alpha's central claim to give people an opportunity to explore the meaning of life – is not actually the aim of Alpha itself.

**Does Alpha offer an opportunity to
explore the meaning of life?**

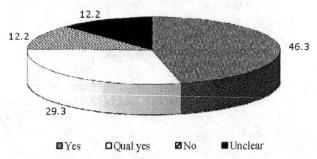

Further, Brian concludes that Alpha does not offer the opportunity to explore the meaning of life, despite the perception of those he himself interviewed: approximately 76 per cent gave a qualified or unqualified yes to this question, in contrast to just 12 per cent who said no (see chart above, taken from Brian[12]). Brian discounts this affirmative response by explaining that it was due to the high percentage of Christians on Alpha. Brian is thus using other criteria to assess his thesis about Alpha's claims.

Brian then suggests that Alpha guests go through a process of 'de-Christianisation'. That is, guests who would have described themselves as Christian before embarking on Alpha are persuaded by the end of the course that they were not 'proper Christians' at all, but had come to be so after completing Alpha. Conversion on Alpha, then, is from one form of Christianity (nominal) to another (Charismatic–Evangelical). Brian argues that Alpha has succeeded in enlarging the Charismatic constituency within churches, and

---

[11] Walker (foreword in Hunt 2001) suggests that Alpha is located in the 'just looking' tradition, similar to the posters of the School of Economic Science lectures on the London Underground. It has the aim of stimulating curiosity by offering the possibility of knowledge and personal growth.

[12] Brian 2003:178.

being a fierce critic of the Charismatic tradition, he finds this alarming.

Brian's thesis is methodologically thin (two pages). His suggestion[13] that his thesis could be classified as 'grounded theory' is doubtful. Grounded theory attempts to allow theory to emerge with initial decisions not based upon a preconceived theoretical framework.[14] In contrast, Brian began his research with particular pre-set questions about Alpha and with an educational theoretical framework. Brian's methodology particularly lacks reflexivity. He places himself within a liberal position compared with the Charismatic–Evangelical theology of Alpha. He comments:

> Nevertheless, every attempt has been made to allow the comments and criticisms voiced by each of the participants in the research to be heard and interpreted as fairly as possible...any observations of Alpha's success or failure in meeting its own claims have been made by reference to those same claims without any external reference to a different (more liberal) agenda.[15]

He seems to be suggesting that his more liberal stance neither affected his selection of data nor his analysis of how effective Alpha was in accomplishing its own claims. This is far too naïve. As I shall discuss in Chapter 4, reflexivity involves self-awareness about one's own interpretative lenses, the effect one has on those being studied, and attentiveness of how oneself is affected by the research. For example, while he criticises Ireland (see §4 below) for relying on the comments of priests, Brian's selection criteria is reliant on rural deans (for which church leaders to interview), and parish priests (for which Alpha graduates to interview). Surely he is not claiming they have a lack of bias?

The main contention Brian has with Alpha is due to a difference between a deductive and inductive approach. Alpha's more catechetical (deductive) approach is about the faithful transmission of Christian faith, whereas Brian's (inductive) educational, and he claims Anglican, method values learning for its own sake and is reluctant to stifle theological exploration. For a potential resolution between these two approaches, see Chapter 7 (§5).

3. Pete Ward

Pete Ward wrote what became a controversial journal article entitled, 'Alpha – The McDonaldization of Religion?'[16] Ward takes George Ritzer's analysis of *The McDonaldization of Society* in order to critique the Alpha course.[17] Ritzer describes McDonaldization as 'the process by which the principles of the fast-

---

[13] Brian 2003:13.

[14] Glaser and Strauss 1968:46; see also Strauss and Corbin 1998.

[15] Brian 2003:132.

[16] Ward 1998.

[17] Ritzer's 1996. See also John Drane's (2000) critique of the production side of consumer religion.

food restaurant are coming to dominate more and more sectors of American society and the rest of the world'.[18] These principles are expressed in four core values. McDonald's 'offer consumers, workers, and managers efficiency, calculability, predictability and control'.[19] Ward contends that Alpha fits with today's consumerist mindset and it can be seen as a significant contextualisation of the methods of evangelism. Like McDonalds, Alpha operates on a global franchising system; it has a recognisable 'product' with a strong brand label; the central organisation of Alpha retains fairly strict social controls on franchisees; it has global ambitions and both McDonalds and Alpha have spawned imitations. Following Ritzer's thesis, Ward suggests that Alpha fits late capitalism. Alpha itself offers consumers, workers and mangers efficiency, calculability, predictability and control.

In Alpha, efficiency is present in the packaging of Alpha material for easy use, and in the streamlining of the content of the course, enabling participants to get to the 'bare essentials' of the gospel quickly. In the process of, in Millar's words, 'stripping down the gospel to its bare essentials'[20] to make the gospel accessible to today's culture, Alpha cuts through ritual and theological complexity. Calculability is about size and quantity. It is experienced in Alpha's predilection for numbers, as seen in most editions of *Alpha News*. 'Alpha has internalised the values of McDonaldization where quantity is self-evident proof of significance and where numbers sell'.[21] McDonalds aims to offer a consistent product in a safe and familiar environment, wherever you are in the world. This predictability even extends to the scripting of interactions between workers and customers. For a church lacking in evangelistic experience, Alpha offers a reassuringly predictable package, including multiple resources and a uniform 'branding'. Thus, the uncertainties associated with Christian outreach are minimised.[22] Ward notes that, 'For the non-churchgoer, this is experienced as non-threatening religion.'[23] Control is expressed through the Alpha resources and through the tight copyright statement that seeks to preserve the integrity of the brand. Ward comments: 'To buy into Alpha is to do it the Alpha way. Alpha thus becomes the cultural producer and creative force.'[24] Ward concludes that McDonaldization should not be baptised uncritically.

Being the Archbishop's of Canterbury's youth adviser at the time, Ward's

---

[18] Ritzer 1996:1.

[19] Ritzer 1996:1. Ward (2005) also looks at patterns of production/consumption in *Selling Worship*.

[20] Cited in Gumbel 2001g:22.

[21] Ward 1998:282.

[22] One church has even offered a 'cash-back incentive to anyone who completes its next Alpha course and doesn't form a relationship with God' (see http://www.starnewsgroup. com.au/story/24386, accessed 3 January 2007).

[23] Ward 1998:283.

[24] Ward 1998:284.

article generated national media attention. He commented on the response of HTB in an interview with Brian:

> The response from Holy Trinity Brompton itself was to try and get me on the *Today Programme* to debate it, so they were like Slap! Bang! into serious anti-spin mode at the highest profile that they could. Secondly, behind the scenes there was an awful lot of connecting with powerful, rich people who had connections with me, and they wanted to shut me up. They manoeuvred powerfully at both levels actually.[25]

Ironically, despite the critique of the McDonaldization thesis, Gumbel himself chose to cite the McDonalds analogy in support of the need for uniformity in Alpha wherever it is offered. He says, 'If I went to McDonalds in Moscow and was given a ham sandwich, I would say that's not on.' Sandy Millar also explains that Alpha aims for 'consistency', so that people can recommend the course to friends in other places with confidence.[26] These comments – stressing consistency, control, uniformity and predictability – further support Ward's thesis. Gumbel counters the McDonaldization charge by suggesting that Alpha does not create monochrome Christians.[27] Rather, diversity comes through the denominational-particular Alpha follow up. Pointing to other (non-HTB) post-Alpha courses to deflate the charge of McDonaldization fails to address the question about Alpha itself. And as Ireland notes below many churches fail to include any post-Alpha follow up.

That Alpha includes elements of McDonaldization now seems a bit of a truism.[28] However, Ward's article fails to account for the ways the McDonaldization thesis is *dissimilar* to Alpha. The McDonaldization analogy breaks down at various points. First, the main drive of rationalisation is economic interests, so profit-making enterprises pursue McDonaldization because it leads to lower costs and higher profits.[29] In contrast, such a motivating factor is completely lacking among the executives of Alpha, many of whom give significant amounts of their own money to AI. Second, McDonalds used the scientific management of Frederick W. Taylor, the aim of which was replacing human with nonhuman technology, and with the goal of employing human beings with minimum intelligence and ability, so as to increase profits.[30] While Gumbel gives quite prescriptive advice about how to lead an Alpha small group, his instructions for choosing leaders could not be further from Taylor's ethos (see Chapter 2 §2.4). Third, a McDonaldized world

---

[25] Cited in Brian 2003:269.

[26] Cited in Ireland 2000:22.

[27] See Ireland 2000:92.

[28] Although, as noted above, Freebury (2001:29) suggests that Alpha has become more like Starbucks, with variations in its core product.

[29] Ritzer 1996:144.

[30] Ritzer 1996:24-25 and 110.

is characterised by superficiality. People pass through McDonaldized systems without being touched by its employees or its products. While this is certainly true for some Alpha guests, many testify to being profoundly affected by experiencing Alpha.

4. Mark Ireland

Diocesan mission adviser Mark Ireland[31] conducted quantitative research on process evangelism courses in 383 churches in Lichfield diocese. His questionnaires received a high (85 per cent) response rate, filled in by the parish priest. Of the 6,334 people who attended these courses twenty-two per cent had, in the judgement of the priest, 'come to Christian faith, commitment, or confirmation'.[32] Of these, Alpha accounted for 992 people (or 21 per cent). Interestingly, the proportion of people coming to faith on Alpha was almost identical to Emmaus and Good News Down the Street courses, and lower than the combined figure for lesser-known and 'home-grown' courses (27 per cent). Ireland suggests that this is due to the ability of clergy to contextualise their courses rather than to their using a pre-packaged product. This puts into perspective any perception that Alpha itself is *especially* endowed with a 'supernatural' anointing.

Brian effectively discounts Ireland's work because it is based upon questionnaires from clergy rather than from Alpha guests themselves. He suggests that clergy have 'invested a great deal of time, energy and emotional capital in it, and are not simply disinterested observers'.[33] This is an unfair criticism of Ireland's work.[34] No methodology is perfect and part of the difficulty of quantitative research is that it is reliant on those, for example, who fill in questionnaires. The same difficulty is encountered by relying on participants themselves, as Brian does. People who convert go through a process of 'biographical reconstruction': they adopt the lexicon associated with that faith, with the new system providing an interpretative framework, offering guidance and meaning to the convert.[35] For example, Beckford's study of Jehovah's Witnesses revealed that what constituted a 'proper conversion' had changed considerably over the movement's 100-year history, based upon its change in character and ideology.[36] In short, data from participants on Alpha is

---

[31] Ireland 2000; 2003.

[32] Ireland 2000:2.

[33] Brian 2003:120.

[34] Hunt (see below) is also unduly critical of reports from church leaders when they mentioned that Alpha was winning converts. He unfairly, I would suggest, applies a hermeneutic of suspicion, dismissing such claims because of their 'vested interest in boasting a thriving congregation' (Hunt 2004:103).

[35] Snow and Machalek 1984; Rambo 1993.

[36] Beckford 1978; see also Heinrich 1977:658.

also subject to a socially constructed subjective interpretation.

Nevertheless, Ireland's work is subject to the critique inherent in any quantitative research (see Chapter 4 §3). That is, in contrast to participant observation, it is limited to an analysis of second-hand accounts (either those of participants or leaders) and that it is unable to observe the subtle and complex social processes involved in human interaction, which unfolds over time. Further, such a method is incapable of accounting for those Alpha guests who left prior to the course's conclusion and thus did not complete questionnaires.

5. Stephen Hunt

One of the most thorough and independent[37] pieces of sociological research conducted on Alpha is by Stephen Hunt. His first book, *Anyone for Alpha?*,[38] was based upon four churches in south-east England and was a sort of pilot study for his more rigorous research, published in a book entitled *The Alpha Enterprise*.[39] Hunt assesses Alpha within the context of what he believes to be an irreversible secularising trend, and questions any claim that within this post-modern context religion is seeing a resurgence. He uses the framework of the commodification of the spiritual market place; how religious groups market themselves to attract 'consumers'. The pilot study included questionnaires, interviews with twenty clergy or Alpha course leaders and partial attendance at three Alpha courses in different churches. Interestingly, seventeen per cent maintained that they had 'committed themselves to the faith' on Alpha.[40] This is not too dissimilar to the Lichfield survey. However, Hunt discounts this figure because the majority of those who responded were already in the church. He, rather arbitrarily, estimated 'true converts' to number between three and four per cent.

Hunt's second research project included a survey of thirty-one churches from various denominations in England and Wales. Hunt experienced methodological difficulties in locating churches to research:

> Every fiftieth church of the first 7,000 listed as subscribing to Alpha in *Alpha News* were selected for contact regarding the possibility of being surveyed. Interestingly, 26 listed had not run the course for a period of time and in some cases several years, and felt unable to contribute. Four listed churches had never been involved with the programme. Twenty churches could not be contacted (neither by phone nor otherwise). Of those that were contactable, 40 (about one in six) were prepared to be involved in the survey.[41]

---

[37] Brierley's research is heavily dependent on figures supplied by HTB.
[38] Hunt 2001.
[39] Hunt 2004.
[40] Hunt 2001:97.
[41] Hunt 2004:93.

This, Hunt observes, contrasts starkly with the 'unrealistic truimphantist propaganda of the national organisers of the Alpha programme'.[42] Of the 1,500 questionnaires administered, 837 were returned (a return rate of 55 per cent). Those interviewed were self-selected: that is, *they* responded to Hunt's questionnaire request. Of the 113 who consented, 50 were selected based upon gender, age, social class, church background and perspective on Alpha. Hunt then describes his participant observation:

> Most of this observation was based on participation through five Alpha courses in different churches over a five-year period (although not always in their entirety). I also attended Holy Spirit weekends, as well as one post-Alpha course and have remained with a church 'cell' (study group) that has continued to meet even as I write.[43]

Hunt takes an outsider sociologist perspective, although he attempts to engage in theological issues that arise with the Alpha phenomenon. Although Hunt positions himself as having 'no axe to grind' and not wanting to be 'unduly critical',[44] he nevertheless uses rather provocative and evaluative language throughout his book, such as 'propaganda', 'Alpha fodder', 'brash triumphantism', 'fundamentalist tendencies'. While Hunt accepts the partiality involved in qualitative work, he tends to shield his methodological 'apparatus'. Apart from describing himself as an 'outsider', his role on Alpha is never made transparent. Was he attending as a guest, a non-participating researcher, or what? He gives hints, but is never entirely clear. On the Alpha day away, he describes several times sitting 'at the back' taking notes, despite this attracting the attention of other participants, and he retained an emotional detachment from participants. All this served to differentiate him from 'the group'. In short, there is a lack of reflexivity in his qualitative research. For example, he shies away from detailing how participating on Alpha affected him. While he portrayed himself as an agnostic in his first research project, he now admits that he is continuing to attend a church cell group. Does this mean he changed his agnostic stance by participating in Alpha?

Has Alpha succeeded, in the religious marketplace, in reducing the increasing marginalisation of the Christian faith? His sobering conclusion is that in contrast to the ecstatic triumphalism of HTB of a sizeable number of conversions, in the context of an increasingly secular society, it is merely a cry in the wilderness with very few hearing the call.[45] The vast majority of Alpha

---

[42] Hunt 2004:92.

[43] Hunt 2004:93.

[44] Hunt 2004:5.

[45] Warner (2003) describes how the tendency to vision inflation among entrepreneurial Evangelicals coheres with other exaggerated assumptions about previous revivals. This gives 'ostensible precedent to aspirations that disregard both the present alienation of

guests, Hunt discovered, 'are already in the church or, at the very least, have something of a church background'.[46] Of the 837 questionnaire respondents, 47 claimed to 'have become a Christian as a result of taking Alpha'.[47] That is a percentage of 5.6. Their previous church background is shown in the chart below.

None	11
Anglican	11
Baptist	10
Pentecostal	6
Roman Catholic	2
Methodist	2
Other	5

Hunt concludes that most of the converts were returning to church later in their lives. So, if Alpha is not reversing church decline, then precisely what is it doing? Alpha's major achievement, Hunt argues, has been in extending Charismatic Christianity to churches previously untouched by the Renewal Movement. In other words, it is an 'internal revival'.[48] With Alpha's diluted version of Charismatic Renewal, Hunt concludes that the Charismatic Movement, after forty years, has finally blown itself out.[49]

Hunt's position is open to the usual critiques of the secularisation thesis.[50] MacLaren outlines some of these criticisms: the theory 'is mere ideology; unfalsifiable; dependent on a prior definition of religion; incoherent; or based on a spurious notion of there being a "golden age" of belief'.[51] A number of areas Hunt points to are unfalsifiable. First, he deems that science is the subject where Christianity has conceded the most ground to secularity.[52] He thus seems to be working with a prior implicit theology of what constitutes advance or decline for the Christian faith, one where religion is opposed to 'the secular'. MacLaren notes that such an approach for sociology is deeply value laden.[53] So,

---

Western European culture from Christianity and the perceived irrelevance and impotence of the Western European church' (Warner 2003:233).

[46] Hunt 2004:170.

[47] Hunt 2004:187.

[48] Hunt 2004:252.

[49] John Finney (2000) suggests that *all renewals* inevitably change, lose their intensity and end in ordinariness. Steven (2002) notes that while the intensity of Charismatic Renewal has certainly waned, many of its features, in particular its worship, have now entered mainstream churches. See Hocken (2004) for its impact in the Roman Catholic Church.

[50] Berger 1999; Cameron 2003; Casanova 1994; Davie 1994, 1999.

[51] MacLaren 2003:67.

[52] Hunt 2004:143.

[53] MacLaren 2003:73.

when scientific tradition is revised in the light of new knowledge it is known as progress, but when religious tradition is revised in the light of that same knowledge it is called defeat! Second, Hunt's thesis defines away the possibility of religious resurgence. As Jackson points out, 'History rarely proceeds in a straight line and it is unwise to forecast the future by extrapolating recent trends.'[54] Alan Gilbert also describes how three centuries on from the Enlightenment,

> ...neither the dechristianisation of Europe nor the construction of an autonomous secular culture is either complete or certain...[reversal is] a possibility about as likely as the prospect, 2,000 years ago, that an insignificant Jewish cult might succeed in turning the great classical world upside down![55]

Third, Hunt describes how the Charismatic Movement in general, and Alpha in particular, display many of the dynamics of secularisation. While this resonates with contemporary culture, it is accommodating to secularisation and is a sign of weakness rather than strength.[56] It seems as though any engagement with contemporary culture, such as the offer of choice, is branded as an accommodating accession to secularisation.[57] But why should this be seen as a weakness? For example, Christian apologists have always drawn from their intellectual surroundings to present the reasonableness of Christian belief.[58] In sum, secularisation is not such a straightforward and predictable process as Hunt would assert.

6. Peter Brierley

Peter Brierley from *Christian Research*, surveyed 8,681 churches during a ten-year period between 1989 and 1998.[59] He reviewed all of the churches listed in *Alpha News* to see how they compared with these churches, how long they had been running Alpha and whether they had declined. Some 1,866 churches had undertaken at least one Alpha course. He discovered that the longer churches kept running Alpha, the less likely they were to decline. This was because churches only started to attract 'outsiders' after running Alpha for three years or more. The report claimed that this provided 'statistical evidence that Alpha courses help congregations to grow'.[60] Backing Brierley's research, Gumbel argues that Alpha is a long-term strategy and that churches should persevere when the overall numbers decline after the first two or three courses, because it

---

[54] Jackson 2002:63.

[55] Quoted in MacLaren 2003:70.

[56] Hunt 2004:39.

[57] See Casanova 1994:220.

[58] See Dulles 1999.

[59] Brierley 2001; see also Warren and Jackson (2001) for an outline of this report.

[60] Brierley 2001:50.

is only when the non-churchgoers go on courses that Alpha proper starts.[61] Nevertheless, even with these statistics, half of the churches who had continually run Alpha were still declining in number. Further, it is highly problematic to suggest a causal link between running Alpha and church growth.[62] As Freebury points out, it might simply be the case that growing churches are more likely to run Alpha.[63]

Brierley's research for the Salvation Army approached 2,900 churches of various denominations, of which 1,125 replied, a response rate of 38 per cent.[64] Of these, 69 per cent had held an Alpha course, the median number of courses being three. Of the 'non-church people', 45 per cent made 'faith commitments'. This is an extraordinarily high figure compared with other research.[65]

7. Summary

Gumbel has attempted what seems to be an impossible task: to present the basics of Christianity, things upon which all Christians agree, in a standardised package, and to be used across the denominational, cultural, socio-economic and intellectual spectrum. What is the result? Alpha is too basic for some, and has too many assumptions for others; it is both too liberal and too conservative; it's theology of atonement is too Evangelical for some and lacking in wrath and repentance for others. Those from the mainline churches are dissatisfied with the lack of teaching on ecclesiology and the sacraments, while those from Pentecostal Churches want more emphasis on glossolalia. It is a result of these perceived deficiencies on Alpha that a plethora of alternative courses have arisen (see Appendix 2 for a list).

There is a huge divergence between the quantitative research of Hunt and Brierley in assessing the results of Alpha. For Hunt, only 5.6 per cent were 'true' conversions whereas Brierley reported how 45 per cent of 'non-church people' made 'faith commitments'. In between these sits Ireland's research in which 21 per cent of Alpha participants had 'come to Christian faith, commitment, or confirmation'. I would suggest that a large part of this disparity is due to counting dissimilarities and to theological differences. Brian raises the question over what 'coming to faith' really means, a phrase that Ireland repeatedly uses. Due to the incommensurable criteria among Christian

---

[61] Gumbel 2004.

[62] When questioned, Brierley conceded that his research did not prove a causal link (see Brian 2003:113).

[63] Freebury 2001:69.

[64] Brierley 2003.

[65] Brookes (2007:139 and 170) questions Brierley's interpretation of his empirical data. He also (2007:141) questions whether courses more committed to running Alpha would be more likely to return questionnaires compared with those that are not particularly active.

traditions, defining what 'becoming a Christian' means is highly contested.[66] What one might call conversion, another will define as de-Christianisation (see Brian above). How one interprets the spectrum between the self-designation of the UK population (72 per cent in the 2001 UK census identified themselves as being Christian[67]), through to attendance, membership, saying a prayer, or having a particular (ecstatic?) experience, depends on one's theological perspective. For example, had those people who 'became Christian' on Alpha been baptised as infants? If so, an Anglican, Roman Catholic and Orthodox understanding would interpret this as being a person's faith coming alive, a faith blossoming into maturity. This would be associated with re-evangelisation rather than to the first time proclamation of the Gospel to the completely non-churched. However, Evangelicals tend to stress the importance of wholehearted personal commitment (see Chapter 7 §3.2). In sum, the difference in the above quantitative research is partly based upon the theological assumptions of the researcher.

These comments raise a number of questions about methodology. First, if, as I have argued, *a priori* assumptions account for the disparate quantitative results on Alpha, it is essential for researchers to make their theological positions clear as part of their individual research. Second, researchers also need to be clear about how they define conversion, and take into account the prior spiritual journey of guests. Lastly, as I shall argue in Chapter 4, an inherent weakness of any quantitative research is that only certain types fill in questionnaires. Approximately 30 per cent of Alpha guests drop out and thus do not complete questionnaires, which are issued at the end of the course. How would the inclusion of this 'silent minority' sway things?

The research on Alpha conducted prior this book has been almost entirely quantitative and/or reliant on interviews. There is almost a complete lack of qualitative, participant observation, research where Alpha is assessed 'on the ground'. This book, to repeat an earlier claim, is intended to redress such a lack. As I shall discuss in the following chapter, participant observation is a way of providing in-depth contextual data, and is unrivalled for uncovering the relatively subtle and complex social processes involved in human interaction. I have attempted in my research to nuance the spiritual journey of those who joined Alpha, their previous religious identity, and account for the polymorphous dimensions of conversion. The only prior participant observation conducted on Alpha has been Hunt. However, my research differs in focus and methodology from Hunt, as I shall outline in the following chapter. My role on Alpha as a 'marginal insider' placed me in a unique position to research Alpha and enabled the undertaking of a rich and detailed account of the course and its participants.

---

[66] Indeed, it is debatable whether it is an appropriate question (see Chapter 7).

[67] www.statistics.gov.uk/cci/nugget.asp?id=293, accessed 11 August 2005.

Chapter 4

Methodology

A number of difficulties with regard to assessing Alpha were accentuated in the previous chapter. I noted that insufficient attention was given to the religious history of Alpha guests, and how a lack of clarity in measuring Alpha's 'achievements' was based on the *a priori* assumptions of the researchers. The most prominent deficiency in the research to date was the dearth of substantial qualitative research, particularly of an ethnographic sort, a lack that this book attempts to redress. In this chapter I shall make clear my personal identity, my epistemology, methodology and methods, as well as including the 'messiness' and mistakes that are involved in participant observation. Ball, Davies and Gillham stress the importance of an autobiographical, narrative approach.[1] Such a style can achieve a clearer representation of how discoveries really take place, although it also carries with it the danger of a study becoming completely self-absorbed with more of a focus on the researcher than those who are being researched. Ball critiques the research methodology that emphasises the technical aspects of data collection and analysis and ignores the stresses and tensions of fieldwork.[2] The difficulties of participant observation are glossed over and coded out, with the researcher exorcised from the research process. Difficulties involve boredom and tiredness, false trails and participant observation syndrome, that wherever you are the action is going on somewhere else. In my methodology and throughout this book, I shall attempt to 'show the hand' of the researcher.

1. 'Insider' Research

For the first thirty-two years of my life, my religious background was rooted in the Pentecostal (Assemblies of God) tradition. My first degree was at London Bible College,[3] a college well-known for being Evangelical, after which I went to work at Holy Trinity Brompton (HTB). I remained there for five years, from 1998 to 2003, working as the publications editor and also producing the Alpha videos. Strauss and Corbin comment that professional experience can be an

---

[1] Ball 1990; Davies 1999; Gillham 2000.
[2] Ball 1990.
[3] Now called the London School of Theology.

excellent source of sensitivity.[4] Although it can easily block perception, it can also enable the researcher to move into an area more quickly because he or she does not have to spend time gaining familiarity with surroundings or events. During my time at HTB, I attended the church and regularly participated as a small group leader on Alpha. This gave me an intimate knowledge of the Alpha course from an insider's perspective. I was very comfortable with the 'grammar' of Alpha: its ethos, theology (both explicit and implicit), the organisational structure of AI and HTB, the resources it produced, and so on. I was also very familiar with the Charismatic–Evangelical social and theological language that was used. My five years at HTB, as a 'quasi ethnographer', helped prepare me for the subsequent period of study during theological college between 2003 and 2006. The question that naturally arises from having such a background, and conducting this particular research, is whether it is at all possible to 'step back' from being a complete insider and becoming a researcher. Is it possible, or necessary, to separate completely these roles? I shall argue that the role I took as a marginal insider gave my research a rich and detailed account; it gave me access to a role that could only be adopted as an insider; it gave me access to 'back region'[5] activities, for example, leadership discussions and team emails. In sum, my ability to trade on my insider role put me in a unique position to research the Alpha course.

While ethnography has its roots in social anthropology, its methods are now used by multiple disciplines. It is also utilised by studies that use the researcher's insider status as the basis for research.[6] This includes, among others, studies in healthcare practice,[7] youth studies,[8] research among Alcoholics Anonymous,[9] Evangelical Christianity,[10] British Wicca,[11] and Information Systems.[12] With every methodology there are strengths and weaknesses. Those who advocate an 'insiders' view argue that one can only get an authentic account by immersing oneself in the field of study. An analysis of social structures and group dynamics requires an 'insider' with intimate knowledge of the language as well as the culture and context in which it is situated. Aguilar describes the positive elements for insider research: there is a lack of culture shock, the researcher is less likely to alter social settings, has greater linguistic competence and can engage in participant observation to a far greater degree. In contrast, the outsider is often seen as an impersonal

---

[4] Strauss and Corbin 1998; see also Jorgensen 1989.
[5] Goffman 1990.
[6] Burgess 1991.
[7] Allen 2004.
[8] Hodkinson 2005.
[9] O'Halloran 2003.
[10] Warner 2006.
[11] Pearson 2001.
[12] Nandhakumar and Jones 1997.

inquisitor.[13]

In their ethnographic studies of children and schools, Adler and Adler describe the positive aspects of being insiders.[14] The researcher who is a true member does not have to negotiate either formal or informal entrance with other members and will be already intimately familiar with many members and the meeting venues. O'Halloran argues that only an AA insider has full access to the meetings closed to non members.[15] Thus the insider has an advantage in terms of access, in that those being researched are less likely to fear being appraised or judged and thus withhold parts of themselves or alter their behaviour in accordance with what they perceive to be the researcher's expectations.[16] This was the same for Calley's research among West Indian Pentecostals where there was no possible role for the outsider:

> One who attends their services is, by definition, either a member or one interested in becoming a member. It is the duty of saints to take every possible opportunity of converting him…When an outsider is present the restraint of all present is marked; the leader preaches more for the benefit of the stranger than for the congregation. Ecstatic behaviour is likely to be restricted to the odd ejaculation of 'Hallelujah', lest the stranger's religious sensibilities be offended.[17]

Critics of insider research counter this by arguing that an 'outsider' position is preferable because it is freer from the potential bias that arises from sustained affiliation with a group or 'going native'. An outsider, it is argued, is a 'disinterested' observer, has a 'stranger value',[18] can raise questions about the way members of the host community see things, and can be privy to secret information because they are a non-interested party.

Such arguments have become polarised and based upon the false positivist epistemology of an objective reality that a detached, unbiased and neutral scientist can observe.[19] 'Bias', asserts Aguilar, 'is the human condition, a danger for both insider and outsider researchers'.[20] Feminists and post-modernists[21] have challenged the ontological and epistemological assumptions

---

[13] Aguilar 1981.

[14] Adler and Adler 1997.

[15] O'Halloran 2003.

[16] O'Halloran 2003. This is not always the case. After five months of participant observation in the 'open meetings' among AA members, 'outsider' sociologist David Rudy developed sufficient rapport to gain access to 'closed meetings' (Rudy 1986).

[17] Calley 1965:146; see also Harding's (1987) research among fundamentalist Baptists in the USA.

[18] Burgess 1991:24.

[19] See Gadamer 1994; Polanyi 1962.

[20] Aguilar 1981:22.

[21] Barbour 1976; MacKinnon 1982; Lyotard 1984; Flax 1987; Lyon 1994; Smart 1993.

foundational to the modernist sort of social science research.[22] 'Objectivity' is viewed as the bias of white, middle-class men.[23] Reason argues for a 'critical subjectivity', which he sees as going beyond the split between subjective and objective. For Reason, while the old scientific ideals of critical and public knowledge are valued, valid inquiry is based upon the critical and self-aware judgments of the researcher. He writes:

> Critical subjectivity is a quality of awareness in which we do not suppress our primary subjective experience; nor do we allow ourselves to be overwhelmed and swept along by it; rather, we raise it to consciousness and use it as part of the inquiry process.[24]

Influenced by post-modern concerns over totalising meta-narratives, and of the links between knowledge and power,[25] my epistemology rejects the modernist disembodied researcher, and questions modernity's 'hegemonic claim to power masquerading as knowledge'.[26] I ruled out an 'empty head' approach, as though a researcher approaches reality as a *tabula rasa*. I approached my research of Alpha as an embodied person, formed through my culture and prior experiences and understandings of the world. I was not therefore attempting to write *the definitive* account of Alpha or to have revealed *the* single insiders truth. As Wolcott warns, '…there is no monolithic insiders view…There are multiple insiders views, multiple outsiders views. Every view is a way of seeing, not *the* way.'[27] While there are multiple possible interpretations of my data, as Kvale stresses, this does not render any one interpretation invalid.[28]

Although I affirm the post-modern and interpretivist critique of positivism, I reject the more extreme relativistic forms of post-modernism[29] and the reduction of epistemology to the construction and reconstruction of our private language worlds. St Paul's words, as Aune points out,[30] hold in tension the modernist/realist and postmodernist/relativist notions of knowledge and suggests a useful Christian epistemology: 'For now we see in a mirror, dimly, but then we will see face to face. Now I know only in part; then I will know fully, even as I have been fully known' (1 Cor. 13.12). It is, with critical

---

[22] Aune 2004.
[23] Kvale (1996:64) outlines twelve definitions for the term 'objectivity': that there is such a lack of agreement over the term underscores it as being a rather subjective concept.
[24] Reason 1988:11-12.
[25] Lyotard 1984.
[26] Wright 2004:24.
[27] Wolcott 1999:137.
[28] Kvale 1996.
[29] Wright 2004.
[30] Aune 2004:44.

realism,[31] committed to a realistic understanding of the world but rejects naïve forms of realism. It rejects, as Wright puts it, 'any simplistic mind/body dualism, in favour of a holistic reading of the world in which reality is made up of mind and matter existing in intimate and indivisible unity'.[32]

Therefore, I view the notion of there being *either* an insider *or* an outsider in an absolute sense as inadequate. The essentialist argument, that *only* insiders can fully access and understand the values, meanings and world-views of those they study, is based upon a questionable premise that there exists a single insider's truth[33] and on an implicit model that characterises all researchers as either absolutely inside or outside a homogenous social cultural system.[34] A more realistic model views the researcher as relatively inside or outside with respect to a multiplicity of social and cultural characteristics of a heterogeneous population. Situations are, Davina Allen argues, 'neither totally familiar nor totally strange, and the researcher's insider–outsider status changes at different points in a research project and is different with different groups and different individuals'.[35] Allen thus rejects *a priori* assertions about the researcher's insider–outsider status in the field and views this as something to be discovered, negotiated and renegotiated as part of the research process.

2. Reflexivity

Allen goes on to stress the importance of the researcher's reflexivity, which includes several elements:

- a concern with how the field of study is filtered through the very particular interpretative lens of the researcher and, as such, reflects their individual history and biography as well as their theoretical perspective;
- an acknowledgement that in actively participating in the field, the researcher will have an effect on the phenomena being researched; and
- a recognition that the field will have an effect on the researcher.[36]

It is therefore important for the researcher to make transparent the processes of their work to augment the rigour of qualitative research and enable both the researcher and the reader to assess the validity of the study findings. As noted above (§1), research reports should thus 'show the hand' of the research and not try to present the findings as the product of a disembodied and omniscient

---

[31] Bernstein 1983; Bhaskar 1989; Davies 1999; Huyssteen 1989; MacIntyre 2004; Polanyi 1962; Taylor 1992; Wright 2004.
[32] Wright 2004:54.
[33] Hodkinson 2005.
[34] Aguilar 1981:25.
[35] Allen 2004.
[36] Allen 2004.

observer.[37] As Bochner notes, they should also reflect the way in which the researchers' experience of themselves have been changed by the social actors as well as the ways in which the researcher may be changing the social actors' experience.[38]

I personally went through a transition during my time at theological college. I moved away from working at HTB. This meant, obviously, that my livelihood was not dependent on AI. I also moved away from attending HTB and the vibrant social network that I had experienced, and very much enjoyed. With Adler and Adler,[39] I experienced pangs of betrayal in writing about aspects of HTB and Alpha that were unfavourable. However, I was aware that one of the dangers of insider researchers is, as Bennett points out, being unable to disconnect themselves from group ideologies and, as a result of a sense of loyalty, take the role of 'subcultural spokesperson', rather than critical analyst.[40] At theological college I was interested in experiencing a different dimension of the Anglican tradition as part of my training and for the first two years was assigned to a liberal catholic church, and for the last year assisted the chaplain at one of the university colleges. During my final year at theological college, I found a curacy at All Saints Fulham, a moderate catholic church, from where I completed this book. While at the start of my research I would have identified myself as an Evangelical I have since moved towards a more broad Anglican theology.[41] Going through such a process has heightened my sensitivity to the taken-for-granted background that underlies Charismatic–Evangelicalism in general and HTB in particular. This practical social knowledge that we take for granted is what Schutz described as 'common-sense knowledge', which comes as part of the 'life-world' belonging to a social group.[42]

3. Methodology

Max Weber critiqued positivist methodologies in favour of *verstehen*,[43] a research approach, or stance, that enabled the researcher to discover the social

---

[37] Altheide and Johnson 1994.

[38] Cited in Jones and Nandhakumar 1997; see also Burgess 1991.

[39] Adler and Adler 1997.

[40] Cited in Hodkinson 2005.

[41] I shall elucidate further on this in Chapter 7. I have been influenced particularly by, among others, Tom Smail 1988; 1995, Christopher Cocksworth 1993; 1997; 2007, Rowan Williams 2000b, as well as those from other confessions including Newbigin 1953, Abraham 1989; 2002; 2003, Gunton 1993; 2002 and Stackhouse 2004.

[42] Schutz 1967b.

[43] The English translation, 'understanding' does not fully convey the meaning of the term *verstehen*, which implies a particular kind of understanding, applicable primarily to human behaviour.

and cultural world of a group being studied.[44] This involves the attempt to gain some kind of empathetic (not necessarily sympathetic[45]) understanding of what the world is like from the point of view of others.[46] It is a process of inquiry where the researcher tries to put him or herself in other people's shoes. He or she attempts to recognise the assumptions or the 'filters' through which their world is seen, so that the actions and perceptions of the people being studied begin to make sense. Or, as Abel puts it, *verstehen* consists of 'bringing to the foreground the inner-organic sequence intervening between stimulus and response'.[47] Weber made a distinction between *erklärendes verstehen*, or the motivational sequences for the behaviour of social actors, and *aktuelles verstehen*, or the meaning they themselves give to their actions.[48] The aim for the researcher is to correctly identify the common-sense constructs pre-selected and pre-interpreted by those who participate in the social world under investigation.[49]

Quantitative research presents a description and analysis of a community at one particular point in time. This, of course, can uncover very helpful data. However, the advantage of a *verstehen* approach, and its associated qualitative research method of participant observation, is its suitability for uncovering the relatively subtle and complex social processes involved in human interaction. This would particularly be suitable for researching the dynamics involved on Alpha. Wilson writes, 'Any social group is full of spontaneous activity which reflects a structure and set of beliefs which are difficult, if not impossible to capture by a formal [for example, a questionnaire] method of questioning'.[50] On Alpha, questionnaires are particularly limiting, in that a number of people drop out of the course before questionnaires are administered. Further, not everyone will fill out questionnaires,[51] and there can be a gender bias as well as other biases.[52] In addition, as Hopewell discovered in his research amongst congregations, 'members participate in religion more readily than they explain it'.[53]

Whyte noticed that a key issue in sociology is *time*,[54] or what Strauss and

---

[44] Weber 1964.

[45] Barker 1984:20.

[46] As Schutz notes, *verstehen* is not a method but rather 'the particular experiential form in which common-sense thinking takes cognisance of the social cultural world' (Schutz 1967b:273).

[47] Abel 1948–9.

[48] Weber 1964.

[49] Steven 2002.

[50] Cited in Steven 2002:39.

[51] For example, Hunt's (2004:93) questionnaire received a 55 per cent return rate.

[52] See Richter and Francis 1998:172.

[53] Hopewell 1988:68.

[54] Whyte 1981

Corbin call *process*: the dynamic and evolving nature of action/interaction.[55] In his 1950s study of Italian street corner gangs in Boston, Whyte writes, 'I was observing, describing and analysing groups as they evolved and changed through time...In other words, I was taking a moving picture instead of a still photograph.'[56] *Process*, then, can be thought of as the difference between a snapshot and a moving picture.[57] This was helpful in uncovering the group dynamics involved during the three months of an Alpha course. How and with whom did relationships develop? How did groups manage discerption? How did conflict affect the group?

Schutz criticised Weber for being excessively individualistic, arguing that humans could only act by drawing upon a shared set of social concepts, symbols and meanings.[58] It is a criticism made of symbolic interactionism,[59] which inspired grounded theory. Yet, as Fine points out in his discussion on symbolic interactionism, the micro–macro debate is seen as misleading with the micro-sociologist (ethnomethodology or symbolic interactionism) also interested in questions of larger institutions, and macro-sociologists (structuralist, Marxist, or institutionalist) accepting a vision of structures ultimately grounded on the actions of participants, even if they do not emphasise the power of the actor as much as interactionists.[60] So, while I favoured an interpretativist approach, with the stress on the micro (face-to-face) interaction among individuals, and aiming at a more 'naturalistic'[61] uncovering of social life than positivists, I was also aware that interaction is set within institutions and an adequate analysis must take structure into account.

As described in the Introduction, my three main aims of this book were, first, to compare and contrast the official version of Alpha, as set out by AI, with what happens 'on the ground'. Second, to research conversion on Alpha, which is one of the primary aims of the course.[62] The third aim complements the sociological investigation of Alpha by assessing its theological foundations. My focus was that of a 'grounded ecclesiology', or 'ecclesiological ethnography'[63]: that is, on the first-hand accounts of local practices and beliefs, rather than relying only on the official discourse.[64] Contrasting with a functionalist method, as Percy points out, such an approach:

---

[55] Strauss and Corbin 1998.
[56] Whyte 1981:323.
[57] Strauss and Corbin 1998:179.
[58] Schutz 1967b.
[59] See Blumer 1969, Charon 2001 and Plummer 1991 for overviews. See Meltzer, Petras and Reynolds 1975 et al. for a critique of symbolic interactionism.
[60] Fine 1993; see also Maines 1977.
[61] Blumer 1969:46.
[62] Gumbel 2001g:110.
[63] Healy 2000:169-85.
[64] Burgess 1991; Geertz 1973; Hammersley and Atkinson 1995.

...moves research away from concentrating on the primary claims of 'pure' or 'central' religion (or its analysis) towards the grounded reality of praxis (e.g., it might assess a number of Roman Catholic congregations and their practices – not ask the Vatican or theologians what such churches should be doing or believing).[65]

Observation was used not so much as to prove a theory. Rather, as Strauss and Corbin describe, one begins with an area of study and what is relevant to that area is allowed to emerge.[66] Being influenced by grounded theory,[67] my aim was also to compare and contrast my empirical data with the 'proven and tested recipes'[68] of Alpha, and to look for further light which might suggest 'alternative views on the phenomena'.[69]

To facilitate analysis of my data, I used a computer programme, NVivo, to help with open, axial and selective coding of my fieldnotes and interviews.[70] This helped in the generation of my empirical chapter content (Chapter 5). Because of the sheer quantity of material, I picked the most prominent themes and, simply for reasons of space, had to discard others (for example, ethnicity and gender play a minor role).

3.1 Generalisation

One of the problems of qualitative research is that of generalisation; whether the conclusions drawn from a selection of cases can say something more general or universal. Wolcott describes how you are 'damned if you do, and damned if you don't'.[71] However, 'generalisation' is not a straightforward concept. Critiquing Geertz's 1979 article 'Deep Play: Notes on the Balinese Cockfight',[72] Malcolm Williams outlines three possible meanings of generalisation. First, total generalisations, as in deterministic laws. Second, statistical generalisations, which is simply the relationship between sample and population. This is the basis upon which most generalisations (other than some in physics and chemistry) in the natural sciences are made. The third type of generalisation, what he calls *moderatum*, are where 'aspects of *S* can be seen to be instances of a broader recognisable set of features'.[73] These generalisations are made in interpretivist research either knowingly or unknowingly. For

---

[65] Percy 2005.
[66] Strauss and Corbin 1998.
[67] Glaser and Strauss 1968; Strauss and Corbin 1998.
[68] Schutz 1964, 1967a, 1970.
[69] Robson 1993:149.
[70] Strauss and Corbin 1998:57-241.
[71] Wolcott 1999:93.
[72] See also Denzin (1998) and Guba and Lincoln (1994), who deny any possibility of generalisation for interpretivism.
[73] Williams 2000a:215; cf. Bassey 1984.

example, Geertz's claim that 'Every people...loves its own form of violence' is an example of such a general feature, which is then reworked and enriched through the specific inferences made about his research of Balinese cockfighting.[74] *Moderatum* generalisations are similar to what Schulz called 'cook-book recipes' or our common-sense knowledge of the *lebenswelt*,[75] which we imbibe through primary and secondary socialisation.[76] Concrete problematic situations we face in daily life are initially formulated in terms of the individual recipe knowledge at hand. Such knowledge has the character of the approximate and the typical, the likelihood, rather than of certainty or even probability in a mathematical sense. Schutz writes, 'The consistency of this system of knowledge is not that of natural *laws*, but that of *typical* sequences and relations.'[77] So by concentrating on six Alpha courses, I attempted to provide a 'thick description'[78] which would provide a database for making judgments about the possible 'relatability'[79] of findings with other milieus. Whyte's street corner gangs study suggests that whatever the individual and group differences were, there were basic similarities to be found.[80] It was not necessary to have to study every corner gang in order to make meaningful statements about corner gangs. Similarly, I did not need to study all of the 7,000-plus UK-registered Alpha courses in order to make meaningful statements about Alpha. A study of one Alpha course is not enough, but if an examination of several showed up uniformities, and if this corroborated other research on Alpha, then this would be relatable to the Alpha course more generally.

4. Method

One of the advantages of ethnography is that it increases researchers' flexibility and brings them closer to those they study. The primary methods I used for my research were participant observation and semi-structured interviews. Secondary methods included some content analysis (made use of in Chapter 2) and what Bryman calls 'opportunistic' interviews.[81]

To retain anonymity for churches and those interviewed, and following the style used by Steven,[82] I have used the following coding:

---

[74] Williams 2000a. Wolcott (1999:93) describes generalisations in qualitative research as being 'tentatively offered'. See Davies (1999:90ff) on generalisation from a critical realist perspective.

[75] Schulz 1964; 1967a.

[76] Berger and Luckmann 1991.

[77] Schutz 1964:73 emphasis in original; see also Schutz (1967b:111-22) on typification.

[78] Geertz 1975.

[79] Bassey 1984.

[80] Whyte 1981.

[81] Bryman 2004.

[82] Steven 2002.

St A = church
LA = Alpha administrator
L = Alpha small group leader
H = Alpha small group helper
S = Sponsor
G = Guest

So, for example, the reference to St D G6 refers to guest number six at the church denoted as St D.

4.1 Participant Observation

Gold classified participant observer roles, which range on a continuum of degrees of involvement from complete involvement with, and detachment from, members of the social setting.[83] The role of insider–outsider has been discussed above (§1). When one actually comes to conduct research, the line between the 'emic', or the insider's point of view, and the 'etic', or outsider researcher's perspective, is blurred.[84] As Agar puts it, 'Ethnographers and others swim in the same interconnected global soup.'[85] The emic–etic paradigm thus seems rather simplistic. While it is helpful to have a clearly defined role, the messy business of participant research means that roles often co-exist. Rather than to see these roles as fixed, it is better to view the researcher's role on a spectrum along which one can move and vary the position as appropriate.[86] Sapford and Judd describe the importance of balancing the insider and outsider roles and combining the advantages of both.[87] Being a 'friend' yet remaining a 'stranger', can be a difficult and sometimes stressful experience, but essential for good ethnographic work.[88]

While I rejected insider versus outsider perspectives in an absolute sense, the terms are helpful in how they characterises the degree of initial proximity between the sociocultural locations of researcher and researched. The role one takes in a field setting very much depends on one's identity, history and culture and what is being researched. For example, Walker was unable to trade on the insider role he took in his research among a Pentecostal group, due to the fact that the believer in such circles is not expected to need elucidation concerning routine activities.[89] In other contexts, being an outsider severely limits

---

[83] Gold 1958. The four he outlined were 'complete participant', 'participant-as-observer', 'observer-as-participant' and 'complete observer'.
[84] Wolcott 1999:135.
[85] Agar 1996:20.
[86] Jorgensen 1989; Spradley 1980.
[87] Sapford and Judd 1996:78.
[88] Hammersley and Atkinson 1995; Ball 1990.
[89] Walker and Atherton 1971.

research.[90] What role should I take on Alpha?

On Alpha, three potential roles can be taken: small group leader, helper or guest. In theory, one could attend as a complete observer. This might have been possible on a large Alpha course. A researcher could attend the course but remain in the background outside a small group. However, many smaller courses take place in homes and so remaining unnoticed in the background would not have been possible. Ball even questions whether such a position is possible: 'The researcher can never be the invisible fly on the wall, as sometimes is claimed, but is always a part of the scene.'[91] Attempting to take a complete observer role would also have severely restricted access to socialising with the guests and to the small group discussions, an essential element of the course.

It would have been difficult for me, in training to be a priest, to have researched Alpha as a guest, unless I went covertly as a 'complete participant', where a sustained observer presence would be concealed. This did not seem necessary, and was ruled out as being unethical, other than in exceptional cases.[92] Participating on Alpha as a leader would have meant that I would have been in danger of being too involved and unable to think theoretically about what was going on. I thus chose the role of a helper as being the most appropriate for my research purposes. My aim throughout was to be sufficiently immersed in this world to know it, thereby providing access to participant perspectives. It was important for me to build sufficient trust and not be cut off from seeing important events or hearing significant conversations. If that trust does not develop, one's analysis suffers.[93] On the other hand, it was critical that I maintained a more or less marginal position, thereby retaining sufficient detachment to analyse what had been seen and lived through. This marginal position minimises the dangers of over-rapport or 'going native', when the task of analysis is abandoned in favour of the joys of participation.[94] This would have been a problem had I participated in the course as a small group leader or speaker.

I sometimes had to be careful in negotiating and maintaining my role as a helper. On two courses, because the small group leader was unable to attend a session, I was asked if I could lead the small group. I politely said that I would prefer if someone else could lead, although I would lead as a last resort. On both occasions, they were able to appoint another leader. My role as a helper meant that I was able to trade on my insider status. For example, I had the privileged position of access to the prayer meetings and the Alpha administrator's 'prep' talk before each Alpha session, as well as being privy to

---

[90] See Calley 1965; O'Halloran 2003; Hodkinson 2005.
[91] Ball 1990.
[92] See the British Sociological Association (www.britsoc.co.uk).
[93] Glaser and Strauss 1968:226.
[94] Hammersley and Atkinson 1995:112.

leadership discussions and team emails. Also, the informal chats I often had with leaders after Alpha sessions were invaluable to my research. The leaders sometimes had contact with participants during the week and they provided their perspective on the guests' spiritual quest, or why some guests had dropped out. Ball points out that key 'informants' are crucial to data collection, but cautions that they offer *a* perspective, one that is embodied in its own distortions and partiality.[95]

The participant-as-observer is the same as the complete participant except that the members of the social setting are aware of the researcher's status as a researcher. At the beginning of each Alpha course, while everyone in the small group introduced themselves, I made it clear that I was a theological student who had come to research Alpha and to help on the course. This marginal role again helped my research. For example, when I conducted interviews at the end of the course, guests seemed willing to confide in me, perhaps because I assured them of confidentiality, and because of the fact that I did not attend the church that was running Alpha and consequently would not be offended by any criticism. Fears and resentments could be expressed to someone who knew the context, yet would neither judge nor 'spill the beans'.[96]

4.2 Interviews

Interview styles range from the structured interview, with set questions and following a clear schedule, through to an unstructured interview with a general intention not to ask specific questions.[97] Reflecting the philosophy of qualitative research, I attempted to listen 'so as to *hear the meaning* of what is being said'[98] rather than to dominate the interview by imposing my own world upon theirs. I decided to conduct a semi-structured interview. This gave me more latitude to probe beyond the answers given and thus enter into a dialogue with the interviewee, yet at the same time providing a greater structure for comparability than that of the unstructured interview.[99] Following the advice given by Kvale, I had a framework of certain questions but would often ask follow up questions, while also allowing space for silence, giving the interviewee the opportunity to reflect and to enlarge upon a particular answer.[100] The interview questions can be found in Appendix 3.

The second aim of this book is conversion, so for the first Alpha course I

---

[95] Ball 1990:164; see also Hammersley and Atkinson 1995:125-26.
[96] Cf. Barker 1984.
[97] Jorgensen 1989; May 1997; Rubin and Rubin 1995; Sapsford and Jupp 1996; Kvale 1996.
[98] Rubin and Rubin 1995:7.
[99] May 1997:111.
[100] Kvale 1996.

researched, I conducted purposeful sampling[101] and restricted my interviewing to the guests and one helper, who had recently converted. However, when the second Alpha course 'dissolved' after five weeks, I decided to interview the leaders to get their perspective on what had happened. Their insights were most helpful and they provided another angle or perspective, which helped with triangulation.[102] On subsequent Alpha courses, I made it standard practice to interview the leader(s) of my small group and a helper, as well as the guests.

The interviews took place in a variety of locations: my home, the interviewee's home, my study at college or, more usually, a quiet coffee house in the city. Spradley stresses the importance of rapport in interviews 'where a basic sense of trust has developed that allows the free flow of information'.[103] I attempted to make participants feel at ease through casual conversation before the interview began, often starting with a cup of coffee or tea. It was obviously helpful to have spent ten weeks on the Alpha course getting to know many of the interviewees, and I was accordingly often able to gain a level of trust. One guest explained how he had become more open:

> [the meal on Alpha]...brought us a situation where we could, like we are talking to you, like we feel we know you, we're more open (St E G1).

I explained to the interviewees what my research was about and that I would be interested to learn a little of their backgrounds and their experiences of Alpha. They were informed that their names would be excluded from the finished book, as would any revealing details in the text concerning identity.[104] I then sought permission to tape the interviews for note-taking purposes. No one objected. I made sure that interviewees understood that they could refuse to answer any question with which they felt uncomfortable.[105] Before the interview began I asked if there were any questions. On completion of the interview I asked participants if they had anything to add. I was aware that asking questions about upbringing, relationships with the family and their experience of Alpha raised sensitive issues that required a careful, respectful approach. With Alder and Adler I experienced 'role confusion'.[106] In four interviews, the interviewees started to cry because of the emotionally sensitive issues they were describing. During one interview, I was asked: 'What is Christian? After you [are] baptised? Because I haven't been baptised. So, can I say I am a Christian?' (St A2 G2) What was to be the appropriate response to such situations? Should I have ignored my researcher role to comfort those

---

[101] Bryman 2004:333.

[102] Sapsford and Jupp 1996:96; Burgess 1991; Hammersley and Atkinson 1995:231.

[103] Spradley 1980:78.

[104] Rubin and Rubin 1995:93-101; Spradley 1980:37.

[105] Hammersley and Atkinson 1995:142.

[106] Alder and Adler 1997; see also Argyle 1983:178.

crying or describe my theological perspective?[107]

Sometimes after the tape had been switched off, an interviewee would reveal further information or views.[108] So, immediately after the interview, I wrote these additional points up and made notes about how I felt the interview had gone. I would transcribe the tapes myself, usually within a week, so as to avoid a large backlog of interviews. Passages of speech from interviews have been quoted verbatim, although, following Aune, for ease of reading, I have employed grammatical sentence construction.[109] Omitted words are denoted by three consecutive dots and my questions in the interview text are signified by [I.] for 'interviewer'.

4.3 Secondary Methods

In addition to the above 'purposeful sampling', I conducted unstructured and untaped interviews, what Bryman calls 'opportunistic' interviews,[110] with staff and church members at HTB. Many of these were my friends and discussion flowed from casual conversations at social events and church occasions. I made known to them my research on Alpha, and after the conversation, would ask whether I could use what they had said, assuring them of anonymity. I would then enter these conversations in my study journal,[111] usually on the same day. I also included content analyses.[112] This included the multiple books, newspapers (in particular *Alpha News*), publicity and worship CDs published by AI, as well as the HTB and Alpha website. I used these sources extensively in Chapter 2 as a means of describing the 'official' Alpha discourse.

4.4 Access

Because of my role as an insider, gaining access was relatively straightforward. There was a list of Alpha courses, searchable by postcode, on the Alpha website.[113] I contacted the appropriate church's Alpha Administrator. These people act as 'gatekeepers' for a course, 'key personnel' with the authority to allow or deny access.[114] I explained that I was a theological student training for ordination, and told them of my background experience at HTB. All of the administrators I spoke to were very open about my involvement with their courses. This is in contrast to Hunt's experience in his being refused access to a

---

[107] Brian (2003) experienced similar difficulties during his Alpha interviews.
[108] Hammersley and Atkinson 1995.
[109] Aune 2004:8.
[110] Bryman 2004.
[111] See Burgess (1991:123f) on the use of personal documents.
[112] Hammersley and Atkinson 1995:127-43.
[113] www.alphacourse.org.
[114] Hammersley and Atkinson 1995:63-68; Burgess 1991:48.

number churches, perhaps because of suspicion of his outsider, agnostic/sociologist status, and for fear of the guests feeling, as Hunt himself puts it, 'like fish in a fish bowl'.[115] However, gaining entry is only the start. As Ball notes, in any fieldwork setting we are confronted with multiple negotiations of micro-access.[116] Of importance here is the development of rapport with all of those being researched.[117] 'Legitimacy has to be won and renewed repeatedly'.[118] For me this included maintaining relationships with Alpha administrators, leaders, helpers, sponsors and guests.

4.5 Church Introduction

Having gained access, I went as a participant observer to six Alpha courses between 2004 and 2005. My aim was to gain as wide an experience of Alpha as possible, although I was constrained in various ways. The course duration is usually over three months, so there was a geographical and financial restriction on how far I could travel on a weekly basis for that length of time.[119] I was also limited to the churches that were actually running Alpha. I experienced some frustration locating courses. Some courses from the Alpha website had no contact details, some churches I called had not run Alpha for some time, and I was unable to get through to other churches because their contact details were incorrect. Hunt experienced similar frustration in locating courses.[120] In wanting to research Alpha in a wide range of denominational contexts, I contacted the Alpha Adviser for the area. I was well acquainted with him and met and discussed my research. He did not know of any Alpha courses running in churches with a more catholic orientation, and reported that 'libo' (liberal) churches were not interested in doing Alpha. Following our discussion, we walked back to his church, and he introduced me to the Alpha administrator of one of the courses I was later to participate in (St C). I also called the Alpha for Catholics adviser at HTB to find out whether there were any Catholic courses in my area. I obtained details of one Catholic church twenty miles away, but did not receive any reply despite leaving four telephone messages enquiring about Alpha.

Another factor in choosing which courses to attend related to advice given by AI, which stresses the importance of churches repeating Alpha over a period of time. According to Gumbel, Alpha 'proper' only starts after several courses have been run. As outlined in Chapter 2, for the first three courses, it is mostly Christians who attend. According to Gumbel, it is usually during the third

---

[115] Hunt 2004:94.
[116] Ball 1990.
[117] Burgess 1991:92.
[118] Ball 1990:158.
[119] Hammersley and Atkinson 1995:39.
[120] Hunt 2004:93.

course that non-churchgoing guests start to join. I therefore decided that research should be undertaken in churches that had completed *at least* three Alpha courses. One church (St B) had run over nineteen courses. An outline of the churches researched appears in Chapter 5.

4.6 Field Relations

Defining and managing a particular role in the 'field', as well as attempting to assess what is going on, is a task not without its difficulties. 'Field researchers have to take roles, deal with relationships and enter into the commerce and conflict of everyday life'.[121] As other researchers have noted,[122] field work is never perfect, yet despite making regrettable errors it is still possible to produce a valuable study. Burgess also describes the 'messy' nature of research. It is not merely a matter of neatly following a linear model of steps or stages but depends upon a complex interaction between the research problem, the researcher and those who are being researched.[123] Ball suggests that it is necessary for the researcher to report the challenges encountered during the fieldwork, particularly the affect of the researcher on the research process.[124] For me, the messiness of research involved losing one week of field notes; falling asleep during one of the Alpha weekend talks; having the audio-tape batteries die half way through an interview; arriving at an interviewee's home to find her barely dressed; attempts by a helper to 'convert' me to his church; social *faux pas* (such as forgetting to take my shoes off upon entering a leader's home) in front of those whose cooperation I needed;[125] being viewed as both an 'expert' and 'critic'[126] – and so on.

It was very tempting to take notes throughout the duration of each Alpha session. This was not feasible during the meal time without being completely conspicuous and intrusive. The actual talk time itself gave me an opportunity to make some 'jotted notes' on such things as conversations had over dinner; attendance; a rough sketch of spatial arrangements;[127] the actual talk being given; and any other information that struck me. For this I used an A5 notepad, it being the same size as the Alpha manual. I discovered on the first course that I was unable to take notes during the small group discussion without arousing the curiosity of others in the group. On the first few weeks, whenever I attempted to jot down what was being discussed, either guests, or leaders would become curious and conscious of my role as a researcher. One helper remarked

---

[121] Burgess 1991:5.
[122] Stringer 1999:15; Whyte 1981:337.
[123] Burgess 1991:5-6.
[124] Ball 1990.
[125] Ball 1990:157.
[126] Hammersley and Atkinson 1995.
[127] Jorgensen 1989:82-83.

to me at the end of an evening, 'You've been very quiet this week...You seemed busy making notes.'[128] I had obviously made people feel self-conscious in my attempt to take notes, so I deferred my note taking until the end of each session when I returned home and immediately wrote up my field notes while the events were still fresh in my memory.[129] The longer the elapsed time between the event and the formulation of a written description, the more one forgets.[130] In these notes I expanded on my jotted notes, as well as including my emotional responses to the evening's events.

I found that in my role as a helper, it was particularly difficult to judge when and when not to speak within my small group. I made mistakes in both directions. I sometimes aroused frustration on the part of the Alpha small group leaders for remaining quiet, despite the Alpha training instruction for helpers to say nothing.[131] One couple did not hear me describe at the beginning of the course that I had come as a researcher–helper, and had certain expectations of me as an ordinand:

> I wondered a little bit about you in actual fact, because you were fairly quiet at the beginning. But I think you were there on a spying mission [laughter]...you were very quiet, for a vicar. And at first, we thought, you're not going to make a very good vicar. You need to push yourself a bit (St E G1).

This is another example of role confusion, which Arygle describes as 'being under conflicting pressures from different groups of people...'[132] While I was officially both a researcher and an Alpha helper, in the eyes of those guests I was also a 'vicar', with all the expectations associated with such a position.

Hammersley and Atkinson notes the problem that the ethnographer can face over how much self-disclosure is appropriate or fruitful.[133] It is hard to expect openness and honesty on the part of participants and informants, while never being frank and honest about oneself.[134] Jorgensen also notes the importance of self-revelation for the generation of rapport.[135] Indeed, it is only when leaders, helpers and guests on Alpha speak that the creation of an open and trusting environment is facilitated. At other times I might have said too much in the small group discussion. The group dynamics were often such that there was a high proportion of Christians present, and it was not uncommon for the discussion to stall, for questions to dry up and for the few non-churchgoing

---

[128] St A1 Week 5.

[129] Sapsford and Jupp 1996:85.

[130] Hammersley and Atkinson 1995:146.

[131] See Gumbel 2001d.

[132] Arygle 1983:178.

[133] Hammersley and Atkinson 1995:91.

[134] See Argyle (1983:204ff) on the negotiation of self-presentation. He stresses that all interactors should present themselves clearly in *some* way.

[135] Jorgensen 1989:77.

guests attending to feel inhibited at having to ask all the questions. So occasionally I might have said too much as an official helper on the course.

Burgess notes how, in participant observation, the possibility can arise of researchers modifying and influencing the research context as well as being influenced by it themselves.[136] Ball suggests that reflexivity involves being aware of how the actors' perceptions of the researcher have influenced what they have and have not said or done.[137] Recognising this, from the third Alpha course onwards, I added a question to my interview for Alpha leaders, asking how my presence affected the course. I received various responses from this question:

> I felt it was absolutely the right balance. I didn't feel there was anything you imposed upon the group in any shape or form or otherwise, and it was just great to have you on board (St E LA1).

However, there was one particular incident where I did affect the course structure in a way that was not beneficial to one of the guests. The course consisted of twelve people and for the first three weeks it was split into two small groups. This resulted in some heavily pressurised questioning-asking of the guests by one of the Alpha small group leaders (see Chapter 5 §4.4.1). At the end of the third week, the leaders and I discussed the small group situation and I encouraged them to have one larger group rather than two small groups. My main concern was that guests were given the opportunity to interact or to remain silent without feeling pressurised. On the whole, I think this was good advice and faithful to the Alpha recipe.[138] However, during an interview at the end of the course, one guest, being particularly shy, would have preferred remaining in a smaller group.

Other difficulties can arise when the researcher's own religious attitude differs from those of the people being studied.[139] On one occasion (see Chapter 5 §4.4.2), the Alpha leaders had *very* strong views about a literal creation account, which generated a lively discussion. Had I remained silent, the guest could easily have assumed that I agreed with the leaders. Yet describing my view meant taking a position which differed from that of the leaders. In this particular instance, I spoke up, siding with the guest.

---

[136] Burgess 1991:80.

[137] Ball 1990.

[138] Gundry also recommends groups of between eight and ten people. Although the group needs to be small, it must be large enough so that guests do not feel threatened and can remain silent if they so wish (Report 1995:114).

[139] Hammersley and Atkinson 1995:91.

5. Summary

In this chapter, I have described my critical realist epistemology and my methodological apparatus. This included using a *verstehen* approach and the importance of participant observation for uncovering the relatively subtle and complex social processes involved in a course such as Alpha. This was augmented by semi-structured interviews. Secondary methods included 'opportunistic' interviews[140] and content analyses,[141] the latter employed as a means of describing the 'official' Alpha discourse in Chapter 2. I outlined the (marginal insider) role that I took in participant observation and the advantage it provided in gaining access to the research field and without having to spend any great length of time familiarising myself with the culture and context of the Alpha course. My ability to trade on my insider role placed me in a unique position to conduct ethnographic work on the course. In a reflexive process I attempted to make transparent my own religious identity and how that has mutated over the course of this research. Also included was an account of the 'messy' nature of research[142] and the fact that while field work is never perfect, it is still possible to produce a valuable study.[143]

The problem for any qualitative research is whether or not the conclusions can be generalised. Williams provided greater nuance to generalisation,[144] his *moderarum* generalisation being similar to Schutz's concept of typification, which has the character of the approximate and the typical, rather than of certainty in a mathematical sense.[145] In sum, it was not necessary for me to study all 7,000 UK-registered Alpha courses to make meaningful statements about Alpha. If an examination of six courses revealed uniformities, which were further corroborated with other research on Alpha, then this would be relatable to the Alpha course more generally. In the following two chapters I shall proceed to outline my empirical data.

---

[140] Bryman 2004.
[141] Hammersley and Atkinson 1995:127-43.
[142] Ball 1990; Burgess 1991.
[143] Stringer 1999:15; Whyte 1981:337.
[144] Williams 2000a.
[145] Schutz 1964; 1967a.

Chapter 5

The Alpha Programme

In this chapter, data from my field work will be used to describe the dynamics of the Alpha course. I shall address the first aim of this book, of comparing and contrasting the official expectations and claims of Alpha, as set out by AI (see Chapter 2), with what happens 'on the ground'. The following chapter will then concentrate on the second aim: conversion on Alpha. The final aim of the book, evaluating Alpha's theology, will remain the task of Chapter 7.

First, I shall provide an outline of the churches in which my research was conducted, its social context, and the numbers of team members and guests. I shall look at the church's previous experience of running Alpha, the pre-Alpha course leadership training, the course environment, and an assessment of how faithfully the courses kept to the official Alpha 'recipe'. Second, I will describe the process of affiliation on Alpha. This will include the attributes of guests, their previous religious backgrounds, significant factors in deciding to join Alpha, and discerption. Third, the courses themselves will be described in some detail, including the role of the meal, worship, talks, the small group discussion and the Alpha day away/weekend. Lastly, what happens after Alpha will be assessed.

1. An Outline of the Churches

While my aim in choosing churches to research was to gain as wide an experience of the Alpha course as possible, I was restricted in various ways. As well as geographical and financial constraint,[1] I was also limited to the churches that were actually running Alpha. Despite trying to find liberal and Catholic contexts, I discovered that most churches regularly using Alpha were Charismatic–Evangelical. Further, for reasons outlined in Chapter 4, I only researched those churches that had completed *at least* three Alpha courses. Nevertheless, there was a wide variety in the churches researched in terms of geographical and socio-economics factors.

---

[1] Hammersley and Atkinson 1995:39.

St A

This is a Charismatic–Evangelical church based in a city centre. It is a 'network' church[2] drawing in people from several miles around the city. The church has an attendance of more than 300 on Sundays and has building plans to enlarge the church to accommodate 700 people. The church includes a large population of internationals, many of whom have come from abroad to study at university or to learn English. In terms of social composition, the church was highly diverse. It has a large network of home groups.

The church's roots are in the Restorationist movement,[3] with its aversion to denominations, but could now be described, suggests Walker,[4] as a denomination. At one Alpha session, after no guests had arrived, the team members attempted to explain their church structure to me. They said that it was funny how their church had become a denomination with a hierarchy similar to that of the Church of England. One helper (St A2 H1) described how this frequently happens: 'Groups often start off trying to get back to how they thought the early church lived, but soon came to have structures.' Defending the church's apostolic leadership, in jocular fashion they pointed out that while Jesus was the foundation, it was the leader of their denomination who took the next place of authority.[5]

Alpha had been used regularly since 1994, and consistently ran three courses a year. According to AI, such a rolling programme was precisely how Alpha should be applied. This church thus seemed to provide an excellent opportunity to evaluate whether or not Alpha was attracting non-churchgoers. The Alpha Administrator had worked at HTB for several years where he participated in several Alpha courses. Since this church was so well established in running Alpha, and concurrently running two quite different courses, in terms of social and geographic demographics, I decided to participate in both courses.

St A1

The first course was held in a home close to the city centre and was predominantly a younger group made up of people in their twenties and thirties. The leaders were a South African couple in their late twenties who were renting a 1960s-built terraced house. The Alpha group was hosted in the sitting room and adjoining kitchen. The social make up of the group reflected the diversity found at the church. It included a postman, a researcher, two teachers, an office clerk and an accountant. The course consisted of two leaders, three helpers (including myself) and two sponsors. The total number of guests throughout the course was five.

---

[2] See Cray 2004; Kay 2007:246-59.
[3] See Walker 1989; Kay 2007. Cf. Kay 2007:Ch.4 and 284.
[4] Personal interview on 23 May 2006.
[5] On apostolic networks, see Kay 2007.

ST A2

The second course was located in a prosperous village several miles from the city. The course was led by a married couple who had moved into the area six years earlier and had bought the five bedroom detached house where the Alpha course was hosted. They had six children, and this reflected the make up of the course, many of whom had school connections with the mother. She (L2) thought that people in the village 'might find [St A] a bit wacky', so they had started fortnightly to attend the parish church. They wanted to do Alpha partly to strengthen relationships within the village and because it also represented an opportunity, L2 said, to 'nail her colours to the mast'. In other words, she wanted to make it known in the village that she was a Christian. Socially, the course was middle-class, reflecting the nature of the village. The course consisted of two leaders, two helpers (including myself), and the total number of guests throughout the course was six. The course was also attended by two of the leaders' teenage children, who tended to assume a helper's role.

St B[6]

This church is an Evangelical Anglican Church based in a large village or small town several miles from a city. Describing the ecclesiological location of the church, one PCC member joked that there was high church, mid church, low church, and St B. It has a congregation of over 300 and has run Alpha courses regularly since 1996. In common with many Evangelical churches[7] St B is an *activist* church (one PCC member told me he had counted over sixty activities with which the church was involved) with the aim of 'putting the Church at the centre of the community'. With such breadth of work, Alpha is simply one of the many evangelistic thrusts in which the church is engaged. The village/town traditionally had working-class roots, but over the past twenty years many professional couples have moved in. Such was the make up of the church, and the constituents of the Alpha course.

The course was hosted in a recently built church hall within the church grounds. Being a modern building, it had excellent facilities. It was warm and comfortable, with good lavatory and kitchen amenities. However, since it was used for multiple purposes, it retained an institutional flavour or character. For example, there were notice boards, photo displays with children and youth activities, and folding tables and chairs that were cleared away at the end of each evening. This made the course environment more formal than a home setting. There were a total of seven team members (including myself) and ten guests on the course, although four of the guests had dropped out by the time of

---

[6] As part of my theological training, I worked full time at this church for four weeks and was able to get multiple perspectives, or triangulation (Sapsford and Jupp 1996:96; Burgess 1991; Hammersley and Atkinson 1995:231).

[7] See Bebbington 1989.

the day away. Initially, two groups were formed, but because of the loss of guests the groups were merged by the fifth week.

St C

This course was organised by two Charismatic–Evangelical city centre churches, both linked to a 'family of churches'. Like St A, they had roots in the restorationist movement.[8] But unlike St A, the churches remained largely independent of any denominational structure, although both were under the leadership of a man who led a church twenty miles away and who is described on their website as an 'apostle and spiritual father'. The host church held their services at the community centre in a working-class part of the city. They had a congregation of approximately eighty. This host church had completed five Alpha courses, some held at the community centre and others at the home of the leader. The whole church did the first Alpha course, along with a few guests. Since then, according to the wife (H2) of the leader (LA1), most of the new Christians in the church had come through Alpha.

The other participating church started as a home group with three people in 1994, and had grown to over 200 (during term time) by 2006. Their high-energy service draws a large number of students from the city's universities. The church was also attempting to serve and evangelise the working-class estate where Alpha was held, in what their website described as 'bridging the town and gown divide'. There was a striking difference between the team members and the guests on the course: the former largely being middle-class, the latter mostly working-class.

The weekly transformation of the community centre, where the course was held, into a warm and inviting room with a 'bistro' atmosphere, was remarkable. Subdued lighting equipment was specially brought in to replace the harsh fluorescent lights; tables were covered with disposable tablecloths, napkins and decorated with candles; and music was played in the background. There were thirteen team members on the course with a total of nine guests, although some of them came only once, and others sporadically. Two small groups were formed, with my group including one leader, three helpers (including myself), one sponsor and a total of four guests.

St D

This church is a 'gently' Charismatic–Evangelical Anglican Church in the city centre. The Alpha administrator at this church had worked at HTB for several years before training for the priesthood.[9] He had an intimate knowledge of Alpha and was regularly consulted by Nicky Gumbel because of the feedback

---

[8] See Walker 1989; Kay 2007.

[9] I took over his job at HTB when he left for theological training.

he was able to give based upon his experience of running multiple courses and in his closely following the 'Alpha recipe'. He was also the Alpha regional adviser and I had previously met him to discuss my research. He joined St D as curate in 2001 and since then the church had consistently run Alpha three times a year. By the time I came to attend the course he had moved on, but not before training the church's student worker, who also became the Alpha Administrator. The church's congregation of over 300 (during term time) had a high proportion of students and targeted its Alpha course specifically at this group.

The course was held in the upstairs section of a McDonalds restaurant in an area reserved for the course and closed to the public. The leaders and helpers brought extra chairs from the downstairs section and arranged four groups around the fixed tables and chairs. McDonalds restaurants are specifically designed not to be comfortable in order to discourage socialising.[10] This meant that the evening was not particularly comfortable or relaxing. The course started with twenty-one team members and fifteen guests, but by the end of the course the number of the guests had fallen to nine. In my small group there were a total of six team members and seven guests, although four guests dropped out after just one session.

St E

The course at St E was held in a village five miles from a city. It was jointly organised by the Anglican Church and a non-denominational Evangelical Church. The Free Church holds a very informal service on Sunday mornings in the school hall. They have met in the village for the past fifteen years and approximately forty families attend the church. The Anglican Church has a congregation of about fifty people, and its background has traditionally been middle-of-the-road Anglican. However, the current vicar, who started in 2001, is a Charismatic–Evangelical and has attempted to bring renewal to the church. This push for renewal had caused serious tensions within the church with the result that it had effectively produced two factions: the traditional churchgoers, and a 'renewal' group, of which many had participated on Alpha. To quote the vicar:

> ...the problem is we did have two, firmly two camps. Those who really do want to move forward and experiencing the Spirit in their lives, and those who are still firmly in their comfort zone and will firmly continue to be regular attenders of a Sunday worship service, but on the basis that there is nothing that will particularly rock their boat...we do have, primarily through Alpha, a church growing within a church (St E LA1).

---

[10] See Ritzer 1996:133.

The vicar had attended several Alpha conferences at HTB and had led over eighteen Alpha courses, five of them at St E. Previous courses were hosted in the vicar's home, but because this was a larger course, it was held in the local school. As with the course at St C, this also included a weekly transformation, with up-lighters, tables covered with disposable tablecloths, candles, wine glasses and napkins all invitingly laid out, with Christian music playing in the background during the meal.

The level of attendance at this course fluctuated between twenty-two and thirty-two people. The total number of team members on the course was fourteen, with the guests numbering around eighteen. Of the four groups that formed, I was in one consisting of two leaders, two helpers (including myself) and three guests. The social grouping of this course was diverse. There were manual workers, a college porter, teachers, accountants and a company director. The course attracted guests from the village itself as well as from several nearby.

Having given an account of the churches in which I conducted my research, I shall now turn to assess how closely these churches followed the Alpha recipe.

2. The Alpha Recipe

AI's aim is to get churches to run Alpha courses according to a prescribed formula. I started my research having heard numerous anecdotes about churches running 'deviant' Alpha courses[11] – that is, changing the course to what the leader perceived to be beneficial to the local context. For example, one church I know inserted two talks from *Searching Issues* – suffering and other religions – because many of the guests did not move beyond these issues in the small group discussions and the leader felt it was appropriate to specifically address them in a talk. In the emerging church 'blogosphere' there have been discussions regarding 'hacking Alpha' so as to adapt it to a particular environment. For example, a university course began its Alpha session with Sunday lunch and then took their discussion agenda from the Sunday paper headlines.[12] Regardless of whether or not this enhances the course, such adjustments contravene Alpha's copyright statement. Further, the advice given by AI is that if the recipe is not followed exactly, then it is unlikely that Alpha will be 'effective'. The logic behind this is that Alpha has been 'tried and tested' for over twenty years, and every part of the ingredient is important. To

---

[11] See also Hunt 2004:154-55.

[12] See http://tallskinnykiwi.typepad.com/tallskinnykiwi/2006/05/hacking_alpha_w.html, 'Hacking Alpha: What Have You Done With It?', accessed 9 February 2007. One of the comments on this blog came from a fifteen-year-old Alpha youth leader who described how leaders should 'always hack [Alpha] and in true hacking style never ask permission'.

avoid making the seven most common mistakes, Tricia Neill suggests the following steps:[13]

1. Attend an Alpha conference. Courses where leaders have previously been to a conference experience 'a far higher degree of success with their course'.
2. Get the right people leading the course.
3. Stay in training.
4. Follow the recipe.
5. Do not cut the weekend or the day away.
6. Plan the talks. A live speaker is best, but the videos provide a 'safety net'.
7. Keep Alpha rolling, to keep the momentum going. This means running the course three times a year, and training new leaders so that existing leaders do not burn out.

So, was AI's aim of standardisation successful? Having been prepared to expect varying levels of deviancy, I was thus surprised to find a high level of conformity to the basic elements of Alpha's 'tried and tested recipe'. That is, the basic methodology was followed, including attending a conference, undergoing training, timing, leadership choice, appropriate seating arrangement, venue, as well as the technique and structure of the actual talks. These are the elements that are reasonably straightforward for a church to follow, although it required a vast amount of energy and labour for the smaller churches (St C; St E). One administrator (St C LA1) commented on how she felt overwhelmed by the advice given by AI, and frustrated at how all-consuming Alpha became if it were to be done properly. And despite a huge amount of effort expended by the Alpha leaders, all of the courses lacked the glitzy and professional production of HTB's Alpha course. By far the most complicated and the most unpredictable element of the Alpha course is the small group discussion, and the role of the team members in embodying the ethos of Alpha. This is where most of the difficulties arose, and where the greatest level of deviancy occurred, as indicated below (see §4.4). Nevertheless, my surprise was not that there was no deviancy, but that there was not more.

3. The 'Process of Affiliation'[14]

Having given an outline of the churches I researched and how closely the courses followed the Alpha recipe, I shall now turn to profiling the guests themselves. In this section, my treatment of affiliation will emphasise the

---

[13] See 'Seven steps to an effective Alpha course', http://alpha.org/runningacourse/support/sevensteps/index.htm, accessed 9 February 2007.

[14] This term comes from Rudy's (1986) research among AA.

process involved in joining Alpha as well as the characteristics of those who join the course. How did people find out about Alpha? Who joined the course? And who left and why? Alpha seeks to recruit guests by means of *attraction*, through friendships, as well as through *promotion* (media).

3.1 Alpha Guest Profile

First, who joins Alpha? In my research, the age range of guests was between 17–71, the average being 36, and this included a course predominantly consisting of students. This is in contrast to the average age of 27 for the Alpha course at HTB. But, as Hunt asserts, this 'merely underlines the unique social profile of HTB rather than a universal tendency'.[15] The mean corresponds with Hunt and Brierley's research.[16] The gender ratio, with Hunt, included a higher proportion of females (55 per cent) on the course compared with males (45 per cent). The over-representation of women is a general feature of churchgoing in Britain,[17] and my data on Alpha simply underscores this. The ethnicity of those who joined Alpha in the area in which I conducted this research cannot be taken as representative of the UK population as a whole. The majority were of white British descent, similar to the 96.5 per cent of the population in this county.[18] There were three of Asian descent (two British born), and three white people from other Western countries.

3.2 Religious Background of Guests

Gumbel suggests that getting 'non-churchgoers' to Alpha is becoming less of a problem.[19] How accurate is this statement and how, exactly, is a non-churchgoer defined? Is it someone who has not been to church for several months or years, or someone who has never been to church? Precise definitions are important at this point. Researchers have tended to settle on measures of church *attendance* rather than membership.[20] According to this criterion, Gumbel's main aim of converting non-churchgoers includes over ninety per cent of the UK population, a relatively easy target to hit.

Using Richter and Francis' research,[21] the *Mission-Shaped Church* report[22]

---

[15] Hunt 2004:165.

[16] The group most highly represented in their research was the 31–40 age range (Hunt 2004:167; Brierley 2006:1).

[17] *Christian England* reported a higher percentage of female churchgoers in the UK (58 per cent in England, 62 per cent in Wales, 63 per cent in Scotland) (cited in Hunt 2004:167).

[18] See http://www.statistics.gov.uk/census2001/s104.asp, accessed 30 May 2006.

[19] Gumbel 2004.

[20] Richter and Francis 1998.

[21] Richter and Francis 1998.

helps to bring some clarity, providing an approximate summary of the different groups in English society:

- Regular attenders, 10 per cent of the population, attend five to eight times in a two-month period.
- Fringe attenders, 10 per cent of the population, may attend church one to three times in a two-month period.
- Open de-churched, 20 per cent of the population. They have at some point attended church, have left but are open to return if suitably contacted and invited.
- Closed de-churched, 20 per cent of the population, who have left church damaged or disillusioned and have no intention of returning.
- Non-churched, 40 per cent who have never been to church except perhaps for a funeral or wedding.

What was the religious background of those joining Alpha? Hunt's research on Alpha is outlined in the chart below (in percentage):[23]

Already in church which is running Alpha	57.8
On fringes of church which is running Alpha	13.6
Agnostics or atheists with some experience of church life	16.3
No church experience, non-believers	8
Belonging to other churches	4.3

Hunt notes that churchgoers are over represented in his research because many churches put their members through Alpha as a 'dry run' before going public. However, he stands by his conclusion that most guests are already in the church or, at the very least, have some kind of church background.[24] The religious background of the guests from my research is outlined below. Drawing upon the *Mission-Shaped Church* profile, and in addition to Hunt, I included another category. That is, those who had been christened, who might have grown up attending church but at some stage had stopped going. In other words, the de-churched.

---

[22] Cray 2004:37. These statistics are based upon national averages and will vary from region to region. It is possible that urban areas in the north might have a higher percentage of non-churched. Indeed, the situation is not static, and other research suggests that the number of non-churched is increasing (Brierley 2000; Mayo, Savage and Collins 2004), with younger generations less likely to be churchgoers than older ones (Davie 1994).

[23] Hunt 2004:171.

[24] Hunt 2004:170.

	Total	(%)
Already in church which is running Alpha	8	16
On fringes of church which is running Alpha	2	4
No church experience, non-believers	5	10
Belonging to other churches	5	10
Christened, might have grown up going to church, but at some stage had left	31	60

Subsumed into this group is Hunt's category of 'agnostics or atheists with some experience of church life'. I did this because it was more faithful to my data, reflecting the broad spiritual journey of many of the guests.[25] These categories are somewhat arbitrary and should not be viewed in an absolute sense. For example, some guests could have fitted either the regular attenders or open de-churched category because they had just started to attend church after a gap. I attempted to choose the most prominent one.

3.2.1 ALREADY IN CHURCH WHICH IS RUNNING ALPHA

Several guests in this group described themselves as going through a difficult stage in life and were looking to Alpha to refresh their faith:

> [The small group] were at a phase where we were Christians and we were drifting a bit, and we needed something, and a lot of people were like that (St B G2).

3.2.2 ON FRINGES OF CHURCH WHICH IS RUNNING ALPHA

Prior to my research I had expected more people from within this category so I was surprised to find so few, although by the start of Alpha several of the de-churched could have fitted within this grouping.

3.2.3 NO CHURCH EXPERIENCE, NON-BELIEVERS

Alpha functioned in a variety of ways for the five people in this category. Three guests (St C G1, G3; St D G10) described their non religious background and designated themselves as either atheist or non-Christian at the start of Alpha, although they had visited a church several times just before the course started.

Two guests with no religious background had recently become Christians. For example, St A1 G5 came from a completely non-churched background and had converted only a couple of months prior to joining Alpha. For him, Alpha functioned as a catechumenate course (see Chapter 7), and he was baptised just as the course ended. Also at St A1, foreign student guest, G2, was also from a non-Christian background and had recently started attending St A. She was unsure how to designate herself. She described how her friend had told her to say the 'sinner's prayer', to 'invite Jesus into my life. But, I don't know. What

---

[25] Hunt (2004:170) also remarks that many guests appeared to be considering returning to the faith (and church) after a fairly long absence.

is Christian? After you [are] baptised? Because I haven't been baptised. So, can I say I am a Christian?' (St A1 G2)

Although these guests had some very recent experience of church, and one or two had converted just prior to the start of Alpha, because of their non-religious background, I have included them in this grouping. For most of them, Alpha functioned as one part of a broader spiritual quest.

3.2.4 BELONGING TO OTHER CHURCHES

This group included St B G4 who, because he worked away from home during the week, attended Alpha at a different church as confirmation preparation. The couple at St C (G7 and G8) had come from another church in order to assess whether Alpha was something that they would run at their church. They were introduced to this particular course by their 'Alphaholic' daughter (St C G4), who also did not attend St C, but who joined the course.

3.2.5 CHRISTENED, MAY HAVE GROWN UP GOING TO CHURCH, BUT AT SOME STAGE HAD LEFT

This category covered a wide variety of people who described themselves quite differently. All of them had been christened, most had grown up with some church background, usually Sunday School, and all had left church at some stage in their life. Leaving has many similarities to the process of conversion. It is often affected by an individual's reference to a group's plausibility structure (see Chapter 6).[26] Richter and Francis note how many young people prefer to belong to their peer group rather than to the church.[27] This was the situation for several people on Alpha (St A1 H2; St B G5; St D G7):

> ...probably because it wasn't cool, which sounds really terrible. But people I was mixing with at that stage in general weren't going to church, so I kind of just drifted out of it (St B G5).

A recent Alpha convert, and helper on the course at St A1, commented:

> ...as soon as you hit secondary school, it's sort of like a stigma attached to religion. And I suppose you follow the flow, and under peer pressure, you buckle a bit (St A1 H2).

For others, leaving church occurred during a period of transition. Bibby's research shows how easy it is for members to stop going to church as they move from one community to another.[28] Those in the midst of transitional social situations are more open (or vulnerable) to new self-definitions and new

---

[26] In research conducted by Jamieson (2002:32), the majority interviewed did not leave church suddenly; most gradually drifted out of the church, only realising in hindsight that they had left.

[27] Richter and Francis 1998:132.

[28] Bibby 1997.

groups.[29] For several guests (St C G2; St B G4; St E G7), this happened when they left home, and for St D G9, when his family moved home:

> …we had a lively church, there was good music there and it was fun going, and I went to Sunday School and things like that…possibly what was the catalyst was that we moved house and we went to an area where the church wasn't so lively (St D G9).

Some guests simply drifted away from church because other priorities (St A1 G3; St E G4, G5), or non-church activities like sailing (St D G4) and banger racing (St E G8), were more attractive alternatives.[30] And for other guests (St A2 G1; St D G3, G4, G12), leaving was a more conscious act and included a 'crisis of belief'[31] during mid-adolescence. Based upon the above leaving patterns, all of the guests in this category could be described as being open de-churched because none had left due to being damaged or disillusioned by the church.

All four guests on the course at St A2 joined Alpha perceiving it to be a place in which they would have an opportunity to ask the sort of questions that they had never been given the chance to ask while growing up. This was similar for other guests (St B G1, G2, G3; St D G9) for whom Alpha provided an opportunity to get back 'on the right track' (St B G3). Other guests commented:

> I saw Alpha as being a way into reviving my faith (St D G9).

> …it was a good way of introducing me back into something that I've always had a belief in (St E G8).

For other de-churched guests, Alpha was part of a broader process of re-initiation with it functioning both as confirmation preparation (St B G4, G5) and as a post-confirmation course (St B G6), a sort of mystagogy (see Chapter 7 §1).

The perception of this group concerning their faith varied considerably. They placed themselves in one of three categories at the start of Alpha: some designated themselves as Christian, others as non-Christian, and those who were unsure how to describe themselves.

Some guests who had been christened had rarely, if ever, been to church since then (St D G5; St E G3, G6). Yet the latter two still designated themselves as Christian. In fact, at the start of Alpha, most in this group viewed themselves as Christian (St A1 G2, G3, G4; St B G2, G5, G6; St D G3, G7; St E G1, G2, G3), with the following responses typical:

---

[29] Borhek and Curtis 1975:96; Beit-Hallahmi and Argyle 1997:118-19.
[30] Cf. Richter and Francis 1998:132-33.
[31] Cf. Richter and Francis 1998:17-18; Jamieson 2002:33.

...rightly or wrongly I've always considered myself a Christian, and its not always been a sort of active Christian but, if someone asked me the question, then yeah, I would say I was (St B G5).

I've never really strayed away from that term purely because I wouldn't know what I would call myself if I didn't say I was a Christian (St D G3).

If the members of the first group self-designated themselves as Christian, the second group, in contrast, described themselves as definitely non-Christian at the start of Alpha (St D G1, G11, G12; St E G7).

The third group in this category found it difficult to know how to designate themselves or to make sense of their previous Christian identity. St D G4 rejected various creedal elements of the Christian faith, yet was confused because he had been baptised and attempted to follow Christian values. 'Religious believer' St D G1 had essentially a non-realist theology, describing how Christianity was the source of symbolism for his own non-institutional and individual path.

Such responses sit uncomfortably with Alpha's theology of salvation, and of the Evangelical emphasis on assurance, outlined in Chapter 2. There is an ambiguity in the data here because of the different ways of assessing religious belief. How exactly is it possible to determine who is 'in' and who is 'out'? For many Evangelicals, the litmus test has been whether or not one has been 'born again' (John 3). The boundary marker on Alpha seems to be determinate upon a particular *experience* (see Chapter 2 §2.1.8). However, the incommensurable criteria for determining whether or not someone is a Christian means that assessment of religious belief is problematic. As noted above, because of a lack of common criteria, researchers have settled on measures of church *attendance* rather than membership.[32]

---

[32] The difficulty is yet more complicated. Francis and Robbins (2004; see also Fane 1999) challenge Davie's (1994) 'believing without belonging' thesis: in particular her use of the word 'belonging' as a synonym for participation in membership and in practice. They suggest that belonging has more to do with notions of identity rather than of participation. Francis and Robbins (2004) take a broader view to include three dimensions of religiosity: 'belonging' or affiliation refers to self-identification, 'believing' denotes self-expressed belief in God, and 'practising' to obtain objective counts of church attendance. Each in its own way is a socially significant indicator of a *different*, but in its own right significant, dimension of religiosity (Francis and Robbins 2004:41). So, self-assigned religious affiliation may be helpful in conceptualising social identity, rather than treating it as an inadequate indicator of religious practice and belief (Fane 1999:122). The difficulty with Alpha's stress on an experiential aspect to becoming Christian is that it discounts or devalues other dimensions of religiosity. Such a perspective lies behind Brian's (2003 Ch.4) critique of Alpha and what he calls its 'de-Christianising' process, whereby guests who had previously thought that they were Christian discovered on the course that they were not 'proper Christians'.

3.2.6 SUMMARY

Corroborating Hunt's research,[33] my data suggests that the vast majority (90 per cent) of people attending Alpha were either churched or had some church background. However, my data differs from Hunt's in the balance of regular churchgoers to those with some church background. While the majority (over 62 per cent) of Hunt's guests were churchgoers, my research discovered that the majority (60 per cent) were from the open de-churched category. This difference could be explained in the shift that takes place when churches continue to run Alpha, and Gumbel's conviction that non-churchgoers start to attend by the third course. Linking my methodology to check this, my research supports Gumbel's analysis. That is, according to Gumbel's definition, more non-churchgoers start to attend Alpha when churches persist with the course. However, the vast majority of these non-churchgoers had some form of Christian background. Interestingly, the open de-churched is the category into which Gumbel himself fits.[34] Perhaps Gumbel's influence on Alpha is partly what makes the course attractive to this group of guests. That is, the course reflects elements of Gumbel's experience, and this resonates with those from a similar background. Although not completely absent, significantly under-represented were the non-churched and the closed de-churched.

3.3 Joining Alpha

What are the ways in which guests discovered, and joined, Alpha? Although it is rarely possible to reduce the joining process on Alpha to just one category, there are usually more prominent factors involved. It is clear from the table below that by far most guests (92 per cent) joined Alpha through the influence of their church, vicar, or friends, the latter being the most prominent. In fact, almost all of the de-churched guests came on Alpha largely through the influence of friends.[35]

		Hunt (%)
Through my church	11 (21%)	66
Friends	30 (58%)	20
Media	1 (2%)	5
Poster	2 (4%)	5
Leaflet	1 (2%)	1
Church leader	7 (13%)	n/a
Miscellaneous	n/a	2

---

[33] Hunt 2004; see also Brian 2003:Ch.4 and 8.

[34] Gumbel 2001e:67.

[35] This is confirmed by other research (see Finney 1992; Brian 2003).

Hunt places a much higher percentage on the church (66 per cent) and then friends (20 per cent).[36] Again, as with the church background of the guests, this discrepancy is probably due to the fact that churchgoers in Hunt's analysis were over represented due to churches first putting their members through Alpha (Hunt 2004:170).

Hunt suggests that the aim of the Alpha initiative was to move away from social networks to direct advertising, and that this strategy has failed.[37] However, Gumbel has never argued that this was the aim of national advertising. Rather, visibility by means of such posters, cinema advertisements, media reports, websites, and so on, puts the course in the public domain. Its marketing strategies have been successful in creating what MacLaren calls a media 'splash',[38] drawing attention to the 'product' and reorienting the focus of what Zerubaevel calls 'optical communities'.[39] So when Christians invite their friends to Alpha, they have already been primed as to the national significance of the course.

Gumbel stresses that the 'personal fringe of people who have done Alpha...is the main way long-term to get people onto Alpha', with seventy per cent of HTB's guests knowing someone who had completed a previous course.[40] My research corroborates AI. I discovered that very few guests joined Alpha directly because of the media, posters or leaflets, although several guests described being influenced by these things. There was often a multi-pronged effect that brought guests to Alpha. Its franchise structure, with multiple and identical courses conducted both nationally and worldwide, helped in the recruitment. One guest at St B (G10) is a good example of the multi-pronged recruitment technique that a global franchise provides and how it fits in with a consumerist culture. His vicar had suggested that he did Alpha as confirmation preparation. He commented:

> I had seen Alpha on notice boards, seen it on the back of buses, don't you? But it hadn't dawned on me what it was all about, so that was the introduction.

Working away from home meant that he was not able to do Alpha at his church so he searched Alpha's website to find the nearest course:

> When I was finding out about it, found on the web 'Alpha' and then you go on the Alpha.org website and you think, 'where shall we go and do this course?' Barbados [laughter] it's just [laughter], really quite a big thing (St B G10).

He narrowed his search down to two courses and then reviewed the church's

---

[36] Hunt 2004:176.
[37] Hunt 2004:177.
[38] MacLaren 2003.
[39] Zerubaevel 1997.
[40] Gumbel 2004.

websites. Based on that research he picked the course most suited to his needs.

A number of other guests joined Alpha primarily through *promotion*, that is, the influence of various media. St C G4 describes how she was inspired to do an Alpha course after having seen the television series, 'Alpha: will it change their lives?' She then 'found' a course when she saw a poster outside a church and telephoned to enrol. This was the same for a couple at St E (G1 and G2) who joined after seeing the Alpha banner, although they had been aware of the course through their committed Christian son. Other guests were unhappy with Alpha's advertising message. St D G4 first noticed Alpha when he saw leaflets and joined the course, for one evening only, when his friends invited him. He said that he gained the impression from the advertising that the course represented an opportunity to explore rather than to convert, and how he felt the advertising was misleading:

> I was kind of attracted to it when I saw the leaflets and it was like, come along, we're not trying to convert you. I can't remember quite what it said, but that's the impression I got, it's to find out more, not to convert you. When I went, the impression I got was that it was more to conver [sic], although they kept saying it was to find out more, basically that was the ultimate aim, I think, was to convert you (St D G4).

While the high media profile of Alpha helped in attracting guests, it did not guarantee trouble-free recruitment, as the courses at St A1, St A2, St C and St D discovered. For example, the course at St A2 'dissolved' after five weeks due to lack of guests. The church at St C had attempted to work with the non-churched for three consecutive years, organising a 'summer blast' activity in a working-class community where the Alpha course was to be held. Despite this extraordinary effort, they were only able to recruit one guest. The leader (St C LA1) described how hard it was to convert the non-churched, and that only one woman from the estate had 'come to faith'.

Even the larger course at St D experienced difficulty, despite using the city's trendiest nightclub to launch the course. Christian guest, St D G2, said:

> They did a lot of advertising beforehand for Alpha, and it was all really down to earth kind of stuff, like doing it [at the nightclub], but even that didn't attract that many. I certainly couldn't manage to get any of my friends to come. I asked and asked them, and they were like, 'No'.

3.4 Discerption

Having looked at the profile of the people who join Alpha and their process of affiliation, we turn now to the topic of discerption. Guests generally leave Alpha during the first three or four weeks. HTB have a drop out rate of 20 to 30 per cent.[41] At 30 per cent, my research tallies with the higher end of HTB's drop out rate. Gumbel suggests possible reasons for this.[42] Half of the guests drop out for good reasons, such as moving. In relation to those guests who leave after the first night, Gumbel admits not knowing the reasons. Some leave because of Alpha's conservative teaching – for example, in advocating refraining from sex before marriage. Others are put off by peer pressure, and yet others, quoting the parable of the sower (Mark 4), because the gospel has not landed on good soil.

Being able to trade on my insider role, I followed up some of these guests and also obtained the leaders' perspectives on discerption. This was one of the advantages over Hunt's 'outsider' research.[43] I discovered four broad reasons for guests leaving Alpha: its conservative theology; pressure exerted by team members; structural difficulties; and miscellaneous causes. A more detailed account of the first three reasons will follow later in the section on the small group discussion. I tried hard to interview as many of these guests as possible. In their not finishing Alpha, it obviously meant that they did not complete the questionnaires at the end of the course. These are the unheard voices, the 'silent minority'. However, some of the guests had left the course upset, and might not have wanted to be troubled by an inquisitive researcher. When I attempted to contact guests who had dropped out, but did not receive a reply, I felt it inappropriate to pursue matters further.

First were those guests who found Alpha's conservative theology off-putting (St A1 G1; St D G4). From a Christian background, St A1 G1 had joined Alpha because she had questions about feminism and homosexuality and wanted a forum in which to discuss these topics. The leaders gave her Gumbel's book, *Searching Issues*, to take home and read:

> I really didn't like the book and it made me quite angry. I thought, if the Alpha
> course is based around this book, and this is who they're going by, I don't want to
> be a part of it (St A1 G1).

The second reason was in relation to the degree of pressure exerted on guests by team members. While St B G7 enjoyed the talk, he was totally put off by the leader's questioning and by being directly addressed. He did not return for the second session. On the same course, another guest (St B G3) said that he almost did not return to Alpha following a conflict on Week 7, where a number of team members vehemently condemned transcendental meditation, with which this particular guest had previously been involved. At St A1, G3 was put on the spot by the leader (L1) several times during the discussion. This is how she describes it:

---

[41] Gumbel 2004.
[42] Gumbel 2001g:92.
[43] Hunt 2004:234.

They believed very strongly. So I did feel a bit pressurised...I felt like I was the odd one out. I actually emailed [L1], saying that I didn't think I should continue with it, because everyone else knew how they believed and everything, and I didn't really... (St A1 G3).

After meeting for coffee with the leader this guest agreed to continue with the course.

The third and main reason for leaving was the structural difficulties of an overwhelming presence of team members and/or other Christians in the group. This tended to suffocate discussion. It was the main reason why guests left at St A2, and resulted in the course ending on Week 5. According to the leaders (L1 and L2), the guests felt that it was very much 'us' and 'them', and that they were outnumbered. On the course at St D, in my small group alone, four guests came for one session but did not return. They were largely from the open de-churched category. One guest's (G4) perception was that the overall aim of conversion on Alpha meant that team members avoided argument. The result of this was that discussions tended to fall flat, which, combined with finding Alpha's theology off-putting, led this guest to leave. This was the same reason that St D G13 left the course. One of the leaders in my group reiterated this (St D L1):

I think that guy [St D G4] who came the first week, I think the reason he didn't come back was, it was just a whole group of Christians.

Fourth, the miscellaneous reasons. St B G8 came for several sessions but left, according to the administrator (LA1), because of family reasons. A churchgoer at St B (G10) decided that she would cherry-pick which talks on Alpha she wanted to go to. She came for the first two sessions and did not return until the social evening at the end of the course. Other guests left but because of a lack of contact details I was unable to interview them.

In contrast to Gumbel's analysis where he suggests that half of those who leave Alpha do so for 'good reasons', very few guests that I researched left the course in that way. Two guests dropped out because of Alpha's theology; another guest left because of the pressure exerted by a group leader, with two others close to leaving for that same reason. But the overwhelming reason for discerption was that guests were put off by the numerous, and what they felt to be stifling, presence of Christians on the course.[44]

3.5 Size Matters

Next, we turn to the group constituency. The ideal Alpha group consists of two leaders, two helpers and eight guests. How common were such groups? According to my research none of the Alpha courses even came near to

---

[44] This is also supported by Brian's (2003:204) research.

achieving this ideal. On all of the courses, the majority present were team members. This imbalance was occasionally extreme. For example, on Week 7 at St A1 there were six team members to a sole guest, and this excluded the three cooks. Similar ratios were not uncommon on other courses. A particular course where the presence of team members became an acute problem was at St A2. Part of the difficulty on this course was the uncertainty of knowing how many guests would join. The leaders had invited many people from the village and while a number expressed interest, few came. Having planned the course with the expectation of a viable Alpha group, arrangements were made for speakers and cooks. Then at the last minute, two of the leaders' daughters were invited to join the group. This further affected the balance between team members and guests. On the first evening the ratio was 7:3. On the second week the ratio was 5:3. But by Week 4 there were six team members and no guests. On the fifth week the ratio was 7:1. Because of the lack of guests, the course was discontinued and the one remaining guest watched the Alpha talks on video at home.

What was it that prevented the groups I researched from attaining the ideal Alpha small group? The difficulty of attracting guests has already been noted. The main struggle in arranging the small groups was that the leaders simply did not know how many guests to expect, with the Alpha Administrators tending to overestimate. For example, at St D, ten people had signed up following the introductory evening in a nightclub, but only two from that evening joined the course. The unpredictability involved in recruitment meant that planning the small groups became problematic. Having fewer guests arrive than expected resulted in an excess of team members. One leader describes the difficulty:

> I think turning helpers away and leaders away would be, because I mean, we said we would help if we were needed, so we wouldn't have minded them saying, we've got plenty of people, go away. I think it was hard, because people don't turn up until the day, it's hard to judge. I think that's one of the hardest things. Certainly on other courses we've fought against having one non-Christian in a group of twelve people. Because, especially when people walk through the door, you don't know where they are (St D L1).

The defection of guests has already been noted. The consequence of this was that it further upset the balance of the small groups. Team members were more committed to the course than the guests, so that when guests left team members continued the course with the result that the disproportion between team members and guests increased. I shall now proceed to give an outline of the actual course itself.

4. The Alpha Programme

In this section, I shall give a detailed description of the Alpha programme.

4.1 Meal

The meal is a significant component on Alpha. Within the Christian tradition, the meal is important in establishing, maintaining and transforming relationships.[45] The meal serves several purposes: it creates group cohesion, helps define group boundaries, and enables the development of strong affective ties both with team members and other guests.[46] The meal plays an important part in the 'forming' phase of the developmental sequence in groups.[47] During this phase there is a high degree of anxiety within the group, as group norms are forged, yet it is also where group cohesion develops.

Three courses (St A1; St A2; St C) did not charge for the meal. Referring to 'exchange theory' Hunt writes, 'A kind of implicit cost–return is involved here in that on being fed...there is a certain obligation for guests to accept, be open to, or at least tolerate what follows on a typical Alpha programme evening.'[48] For two of the guests the offer of a free meal raised suspicions, describing how they felt uncomfortable because of the sense of obligation that a free meal had made (St A1 G1; St A2 G1).

St A organised the meal for their two courses centrally, as a church. Each week, between one and five people from a different home group organised the purchasing of food and cooking the meal. They brought the food to the venue and helped to clear up afterwards. Their role was that of the Alpha 'taskforce',[49] relieving the leaders of the stress of catering. Being a large church with multiple home groups meant that it did not impose a strain on the church's human resources. This expense was entirely covered by St A. While on some courses, having a meal provided was an incentive (see St A1; St C; St D), the meal for the guests at St A2 was rather a disincentive because it was too difficult for people to feed their children, get them to bed, and then rush out for a full meal.

Because many of those who attended the course at St B were either professionals with busy jobs or women with children needing to be put to bed, the Administrator adapted the course, starting it a bit later, at 7.45pm. Instead of a meal, the evening began with a home made dessert with coffee and tea. The dessert served the same function as the meal, in that it helped create social cohesion.

---

[45] Webber 2003.
[46] See Mintz and Bois 2002.
[47] See Tuckman 1965; Tuckman and Jensen 1977. The five phases are forming, storming, norming, performing and adjourning.
[48] Hunt 2004:58.
[49] Gumbel 2001g:179-80.

In contrast to St A1 and St A2, where two of the guests felt uncomfortable about receiving free food, several of the guests on the course at St C said they appreciated the free meal, and did not question the motives of the providers:

> I think [the food] was the only reason I went, to have a meal with my mates. It was quite good because it was more social that way (St C G3).

The working class context at St C created some socially awkward dynamics. There are various ways in which to interpret this difficulty. Argyle notes the difficulties that class difference can bring, including language.[50] Argyle outlines Bernstein's (1959) research, suggesting that certain working-class people tend to use what he called the 'restricted code', employing little linguistic symbolism, while middle-class people are able to use what he termed the 'elaborated' code as well as the 'restricted code'. So, in the context of an Alpha meal, the middle-classes were more able to handle and maintain conversation for an extended time through the use of language that was more impersonal, more complex and suited to maintaining relations in face-to-face groups.[51] The middle-class style of dining on Alpha was rather incongruous on this course of mostly working-class guests. Another way of assessing the difficulty of social classes, observes Argyle, is that they are ranked in a social prestige hierarchy, so that people react to those from other social classes as if they were superiors or inferiors.[52] Where there is some established role-relationship, as in the Alpha small group discussion, there can be a perfectly easy exchange between members of different social classes, whereas in a purely social context, like the Alpha meal, inter-class difficulties appeared. The conversation during the meal at St C was always slightly awkward, with all of the initiative and effort coming from the (socially and linguistically superior?) middle-class team members. I tried chatting to the guests each week, but after several questions and one-line replies, the 'conversation' would soon end. Of course, I was part of the 'problem' because, being part of the Alpha team meant, almost by default, that I was perceived as being middle-class. This was all part of the messy nature of participant observation research.[53]

The most controversial of the meals was the food served at St D: McDonalds. A number of guests never ate on that course. Several of them had watched *Super Size Me*, a film in which an American presenter for thirty days ate only at McDonalds and whose health declined dramatically. Perhaps unsurprisingly for students, the option to capitalise on the offer of subsidised or even free food was appreciated. While one guest enjoyed the food (G3), most

---

[50] Argyle 1983.

[51] However, not all of Bernstein's colleagues at London University's Institute of Education agreed with his assertion. For a critique, see Harold Rosen (1974), who studied the richness of working class speech.

[52] Argyle 1983:188-89; see also Napier and Gershenfeld 1985:51-52.

[53] See Burgess 1991.

objected:

> Personally I wouldn't have chosen McDonalds. [I. did you eat any of the food?]
> No, that was kind of a principle thing, and based on taste (St D G4).

> I'm a veggie, and I don't eat at McDonalds (St D G12).

The Alpha administrators at St E had organised a rota where various church members took turns to make the food and bring it to the school hall. Every Alpha session was a major operation, with plates, cutlery, wine glasses, candles, disposable tablecloths, napkins, and so on, brought in. This was labour-intensive and the cause of much stress for the administrator (LA1), exacerbated when church members on the cooking rota dropped out at the last moment.

In summary, all of the courses I researched included a meal at the start of each Alpha session, apart from St B where a homemade dessert was served instead. While guests were anxious at the start of the course, by the third or fourth week, they had begun to relax. This was noticeable by the increasing amount of laughter heard within the groups from this point onwards.

4.2 Worship on Alpha

Following the meal, AI instructs courses to include sung worship. How do Alpha guests find this element of the course? Gumbel describes how guests find worship difficult to begin with, but by the end of the Alpha course, 'they often find it is the part they value most…[and it] helps people to make the step from Alpha to the church'.[54] How did this advice relate to my research?

None of the courses I researched had worship from the beginning of the course. Various elements of worship were introduced at the Alpha weekend or day away (see below) following which, only St B continued to include worship throughout the remainder of the course. The worship was of the Charismatic Renewal variety, which I shall discuss further in Chapter 7 (§3.4). There was a general assumption on the courses that guests knew the appropriate etiquette for prayer. Without introduction, leaders would often launch into prayer. Keeping my eyes open during these times, I often noticed some bewildered looks from guests as they glanced around, clearly not being used to church environments. These prayers were always extemporaneous. With almost all religious renewal movements, Charismatic–Evangelicals have tended to reject 'eternal forms', such as set prayers, that come in standard units, polished with constant use.[55] Instead, they value, as Mary Douglas puts it '…a man's inner conviction. Spontaneous speech that flows straight from the heart, unpremeditated,

---

[54] Gumbel 2001g:62.
[55] Martin 1981:54; Douglas 2003.

irregular in form, even somewhat incoherent, is good because it bears witness to the speaker's real intentions.'[56]

While for Christian guests, worship tended to be a positive part of the course, others, particularly the open de-churched, objected:

> What I found surprising during the day [away], a little bit, was that they introduced singing hymns, or songs, and prayer...I thought, on a course, it wasn't really appropriate. I was just a bit surprised. I didn't really want to sing songs. I didn't know them for a start...Fifteen people sing[ing] songs just seemed a little bit strange. And I also felt they were making a little bit of an assumption that we all want to do that. And I felt from then on in the course, to be honest, it was almost like, well, we've converted them all now, or they're all fully fledged Christians now, so we can have prayer and songs and everything. And that's when I started to get a little irritated...I mean if there were some real agnostics on that course, they wouldn't be happy singing hymns and praying. And so if we're all praying in the group, and they don't want to, it would have been a little bit awkward for them. And the danger is, then, that you stop coming (St B G3).

The difficulty, as G3 noted, is that some guests might drop out. It was the rapid pace of this course that caused G6 to leave. Catholic de-churched guest, St D G3, described how she was put off attending the weekend away because of the fact that it included a lot of 'mass worship' and what she described as, 'the whole kind of stereotype of New Age Christianity'. She also found the introduction of prayer difficult:

> Everyone seemed to be praying, and seemed to be Christian and, its like, do you presume that everyone comes to this as a Christian?...and we prayed in our group, which freaked me out. I'm not good with prayer, I'm really not good with it...That alienates people who aren't Christian, and who don't know what they think. It's a bit kind of, you have to join in or otherwise we're really singling you out...and because everyone is praying, you can't get up and wander off somewhere. So you have to sit there and go, well, everyone's praying and I'm not comfortable with this.

This is corroborated by Hunt's research.[57] He also describes how some attendees found that the inclusion of sung worship reminded them of what they most disliked about church.

4.3 Alpha Talks

The next part of an Alpha session, following worship, is the talk. In this section, I shall compare the talks given on the Alpha courses I researched, with the official Alpha talks, outlined in Chapter 2. I shall highlight any differences

---

[56] Douglas 2003:54.
[57] Hunt 2004.

or idiosyncrasies, and give samples of guests' responses.

There was variety in how the talks were delivered. St E only used the Alpha DVDs, apart from their weekend in which they invited a local speaker. Three courses (St B; St C; St D) had a live speaker for every evening, and other courses (St A1; St A2) had a mixture of video and live speakers. Guests tended to react in polarised ways to Nicky Gumbel's talks. Many were impressed by his communication skills, his mannerisms, and would laugh at all of his jokes. They even noticed his customary blue shirt, which he wears in most of the Alpha videos. This adulation is confirmed by other research.[58]

Others reacted negatively to Gumbel. One guest thought he was 'a bit too much of a showman' (St E G9). Another guest questioned the veneration that came from others in his group:

> [S]ometimes you think, who's this Mr Gamble [sic] [laughter]. He's like God...I sometimes look around at the faces of some of these people there [laughter] and they were transfixed with him. And I'm thinking, he's a Christian, but he's not God (St E G4).

While appreciating the clear presentations, one guest felt that Gumbel lost credibility with some of his 'extreme' anecdotes:

> The one in particular I'm thinking of is when he said he needed to get to London and suddenly the doorbell rang and there was a taxi driver for him. You know, that sort of makes you think he's making it all up and that undermines the credibility for the rest of the stuff he says (St E G3).

The use of such devices is not uncommon in the Pentecostal–Charismatic tradition. For example, there was a season in the 1940s in the United States where the claimed sightings of angels was a common occurrence following William Branham's insistence that he had had angelic visitations.[59] Walker notes how particular fads can influence groups: 'Crowds capitulate to fashion and once words of knowledge appeared on the charismatic scene, they became *de rigueur* in the renewal and in the so-called new churches.'[60] Colin Urquhart also gives multiple illustrations of fantastic miraculous accounts. On one occasion, he described how he had lost his car keys five months previously and the only spare set was with his wife, who had gone out. After praying, Urquhart explains what happened next:

---

[58] Brian 2003:152; Hunt 2004. Hunt (2004:62) suggests Gumbel almost has a cult following among older ladies. One lady describes how meeting Gumbel 'was one of the greatest days of my life'.

[59] Hilborn 2001.

[60] Walker 1995:128-29.

'Well, Lord, I'm going out to the car and somehow I trust you to start it.' I put my anorak on, shoved my hands into the pockets, as I usually did, and found that my left hand was clenching a bunch of keys![61]

Similar accounts to those of Gumbel were related on other Alpha courses. For example, the speaker at St C (Week 5) described how she had experienced financial difficulty as a student and very shortly after praying about it a friend came and gave her £600, the exact amount she needed. Such accounts are part of a well-worn Charismatic subtext: it is a world of crises; a world where God breaks in all the time. The perception is that one prays for something and it happens. Walker[62] points out that this is a world where the supernatural bypasses natural processes; coincidences are imbued with religious meaning; *ergo* God is amazing when you come to know him. This is the thrilling world within the Charismatic narrative, where God's providence 'accompanies the self who launches out toward God in an exciting romantic adventure'.[63] However, unless one is part of this sub-culture, where such experiences are normative, these accounts seem unreal and unbelievable. Its significance here is that Gumbel's account had the opposite effect to that intended. Rather than impressing those on the 'outside', these were precisely the points that were likely to invite discerption.

Courses that made use of a live speaker closely followed the Alpha syllabus, although compared with Gumbel's talks there was a general lack of humour and some of the speakers lacked theological sophistication. The talks were full of Christian jargon and there was present a general assumption of some basic understanding of Christianity. This included such basics as assuming that guests knew that there is an Old and New Testament (which one guest did not know), a basic understanding assumed of trinitarian grammar, and other Christian argot such as 'tracts' and 'Calvary'. One administrator who was attempting to work with the non-churched felt frustrated with what she perceived was the knowledge expected and assumed on Alpha (St C LA1). She said it was unlikely they would run another Alpha course because of this.

As noted in Chapter 2, in the first three weeks of Alpha, Gumbel goes for 'closure', where there is an opportunity for guests to say the 'sinner's prayer'. This was replicated on the courses that had live speakers but sometimes with a higher degree of intensity (St A1 and St B). The speaker at St B (LA1) is a good example of this. On the second session, with a group of fifteen people, she addressed the guests directly several times throughout the talk. Mel Gibson's film, *The Passion*, was described to emphasise the cruelty of the crucifixion and arouse the emotions:

---

[61] Urquhart 1974:53.
[62] Interview 23 May 2006.
[63] Hopewell 1988:76.

We can't be acquitted, we've broken God's laws…Does it make personal sense to
you, you, you [looking at different guests in the group], me?…What a way to treat
love than to take a rain check on Calvary…If you would like to say a simple
prayer, please speak to me or the other leaders (St B Week 2).

I personally felt most uncomfortable over the forcefulness of this talk. The
directness and intensity continued the following week, with the rhetorical
questioning of guests, and a prayer of commitment at the end where guests
were exhorted: 'If you pray this prayer you can become a Christian'. From
Week 4 on, there was an assumption that all of the guests were Christian,
although on Week 8, LA1 again went for closure, targeting guests who might
not be sure whether or not they were Christian.

The reaction of guests to the talks and theology of Alpha was polarised. The
Christian guests were positive about the talks with the following responses
being typical:

I think the talks were good. I found [LA1] really interesting to listen to (St B G5).

There were one or two that were really, really excellent; I got a lot from them (St
D G6).

Those who were not regular churchgoers were more critical, viewing the
theology that they found on Alpha as being too 'black and white':[64]

I think Alpha comes across as being a very black and white thing. I think it puts
you into a position where you have to think in quite a black and white way, which
I tend not to. I'm more of a grey thinker, although having said that, I think you
can sit on the fence too long…I find some aspects of Alpha, because it's so black
and white, a bit simplistic. Topics of discussion I couldn't contribute that much
because, it was quite, 'plonk', there it is, this is how it is (St A1 G4).

[T]here was [LA1] and [L2], and to me they pretty well believed it 100 per cent.
They'd deny that…didn't seem to leave much room for manoeuvre. To me there
are grey areas where you can't be definite about things, and I took it upon myself
to challenge them on some of those things…[S2] told me if I doubted something it
was the devil. For God's sake, you know, I mean. I felt there was a bit too much
black and white and there are a lot of grey areas and it's nice to discuss the grey
areas (St B G3).

One guest felt 'a bit alienated' because of Alpha's theology (St D G5) and, as
noted above (§3.4), another (St A1 G1) left after reading *Searching Issues*:

[Gumbel] said [AIDS] was an indirect result for not following God's word as
giving AIDS. And I just thought that to make any connection there was just

---

[64] For how this relates to 'stages of faith', see Fowler 1981; 1984 and Jamieson 2002.

outrageous. Especially since lesbians don't get AIDS through sex as well. So the logic wasn't there. I just thought that was really off. And some people have found it beneficial to have counselling if you're gay. And I thought that was a very, very old fashioned view, which was ridiculous. The other religions and New Age parts of [*Searching Issues*] wound me up, because I do yoga, and I don't think that's ungodly and I don't think demons are going to come into my mind when it's blank (St A1 G1).

One de-churched theology student, while generally enjoying the course, thought that Alpha was 'theologically dubious':

I thought it was really nice that they were really friendly, good group atmosphere and stuff. I didn't like the theology from the start. I didn't like the message, no, no, I didn't like the theology. I remember in the first few sessions they would try to prove the historical authenticity of Jesus Christ…there's no way you can prove God like that, it just didn't really make sense from a faith perspective, it doesn't really make sense from a historical perspective, so what's the point. So that annoyed me…

4.4 Small Group Discussion

Remaining faithful to the Alpha recipe is perceived by many to be relatively straightforward.[65] For example, attend an Alpha conference, carefully pick and train the team members, prepare a meal, follow the rule of 'no religious talk' during the meal to encouraged the development of affective relationships, put on a video/DVD, and include an Alpha weekend. Supporting each course is the multitude of Alpha resources, nationwide regional advisers and a central headquarters, with a large and highly skilled team. AI has provided immense detail to help churches to 'correctly' conduct Alpha. For churches with little or no evangelistic experience and little confidence that they have the appropriate skills for evangelism, this type of prescriptive advice enables them to evangelise in a reassuringly predictable way, hence Percy's article entitled, 'Join-the-dots Christianity'.[66] There is certainly a similarity between the way McDonalds and Alpha attempt to assert control through things like materials, skills, knowledge, rules, procedures and techniques. However, like McDonalds, the most unpredictable element in a franchise is the human dimension.[67]

The area that is the most unpredictable on Alpha is the small group

---

[65] See Hunt (2001:251), Ball and Grundy (2000:15) and the endorsements from church leaders in Appendix F of *Telling Others* (Gumbel 2001g).

[66] Percy 1997. Ritzer (1996:102) gives the same description in his McDonaldization thesis: 'Cooking fast food is like a game of connect-the-dots or painting-by-numbers.'

[67] Ritzer (1996:101) writes, 'The replacement of humans by machines is the ultimate stage in control over people – people can cause no more uncertainty and unpredictability because they are no longer involved, at least directly, in the process.'

discussion. To help team members is Gumbel's book, *Searching Issues*,[68] which attempts to address the seven most discussed topics that have come up on previous Alpha courses. Detailed instructions are also given in the Alpha training about how to lead groups (see Chapter 2 §2.4). This includes a participatory leadership style:[69] hosting discussions in an open and non-pressurised way and allowing guests to articulate whatever questions they desire. However, given the variable nature of human interaction, it is impossible to completely predict the questions guests might ask, and the way that discussions unfold. It is to a description of the Alpha small group discussion that we now turn. How did the discussions evolve over the duration of the course? Were guests able to ask *any* question they had? Were guests able to answer their own questions (*pace* Gumbel[70]) rather than looking to the leaders? What was the role of the team members? Who controlled the agenda?

4.4.1 ST A1

Throughout this course, the small group failed to achieve the type of discussion envisaged by Gumbel. Despite the forty-five minutes allocated for small group discussion, it sometimes lasted as little as fifteen minutes. The main difficulty seemed to be the directive leadership style of L1, which stifled discussion. L1's coercive push for conversion seemed to inhibit a more open spiritual exploration. For example, on the first week, L1 did approximately 80 per cent of the speaking. She became very nervous when she asked whether the guests had any questions, and filled up the momentary silence with further talk about Jesus and whether he was the Son of God. L1 thus gave very strong direction to the discussion, with direct questioning of particular guests. Because G2 and G3 were perceived to be the non-Christians in the group, the leader asked them what they thought of the talk and whether they believed that Jesus was the Son of God. I was surprised by such directness and felt very uncomfortable in this group. The intensity and directness of the questioning came close to being coercive. This continued the following week. Perhaps because L1 was unsure about where to locate G1 spiritually, she asked, 'Knowing about our sin now, and about God's forgiveness, how do you feel about opening yourself up to God?' She said that she had 'a word' [word of knowledge] and went on to mention Gumbel's *Why Jesus?* booklet in which there is a prayer in the back, inferring that G1 should offer the prayer. The sponsor (S1) for G3 noted this intensity in the questionnaire. To the question 'Is there any way you think the course could be improved', S1 replied:

---

[68] Gumbel 2001f.

[69] See Lewin, Lippitt and White 1939; Lewin 1947; White and Lippitt 1968; Van Vugt et al. 2004.

[70] Gumbel 2006.

> By not putting people on the spot and intimidating quiet people! Going round and having to give an opinion can be intimidating to some.

The leaders also experienced difficulty knowing how to handle more difficult questions, such as homosexuality. This issue was briefly discussed on Week 2, mostly by L1, who made it clear that God sees the whole picture and that to believe that homosexuality was all right was putting oneself in the place of God. L1 ended the discussion, telling G1, 'if you believe [that homosexuality is okay], it probably means you are under the trap of the devil'. G1 was given *Searching Issues* to read. She returned the following week to inform the leaders that she would not be continuing the course. She was offended by the material in *Searching Issues*, especially the homosexuality chapter.[71] Since the book was written by Gumbel, she did not want to continue the course. Because of the loss of one guest over questions about homosexuality, the way L1 dealt with the subject later in the course changed to that of avoidance. G4 explains:

> One of my questions that I felt absolutely wasn't answered was the homosexuality issue, which I felt was definitely swept under the carpet. [I. How was that dealt with?] I think we moved on to another topic. It was definitely avoided.

The various responses that guests gave to how they felt the discussions went can partly be explained based upon the different constituents of the group. For two guests (G5, G2) Alpha functioned like a (pre-baptismal) catechumenate. Both were positive about the discussion. The de-churched guests, who were on a more open spiritual quest, found the discussion unsatisfactory. The guest who dropped out described in an interview a desire for the group discussion to be 'more open...and less prescriptive, because I think what it boiled down to were those things, well, this is wrong that is wrong, that's wrong' (G1). G4 also expressed frustration at the lack of genuinely open discussion:

> I didn't know how far they were willing to give to the process of discussing as a group...I felt the group dynamic, I don't know how far it gelled that much throughout the course of ten weeks...I mean the open discussion was encouraged a lot, but I don't think that it actually happened (St A1 G4).

4.4.2 St A2

All of the guests on this course were de-churched. They had a Catholic or Anglican background, were unsure of their faith and wanted an opportunity to rethink and question the faith they were brought up in. The first two weeks included some lively discussion, with topics such as Jesus's divinity, suffering, and the relationship with other religions. However, over the next two weeks, guests stopped attending so that by Week 4 there were no guests at all. LA1 interpreted the lack of guests as a spiritual attack, and thought it might have

---

[71] Cf. Hunt 2005.

been because the church had not been praying enough for the course.[72] The fifth and final session on this course was one of conflict over the subject of evolution. L1 said, 'those who believed in evolution could only do so by committing intellectual suicide'. G1 had conducted scientific post-doctoral research at university, so quickly took the bait. The leaders believed the Genesis account was historical–scientific and not, as H1 suggested, a 'poetic account'. I felt that I should give my view, and agreed with H1 and G1. As Bion writes, 'There is no way in which the individual can, in a group, "do nothing" – not even by doing nothing.'[73] Silence in this situation would probably have been interpreted as agreeing with the leaders. G1 gave a sophisticated yet accessible account of how evolution occurred; how mutations happened and continued to occur. However, she did not have difficulty in both maintaining this view and a belief in God. The tension in this discussion mostly came from the leader (L1), who 'went native', that is, changing his role from hosting a discussion to full participation as a guest.

In the interview with G1, she described the difficulty that the evolution discussion caused for her:

> It could be, at the same time as evolution you could be a Christian [I. hold them together] hold it together. Whereas I very much felt like, if you read the Bible and believed the first few chapters on creation, then you couldn't believe in evolution. I found that very difficult. I really like [L1 and L2] and their approach to life, and when this came out, I was almost in shock. It was like, I can't believe these two people that I know, that they were so adamant about something, but to them it must be true. To them it must be really, really true. But I felt, okay, that's fine, you can have those beliefs, but do not force them on anyone else. You just need to calm down on this belief.

From G3's comments, it seems that the discussion on Alpha triggered difficulties that had previously not existed for her.

This was the last Alpha session; a viable course was simply not possible with only one guest and six team members. As noted above (see §3.4), the guests who left told G1 they felt it was very much 'us' and 'them', and that they felt outnumbered. The leaders (L1, L2) described how one guest (G2) who dropped out after the first week thought that there should have been more open discussion on the course, but felt that the agenda was controlled by the Alpha material, which they felt obliged to go along with. G1 noted the frustration that this caused:

> I suppose I was a bit disappointed that the proportions, there were a lot of people who were at the church already. So I found that very one sided. You almost feel you are being coerced into this...I think you need more of a dynamic. I'm quite

---

[72] Cf. Hopewell 1988.
[73] Bion 1961:118.

open to listen to what people have got to say, but I feel it was a bit one sided (St A2 G1).

This loss exacerbated the problem and left the remaining guest (G1) feeling very much alone. In the interview, the leaders expressed a sense of failure over the course: L2 said, 'I tried not to see it as such, but I did feel that it had failed.' In short, the defection of guests was due to the overwhelming presence of team members, which had a stifling effect on the group dynamics and discussion.

4.4.3 St B

The perception of both team members and church-going guests was that their church and home group were not the places to ask questions and express doubt. This led a number of Christian guests from St B to join Alpha. The course's broad reach of mission and spiritual formation gave rise to difficulties within the small group context, with a clash of agendas between the guests. The group's main task seemed to be affirming, or re-affirming, the faith of the majority who were regular churchgoers. This group enjoyed the discussion, with one guest describing it as the most positive aspect of the course (G1). In contrast, the open de-churched guests (G3, G7, G9) came with a different agenda, that of spiritual exploration. They were the most dissatisfied with the discussion, with two guests leaving the course and others feeling inhibited to ask questions. Janis notes how subtle constraints, which the leader may reinforce inadvertently, prevent members from fully exercising their critical powers and from openly expressing doubts when most others in the group appear to have reached a consensus.[74] The difficulty was made worse by the directive leadership style of L1 whose control of the agenda stifled discussion. For example, on the first week the leader (L1) was finding it hard to get the discussion going. After a few minutes, he asked, 'If Jesus were here now, what question would you like to ask him?' No one responded, so he directed the question to G7, who replied that he did not want to say anything. However, being directly focused upon, he related how he had been brought up by his mother to go to church but stopped going at the age of twelve. Because of this encounter, G7 did not return to the course. I later learned from the administrator (LA1) that '[G7] hated the small group discussion, led by [L1]. He felt that it was too harsh, too structured'.

The group's primary task, spiritual formation, meant that the de-churched guests had four options: conform to the group norms, challenge the norms, remain a 'closet deviant', or leave.[75] Argyle notes the difficulty of changing group norms, suggesting that it requires at least two 'deviants' who are unanimous, and who display conviction.[76] Two de-churched guests decided to

---

[74] Janis 1982:3.
[75] See Napier and Gershenfeld 1985:131; cf. Martin 1984:64-65.
[76] Argyle 1983:170.

leave: G7 after just one week, and G9 just before the day away because she felt nervous about the rapid pace of the course. Her partner said that 'she felt it took off and that she was left behind...like a horse and cart and the horse had gone off and left the cart. And from then on she felt uncomfortable' (G6). The other open de-churched guest (G3) challenged the group norms on Week 7, the 'storming' phase of the developmental dimension in groups.[77] The subject was evil and G3 raised a question about transcendental meditation.

Schachter showed how the more cohesive the group the greater the inclination of its members to reject a nonconformist.[78] Placing a high value on the maintenance of the group, and perceiving G3 to be a threat, the group as a whole seemed to attack the deviant. Although the leader (L2) suggested that there were a variety of views held by Christians on those types of issue, S2 was most forceful in condemning such things. G4 asked why such a practice was necessary if one was a Christian. Then S1 said it was better to stay clear of such things. This eventually led to an outburst by G3 who had become increasingly agitated by the onslaught. He said, 'you mention that things are not black and white' and proceeded to tell the group that not everyone was as advanced as 'you all'.

Although tempted to leave, G3's response was to challenge the group norms. Because G3 had prestige, and therefore influence in the group,[79] his comments tended to carry greater weight compared with guests of lesser status (G7, G9). The following week, there was still an atmosphere of tension. G3 said, his voice full of emotion, 'I still have questions...I do still have doubts.' He described how he almost did not return because of what happened on the previous week:

> To be given trite answers is not helpful and that's what I got last week, trite answers. I don't mind if you tell me you don't know the answers but to be told that my doubts were from the devil...they are things I've thought about.

He described how he had expected to find a group of agnostics on Alpha and to have much more debate. He raised an interesting question regarding Alpha's multiple aspirations:

> I don't know why you are all on the course, you all seem to have a strong faith...At times I thought, are they really running this for themselves, for their own enjoyment or whatever, or are they really doing it for us...I think they need to think who they're aiming it at and being a bit more sympathetic to the people who aren't believers and who could well be agnostics (St B G3).

---

[77] See Tuckman 1965; Tuckman and Jensen 1977.
[78] Schachter 1968; see also Cartwright 1951.
[79] Cartwright 1951:389; Festinger 1968:221.

4.4.4 St C

My small group at St C started with a greatly disproportionate ratio between team members and guest: seven to one. The only guest, G3, said that she had questions but, 'I don't want to criticise you...I mean I want to criticise, but I don't want to be rude'. Several team members said that they would not be offended and encouraged G3 to criticise. G3 proceeded to ask a variety of questions including the difference between the Old and New Testaments, C. S. Lewis' argument, halos, how God could have created hell, because hell is evil and God could not create evil. Despite the group imbalance throughout the course, this did not perturb the two non-churched guests from asking questions. They asked a variety of them, some relating to the week's talk, and others completely at random. The de-churched guest (G2) rarely spoke, although she often had conversations with the leader on the way home.

When a question was asked about the reliability of the Bible, the two helpers expressed opposing views. H1 said that there were no errors. H2, who was studying English at university, described hermeneutical difficulties, and how one could never know for certain whether hers or other interpretations of the Bible were accurate. No one in the group had the theological resources to know how to deal with this question and it was effectively ignored. From Week 3 onwards, the discussion changed to include more affective and personal issues. G2 became tearful as she described how she felt God had healed her on the bus coming home from work, and how her back pain immediately left her. Everyone in the group was moved, some to tears. Non-churched guest, G3, then said that she now believed, and that she felt that she was a Christian, despite still having questions. She asked whether Christians were baptised. L1 said that it was a Baptist thing but that it was also biblical and a good idea to get 'dunked'.

While there were some lively discussions, awkward periods of silence were not uncommon. The leader (L1), felt that the discussion did not go very deep, by which she meant people 'sharing from the heart'. She said this was because there were too few guests and too many team members. She also described the difficulty of following the Alpha recipe (by not speaking too much), yet needing to 'fill the gap up':

4.4.5 St D

At St D, the group discussion varied depending on the group, with one group very positive about the discussion time and two groups dissatisfied. During the first three weeks in my group, four open de-churched guests came for one session but did not return. They came with many questions, but left feeling frustrated with the lack of discussion. On the first week, C. S. Lewis' trilemma argument was raised, with open de-churched guest (G4) unconvinced by it. He was apologetic about asking all the questions, but with such a large contingent of Christians in the group, without his questions, the discussion kept drying up. He dropped out after the first week. The second week was dominated by non-churchgoing guest G13. He fired questions at a rapid pace throughout the discussion and his honesty stimulated others in the group to open up. When he asked why everyone had joined the course, the response from the team members was 'so that people will become Christian'. Unimpressed by this, G13 responded, 'I see God as being much bigger than Christianity'. On Week 3, various guests raised Freud's description of religion as being wish-fulfilment, and how a crisis always precipitated a spiritual quest. However, the conversation tended to quickly stall, with questions not discussed to any great extent. From Week 4 onwards, the group settled down to four team members and three guests, one of whom was a Christian (G2), another a non-practising Catholic (G3) and one a non-churched guest (G10). With so few non-churchgoing guests, there was difficulty in generating and continuing discussion. Nevertheless, despite making comments on the difficulty of getting a discussion going, G3 described it as being the most enjoyable aspect of the course.

I interviewed guests from other groups at St D. Several guests (G1, G5, G8, G9) from the same group were all positive about the discussion. Alpha convert, G5, describes his experience:

[W]ithin our group we talked about whatever we felt like. It was always led around Christianity, but it was exactly tailored to the people in the group.

Although theological student, G1, had questions about Alpha's theology, he enjoyed the discussions very much and found them helpful as a way of structuring and clearing his thoughts:

I did enjoy it, I can't deny it. I had fun and the people were great, but theologically questionable, in my opinion (St D G1).

The positive response from the guests in this small group was largely due to a highly social and skilled leader.

However, most of the other guests I interviewed were dissatisfied with the discussion time. Again, Alpha's multi-pronged aim of mission and spiritual formation meant that guests were at a different place spiritually and with varying questions. This caused frustration for both the open de-churched guests, many of whom left after just one session, *and* the Christian guests, who felt inhibited in asking questions for fear of creating further difficulties for the guests that they were attempting to convert. L1 and L2 described how some of the guests who dropped out had been 'a bit freaked out by there being so many Christians in the group'. Open de-churched guest, G12, expressed this frustration. Being conscious of the presence of Christians in the group, she was concerned about not offending people:

[I]n my little group, I was the only one who wasn't [a Christian], so my first impression was like, 'Oh dear, on my own!' [laughter]...I did feel when the discussion groups came, I was a bit, its just me here ploughing this little furrow [laughter]. I was interested to find out. I have to ask the obvious or belittling questions, you know, why do you believe in God? And some of them, they just sat there and it was like, 'okay, strange girl' [laughter]…When I said, how can you believe in something that you don't see, you don't feel, don't hear, and it was just like, 'Well, its God, you know, what are you, how can we not'. And I was like, yeah, I understand that you can, but tell me why or how or something. I found the discussion group quite awkward sometimes.

[M]aybe I'd felt happier if I'd known that there were other people in the group who felt the same as me and so I could ask more questions. When they were asking questions, it was discussing how strong a faith as opposed to no faith…it didn't crack the core questions for me (G12).

Another difficulty was based upon Gumbel's advice for team members to both avoid answering questions and debating with guests. Both of my leaders were confused by such instruction:

I think the training in some ways is really quite unhelpful, because it does sort of say, don't answer people's questions…but it seems that sometimes you do need to do that, and we haven't been very good at that because we've been so, oh we mustn't do that, and we mustn't do that…so I'm not sure exactly where it should be (St D L1).

This advice stems from Gumbel's concern that leaders should not give further teaching and accordingly he instructs leaders to open the question for others in the group to answer. As the above leaders testified, this advice was sometimes problematic. G6 expressed frustration with her leaders who kept to the Alpha recipe and described how the discussions would often 'fizzle out'. This was also a disincentive for G4 who left after one week. His perception was that Alpha's aim was to convert people and that the team members were afraid to argue for fear of putting him off. He comments:

I was trying not to be too provocative, but I was trying to ask questions about things that maybe were contradictory to Christian views, and I was hoping someone would defend it a bit. But not that many people did. I wanted a bit more discussion rather than, I kept saying things and then people kind of agreed, and then that was it…Some of them didn't really seem to know quite what it was they believed in, it was just sort of [hand clap] Christianity, and that's what you believe in. Maybe that was why they didn't argue back very much, because they didn't really know what to argue (St D G4).

4.4.6 St E

The group discussion at St E was varied. On some evenings the discussion was lively and the time to end the session arrived too soon; on others, the discussion was slow, with periods of silence. In my group, a couple's recent bereavement dominated much of the discussion throughout the course. They had come to

Alpha looking for answers. As Cartwright notes, a group becomes particularly attractive when it satisfies the needs of its members.[80] However, particularly detrimental for G1 was the dramatic testimonies and healing stories in the AI book, *The God Who Changes Lives*, which he had been given to read. He said, 'I couldn't relate to it. I feel as though I've taken a step back after reading that. I wish I'd never read it. I mean, why weren't my prayers answered?' (G1) I later suggested that he should read some of the Psalms.

Guests asked a number of questions that neither the leaders nor the group were able to address. For example, on the first week, G3 said that his question, coming from a scientific background, was not so much who was Jesus, but rather whether there was a God. He said, 'If God exists, then I could believe that Jesus was the Son of God, but I'm not sure there's a God. My question is one step back.' The leaders did not know how to respond to such a question and it resulted in a bit of banter between L1 and G3. L1 retorted with another question, asking G3 what he thought about Jesus. He replied that Jesus was a good man, that he taught good morals. L1 responded, 'But where did he get those morals from?' G3 then described how the biblical writers were from a pre-scientific world but that today there were many other explanations about the universe that did not rely upon God. The discussion moved on to questions about evolution and G3's original question was evaded and it was never asked again.

Again, the role of the leader played an important part in group dynamics. For much of the discussion time, the agenda was controlled by the leaders. The administrator gave them a list of questions at the beginning of each session which largely determined the discussion. Consequently, G3 felt that he lacked the opportunity of asking questions. He put this down partly to the leaders' inexperience at hosting groups. While he valued there being opening questions set by leaders, he expressed frustration over the lack of opportunity to ask questions not related to those on the Alpha agenda:

> [Q]uite often, the questions coming up in my mind were not related to the subject of the evening. And I felt reluctant to ask them because it was taking the conversation away from what I thought we were supposed to be talking about this week and, certainly in business meetings, when someone starts talking about something that isn't on the agenda, I find that very frustrating. So I didn't want to be the cause of it in the Alpha setting. But apart from the conversations, the opportunity to network over coffee at various points in the evening, there weren't any other opportunities in the Alpha set up to ask those questions.

In another group, G8 was positive about the discussion and wanted more time for it. In contrast to G3, G8 felt able to ask questions not related to the evening's topic. In yet another small group, G4 and G5 described how their leaders 'shied away' from difficult questions saying that they would be

---

[80] Cartwright 1951:388.

discussed in a later session, but they never were. So, although G5 was a university scientist, the subject of evolution was never raised during the discussion:

> Alpha is focused on Jesus and thereafter, so I think it didn't really delve into the very beginning of the world (G5).

> I don't think you'd dare mention evolution with that [small group leader] there...because it's probably a difficult a subject, isn't it? They don't want to raise it [laughter] (G4).

They described how feelings of inhibition prevented a more open discussion.

In summary, the most unpredictable part of Alpha was the small group discussion and it was this area where the greatest deviancy occurred. There were various reasons for this. In Chapter 2, it was observed that Gumbel merged the pre-Alpha course conducted at HTB into Alpha and, in particular, into the small group discussion.[81] The result was that the most difficult questions were discussed within a small group context, where the leaders lacked formal theological training. Further, Gumbel's vision of guests answering their own questions foundered when these more complex questions were tackled. This is further supported by other research.[82] For example, no one knew how to answer one guest's question regarding trinitarian grammar.

On the whole, leaders were unable to assimilate the participatory style of leadership that Gumbel outlines.[83] Some leaders (St A1 L1; St B L1) were directive and pressurising. This resulted in stalled conversation, with questions put by guests going undiscussed. Others (St A1 L1; St E L1 and L2) controlled the agenda through their list of questions and were not attentive or sensitive to quiet guests. Two leaders (St D L1 and L2) were simply confused by Gumbel's instruction on how much they should, and when not, contribute to the discussion.[84] Another difficulty leaders had was in how to manage debate and conflict. When leaders, following Gumbel's advice, avoided debate (St D L1, L2, LA1), the discussion tended to grind to a halt, with rather awkward periods of silence. Watts, Nye and Savage make clear that conflict is often considered to be taboo within church contexts because there is an expectation that the

---

[81] Gumbel 2006.

[82] Hunt 2001; Freebury 2001:20-21; Brian 2003:200. Hunt (2001:91) quotes one leader who described the small group as 'a bit like the blind leading the blind!'

[83] See also Brookes 2007:98-100.

[84] Festinger (1968:301-17) points out that the style of leadership should change according to a particular situation. What might work in one context cannot be guaranteed to work in another simply by having a set of 'rules of leadership' – for example, Alpha team training. He suggests that a 'situational' approach to leadership is required.

church should be a perfect, conflict-free environment.[85] The successful management of conflict requires knowledge, expertise and experience, being attuned to such things as personality, gender and culture. Communication skills are essential, as well as a grasp of conflict resolution styles. All this requires sensitive interpersonal skills that are not easily acquired in two or three Alpha training sessions.[86]

Another difficulty lay in Alpha's broad aim of attempting to hold together both mission *and* spiritual formation (see Chapter 2). This multi-pronged focus meant that Alpha guests came from a wide range of backgrounds with differing, and sometimes conflicting, motivations for participating on a course. This regularly resulted in a clash of agenda between those regular churchgoing guests who viewed the course as a way of vocalising doubt and to refresh or galvanise their faith, and those on a more open spiritual quest. This caused frustration for both groups. From the perspective of the Christian guests, there was a feeling of impatience at having such basic apologetic talks, and a desire for more Bible study. They also felt inhibited in asking questions because they did not want to create further difficulties for the guests whom they were attempting to convert. In contrast, there were those who had limited or no church background, and who found Alpha's starting point difficult. Several team members (St B L1; St D H1, L1) described how Alpha presumed that people knew the basics. They thought that the course would be more beneficial if it started further back, for those who had 'never even stepped into a church'. The group agenda was controlled, perhaps simply by default, by the majority of Christians present. And with the group's primary task being spiritual formation, guests on a more open spiritual journey had four options: conform to the group norms, challenge the norms, remain a 'closet deviant', or leave.[87] At various stages of the courses, guests responded in all four ways.

4.5 The Alpha Weekend/Day Away

The remaining element of the Alpha course itself is the weekend or day away, which is scheduled to take place halfway through the course. Four courses offered an Alpha day away and two included a weekend. One course (St D) joined HTB's weekend, and this provided me with the chance of doing some comparative analysis. I discovered a stark contrast between St D's course, which joined HTB's Alpha weekend, and the day away/weekend on the other

---

[85] Watts, Nye and Savage 2002:232; they develop Kilmann and Thomas' five styles of conflict resolution: competition, accommodation, avoidance, compromise and collaboration.

[86] Meadows (2007:410-11) argues that churches have used Alpha as 'technique' and to be satisfied with 'a mere simulacrum of real evangelism', rather than its leaders being 'apprenticed in a practice'.

[87] See Napier and Gershenfeld 1985:131.

courses.

On all of the courses, there was a distinct lack of 'hype' in the lead up to the weekend. Leaders tended quite nonchalantly to announce the plans for the day. Even so, there was usually some expectation of potentially dramatic and supernatural occurrences. For example, one guest (St A1 G4) prior to the day away had expressed interest in the Holy Spirit, but was scared that her 'body would be overtaken'. The administrator (LA1) reassured her, saying that the Holy Spirit was 'a gentleman' and would not force himself upon anyone.

The style of worship on all of the weekends had been influenced by Charismatic Renewal. It involved a flow of uninterrupted worship songs, each taking one more step towards intimacy with God (see Chapter 7 §3.4). Two churches (St B; St C) introduced Anglican elements. At St B, Charismatic worship songs were set within an Anglican liturgical framework. There was a prayer of preparation; a confession, followed by a period of silence; a kind of absolution (1 John 1.9) said by the administrator; a time of extemporaneous prayer; and a simplified creed. This was all intermingled with relatively modern worship songs including 'Majesty',[88] 'You laid aside your majesty',[89] and 'Be still for the presence of the Lord'.[90] The period ended with the song 'Spirit of the living God fall afresh on me'.[91]

While there were often tears, and tongues were spoken on two courses (St A and St C), there were no dramatic conversions and a general lack of 'physical manifestations' despite an attempt by the leaders to give space for this to happen. For example, St C's day away included two other churches. At the end of the day came the 'prayer ministry' time and the leader prayed for the Spirit to come. There was silence for over five minutes. Two group leaders started to move physically, one dramatically waving his arms. Several people quietly started to speak in tongues. One woman started to cry. The speaker then asked if anyone had a word from God. A group leader from another course said that she 'had a picture of a field; a green meadow with a fence. And that God wanted someone to go through the fence'. The other leader, who had been shaking with big arm movements, prayed that God would, 'lead me through the fence'. Following this, permission was given by the speaker to move around and pray for one another. This continued for more than thirty minutes. Despite the opportunity given for 'prayer ministry', the guests from St C seemed to experience very little. Two blamed themselves for this:

> ...hearing people speak in tongues was quite, I didn't know what to make of it at first, and I started laughing. I kind of got used to it...It was quite good to learn because after that I kept trying and trying to do it, but it just didn't come, didn't

---

[88] *Songs of Fellowship* [SF] (1998), No.379.

[89] *SF* (1998), No.633.

[90] *Mission Praise* [MP] (1990), No.50.

[91] *MP* (1990), No.613.

work... [I. How did that make you feel?] I don't know. It's my own fault because if I had followed it more in the first place then I would have probably got it... (St C G3).

G4 also did not 'experience' anything during the day:

I'd like to say I did but in all honesty I don't think I, not really. And I keep wondering if that's my fault because I'm sort of so desperately sitting there thinking something's going to happen, then it doesn't...I kept hoping that something would partly because I'd done Alpha before...it seemed to be just myself and my friend who went, and we were the only people that weren't touched by the Holy Spirit that day. Everyone else was suddenly talking in tongues and falling to the floor in floods of tears and all that sort of thing, and we just sat there totally baffled to be honest...[I] sort of felt more ready to make a commitment and the whole lot. I really wanted something to happen but, I don't know, it's weird... [I. Were you disappointed by that?] I was disappointed yeah...maybe it was just me. Maybe I expected too much (St C G4).

In sum, guests remarked on how they appreciated the social aspect of the weekend, but no one described it as a life-changing experience. Some guests felt that a whole day was too long, and one guest even found the day 'quite boring' (St C G3). Several guests were disappointed at not having an experience of the Holy Spirit and blamed themselves for this. There was nothing on these weekends that could be regarded as 'power evangelism' (see Chapter 2 §1.5-1.6) where the experience of God – through words of knowledge and healings – overcomes resistance to the gospel and brings about conversion.

This is supported by other research. Hunt found the Alpha weekend that he attended 'a bit of an anticlimax' and noted a sense of disappointment among the leaders.[92] In Lewis' research of nine Methodist chapels over the course of four years, he described how he followed Alpha's 'seven tips on making the most of your course' and did everything by the book but did not see the sort of results advanced by HTB that one could expect. The day away that he ran did not produce any 'gifts of the Spirit' or Charismatic Renewal and this resulted in confusion and disappointment.[93] One leader reported that there were no outward signs of the Spirit but there was a sense of the presence of God, 'a general niceness'. Lewis interpreted this to be the Holy Spirit working, but in different ways from HTB, including the feeling experienced by people of God's blessing, or an affirmation of their place in his love. He concluded that the pattern that works for HTB does not easily translate to other contexts. Watling describes an Alpha weekend at a Church of Scotland where no-one requested

---

[92] Hunt 2004:244.
[93] Lewis 2001:42.

the 'infilling' or 'refreshing' of the Holy Spirit.[94] The minister stated that the room was full of peace and did not require any dramatic infilling.

All of this contrasts starkly with the St D/ HTB weekend. Only one Christian guest in total signed up for the weekend and none from my small group. I sensed that guests did not wish to attend the weekend, rather than their being unable to do so. This was confirmed later in the interviews. Some had legitimate reasons for not going (G1, G9). Others (G3, G10) were put off because it involved not only a whole weekend, but the idea of worship (G3), the overwhelming presence of Christians (G12), and nervousness about going away with people they hardly knew (G2, G6).

The HTB organised weekend included several groups from other churches and universities, with those from HTB making up a third of the total. With approximately 300 people present there was a marked difference in group dynamics compared with other weekends. Because I had friends from HTB who were leading small groups, I was able to spend time with them and some of their guests. As one might have expected, the weekend ran exactly to the Alpha recipe. The talks kept very close to Gumbel's Alpha addresses, usually with the same illustrations. They were interspersed with well-told jokes, some of which got applause. These had the effect of helping to relax and disarm guests. A recurring theme throughout the talks, and in contrast with other courses, was that speakers continually 'primed' guests, or built up an expectancy that things would happen later during 'ministry time'. This included repeated comments such as, 'We'll do a bit of that later.' Various physical manifestations that might happen were suggested, including shaking, falling over, feelings of fire or 'liquid heat' in the body, or hands tingling. This was explained as a 'deeper spiritual work with physical manifestations'.

The worship slowly increased in length and intensity throughout the weekend. By late Saturday afternoon there was an extended time of sung worship in classic Vineyard style. During the first song people started clapping, raising their hands and some started to dance. This was followed by another song, 'Your love is amazing, steady and unchanging, I can feel this love song rising up in me'.[95] Then the hymn 'Amazing grace' followed. During this there were shouts of 'hallelujah', 'Jesus', and 'Thank you Lord', mostly from the black contingent. The pace of the songs then slowed and quietened down.

The first 'prayer ministry' time followed the next talk. The speaker instructed guests to put their hands out in front of them, and prayed: 'Lord, let your power come upon us...pour out your Spirit...we claim that promise.' The speaker then suggested possible responses: 'you might feel heat...shaking'. There was silence. 'You might like a gift from God...tongues. We're going to sing in tongues'. The speaker then started singing in tongues and was joined quietly and harmoniously by others in the group. This lasted for about four

---

[94] Watling 2005.
[95] *Survivor Songbook No.1* (2001), No.197.

minutes. There were more suggested responses to the Holy Spirit. Various 'words of knowledge' were given: someone with a particular back problem (a technical name for it was given); someone who felt abandoned in life. People responded to these things and the speaker asked for them to be prayed for. It was at this point that permission to leave was given. Various people from St D prayed for one another. Then a woman started to scream and was held up by two people as she entered a trance-like state shouting out 'Jesus'. Many other people were in tears; there was hugging and 'group hugs'. During this time worship was quietly being played and one of the HTB organisers walked around with a box of tissues. Another opportunity for 'prayer ministry' was given after Holy Communion on the Sunday.

Very different responses to the weekend were given by those from St D. The one guest who went on the weekend was positive about it and described how she 'felt something':

> I thought it was quite amazing actually hearing people sing in tongues...I suppose I just felt something, I don't know how to explain it, sort of something inside, some sort of feeling, like warm, not really sure how to explain it more. Like a presence maybe (St D G7).

The helper (H1) from my group also enjoyed the weekend, but thought that it would have been too intense for her friend (G3). Others had a negative time. A helper (H2) found the Saturday ministry time difficult because he had not 'felt' anything. Also, one of my small group leaders had a spiritual crisis following the 'ministry time', although he was reluctant to talk about it. A small group leader from HTB told me that her group had been somewhat negative about the 'ministry time'. While they enjoyed being prayed for, she said, 'They felt that the speaking in tongues had been engineered.'

So, what exactly is it that makes HTB's weekends so different? To begin with, the HTB weekend was much larger than the other courses. Those guests from HTB seemed to arrive with a higher degree of expectancy.[96] One HTB guest described how 'the whole course has been building up towards this weekend'. The sense of anticipation grew during the talks given by the HTB speakers. A recurring theme was the 'priming' of guests and building an expectancy that things would happen later during 'prayer ministry'.[97] Being 'physically encapsulated' (see Chapter 6 §6.1) for a whole weekend also gave group members more time to bond, for guests to feel relaxed and thus more 'open' to a life-changing experience of the Holy Spirit. During the weekend, the length and intensity of worship increased, with the emotional and spiritual temperature reaching a crescendo during 'prayer ministry'.

---

[96] See also Watling 2005.

[97] The only course which had similarities to HTB's weekend was St E where, like HTB, the speaker suggested various responses to the Holy Spirit.

I am inclined to think that the events surrounding HTB's Alpha weekend resonate with Walker's assessment regarding the Charismatic phenomenon: that is, they are often psycho–social constructions.[98] Walker notes, 'large audiences are receptive to platform cues and crowd happenings, and the power of suggestion in such an atmosphere of excitement is strong…That the phenomena are strange does not mean they cannot be from God, but it does not mean that they are either'.[99] Scotland viewed the Toronto Blessing as 'a mixture of the Divine, the human and the psychologically-induced'.[100] I would suggest that the same might be true for the Alpha weekend at St D/HTB.

4.6 After Alpha

As described in Chapter 2, the main aim of Alpha is conversion, with the broader intention of spiritual maturity (Col. 1.28-29). Gumbel recognises that this takes longer than a ten-week course, hence his follow on courses. Officially, Alpha is part one of 'a two-year programme of adult Christian education'.[101] How did this relate to the churches that I researched? What were guests offered post-Alpha?

Despite a number of guests being open to continuing their spiritual journey, specific post-Alpha follow-up was almost non-existent at St A, St B, St C and St D, other than attending church and joining a home group. St A had no post-Alpha follow on course but did have an informal process of initiation for those who converted. The two converts on this course (G2 and G5) had just started to attend St A before Alpha began and baptism was seen as the next step for them. G5 was baptised towards the end of the course, but the leaders did not feel that G2 was ready for baptism. However, nothing specific was available for the de-churched guests (G3, G4). One of them (St A1 G4) described how her faith was 'reawakened' on Alpha, yet was not offered any way of continuing on her spiritual journey.

All of the guests at St B had been christened and others were making use of Alpha as a confirmation preparation, so it was perceived that home groups were a suitable forum for them to continue, although one guest (G3) had been put off such groups because of negative experiences during the small group discussions.

The Alpha administrator and church leader (LA3) at St C had written and self-published discipleship courses. However, in contrast to the church's official discourse, this course was conspicuous for its lack of follow on

---

[98] Walker 1995; see also Noakes 1984. Hunt (1998:80-82) compares it to non-Christian faith healing and Kundalini yoga, which include similar 'manifestations' (see also Hand 1998:82).

[99] Walker 1995:128, 158.

[100] Scotland 2000:249.

[101] Gumbel 2004.

procedures. There was no official follow-up for the two non-churched guests (G1, G3), one of whom converted on Alpha, although both were informally followed up by church members. Open de-churched guest, G2, was distressed that Alpha had finished but felt that the church services at St C were too intense, with everyone 'praying and speaking in tongues'. According to my group leader (St C L1), the Alpha administrator had 'forgotten' to follow her up.

It was the same for St D. The church neither contacted guests after Alpha, nor invited them at the end of the course to join the church's weekly student group. A number of guests were regular churchgoers, or had recently started to attend church (G2, G5, G6, G7, G8, G14). Those who were not regular churchgoers were left in limbo. Non-churched guest, G10, and de-churched guests, G3, G9 and G12, completed Alpha without converting and none was officially followed up. Yet G3 said that she would have been open to continuing what had begun on Alpha:

[I. Have you been contacted since by the church?] Not at all. [I. Would you want to continue discussing stuff?] Yeah, in a way. I quite liked the discussion aspect...the only contact I've had is [H1], going 'Come to church and see everyone' (G3).

St E had by far the most well thought through follow-up options post-Alpha, with most of the guests involved in some way or another. This included two Bible study groups, a *Christianity Explored* nurture group for guests not ready to join a home group, and a men's group that met in a pub. A number of guests (G1, G2, G4, G5, G8) were grateful at being able to continue what they had started on Alpha. G1 and G2 appreciated being able to continue their spiritual journeys. They actually hosted the *Christianity Explored* group and reported that it had already increased in size:

I think we would be a bit empty if we lost this, personally...We're not starting our own church [laughter]. We might have to knock a few walls down, but, no, we look forward to it (G1).

Moving Alpha guests into a home group context was off-putting for G8, although he was keen to continue his spiritual journey. His partner had previously completed Alpha, but he described her regret at how nothing was offered afterwards for her:

...she said she always felt she wanted more afterwards, to keep going with it, but...there was no follow on for her, she just stopped. And with that in mind, I said the same thing at the Alpha group last year, and they said, 'Oh, we can run these home groups'...And to be honest, I went to the first one and I felt...like I was a non-believer, and everyone else was in a different place and I didn't enjoy it. Whereas going to the pub last week with [LA1] and a bit more relaxed atmosphere, maybe with it being all men as well, it felt a bit more akin to my own lifestyle, and I found that more enjoyable... (G8).

Although not all of the guests from St E had made the transition into the various groups, some purely for practical reasons, there were numerous options.

5. Summary

In this chapter, I first gave an outline of the churches in which I conducted research. It was noted that I experienced difficulty locating churches running Alpha courses other than Charismatic–Evangelical ones. Although I was constricted denominationally, I was able to research a wide variety of courses in terms of socio–economic demographics.

I next looked at how faithfully courses kept to the Alpha recipe. Having expected a high level of deviancy, I was surprised to find conformity in terms of Alpha's basic methodology. This conflicted with stories of 'hacking Alpha' about which I had previously heard. However, serious difficulties arose in the small group discussion.

The third section assessed the process of affiliation. While the vast majority (90 per cent) of people attending Alpha were either churched or had some church background, it was suggested that Gumbel was correct in his conviction that non-churchgoers start to attend Alpha when churches persist with the course. However, the majority (60 per cent) of these non-churchgoing guests were from the open de-churched category – that is, they had been christened, had some experience of church, but at some stage had left. Significantly under-represented were the non-churched and the closed de-churched, which, according to the *Mission-Shaped Church* report, constitute sixty per cent of the UK population.[102] This raises the question of whether Alpha should start further back.[103]

The vast majority of guests (92 per cent) joined Alpha through the influence of Christian friends, church or church leaders. The high profile of Alpha gained through its marketing strategies was successful in achieving public recognition for the course. This has resonance with what MacLaren terms 'consumerist religion'.[104] Guests often joined based upon a multi-pronged dynamic including friends, website, leaflets, posters and so on. Yet despite considerable effort, four of the six courses had continuing difficulty in recruiting guests. My research revealed a defection rate of 30 per cent, which tallies with the higher end of HTB's drop out rate. While Alpha's theology and the pressure exerted by leaders caused some discerption, most left because they were put off by the overwhelming and stifling, presence of Christians on the course. This became

---

[102] Cray 2004.
[103] See also Hunt 2004:253-54; Murray 2004:160-63; Brookes 2007:74.
[104] MacLaren 2004:172-82.

so acute on one course that it dissolved after the fifth week. Part of the difficulty here related to the unpredictability in recruitment. It was common for fewer guests to attend than the Alpha administrators expected, resulting in an excess of team members. This state of affairs was exacerbated by the presence of Christian guests, Christian sponsors, and by the defection of guests.

The fourth section described the actual Alpha programme, including the meal, worship, talk, discussion and the weekend /day away. The meal was significant in that it facilitated the development of group cohesion and enabled the development of strong affective ties. The meal was fraught with difficulty for several courses, and for various reasons: the actual food and location (McDonalds), the working class context of one course, the stress involved for two administrators in providing food, the difficulty of young mothers in organising their children's night time routine and getting to the meal on time. Lastly, the offer of free food on three courses met with mixed responses, with some guests appreciating it, while for others the offer aroused suspicion.

Although sung worship was only partially used, its style was influenced by Charismatic Renewal. This fitted the Charismatic–Evangelical spirituality of those churches that I researched, although it had caused serious tensions within one church (St E) where it created two factions: the traditional churchgoers, and a 'renewal' group, many of whom had previously participated on Alpha. While the church-going guests generally appreciated the worship, several of the de-churched guests thought that the inclusion of worship was inappropriate and felt alienated by it. This conflicts with Gumbel's comment that by the end of Alpha guests usually become accustomed to worship, although perhaps this difference is due to the fact that HTB includes worship from the very first evening.

Those courses with speakers kept faithfully to the Alpha syllabus. This meant that key themes came through including penal substitutionary atonement; a push for conversion (especially for the first three weeks), which was primarily described using 'born again' language; a strong sense, or *feeling*, of assurance; a Charismatic experience of the Holy Spirit and a particular (canonical and proof-texting) approach to the Bible. Like the official Alpha material, the talks were full of jargon and assumptions about Christian belief, although this did not seem to pose a difficulty because most guests had a church background. However, the speakers differed from Gumbel in a number of dimensions: an absence of humour; two courses had a much higher intensity; and there was sometimes a lack of theological nuance. A reoccurring theme on the courses was that Alpha's theology was too 'black and white'. The theology of the churches that I researched tended to be more conservative than the theology found in the Alpha resources.

The small group discussion was the most unpredictable part of Alpha and was where the greatest deviancy occurred. There were various reasons for this. Gumbel's deferral of the more difficult questions to the small group, and to leaders lacking formal theological training. His vision of guests answering their own questions foundered when these more complex questions were tackled. Leaders were generally unable to assimilate the participatory style of leadership that Gumbel outlines. This resulted in stalled conversation, with questions put by guests going undiscussed and the inability of leaders to appropriately manage debate and conflict. Another difficulty lay in Alpha's broad aim of attempting both mission *and* spiritual formation (see Chapter 2) with neither adequately accomplished (see also Chapter 7). Guests often had conflicting motivations for joining. There was a distinction between regular churchgoing guests, who viewed the course as a way of refreshing their faith, and those on a more open spiritual quest. Such positions were at odds with each other.

The contrast between St D's course, which joined HTB's Alpha weekend, and the day away/ weekend on the other courses was noted. In short, the weekends lacked 'power evangelism' where the experience of God overcomes resistance to the gospel and brings about conversion. Guests appreciated the social aspects of the day away, although some of them were disappointed at not having an experience of the Holy Spirit, for which they blamed themselves. This is supported by other studies.[105] I have concluded that the dramatic accounts at HTB's weekend resulted from a variety of factors: the high degree of expectancy in the build up to the weekend, the reception of a large audience to platform cues and crowd happenings where the power of suggestion is strong,[106] the gradual increase in intensity during worship and the pressure to conform to group norms, which is heightened in emotion-producing situations. In short, I have suggested that Scotland's analysis of the Toronto Blessing also relates to the Alpha weekend: that it is perhaps a mixture of the Divine, the social and the psychologically-induced.[107]

Finally, there is the topic of what happened afterwards. Gumbel's aim for Alpha to be part one of a two-year programme of adult Christian education was for the most part unsuccessful. Although a number of guests expressed an interest in continuing their spiritual journeys, specific post-Alpha follow up was practically non-existent in relation to five courses. The general lack of follow on from Alpha has been identified by other researchers.[108] As I shall discuss in Chapter 6, conversion is profoundly precarious, and plausibility collapses unless it is maintained continually and consistently through socialisation and conversation.

Having assessed the first aim of the book – to compare and contrast Alpha as it is 'on the ground' with the official version – I shall now proceed to assess the second aim. This is to investigate the course's primary goal of conversion. To help facilitate this analysis, I shall make use of the framework of the sociology of conversion.

---

[105] Lewis 2001; Hunt 2004; Watling 2005.
[106] Walker 1995.
[107] Scotland 2000.
[108] Ireland 2000:42-43; Hunt 2004:72.

Chapter 6

Alpha and the Sociology of Conversion

Alpha's primary aim is to convert non-churchgoing guests. To what extent does the course succeed in achieving this? And how is conversion to be understood? In this chapter, I shall relate theories in the sociology of conversion to describe the conversion process on Alpha. I shall first outline the different types of conversion. Then the various *processes* involved in conversion will be described, seeing subjects not necessarily as passive victims, nor as being psychologically deficient, but rather as people often on an active spiritual quest. Lastly, conversion will be examined through the matrix of three interweaving explanations: social–psychological explanations attempt to describe conversion in terms of human need; structural explanations locate the explanation primarily within changing social structures; and cognitive explanations describe it in terms of the perceived logic of the beliefs themselves. I shall employ them as a theoretical framework in helping with the attempt to decipher conversion on Alpha.

1. Defining Conversion

One of the inherent difficulties in the sociology of conversion is linguistic. How does one define conversion? Is it accurate to define it as 'a change in which one adopts a new religion'?[1] or limited to *radical* personal change.[2] Richardson notes the faddism present among sociologists, in particular how such *a priori* assumptions slant how they portray conversions, emphasising certain features more than others. For example, it is highly likely that affectional ties developed from meaningful interaction have been an aspect of conversion and recruitment for a long time and in different settings, yet researchers have not noticed this until recently because of the blinders of the traditional 'Pauline paradigm'.[3]

---

[1] American Heritage Dictionary 2000.

[2] Heinrich 1977:674; Snow and Machalek 1984; Pargament 1997. See also A. D. Nock's (1933) seminal work on conversion. He views conversion as involving 'a consciousness that a great change is involved, that the old was wrong and the new is right' (Nock 1933:7). He refers to other 'lesser' transformations as 'adhesion'.

[3] Richardson 1985:175. The recent stress of plausibility structures, see below, and the significance of wider society and religious groups in conversion is a helpful corrective to the individualistic accounts of William James (1902) and A. D. Nock (1933).

Further, within the sociology of conversion, there has been a fascination with the more 'deviant' or fringe types of conversion to NRM, which only account for one per cent of religious believers,[4] rather than an interest in mainstream religious traditions.[5] This has led to a rather skewed perception of personal religious change and has resulted in a form of selection bias, reflecting the different areas of emphasis of researchers.[6] As Suchman maintains, studies of the most glamorous and all-encompassing forms of conversion must be supplemented by investigations of more pedestrian and restricted realignments.[7]

Lewis Rambo's seminal work on conversion generates a much richer and diverse way to expand the understanding of religious change. He outlines five types:[8]

1. *Tradition transition* refers to conversion from one traditional religion to another.
2. *Institutional transition* occurs where a person changes allegiance, for example, from one denomination to another within the Christian tradition. This can be based simply upon geographical convenience or on a shift in spirituality or belief.
3. *Affiliation* conversion takes place when one moves from a position of no previous religious belief or commitment to becoming involved with a religious community.
4. *Intensification* refers to a renewed commitment within an existing religious affiliation, or an intensification of a faith that was formerly present in the form of a seed, and which blossoms into full flower.
5. *Apostasy* refers to the rejection and defection from a previous religious group. This may or may not involve the adoption of a new religious system. Of course, apostasy is in the eyes of the judge, not the convert.

All of these types of conversion involve different degrees of change and a different process of conversion, depending on the beliefs and practices of both the group being converted to and the convert.

---

[4] Beit-Hallahmi and Argyle 1997:8.

[5] For recent discussion in the sociology of conversion, see Anthony and Robbins 2003; Batson and Ventis 1982; Beckford 1978; Beit-Hallahmi and Argyle 1997; Davidman and Greil 1993; Greil and Rudy 1984; Heinrich 1977; Lofland 1966, 1977, 1978; Lofland and Skonovd 1981; Percy 2000; Richardson 1985, 1993; Savage 2000; Snow and Machalek 1983, 1984; Stark 1965; Stark and Bainbridge 1980; Straus 1979; Ullman 1982.

[6] Kilbourne and Richardson 1989; Suchman 1992.

[7] Suchman 1992:S16.

[8] Rambo 1993:12-14.

2. Conversion on Alpha

How does all this relate to Alpha? Hunt's quantitative research revealed that of the 837 respondents who returned their questionnaires, 47 stated that they had 'become a Christian as a result of taking Alpha'.[9] And of those 47 converts, 11 had no church background. Hunt concludes that Alpha is 'rejuvenating those already in the church through charismatic teaching and culture'.[10] Using Rambo's categories, my research gives greater nuance to Hunt's findings (see below table). It agrees with Hunt's analysis that the majority (90 per cent) of those who attend Alpha have some church background, although it differs in the balance of those who are regular churchgoers compared with those with some church background. I noted in Chapter 5 (§3.2) that most people (60 per cent) attending Alpha come from the open de-churched category.

Conversions

Tradition transition	0
Institutional transition	0
Affiliation	3
Intensification	17
Non-conversions	34

The religious background of the guests on Alpha corresponded to the majority of conversions being of the intensification type:

> I think it's affirmed and probably reaffirmed what I knew or had as a child, but then you leave home...and get into the student way of things. So I think it's probably reawakening something that was started as a child (St A1 G4).

> I've started afresh... (St B G5).

It is important to stress here that a number of these conversions (St B G4, G5; St D G5, G7, G9) were the result of a wider process of reinitiation in which Alpha played just one part. For example, one guest (St B G5) had started a quest at St B eighteen months prior to Alpha and had already been confirmed. Further, several of these conversions included guests who were regular churchgoers and whose faith was intensified on the course (St B G1, G2, G4; St D G7; St E G10).

Interestingly, of the five non-churched guests on the courses that I researched, three converted. Two did so several weeks prior to the start of Alpha (and so not directly as a result of the course) and one during the course, although the latter described how she was unsure of the commitment that she had made. These are classified as 'affiliation' conversions.

---

[9] Hunt 2004:187.
[10] Hunt 2004:195.

Most of the guests on Alpha did not convert. Of this group, at least fifteen left the course. Also in this group were eight regular churchgoing guests. Noteworthy here is that a number of guests who did not convert (St C G1; St D G10; St E G3) described how, although not making a 'commitment', they felt that they had taken a step forward in their faith journey. This was the case even despite Alpha, including two guests who left the course (St A1 G1; St D G11) and one guest (St A2 G1) where the course ended after the fifth week.

Having outlined the types of conversion on Alpha, what were the processes involved in them? Did the guests experience conversion gradually or as a dramatic event? Further, how active were they in pursuing a spiritual quest?

3. Process Theory

There has been a move away from 'psychopathological' explanations of conversion[11] where conversion is reduced to the amount of coercion involved, with vulnerable converts seen as passive victims with little control over manipulative groups. In contrast, contemporary studies of conversion have emphasised the convert as being an active searcher and the consideration of conversion as being more of a 'process',[12] 'a marathon, not a sprint'.[13] Rambo includes a process model that gives space to the social or corporate nature of conversion. He defines conversion as 'a process of religious change that takes place in a dynamic force field of people, events, ideologies, institutions, expectations, and orientations' and outlines various stages: context, crisis, quest, encounter, interaction, commitment and consequences.[14] These should not necessarily be understood as successive stages. For example, a personal crisis might come *after* the quest stage. In adopting Rambo's model, I shall follow McKnight's preference for using the term 'dimensions' rather than 'stages'.[15] A stage can imply either a sense of a deterministic march to conversion or process of maturation.

First, Rambo notes the *context*, that which shapes the convert as well as the process of conversion, including the social, cultural, religious and personal circumstances of the individual. Since this is the necessary backdrop or condition to all human beings, it is questionable whether context should be viewed as a particular dimension of conversion. Second, there comes some kind of *crisis*. Some crises call into question one's fundamental orientation to life, and others in and of themselves are rather mild but are the 'proverbial straw

---

[11] Stark 1965; also see Barker 1984; Kilbourne and Richardson 1989; Richardson 1993; Anthony and Robbins 2003; Shinn 1992.

[12] Lofland and Skonovd 1981; Rambo 1993.

[13] Percy 2000.

[14] Rambo 1993:5. Rambo's theory has received positive quantitative support in Kahn and Greene (2004).

[15] McKnight 2002:49.

that breaks the camel's back'.[16] A crisis provides the opportunity for a new option, stimulating a quest to resolve conflict, or to fill a void. On Alpha, all of the guests who converted, except one, described various crises they had suffered. These ranged from bereavement, marriage crisis, engagement break up, divorce, illness, to more general angst or dissatisfaction about life:

> I'd just separated with me wife. I started to question myself quite deeply and think, where's this all going...you know, what is the meaning of life (St A1 H2).

> Slightly disorientated cause I'd just split up with my fiancée, which was my decision, but...feeling slightly fragile about approaching thirty...there is that mild anxiety, oh, I'm single, oh, would I like children, oh, but you need someone first. General anxiety (St A1 G4).

> [L]osing my dad made me turn a bit more back to church...made me want to question religion and made me think about where my dad was at now and stuff like that (St B G5).

> I suppose what made me start thinking about God and the church was because I was ill. I found out that I'd got cancer...I was told if I didn't have this operation I had a year to live (St C G4).

Other guests were in a highly vulnerable emotional and psychological state:

> I tried to kill myself. It was that or [my boyfriend would] kill me. And he got put in mental hospital because he got brain damage...I had two breakdowns and a lot of problems afterwards. Even now I'm edgy. And I had a breakdown a year ago, and I was in hospital (St C G2).

Of course, everyone experiences stress and crisis from time to time, yet not everyone converts.[17] Thus, crisis *by itself* is insufficient to predict conversion.

The third dimension following crisis is that a person *quests* for answers to needs. Before Alpha began, the quest dimension was lacking for a number of guests who converted.[18] For them, Alpha itself was a part of the quest. They tended to go straight from the crisis dimension to an encounter, quest and interaction, either in their church or on Alpha. For others a quest had begun

---

[16] Rambo 1993:46.

[17] Heinrich's (1977) research comparing converts to 'Pentecostal Catholicism' and a control group of 'non-Pentecostal Catholics' found that both groups reported stress. This is supported by Greil and Davidson's (1993) study of secular Jews converting to Orthodox Judaism. They discovered that the large majority converting did not experience a crisis. They suggest that the difference was due to their adoption of a relatively less deviant world-view in contrast to previous studies, which have concentrated on conversions to more deviant groups.

[18] St A1 H2, G1, G2; St C G2; St D G7; St E G1, G2, G4, G5, G7, G8.

prior to Alpha (St B G4, G5, G6). One guest (St A1 G4) had a weekly Bible study with a Christian work colleague. For another guest (St A1 G5), it was the film *The Passion* that led to a quest, asking a friend (S2) whether he could attend church with him. Three guests had pursued other religions in their quest (St C G1, G3; St E G3). For St C G3, this included a superficial interest in Satanism and Buddhism:

> I had interest in quite a few religions: Satanism because it was quite controversial...and Buddhism because it didn't actually have a god, it had a real man.

For others the quest was quite proactive and longer term:

> I started going to church about a year ago, quite regular. I met people there and talked about Christianity. So I sort of compared that with the Mosque (St C G1).

> I first of all came across something called Tantra. [It] comes from the East, from India, and it's not a religion, it's a sort of way of meditating and breathing, and looking at life in a different way. And I found that very therapeutic and helped me sort myself out, what I really wanted. But also there was a spiritual aspect to it. Very gently done...up until I started that, I wasn't at all spiritual. In fact I didn't even know what it meant to be spiritual. I had a scientific career, and in a sense I guess I've always been too analytical and I will have discarded things I couldn't see and touch and measure without giving it much thought. But through the Tantra course...my mind just opened up a little bit and I thought, well, there's no harm in it, why not explore and see what happens...I was in this mode of discovery when I was talking to [L2]...and I mentioned the fact that I'd like to know more about Christianity... (St E G3).

As with a crisis, the quest dimension did not lead inevitably to conversion for a number of guests (St D G1, G3, G4, G10, G11).

Fourth, a person *encounters* an advocate. This may be a charismatic leader, who can have a considerable effect on a decision whether or not to convert, or a group of people, who offer a solution to the various needs of a convert. I have given an account of the process of affiliation on Alpha in Chapter 5 (§3). The vast majority of guests (92 per cent) joined Alpha through the influence of friends, church or church leaders. Following this was the initial encounter with the Alpha group. Rambo argues that what makes any voluntary conversion process possible is:

> ...a complex confluence of the 'right' potential convert coming into contact, under proper circumstances at the proper time, with the 'right' advocate and religious options. Trajectories of potential converts and available advocates do not

often meet in such a way that the conversion process can germinate, take root and flourish.[19]

Following the encounter, the next dimension is *interaction*, the most potent avenue of connection to new religious options. This allows time and space for the potential convert to learn more about the belief system of the group and its way of life. During this dimension, there is a 'spectrum of passivity and activity by the potential convert, as well as manipulation and persuasion by the advocate'.[20] This was the primary dimension at work on Alpha.[21] Having joined Alpha, guests became a part of a small group where interaction was intensified.

The sixth dimension, and the fulcrum of the change process, is *commitment*. Rambo notes: 'A specific turning point is often required and/or experienced, and this commitment is often dramatised and commemorated.'[22] As described in Chapter 2 and 5, there is an expectation of commitment on Alpha throughout the course, but especially on the first three weeks and at the Alpha weekend. This commitment is expressed in various ways: in saying the 'sinner's prayer' and opening up oneself to a charismatic encounter with the Holy Spirit.

Of those who converted on Alpha, four made a specific commitment: three (St A1 G2, G5; St B G5[23]) saying the 'sinner's prayer', and one (St B G4) using Alpha as part of a wider sacramental process (confirmation). The majority of guests who converted (80 per cent; cf. Finney 1992) did not make a specific 'commitment', but described how their faith was deepened, got 'back on track' (St B G1), over the duration of the course. Other guests described how Alpha was the beginning of a journey:

I feel like it's a mountain and I've just started climbing it (St E G8).

Two guests at St B described the gradual development of their faith, one of them drawing an analogy with a dimmer switch, which was progressively being turned up (St B Week 3). One of these guests (St B G3) related his journey:

…during the summer, I'd have to say that I was an agnostic. By September, I was becoming, 'Okay, I think I'm pro-Christians here,' and going to church as well. I would say that I am a fairly new Christian now…it was a gradual thing.

Another guest, a retired builder, told how Alpha had laid a foundation, but admitted that this was only the beginning:

---

[19] Rambo 1993:87.

[20] Rambo 1993:102.

[21] Ferguson (2001:230) views interaction as describing the catechumenate of the ancient church (see Ch.7).

[22] Rambo 1993:124.

[23] While I have included St B G5 as saying the 'sinner's prayer', she was also using Alpha as confirmation preparation.

I can only explain it as a wonderful foundation. And we've been lucky enough that people have helped us lay the first course. So the foundation has been put into place, and the group we're please that we were able to continue is starting the building. We're a little way from putting the roof on. But without the foundations you haven't really got anything, whatever you do in life (St E G1).

One guest felt frustrated at not experiencing a 'lightning bolt' type of conversion:

I've always thought, if you're going to be a Christian, you need to have that kind of bolt of lightning hit you, set you off. I'm still slightly waiting for that kind of kick. Some people get it, some people don't. But, perhaps I need it (St D G9).

His expectations were the result of a previous off-putting encounter with a group of charismatic Christians where everyone was crying and falling over, but where he 'felt nothing'.

Last, there are the *consequences* of conversion. 'Conversion is precarious; it must be defended, nurtured, supported and affirmed. It needs community, confirmation and concurrence'.[24] Rambo notes how Evangelicals are less well equipped to deal with post-conversion maintenance procedures, resulting in many converts dropping out a few months after their conversion experience.[25]

To develop the sociology of conversion further, I shall make use of Duncan MacLaren's recent work.[26] I have chosen MacLaren for two reasons: his theoretical framework for conversion was, in my opinion, the most sophisticated account that was available and because there was a strong fit with my fieldwork. MacLaren elaborates on Berger and Luckmann's thesis on plausibility structures and outlines three broad types of explanation with which to unravel conversion and commitment. First, social–psychological explanations attempt to explain it in terms of human need. Secondly, structural explanations have been offered which locate the explanation primarily in changing social structures. Thirdly, cognitive explanations describe commitment and conversion in terms of the perceived logic of the beliefs themselves. These three approaches should be seen as interweaving dimensions rather than being viewed as if they were exclusive of one another; to some degree, all three are involved in any individual case of conversion. The advantage of this approach is that it recognises the social structures and pressures inherent in group dynamics while also taking into account the meaning that converts themselves give to their actions – what Weber termed *aktuelles verstehen* (see Chapter 4 §3).[27]

---

[24] Rambo 1993:167.

[25] Rambo 1993:136.

[26] MacLaren 2003; 2004.

[27] Weber 1964. From this point on, I shall also include references to several Alpha team members who had converted on previous courses.

4. Social–Psychological Explanations

This theory looks to the affective reasons for conversion. It can include the appeal of beliefs that satisfy an affective need, or it can be the believing community itself that meets the needs of an individual. For example, someone in need of community is likely to find the beliefs of a welcoming community more plausible than alternative beliefs that exist in a vacuum.[28]

4.1 The Need for Identity

The idea of voluntarily choosing a marriage partner, or a different religious identity from that which one has been brought up in, is relatively novel. Prior to the Reformation in Europe, religious identities were ascribed to the individual through the various processes of socialisation, and the options for change were extremely limited.[29] Charles Taylor traces the shift, noting that the onset of secularisation was not particularly through people becoming highly educated, with the consequent advancement of science. This had some effect, but it was not decisive. Rather, the key factor lay in the plurality of sources, including those that did not necessarily presuppose a God. Along with the rejection of religious authority, all outlooks by then looked uncertain in a way that religious faith in earlier times did not.[30] Beit-Hallahmi and Argyle describe how such uncertainty puts an enormous strain on the old notions of self, relationships, communities and convictions. Other factors leading to vulnerability include a limited network of social support and individuals undergoing dramatic life changes, thus finding themselves in the midst of transitional social situations.[31]

As well as societal changes there are also developmental changes, where the question of age naturally arises. Over the course of forty years researchers correlating age with conversion have found that mid-adolescence is generally the peak time,[32] and certainly no older than thirty.[33] At that time of life cognitive systems are being built with which to make sense of the world. Seeking security and developing an individual adult identity are also part of this.[34] Conversely, this can also lead to the de-conversion of teenagers from the faith under which they were raised.[35]

The religious quest is not confined to adolescence, but can come at any point in life. Savage notes that Jung and Erickson viewed religious development as a

---

[28] MacLaren 2003:90.

[29] MacLaren 2003:95; see also Wilson 1973.

[30] Taylor 1992:313, 338.

[31] Beit-Hallahmi and Argyle 1997:118-19.

[32] Savage 2000:5.

[33] Beit-Hallahmi and Argyle 1997:115. In the UK, the average age has now risen to 18.11 (Brierley and Wraight 1997).

[34] Beit-Hallahmi and Argyle 1997:116.

[35] Richter and Francis 1998.

kind of spiritual puberty and the task and prerogative of middle age.[36] Conversion among adults implies a change of identity after an earlier period of identity-formation. Such conversions have often been correlated to the incidence of various psycho–pathological states, with the conversion experience providing a resolution to some of this anxiety, unhappiness, depression or uncertainty. Conversion thus helps the formation of a more stable and competent ego.[37] More positively, Conn sees conversion not so much as a coping mechanism but rather as a process that is integrated into healthy growth and quest.[38] Whether such conversions are developmental, societal or have a theological basis, they are explained here in terms of the benefits of a new identity to the convert.[39]

4.2 The Need for Community

Allied to the need for identity is the need for community. Identity is formed in the mirror of others' definitions of who we are.[40] The need to belong is a fundamental, powerful, and extremely pervasive motivation.[41] Only in the context of belonging within some social group can we arrive at an understanding of our own identity. Friendship networks, especially a loving, caring community, are influential in the *resistance and rejection* of conversion.[42] If the need to belong is not met, an individual might be led to seek it within any number of social groups, including religious, radical political or activist groups. The religious group may be particularly conducive to meeting this need because it offers not just a sense of belonging, but of purpose, and even a whole universe of meaning within which the convert's new identity and purpose make sense.[43] Barker's research into Moonie converts found that many of them expressed psychological or emotional relief and comfort after finding an atmosphere where they felt 'at home'. Many said that it was the friendliness or the showing of love that had made them want to join.[44] As Lofland and Stark reported in their research of a cult: 'The development or presence of some positive, emotional, interpersonal response seems necessary to bridge the gap between first exposure to the D.P. [Divine Presence[45]] message and accepting its truth...final conversion was coming to accept the opinions of one's

---

[36] Savage 2000:6.

[37] Beit-Hallahmi and Argyle 1997:121-22.

[38] Conn 1986.

[39] MacLaren 2003:96.

[40] Berger and Luckmann 1991:44.

[41] Baumeister and Leary 1995.

[42] Rambo 1993:108; Barker 1984:245.

[43] MacLaren 2003:97-98.

[44] Barker 1984:163.

[45] The Divine Presence cult is now widely assumed to have been the Unification Church.

friends'.[46]

Borhek and Curtis observed that groups which set out to recruit converts were likely to make appeals to those suffering isolation or dissatisfaction with interpersonal relationships, since such people are particularly receptive.[47] Beit-Hallahmi and Argyle note how vulnerability is tied to a limited network of social support. Those in the midst of transitional social situations are more open (or vulnerable) to new self-definitions and new groups. When social support is weak, those who do not feel a sense of belonging to any immediate or primary social group, are likely to feel detached from wider ideologies and to be open to new ideas.[48] Such vulnerability is intensified in times of stress or crisis. Mormons have recognised that any new arrival in a strange city will naturally seek human community. The first step in their recruitment techniques, out of a list of thirteen, is to befriend families 'who have moved into the neighbourhood and thus have no strong ties of friendship in the neighbourhood'.[49] Conversely, as indicated in Chapter 5, Bibby discovered that moving location was also a reason for *de-conversion*.[50]

The need for community provides answers that may appear particularly plausible, not necessarily as coherent belief-systems, but as attractive social solutions to the pain of loneliness. 'The beliefs of such a nurturing group will derive affective plausibility as a consequence of their association with the group'.[51]

4.3 The Need for Compensation

It is possible to discern two areas where the need for compensation is required. One is related to childhood relationships and the other to particular beliefs. Attachment theory asserts that individuals form emotional ties that reflect their connections with their original primary caregivers.[52] Ullman[53] and Allison[54] found that a major motivating factor for converts was to do with the emotional – involving problematic relationships with fathers, unhappy childhoods and past histories of disrupted or distorted personal relationships.[55] Here the love

---

[46] Lofland and Stark 1965:871; see also Gerlach and Hine 1970:79-97; Stark and Bainbridge 1980.
[47] Borhek and Curtis 1975:96.
[48] Beit-Hallahmi and Argyle 1997:118-19.
[49] Stark and Bainbridge 1980:1387.
[50] Bibby 1997.
[51] MacLaren 2003:98.
[52] Kirkpatrick 1997; Granqvist and Kirkpatrick 2004.
[53] Ullman 1982.
[54] Allison 1967.
[55] It is also possible to interpret this data as the overcoming of a previous failed attachment rather than as compensation. In pastoral practice, Frazer Watts has observed that people's image of God and style of religion more often *reflects* a basic outlook on

and security that is lacking in the lives of the insecurely attached, perhaps due to insecure attachments to parents during childhood, finds compensation in the love and acceptance received from God, or from a member or members of a religious group. Indeed, the God of most Christian theology seems to correspond closely to the idea of a secure attachment figure.[56] Alternatively, the need for compensation can occur when basic human needs go unfulfilled or are restricted. Again, these needs can be met when they are offered, for example, by a significant other, or others, within a religious group. It is in times of severe emotional distress, and particularly distress associated with disrupted attachment relationships, when attachment history exerts its strongest influence.[57]

The other need for compensation is related to particular beliefs, especially when a situation of loss arises. Compensation is desired not only in the act of suffering but also in the face of death, tragedy, or meaninglessness. Here it is the beliefs themselves that meet the affective need. In *A Making of a Moonie*, Barker relates how, for a young woman whose husband had been killed in a car accident, the opportunity to talk about the spirit world and life after death had brought a feeling of immense relief. The belief in an after-life, or a forum in which to discuss the 'spirit world', provided the desired compensator to someone faced with such tragic loss.[58]

4.4 The Need for Certainty

Some converts are seekers who are dissatisfied with the answers they have previously received. This need for certain knowledge is different from the kind of cognitive explanations in that the former is basically need-driven and, developmentally, represents an immature or compulsive need for a totalising explanation of everything. Plausibility here is 'constructed around an island of meaning which offers a place of cognitive terra firma'.[59] Ali Köse's research into native British converts to Islam pointed to their feelings of disillusionment with an unstable and permissive secular West, the perceived compromising of the church, and to their preoccupation with what is right and wrong. Their search for a religious outlook brought them to Islam, which offered them an

---

life rather than compensating for it. For example, it is more natural for a person who has experienced a punitive, rejecting father to see God in similar tones, rather than as a compensatory warm, forgiving and all-loving God (cited in Savage 2000:7; cf. Rambo 1999).

[56] The theologian Kaufman has noted this correspondence, and concluded: 'the idea of God is the idea of an absolutely adequate attachment figure...God is thought of as a protective parent who is always reliable and always available to his children when they are in need' (Kaufman 1981:67).

[57] Kirkpatrick and Shaver 1990:329.

[58] Barker 1984:158.

[59] MacLaren 2003:201.

encompassing religious world-view with which to satisfy their cognitive needs.[60] Such plausibility is not rational, in the sense of being derived from a thorough investigation, but is based upon an affective need for cognitive security. 'The seeker in this instance needs an answer, and, if necessary, at the expense of genuinely open inquiry'.[61]

5. Social–Psychological Explanations and Alpha

The above types of conversion are explained primarily as need-based – identity, belonging, compensation and certainty – the resolution of which potential converts believe resides in God, a charismatic leader, priest or guru, or in certain faith communities. How do these relate to Alpha? What are the prominent dimensions for those who converted?

I have not used the themes of identity and certainty because in the 52 Alpha sessions in which I participated and in the 51 interviews conducted, they were found to be insignificant factors.

5.1 Need for Compensation

The need for compensation was a prominent factor for a number of converts (St A1 G2, H1; St B G2; St C G3; St E G1 and G2, L1). Four of these described difficult parental relationships and as a result formed strong emotional ties to the Alpha group. It was the Christian community experienced on Alpha, and/or belief in God, that compensated for the insecure attachments to parents during childhood. Foreign student guest, St A1 G2, describes her upbringing:

> I don't have a close relationship with my father, because my father is unreliable. He never consider me, never care[d for] me...My childhood, it was very, very sad. I feel I was growing up in darkness...My older brother [and] my older sister, both of them didn't like me. Only my mother cared [for] me, but my mother was very busy...

This guest had recently moved to the UK as a student and had high affective needs for community. Experiencing a marriage crisis and anxiety concerning her future, the attraction of a welcoming community was powerful. It was the Christian community rather than a particular belief in God that was referred to as offering support. In participating in Alpha, this guest described how she discovered a new family. Its members were kind to her and paid her attention, the attention she lacked in growing up:

---

[60] Köse 1999.
[61] MacLaren 2003:102.

But I can feel from you, from everybody – I can't feel God because God is invisible – but you are visible. So I can feel something when I am with you…And I know I have many brothers and sisters. I have big family [and] that's very nice.

For one helper (St Al H2), an affiliation convert on a previous Alpha course, it was the combination of the need for compensation and being 'overwhelmed' by the Christian community that resulted in conversion. It was first sparked by his marriage crisis, which was exacerbated by another relationship where he was 'conned out of a lot of money'. He described his feelings before the Alpha course as being 'extremely disillusioned':

…my dad was never there…Something happened to my mum when she was a child, so that gave her the IQ of a ten-year-old child, and she actually behaved like one. You'd walk through the door and you didn't know if mum was in a good mood or in a bad mood: if she was in a bad mood, you'd get plates, saucepans thrown at you, stuff like that. It was very difficult because we couldn't have any friends around. It was too unpredictable, too volatile…If it happened now, we would have been put into care…

His portrayal of the commitment stage involved a pragmatic 'show me' attitude[62] where people try on a new religion like a pair of shoes:

I was still sceptical but the way I thought was basically, if you don't try it you don't know, so I thought I'd…try this out…I became a Christian during the course. On the Holy Spirit day at [St A]; it's the 6th June. I gave my life to the Lord and I thought, well, I've got to trust in something, and in order to keep my sanity…and that's probably what I needed, is to know that there were actually somebody there who did care for me, no matter how small it was. At that point in time I felt that nobody actually cared for me.

As well as belief in God compensating for his affective needs, of value and to be cared for, the Christian community was also influential. H2 continues:

You can always go to any other Christian in the church and they will try to help you, if they can…the sense of the community, real community, that's the essence of it all. Because you don't need the church to pray but you need other people to interact with, so you feel a part of a community and…you feel worthwhile, you've got some sense of worth. And it gives great strength and great peace (St Al H2).

This conversion account highlights a variety of motivational factors. As Rambo notes, 'it is imperative to recognise that motivations to conversion are multiple, complex, interactive and cumulative'.[63] For someone with distorted parenting patterns during childhood, compensation was 'supplied' by both God and the

---

[62] Lofland and Skonovd 1981.
[63] Rambo 1993:64.

Christian community, who offered love and security in a time of crisis – this, and a pragmatic willingness to try out Christianity.

Continuing with the need for compensation, Alpha guest (St B G2) described how she had been sexually abused by her father while growing up, which she had previously attempted to resolve through therapy. A committed churchgoer, she described feelings of loneliness and unmet affective needs for support, compensation for which the Alpha small group was able to offer. In the interview this guest frequently used the word 'support' in describing her experience on Alpha both in terms of the community and beliefs:

> It was a support really, with what was happening with my family and it just felt right. And I think that some of the Scripture that we looked at really supported what I was feeling...especially about the evil...I found that useful and I found it supported what I was thinking...it has [helped] in terms of support; it gave me a lot of strength at that time (St B G2).

For this guest, compensation functioned at the level of both the Alpha group and the beliefs themselves. This combination of belief and community is heightened in a situation of loss, and related to the couple (St E G1 and G2) who suffered bereavement just prior to Alpha. They wanted to know that they would see their loved one again in the afterlife. Interestingly, G1 recognised his own mixed motives and described how he felt a bit of a fraud in his desire to see his loved one again rather than 'just wanting Jesus' (St E Week 3). The strong tie with the Alpha small group was the other factor for this couple:

> I don't know what we'd have done without these people, I really don't...I think we would be a bit empty if we lost this, personally. And I know, [H2], her Christmas card [said], 'It was lovely to make two more friends' (St E G1).

The same combination of belief and community, or a 'significant other', in a situation of loss can be seen in the conversion of one of the leaders at St E. She converted on a previous Alpha course in the mid-1990s. The loss of her mother led her on a quest:

> ...my mum had died a couple of years before. I think I was still grieving for her...I think that set me on a path of wanting to have that certainty that she had and knowing that I'd see her again. So that's what took me to Alpha the first time 'round... (St E L1).

On Alpha, she developed strong ties with the small group leaders, who became, and still remain, her 'mentors'. For the latter two cases, the beliefs themselves met an affective need. That is, a desire for a belief in the afterlife compensated for the bereavement. The community further compensated for this loss, offering emotional and social support.

5.2 Need for Community

While the need for compensation was a strong factor in the conversion of seven people, the most prominent characteristic for the social–psychological explanations for conversion was the need for community, although it must be re-emphasised that there exist a number of interrelated factors between these dimensions. Socialisation and the conversion process is facilitated through the affective ties with significant others.[64] As noted above (§4.2), the need to belong is a fundamental human need and when this need goes unmet, individuals may seek it in various social groups such as Alpha.

Many of the guests highlighted the friendliness that they experienced, with the following comments being typical:

> I think the people...were very friendly (St A1 G4).

> I thought it was really nice that they were really friendly (St D G1).

Even one guest who left the course was positive about this aspect of Alpha:

> Yeah, the people were so nice...I felt really quite bad leaving, because the people were so nice (St A1 G1).

The effect of having a course spread over three months meant that affectional bonds are given a lengthy period to develop. On arrival at the first night of Alpha, guests tend to be apprehensive, nervous and even suspicious. As Napier and Gershenfeld note, any new group will be charged with tension as individuals test out their environment and observe the various personalities involved.[65] Leaders often tried to introduce people to each other, but the guests were usually particularly tense. By the third or fourth week, tension had eased and rapport had developed. Most of the discerption had occurred by then, with the small groups becoming stabilised. Guests tended to be much more relaxed, friendly and pleased to see one another, with increasing levels of laughter. An Alpha helper describes how this happens:

> [T]he most enjoyable part of it is seeing total strangers on week one, being very negative, they sort of block themselves off and their body language says, I'm a barrier and don't come through. By week four, they open their arms, and don't cross their arms and stuff like that. They start to talk and be more open. And by week ten they don't want the course to end (St A1 H2).

In Alpha small groups, high value is placed on group cohesiveness and affective bonds. Many of the guests expressed the importance of the Alpha

---

[64] Gerlach and Hine 1970; Heirich 1977; Lofland and Skonovd 1981; Snow and Machalek 1984; Stark and Bainbridge 1980.

[65] Napier and Gershenfeld 1985:43.

group and a sense of belonging that they felt on the course. The following comments by guests were typical descriptions of the most enjoyable aspects of the course:

> I think meeting new people…a sense of community, a sense of belonging, which is nice (St A1 G4).

> I suppose meeting people and discussing (St E G4). Feeling part of something, building deeper friendships with the people that were there (St E G5). Feeling part of the community (St E G4).

The importance of personal affect, trust, and respect for the Alpha team members was crucial for conversion. To quote Lofland and Stark again, '…conversion was coming to accept the opinions of one's friends'.[66] The Alpha team offered not only friendship and a sense of purpose but, as MacLaren puts it, 'a whole universe of meaning within which the convert's new identity and purpose make sense'.[67]

The importance of strong ties with a sponsor or leader was noted by St B G5, as it was by the following guest:

> I had a very good leader, who's at my college…I told him all my problems, and he just sat me down and said, 'Right, answer these questions. If the answer's yes, you're a Christian, don't worry about it' [laughter] so that's what got me into it (St D G5).

As well as a general need to belong, during times of transition social support is weak and people are more open (or vulnerable) to new self-definitions and new groups. A number of guests had gone through such transitions, had feelings of loneliness, and high affective needs for community. Five guests had recently moved into the area where Alpha was running (St A1 G2, St B G3, G5, G6, St E G7), two of whom had been through a divorce. St B G6 described feelings of isolation following a 'very messy divorce':

> [T]he thing is, you tend to live a rather isolated life. You go to work, you drop the kids off in the morning, you go to work, come back, pick your kids up from the childminder, come back here, feed children, and that's it…And it was getting, to gain friends and all the rest of it, and get into the wider community, and [S2] said, 'Do you fancy bringing [your children] to church?' And I thought yeah, the kids might like that.

For this guest, it led to an eighteen month quest and process of re-initiation into the church, culminating in confirmation. For him, Alpha was a sort of mystagogy, or post-confirmation class (see Chapter 7 §1–2). This group also

---

[66] Lofland and Stark 1965:871.
[67] MacLaren 2003:98.

included two young mothers who had recently relocated. St E G7 described the openness that the transition brought:

> We had quite a major change in coming here, so it was all quite positive. A few things that had happened in the fairly recent past that I wanted to forget and get over and…I do think that when we came to [St E village], it was like a change in life and a moving on…I felt quite a positive mood anyway and wanting to open my mind a bit more into things, and think about things again.

5.2.1 LOVE BOMBING

People who have high affective needs, whether for identity, certainty, compensation or community, are often in a vulnerable condition and potentially open to manipulation. Among some groups, a common technique for recruitment is what is known as 'ingratiation',[68] or the more popular term, 'love bombing'.[69] Lofland notes how a 'hooking technique' for a group's successful proselytisation stems in part from the self-conscious manipulation of a loving atmosphere.[70] This is one of the tactics employed that Barker found in her research into the Unification Church. Moonies shower their guests with an unusual degree of friendliness.[71]

Christians attempt to follow Jesus's command in the Great Commission (Matt. 28:18-20), and one of the strongest motivations for mission is simply a desire to help people.[72] In their attempt at this, do Alpha team members 'love bomb' guests, even if inadvertently? On some courses, there was a noticeable contrast between the preparation time among team members, compared with when guests arrived, in which an unspoken 'hospitality mode' was assumed. I noticed this at St C one evening when I arrived to help set things up. All of the team members ignored me, busy with their task of creating the right ambience. I joined in the preparation, until the venue was ready and the team grouped together for prayer. Even then, there were no greetings, just the odd eye contact and acknowledgement. However, when guests arrived mid-way through the (intensely charismatic) prayer time, there was an abrupt 'conversion', and the team members switched mode to focus on the guests. This is similar to Goffman's description of 'front region' and 'back region' areas, as in a restaurant, where in the kitchen, the 'back region', there is a scene wholly

---

[68] Jones 1964.

[69] Hassan 1988.

[70] Cited in Rudy 1986:32.

[71] Barker 1984. Yet such love bombing techniques resulted in mixed responses. Barker noted how some guests reacted quite forcefully *against* what they saw as the over-effusiveness of the Unification approach; there have been guests who were attracted to the Moonies, yet despite this, they decided not to join the movement. In other words, love bombing is not an irresistible technique which inevitably secures conversion (Barker 1984:180).

[72] Rambo 1993:75.

different from the elegant reserve displayed in the dining area.[73] When Alpha guests arrived, team members were suddenly 'on stage', seeking to create a certain ambiance – welcome, friendliness, attentiveness – in order to facilitate conversion. The general friendliness on Alpha has already been described above. This was a sort of unspoken *modus operandi*.

Barker also noted the high proportion of 'members' to 'non-members' and the attention that was then directed to the 'non-members'.[74] A 'normal' Alpha course with eight guests and four team members might avoid this problem. But according to my research there were no 'normal' Alpha groups, and similar to the Moonies, there was a high proportion of 'members' to 'non-members'. Team members often went out of their way to welcome people and tend to the guests' needs.

The course which had a number of love bombing elements was St A1. Almost all of the socialising was between team members and guests, rather than between guests. Even by week six, there was very little rapport between the guests; they rarely spoke to one another. This meant that each guest received a lot of attention from the team members. One foreign student guest described how she came to be on the Alpha course. She had bought a television set and was attempting to take it home on her bicycle. A member of St A stopped her car and offered to help:

> On the way [home], she asked me, 'Have you been to church?' I told her, 'Not yet'. So she asked me, 'Do you want to go to church on Sunday?' I answered her, 'Yes'. So, next Sunday, she came to my house and took me to church (St A1 G2).

This guest was then picked up by car and dropped home for each Alpha session. She received a high degree of support and attention both leading up to Alpha and during the course itself. Showering people with friendliness was not uncommon at this church. An Alpha convert describes being suspicious about the over-effusiveness of the Alpha group:

> My first impressions on Alpha were, they're too nice to be true. What's the catch? I kept looking for the catch that was gonna come, and I honestly thought people can't be this nice and this honest with you and they don't want anything in return. [I. So you were a bit sceptical at first.] Extremely sceptical at first, yeah. I was just waiting for the bubble to burst (St A1 H2).

How is it possible to draw a line between Christian team members on Alpha simply being friendly and the techniques of love bombing? Guests on Alpha certainly received a high degree of attention, but does that in itself constitute ingratiation? Perhaps the dividing line is the *motivation* for giving special attention, and whether guests are viewed instrumentally. Is the enormous

---

[73] Goffman 1990.
[74] Barker 1984.

amount of individual attention manipulative? Are guests seen as a means of notching up another conversion and increasing church membership, or even gaining in spiritual status within the Alpha group and church? For Moonies, there is clearly a certain status attached within the movement to acquiring 'spiritual children'.[75] Barker also notes the stark instrumentalism seen on the Moonie workshops: 'Once the hosts are convinced that they cannot persuade a guest to change their mind, the guest who insists that he or she does not wish to continue to the next stage tends to get fairly sharply dropped'.[76] Of course, the difficulty is that it is not possible to know the motivation of each Alpha team member. Some might offer genuine affection and friendship while others may see it as a means of increasing church membership.

If there were minor levels of love bombing on some of the Alpha courses, there were also dissimilarities. Tourish and Pinnington describe how cults encourage the fallacious notion that all members are more alike than they really are, and are more dissimilar from non-members than is actually the case. The objective here is to create an overwhelming sense of group identity, infused with a spirit of cohesion, loyalty and commitment to the group's goals.[77] Joining a group then seems a natural and risk-free next step. The *intentional* construction of such group dynamics is absent in AI discourse and in the Alpha groups that I researched, although guests often felt themselves to be under pressure to conform to group norms owing to the disproportionate number of Christians present (see Chapter 5). Another dissimilarity to love bombing cults was the level of intensity. For example, there was a stark difference between Alpha's one session per week compared with the Moonies, where non-members lived in an isolated community where it was difficult to communicate with other non-members.[78]

In sum, while a 'normal' Alpha small group would obviate characteristic ingratiation techniques, the ratio of team members to members in the courses that I researched gave rise to some of its tendencies. If there were elements of love bombing on Alpha, and I think in some groups there might have been, it was relatively low in intensity.

6. Structural Explanations

While social–psychological explanations focus on the various needs of the individual, structural explanations attempt to tie in patterns of commitment to

---

[75] It is a rule (in theory, if not always in practice) that a couple cannot consummate their marriage until each partner has at least three spiritual children! (Barker 1984:186) Motivation indeed.

[76] Barker 1984:114.

[77] Tourish and Pinnington 2002.

[78] Barker 1984:114.

wider social and cultural phenomena.[79] Drawing on the work of Schutz,[80] Berger and Luckmann's *The Social Construction of Reality*, originally published in 1966, suggested that the social context was the thing that supplied a whole pattern of beliefs that in general nobody questioned.[81] It is taken for granted that this is the actual nature of reality. In a process that Berger calls 'cosmisation', religion has traditionally served to reify the social world, to make the contingencies of social arrangements look as if they are immutable absolutes.[82] Modernity is the story of the collapse of religion's legitimating force, the 'sacred canopy',[83] bringing with it a plurality of sources.[84] Religion's definitions of reality are no longer taken-for-granted and this implies that it is forced to compete with secular options.[85] Religion itself becomes a matter of choice, a 'heretical imperative'.[86] The survival of religion in a pluralist context depends on three factors: plausibility structures, maintenance processes and legitimations. Each of these is crucial for understanding how conversion is facilitated and maintained.

MacLaren makes a marked improvement in his modification of the account of Berger and Luckmann. He also augments their insights using the cognitive sociology of Zerubaevel.[87] It is MacLaren's modification of plausibility structures that is relevant to my book and it is *his* explanation, rather than that of Berger and Luckmann, upon which I shall rely in the course of this study.

6.1 Plausibility Structures

This element recognises that it is the local context that defines what is to be accepted as knowledge, or what Berger and Luckmann call 'plausibility

---

[79] This is not to be identified with structuralism. MacLaren (2003:103) calls this theory structural rather than structuralist, because the latter tends to imply that 'social phenomena alone offer sufficient conditions for belief', a perspective he wishes to avoid.

[80] Schutz 1964; 1967; 1970.

[81] Berger and Luckmann 1991

[82] Berger 1967:28.

[83] Berger 1967.

[84] Taylor 1992. Berger has slightly revised his theory. He now views pluralism, which he had previously identified as being linked with decline in religious belief, as changing the way *how* we believe rather than *what* we believe (Berger 1998, 2001:194). This must now entail an 'epistemological modesty' rather than absolute certainty (Berger 2000).

[85] MacLaren 2003:104.

[86] Berger 1980.

[87] Zerubaevel (1997) describes three virtual or imagined 'thought communities': mnemonic communities refer to how our *memories* are maintained as plausible; 'optical communities' are those which influence the scope of our *attention*; 'visionary communities' include those who *imagine* the future (see MacLaren 2004:112-17).

structures'.[88] Plausibility structures are social structures; they point to the 'social location' of thought. It is a problem contained *in nuce* in Pascal's statement that what is truth on one side of the Pyrenees is error on the other.[89] Knowledge is acquired in the course of socialisation and that 'mediates the internalisation within individual consciousness of the objectivated structures of the social world'.[90] The structures that mediate knowledge include family, school, church and workplace. These lend plausibility to an assemblage of maxims, morals, beliefs, values and myths, to those who inhabit the structure.

Any radical departure from these taken-for-granted norms appears as a departure from reality. MacLaren writes:

> Plausibility is constructed not on the basis of affect or reason, but on account of the relatively uncontested, taken-for-granted meanings offered within the local context of the plausibility structure.[91]

The two basic functions performed by the plausibility structure, MacLaren notes, are *cohesion* and *exclusion*.[92] These provide the 'walls' around a faith community, containing the believers and their beliefs, while also limiting or excluding threatening influences from beyond the structure.[93] Cohesion can include the social structure of a group, which brings with it a strong sense of belonging,[94] and the presence of 'significant others' with whom affective bonds are forged. Mention has been made (§4.2) of the research of Lofland and Stark into the Divine Presence cult.[95] They found that interpersonal involvement leads a person gradually to accept the beliefs of those people he or she has come to trust. These significant others are the guides into the new reality; they mediate the new world to the individual.[96]

Cohesion can include the extent to which members share the same 'cognitive subculture'[97] or the extent to which their beliefs comprise a coherent whole. Cohesion, MacLaren notes, 'may also be achieved through legitimating practices such as apologetics, which seek to demonstrate the inner rationality of belief systems in the face of competition'.[98] For some groups, a 'charismatic

---

[88] Berger and Luckmann 1991.

[89] Cited in Berger and Luckmann 1991:17.

[90] Berger and Luckmann 1991:83.

[91] MacLaren 2003:106.

[92] MacLaren 2004:111.

[93] Borhek and Curtis 1975:43; Greil and Rudy 1984:263.

[94] Cartwright 1951.

[95] Lofland and Stark 1965.

[96] Berger and Luckmann 1991:177.

[97] Zerubaevel 1997:12.

[98] MacLaren 2004:111. Christian apologists Josh McDowell (see www.josh.org) and Ravi Zacharias (see www.rzim.org) are two examples.

leader'[99] can be an important element in apologetics. Indeed, new religions are rarely initiated by committee. Usually there is a founder or leader who is believed to have some special powers or knowledge, and to whom his (or, occasionally, her) followers are, as a consequence, willing to accord a special kind of authority over them.[100] The charismatic leader might not have direct involvement with the convert but the perceived power and energy of the charismatic leader – actual or imagined – are powerful catalysts in the conversion of many people.[101]

For exclusion, there are various strategies. Greil and Rudy describe the process of 'encapsulation', where the potential convert is invited and/or persuaded into a self-contained world in which the process of conversion begins or is strengthened.[102] Of course, this can sound sinister. Nevertheless, it is a procedure employed to some extent by everyone who wants to teach something new. Every classroom is a form of encapsulation in that it creates an environment within which 'there can be concentration on the topic at hand, control of noise and competing ideas and minimal interruption'.[103] The three varieties of encapsulation are physical, social and ideological, which overlap and reinforce one another. As Greil and Rudy put it, they act like *'social cocoons* in that, like cocoons, they coat themselves with a protective covering to protect the process of transformation going on within from interference from the outside'.[104]

6.1.1 SOCIAL ENCAPSULATION

Social encapsulation is the term ascribed to those means directing the potential convert into life-style patterns that limit significant contact with 'outsiders'. The theology of the group can control the degree of social interaction and communication within and outside it. Sects tend to view the world as the domain of evil, have a 'blame the devil for everything' outlook,[105] and socially isolate themselves and potential converts from the contamination of 'the world'. Alternatively, simply the amount of time required for involvement in a group acts as a social mechanism that creates a boundary between insiders and outsiders. For example, AA members are challenged with the '90/90 rule', which means attending 90 meetings in 90 days. With such a requirement, the AA member does not have time to hang around with drinking buddies.[106]

---

[99] Weber 1964.
[100] Barker 1989:13.
[101] Rambo 1993:113.
[102] Greil and Rudy 1984.
[103] Rambo 1993:104.
[104] Greil and Rudy 1984:264.
[105] Scotland 2000:14.
[106] Rudy 1986:34; Greil and Rudy 1984:265.

6.1.2 IDEOLOGICAL ENCAPSULATION

Ideological encapsulation involves the cultivation of a world-view and belief system that 'inoculates' the adherent against alternative or competitive systems of belief.[107] Ideological encapsulation gives permission and provides a space for such experiences to be talked about and valued. Berger notes how, in today's modern society, the supernatural as a meaningful reality is only held by a cognitive minority. This is invariably an uncomfortable position – not necessarily because the majority is repressive or intolerant, but simply because it refuses to accept the minority's definitions of reality as 'knowledge'.[108] And with the marginalisation of religion to a private sphere people increasingly struggle to talk openly about it.[109] Zerubaevel notes how it is society that determines what we come to regard as 'reasonable' or 'nonsensical' and it usually does so by exerting tacit pressure which we rarely even notice unless we try to resist it. Such sociomental control is one of the most insidious forms of social control.[110] For example, although many people have had what they would describe as a religious experience,[111] there is a reticence to talk about such things, for fear of being labelled 'nutty'. Indeed, it is not uncommon for even the Church to frown upon such experiences! Barker suggests that had Freud been studying present-day students in Britain rather than late nineteenth century matrons in Vienna, he might have concluded that it was spiritual rather than sexual repression which lay at the root of many current frustrations. It is, after all, often quite acceptable for a student to tell his friends whom he slept with the previous night. He is far less likely to tell them that Our Lady appeared while he was saying his prayers.[112] However, if ideological encapsulation is the only mechanism of encapsulation, a group's continued viability is unlikely, because the world-views and identities of its members would not receive sufficient social confirmation.[113]

6.1.3 PHYSICAL ENCAPSULATION

Physical encapsulation may be achieved by removing people to distant or remote locations or by actual barriers other than distance, as in monasteries, mission compounds and religious communities and ghettos. Moonies, the Jesus People and Hare Krishnas have all used these means.[114] Here, cohesion and socialisation of both beliefs and relationships is facilitated more powerfully

---

[107] Rambo 1993:104-106.
[108] Berger 1970:18-19.
[109] Berger 1967:137.
[110] Zerubaevel 1997:13-15.
[111] See Hay 1990.
[112] Barker 1984:220.
[113] Greil and Rudy 1984:269.
[114] Greil and Rudy 1984:265.

through living within a community.[115] For example, Barker notes the importance of intensive interaction during Moonies 'workshops'. These lasted anything between a weekend to twenty-one days and have been the sect's main recruitment technique.[116]

In summary, encapsulation provides a 'social cocoon' that excludes or minimises interference from the outside. Apart from extreme groups, there are very few cases of complete physical or social encapsulation. Most recruiters use a combination of all three encapsulation mechanisms.

6.2 'Plausibility Shelters'

MacLaren critiques Berger's and Luckmann's theoretical explanation of plausibility structures. While they are helpful in describing how a particular religious community's 'walls' contain their believers and beliefs, the situation of late modernity, MacLaren notes, has created an extremely complex situation with increased competition between a plurality of plausibility structures.[117] The greater the competition, the harder it is for any one plausibility structure to maintain a sense of reality-taken-for-granted (or even reality-convincingly-explained) for its participants, since the available options present a continual challenge. The 'walls' of such structures are fluid, which makes difficult the task of cohesion and exclusion. MacLaren suggests:

> Perhaps a more accurate term might be 'plausibility shelters' – derived from the image of the bus shelter, which has some walls, and a makeshift roof, but is less than watertight![118]

Contemporary people inhabit a bewildering multiplicity of such shelters, and move freely from one to another on a global scale. What seems plausible in the family, the workplace, or in the mass media, may vary widely. Therefore, a simplistic account of plausibility structures must be avoided. Apart from extreme cases such as world-denying sects, plausibility structures are likely to be undermined and influenced from a number of directions, which means it can only ever provide a partial explanation.[119]

6.3 Maintenance Processes

Berger and Luckmann comment: 'To have a conversion experience is nothing much. The real thing is to be able to keep on taking it seriously; to retain a

---

[115] Lofland and Stark 1965:12.
[116] Barker 1984.
[117] MacLaren 2003; 2004.
[118] MacLaren 2003:109.
[119] MacLaren 2003:110.

sense of its plausibility.'[120] In a modern, pluralist, mobile and individualistic society, maintaining commitment to *any* group is always problematic. Berger suggests that the two most important processes for the ongoing maintenance of plausibility within plausibility structures are 'socialisation' and 'conversation'.[121] Conversation maintains beliefs as plausible over time, while socialisation ensures continued plausibility between generations, or from 'insiders' to 'outsiders'.[122]

6.3.1 SOCIALISATION

Socialisation is about the way people learn, or acquire, a culture so that they are able to function within it.[123] The most obvious and powerful element of primary socialisation is the family, but other 'secondary' forms of socialisation include such things as school, work, church, and interest groups.[124] Conversion involves a socialisation where seekers are initiated into the society of which they become a part, although for intensification conversions, it is rather being *reinitiated*. Berger and Luckmann describe how this involves a radical transformation of their subjectively apprehended social reality, which is similar to that of primary socialisation, except that it is considerably more complex for a convert. This is because the primary socialisation of the subject must now be reinterpreted or even destroyed in order to give the person concerned a new social identity.[125] As noted above (§5.2), this process is facilitated through the affective ties formed with significant others. Such ties facilitate the transmission of beliefs, perhaps due to dependence, the desire for approval, or the facilitation of trust within the relationship.[126] As Wilson notes, in the process of resocialisation, 'the convert learns a language and a life-style which become a part of himself as he takes on a new definition of his own individuality and personality and of the social collectives in which he participates'.[127] If socialisation ensures the transmission of beliefs from generation to generation, or from insider to outsider, conversation ensures the ongoing plausibility of beliefs over time.

6.3.2 CONVERSATION

The most important vehicle for reality-maintenance is conversation.[128] Those who are least 'encapsulated' are most likely to drop out.[129] The most important

---

[120] Berger and Luckmann 1991:177.
[121] Berger 1967.
[122] MacLaren 2003:116.
[123] MacLaren 2003:117.
[124] Berger and Luckmann 1991:183-93.
[125] Berger and Luckmann 1991.
[126] Elkin 1963:30; MacLaren 2003:118.
[127] Wilson 1982:119.
[128] Berger and Luckmann 1991:172.
[129] Greil and Rudy 1984:273.

content and instrument of ecclesial socialisation is learning the language of faith, which presupposes ecclesial socialisation. Therefore, for religious faith to remain plausible, conversation must be continual and consistent.

> This reality-generating potency of conversation is already given in the fact of linguistic objectification...In the establishment of this order language *realises* a world, in the double sense of apprehending and producing it. Conversation is the actualising of this realising efficacy of language in the face-to-face situations of individual existence.[130]

If it is the religious community that provides the indispensable plausibility structures for the new reality, this community is also where discourse comprising these beliefs is continually rehearsed in everyday conversation, helping to generate the reality of the phenomenon being described. Literal conversation is a significant way in which beliefs are continually maintained as plausible, but the notion of conversation also includes the non-verbal or symbolic reaffirmation of belief. MacLaren describes how the presence of a great cathedral in a small town may continually affirm and 'speak' of the power and immediacy of the beliefs which it represents. Likewise, the rituals which take place within the cathedral form a kind of ongoing conversation that continually make present the realities they are intended to signify.[131]

In a world where religion faces competition from a social rhetoric that is often profoundly antagonistic towards religious truth claims, conversation, and the reality that it maintains, is profoundly precarious.

> The ongoing maintenance process of conversation needs to be sustained at quite a high level if the religious world-view is to remain plausible to those who participate. This may be achieved through the 'conversations' of liturgy, ritual, preaching, Bible-study, conferences, literature, social interaction, and so on.[132]

The longer a person is isolated from face-to-face conversation, the world as apprehended by that individual may begin to crumble. Fichter's investigations reveal that of the Catholics who no longer participated in the activity of their church, more than 75 per cent received no religious instruction.[133] From this, Carrier concludes that catechesis is the very condition of the survival for a religious group; it is not only an educating function that it performs – it is a way of integrating and rooting the faithful within the community.[134]

---

[130] Berger and Luckmann 1991:173.
[131] MacLaren 2003:121.
[132] MacLaren 2003:122.
[133] Cited in Carrier 1966:139.
[134] Carrier 1966:139.

6.4 Legitimations

The last factor in the structural explanation for conversion and the construction
of plausibility is to be found in legitimations. MacLaren writes:

> It is not enough for beliefs merely to attract commitment; they must also achieve
> subjective validity. While they may achieve commitment independently of their
> validity at some point their validity must be addressed in order for this
> commitment to be maintained. Legitimations may, therefore, function as *post hoc*
> rationalisations for beliefs which are already held. Equally, they may simply seek
> to deal with the discrepant experience which confronts every belief system in
> varying degrees.[135]

Berger and Luckmann outline four analytical levels of legitimation.[136] The first
is the 'incipient' and most basic level of language. The second level contains
theoretical propositions, such as myths and proverbs. The third level consists of
explicit theories, such as scientific accounts or religious doctrine. The fourth
level is the 'symbolic universe', those all-encompassing explanations, a 'world-
view', which aim at encompassing all institutions in a symbolic totality.
Legitimation becomes important when there is a 'problem': in a multi-cultural,
multi-religious and competitive environment, a clash in one's 'symbolic
universe' raises question marks over previously unquestioned beliefs.
Legitimation is concerned with the process of *explaining* and *justifying*, which
serves to maintain socially constructed reality.[137] Religious communities are
forced to deal with opposing counter-claims, what some philosophers call
'defeaters', by constructing sophisticated apologetic strategies. These can
involve any of the four levels of legitimation.

While these legitimations may consist of reasons for belief, they tend to be
used to *sustain* rather than to *generate* commitment. The two main approaches
employed in the act of legitimations are those of *nihilation* and *hermeneutic*.
Christian apologists see both of these strategies in the NT: 2 Corinthians 10.4-
5, which is the offensive approach, and 1 Peter 3.14-16, which emphasises
making a defence (*apologian*) of the faith. The former, more offensive,
approach attempts to 'annihilate', or render powerless, threatening hostile
interpretations. For example, Freud's thesis that religion is based on wish-
fulfilment, is 'swallowed up' by Plantinga, who argues that even if wish-
fulfilment is the source of theist belief, it would not be enough to establish that
the latter had no warrant. 'Perhaps this is how God has arranged for us to come
to know him'.[138] In such a way, the strategy of nihilation attempts to discredit
its opponents. In the second, more constructive hermeneutic approach, a belief-

---

[135] MacLaren 2004:121.
[136] Berger and Luckmann 1991:110-46.
[137] Berger and Luckmann 1991:83.
[138] Plantinga 2000:197.

system interprets as much of the world as possible within its own terms, to advance its claim to be the true interpretation.[139] It seeks to provide a 'cognitive map' into which new experiences can be placed, or absorbed.[140]

No belief system is totally able to avoid disconfirming experience. MacLaren suggests that the way religious communities have coped with this is 'through avoiding empirical conflict, allowing attrition of peripheral beliefs to save the centre, or employing any number of hermeneutical schema to interpret reality, as far as possible, in terms of themselves'.[141] For example, Festinger describes the cognitive dissonance felt by members of a UFO doomsday cult when the leader's prophecy of Earth's destruction failed. Through a process of secondary elaboration – by accepting a new prophecy that the aliens had instead spared the planet for their sake – the dissonance was lessened. Through a hermeneutical schema, the cult continued 'with their faith firm, unshaken, and lasting'.[142]

7. Structural Explanations and Alpha

How do the structural elements in the above discussion relate to Alpha? How is plausibility constructed on the course, what forms of legitimations are used, and what is the maintenance process? First, how is plausibility constructed on Alpha?

7.1 Plausibility Structures

Several people described their situation of living in multiple and competing plausibility structures. Some mentioned the difficulties working or studying in an 'atheistic' environment had for their faith:

> I had my course the day after [Alpha], and I found it really hard on my course to defend what I believed; there's a lot of strong atheists on my counselling course. And it gave me strength to go the next day and say what I felt...it just felt a support (St B G2).

> I'd been working in a scientific environment and a lot of people are vociferous atheists...And after a while you start to think, do I actually still believe in God? So, working in that environment day in day out is actually very tough (St C H1).

For these Christians, the Alpha group was a source of comfort and strength in a world that they felt was hostile to religious belief. Alpha functioned as an alternative plausibility structure, facilitated through strong affective

---

[139] MacLaren 2004:123.

[140] Borhek and Curtis 1975:9.

[141] MacLaren 2003:127.

[142] Festinger, Riecken and Schachter 1956:5.

relationships, with talks by a charismatic figure (if by DVD), and intense group interaction. Structurally, Alpha includes all three processes of exclusion, or encapsulation. Social encapsulation can be seen working throughout the course: on the weekly Alpha sessions and on the Alpha weekend or day away, which is where physical encapsulation is also experienced. It is through the Alpha talks and small group discussions that ideological encapsulation occurs.

First, there is social encapsulation. Gumbel stresses the importance of the Christian community on Alpha, and places its evangelism strategy within the context of the church community. As noted, in Chapter 2 (§1.1), this is quite different to the evangelistic campaigns of Billy Graham, Luis Palau and others, where big events were held in football stadiums. Alpha's approach is more akin to the early church catechumenate, where the church acts as a mother in whose womb people come to faith. Miroslav Volf's attempt at a Free Church ecclesiology has some resonance for Alpha groups, and how they might function as a plausibility structure. He notes the importance of 'significant others' (family or friends) rather than church 'officeholders':

> The 'significant others' function in the life of a Christian as the main players in the performance surrounding the person's Christian identity, while the 'rest of the others' function as a kind of chorus. And the mediation of faith is supported by the life of all the members of the church (the 'remaining others'), who among other things also create the plausibility structures for the mediation of faith.[143]

By joining an Alpha course, guests actually experience something of being a part of the Christian community. The meal, talk and the small group discussions facilitate the creation of a plausibility structure for the mediation of faith. The meal serves several purposes: it creates group cohesion, helps define group boundaries, and enables the development of strong affective bonds within the small group. The small group discussion further facilitates this bonding process. One guest (St C G6) had alcohol problems and so attended Alpha intermittently. He described how, for him, Alpha was good because it was another evening when it kept him off the drink. Similar to the AA 90/90 rule (see §6.1.1 above), Alpha served as a social mechanism that kept this guest from drinking, although the structure on Alpha was not strong enough to keep him off alcohol.

While Alpha stands in contrast to revivalist and coercive conversion, the small group brought an element of pressure, especially for the vulnerable. The couple at St E (G1 and G2) who had recently suffered bereavement seemed aware of being 'pulled along' by the group. For them, pressure existed as a 'support' rather than as an 'inducement' to convert:[144]

---

[143] Volf 1998:167. See also Lesslie Newbigin (2000:Ch.18) and his description of the Christian congregation as the 'hermeneutic of the gospel'.
[144] Cf. the 'affectional conversion' motif in Lofland and Skonovd 1981.

If there'd been...several of me, your hands would have been full. Do you understand? We were pulled along quite easily and gently (St E G1).

Another guest described the process of change during his conversion and the importance the religious community had for him:

If you would have said to me before how I would have found it, and you were to list it as bullet points and said, okay, this is what's going to happen to you in the next six months...I would have never had said it would have been possible...I wouldn't say it's been a bed of roses since I've become a Christian. I've had phases where I've had either temptation put in front of me, or I've had something that's got in the way. And I think sometimes, when you go to Alpha, or you go to your cell group, and you actually talk through it, you actually find out it challenges the way you look at things really (St A1 G5).

For this guest there were minor legitimating factors present. For example, he describes how he had 'skip read around in the Bible...because I couldn't read whole chunks'. However, he was unable to understand, at least at this stage in his conversion, how exactly the change happened:

I just felt something inside just saying, 'Yeah, that's what you've been looking for.' It's bizarre how it happened (St A1 G5).

This guest was gradually resocialised into Alpha's alternative plausibility structure through prolonged group interaction.

One guest described the confrontation he experienced in attempting to talk about his spiritual life with his work colleagues and how, in contrast, the Alpha small group provided the space for him to be able to discuss such things without being mocked. By the end of the course, he described how at work he no longer felt pressurised to conform to his colleagues' expectations of what was appropriate conversation:

I think it's actually sharing the experiences with everyone else around in your small groups, you can say, well, this happened to me today, and did it happen to you. And it makes you able to talk about it without being, I know it sounds awful, but being laughed at. I talk to my friends about it and they all laughed at me, saying, '[G8], you've been a womaniser, you've smoked, you've drank, you've gambled, you have this, not wild lifestyle, but I've had an active life...and I'm shocked at my friends reaction that I'm actually interested in something like this. I don't feel peer pressure to conform with them anymore... (St E G8).

While the social and ideological encapsulation on Alpha was appreciated by these guests the overwhelming presence of Christians on Alpha, as noted in Chapter 5, was also the main reason that guests gave for leaving the course.

The power of a group's plausibility structure, and its ability to influence, is intensified at the Alpha weekend or day away, where guests experience physical encapsulation. Gumbel is conscious of the 'alternative' plausibility structure on Alpha and how it is far more 'effective' if a course includes a weekend rather than just a day away. Gumbel states:

> I have found many make as much progress spiritually during the weekend away as in the rest of the course put together.[145]

> [I]n an environment like this, the pressure is all to be Christian. But the moment we get back to wherever we go in the world, the pressure is all the other way.[146]

Gumbel goes on to note an experiment[147] where seventy-five per cent of people assessing the lengths of lines on paper were influenced by the (in) group. It is interesting that Gumbel actually is aware of the potential 'pressure' on the weekend. This is despite his assertion that Alpha is a low-key unpressurised introduction to the Christian faith.[148] It is primarily at the weekend that the dramatic conversions reported by AI occur (see Chapter 2).

It is difficult to convey the intensity of an HTB Alpha weekend. As described in Chapter 5, as well as the 'priming' of guests by the speakers with suggestions and carefully constructed music, together with physical encapsulation, participants are isolated from their regular social contexts, leaving them open or vulnerable to various pressures that could induce conformity.[149] Pressure to conform is heightened in emotion-producing situations.[150] Such situations are often novel and outside the realm of past experience. It could thus be expected that the emotions would be particularly vulnerable to social influence.[151]

An Alpha administrator's attempt to induce conversion on a bereaved couple (G1, G2) at St E's weekend is an example of the potential pressure exerted on guests. During the worship songs the couple started to cry. The small group gathered around them and the leaders (L1 and L2) also became tearful. After twenty minutes they were brought coffee and were joined by the two administrators (LA1, LA2). They started crying again and at this point LA2 attempted to push for a confession or prayer of commitment: 'God knows your pain because Jesus died on the cross. How do you think God feels about his Son dying on the cross?' He encouraged G1 to 'give in to God', to give his life to God. He then suggested that G1 pray out loud, but G1 said that he was not quite ready for that. There were seven of us around the couple, all offering comforting words and praying for them. It lasted for about forty minutes and

---

[145] Gumbel 2001g:64.

[146] Alpha Weekend Talk 4.

[147] Although no source is given, it is likely that this refers to Asch's (1956) research.

[148] Gumbel 2001g:38.

[149] Cartwright 1951; Festinger 1953; Napier and Gershenfeld 1985; Zerubaevel 1997.

[150] See also Brian 2003:182.

[151] Napier and Gershenfeld 1985:136.

was highly visible and intense. I felt most uncomfortable with what LA2 was saying to G1. He seemed to be interpreting the couple's tears as a spiritual experience and potential conversion. What was happening, according to this couple, was a release of grief. Another guest (G7) at this weekend described feeling pressured and uncomfortable at being there:

> I didn't feel all that comfortable with what was going on...And also feeling a bit under pressure that you should feel something, and if you didn't, there was something wrong, so I did feel a bit uncomfortable with that part. [I. Did you feel anything, or sense anything?] No, no, which was probably because I was really up tight thinking, I must be really bad [laughter] (G7).

The above accounts highlight the more extreme aspects of the Alpha day away or weekend. Conversely, most of them were undramatic and relatively subdued affairs (see Chapter 5 §4.5).

Part of Alpha's success in its attempt to convert guests is because it includes all three forms of encapsulation – social, ideological, physical – and thus is able to create the plausibility structures for the mediation of faith. The course provides a social cocoon necessary to *exclude*, to a degree, threatening influences from beyond the structure and in which the process of conversion begins or is strengthened.

7.2 Legitimations

The most prominent channels of ideological encapsulation, and the employment of legitimations, are the Alpha talks and what occurs in the small group interaction. In contrast with the theory of legitimations, explained above (§6.4), when they are used on Alpha, the aim tends to be to *generate* rather than to simply *sustain* commitment. This is why I have included legitimations prior to the maintenance processes. Indeed, the overall aim of Alpha is to convert guests.

The Alpha talks contain relatively few apologetic legitimations, the main content being spiritual formation (see Chapter 2). Still, both the hermeneutical and nihilation approach to legitimations are employed during the first two weeks. In the former, religious belief-systems attempt to make sense of the world in their own terms. Throughout the talks, Gumbel constructs a (particular) Christian world-view. What is important here is that there is a *perceived* logic. Gumbel does this by a collection of disparate references to high profile personalities, including Prince Charles, Princess Diana, Bernard Levin, 'greatest columnist of this generation', Freddie Mercury, Robert Louis Stevenson, and so on. He also makes reference to various Christian scholars, writers, scientists, and lawyers, including Leo Tolstoy, C. S. Lewis, Professor Arnold 'chair of modern history at Oxford University', the late Professor F. F. Bruce 'who was Rylands professor of biblical criticism and exegesis at the

University of Manchester', F. J. A. Hort 'one of the greatest ever textual critics', Sir Frederic Kenyon, who is 'a leading scholar in this area', and so on.[152] Following is an example of the way Gumbel constructs plausibility, taken from the Alpha Supper talk:

> I hadn't realised how many of the pioneers of modern science were believers: Descartes, Newton, Kepler, Galileo, Locke, Copernicus, Faraday, Boyle, Mendel, Kelvin, Pasteur, Lister, Maxwell, Simpson. Professor James Simpson, the brilliant scientist whose discoveries paved the way for safe, painless surgery. Someone once asked him: 'Professor Simpson, of all these discoveries you've made, which of them was the greatest?' And he said 'Well, actually the greatest discovery I ever made was the day I discovered Jesus Christ.'
>
> Lawyers. Perhaps the greatest lawyer of the second half of the twentieth century was Lord Denning. Lord Denning towered, really, over the legal profession for fifty years. He was also the President of the Lawyers' Christian Fellowship. He'd looked at the evidence, and come to the conclusion it's true.

The legitimation here is that these highly acclaimed people are Christians, they are convinced in the *evidence* for the truth of Christianity, *ergo* there is intellectual respectability in being a Christian. It is a moot point whether the list of scientists are Christian. Many had an understanding of the Christian faith quite at odds with Gumbel. For example, Descartes was a proto-Deist, and Locke was a rationalist,[153] whose concept of the miraculous could not be further from that found on Alpha. This is irrelevant for Gumbel, whose primary task in the employment of hermeneutical legitimation is to interpret as much of the world as possible within his own terms, thus claiming to be the true interpretation. In the talk on evil, there is an expectation given of a disconfirming world, which is cynical about faith, and of a personal devil who has become interested in guests since they started their spiritual quest.[154] Here the mundane world, where people experience difficulty in everyday life, is interpreted as reflecting a supernatural realm. Doubts no longer become merely an intellectual grappling but are the result of the devil.[155] Such is the 'romantic adventure' in the charismatic narrative.[156]

In Chapter 2, Gumbel's rational approach to apologetics was noted, including the way he set up 'straw men', caricaturing 'objections' to faith, before demolishing them.[157] Gumbel himself describes each of the talks on Alpha as 'attacking shots'.[158] This is the offensive, nihilation, approach to

---

[152] Gumbel 2001e:11-39.
[153] Thiemann 1985.
[154] Gumbel 2001e:159.
[155] Gumbel 2001e:161.
[156] Hopewell 1988:76.
[157] Percy 1997.
[158] Gumbel 2006.

legitimations where the carriers of competing belief systems are discredited. Christianity is not a 'blind leap of faith...but a step of faith based on firm historical evidence'. 'The science of textual criticism' demolishes the claim that the Bible has changed over the years.[159] The use of logic against epistemological relativism,[160] and so on.

Continuing with the theme of legitimations, the aim of the Alpha small groups is that they give permission and provide a space for the discussion of the talk and the experiences and questions of guests, although the dysfunctionality of groups on several of the courses has been noted. In the Alpha talks, Gumbel avoids dealing with some of the central 'defeaters' of the Christian faith.[161] The effect of this meant that the most difficult questions were discussed in a small group context with leaders lacking theological training. It is here where the employment of legitimations broke down. The problems this caused have already been referred to (see Chapter 5 §4.4). Still, a number of guests described the importance of the small group:

> ...the good thing about Alpha was that if you did have a question, you could ask it. And people would actually answer it. Well, they wouldn't answer it maybe totally, but they would give you how they found things...I think that was the best part, the fact that we did have the chats afterwards, and we'd gone through a lot of issues... (St A1 G5).

It was important that the guests at least perceived an opportunity to exist to discuss questions, and frustration was expressed when this was not allowed.

> Yeah, it did [answer some questions]. It's hard to say exactly how but it just felt that it did (St B G2).

On the subject of creation and evolution, the perception of one guest (St B G4) was that the group had a 'good discussion about it', even though the discussion lasted for only a few minutes before fizzling out. In sum, Alpha guests go through a process of socialisation, or re-socialisation, particularly in the context of the Alpha small group. It is in these groups where they have meals, socialise and have discussions. Alpha guests thus begin to learn to look at the world through 'Christian lenses'. During the course, the Christian story is not something which guests look at in order to gain meaning, but one that they look through in order to make sense of the world.[162]

To what extent was this able to be maintained when Alpha itself ended?

---

[159] Gumbel 2001e:23-27.

[160] Gumbel 2001e:16-17.

[161] These are contained in his book *Searching Issues* (Gumbel 2001f).

[162] This is classic reformed epistemology and is the strategy used by today's foremost Reformed epistemologist, Alvin Plantinga (1993; 2000).

7.3 Maintenance Processes

For guests who had friendships with team members prior to Alpha, the ongoing maintenance of plausibility through socialisation and conversation was able to be sustained in varying degrees. For example, one guest (St A1 G3) was very good friends with the leaders, playing rugby with them on a weekly basis, and had a weekly Bible study with a Christian work colleague. She sensed that she would not feel comfortable attending St A because it was a charismatic church, and expressed a desire to find an Anglican church. However, as noted in Chapter 5, the maintenance processes at work post-Alpha were particularly weak.

One helper (St A1 H2) had converted on a previous Alpha course and expressed his disappointment that there was no follow on to Alpha:

> I think there should be a follow on for new Christians. This is where I felt disappointed, is that you do the Alpha course and then you become a member of the church, if you choose to, and then there is nothing, nobody there to sort of ask. I suppose you need...three or four people come up to you once a week and say, would you like to read the passage in the Bible...I suppose you're like a little baby and you need to be wet-nursed for a little while... (H2).

He went on to say how he almost left the church because of this lack. One of the leaders at St C (L1) described herself as being more of a pastoral person, and was therefore upset at the lack of follow up in the church and at how many people had left due to lack of any form of maintenance processes:

> Ideally, our thinking was that if enough people went into the Alpha and then came out of the Alpha, if there was enough, we'd do a nurture course after that. I suppose that's the other area that Alpha falls through doesn't it? It doesn't have a nurture...I think we're very aware that we've lost probably a lot of people through the net, 'cause we've had lack of nurture. If you're an evangelistic person, it's like, 'lets get 'em in, let get 'em in, let's get 'em in'. But the pastor is like 'Yes, let's get them in, but let's look after them. Let's not be on to the next, 'get 'em in, get 'em in, get 'em in'. If we're going to keep them, God's not going to give us loads more if we can't look after ones...So ideally, I suppose the ideal pattern should be someone becomes a Christian, disciple and nurture them for two years.

In contrast to Alpha's aim of being part one of 'a two-year programme of adult Christian education',[163] the overwhelming situation for guests post-Alpha contradicted this. HTB itself has experienced difficultly here. At the UK Strategy Day,[164] HTB's post-Alpha follow on plan was described by John Parmiter. Interestingly, there was no mention of any of the AI follow on courses. He described how they had tried an Alpha 2, but that it lacked the

---

[163] Gumbel 2004.
[164] On 25 February 2005.

'buzz' of Alpha. Instead, their preference was to keep the Alpha small groups together, and to introduce them into one of the pastorates. These are a collection of three or four home groups. Parmiter admitted that many did not make it to this next stage and suggested that this was either because, quoting the parable of the sower, the seed had not fallen on good soil, or because the pastorates lacked the 'speed' and 'buzz' that guests had experienced on Alpha. Several HTB staff members have told me that, according to HTB's own research, only four per cent of guests make the move from Alpha into pastorates.[165] What struck me during this session was that there was an awareness and concern about the need for discipleship, or maintenance processes, but also a complete loss as to how to go about doing it.

The lack of maintenance processes is significant, because if plausibility is not maintained continually and consistently through socialisation and conversation, people stop believing. Indeed, conversation and the reality that it maintains is profoundly precarious; it needs to be sustained at a high level to remain plausible.[166]

8. Cognitive Explanations

The third type of explanation for conversion points to intellectual grounds, in contrast to the affective and contextual groups.[167] While the latter two grounds are not irrational, they also have their reasons, cognitive explanations have to do with the logical force of the beliefs themselves, rather than with any circumstantial factors that might make the beliefs attractive.

People tend to assume that they have carefully thought-out beliefs. They must think their faith to be well-grounded, justified by evidence, rather than based upon some fantasy, otherwise it loses its force. Clifford's phrase, in *The Ethics of Belief* (1877),[168] is still potent: 'it is wrong, always, everywhere, and for anyone to believe anything upon insufficient evidence.' Kenworthy notes the evaluative dimension to such reasoning, suggesting that people view beliefs arrived at through an internal and rational process as being *positive* and beliefs arrived at through an emotional (because it is emotionally reassuring) and external origin (friends, family, media, and so on) as being *negative*.

---

[165] This is based on discussions with HTB staff members on 20 August 2004 and 11 September 2004.

[166] This is one of the difficulties for plausibility structures: from a religious point of view, it needs a sect to hold it together. MacLaren (2004:126ff) suggests the need for 'benign sectarianism', which works well as plausibility shelters but avoids the abuses of sects. Walker (1992) also suggests that sectarianism will increase at the expense of traditional Christianity over the next thirty years. He writes (1992:55): 'It is true that sects have a bias towards triumphalism and exclusivism, but they are a recipe for survival in a situation of either persecution or adversity.'

[167] MacLaren 2003:128-30.

[168] See *The Ethics of Belief, and Other Essays* (Stephen and Pollock 1947).

Furthermore, when asked to evaluate those who held opposite beliefs, it was assumed that they did so because of external and emotional factors.[169]

Much research on conversion by the human sciences has been based upon the *a priori* assumption that people convert solely because of social and psychological influences.[170] However, the beliefs in themselves can be a significant factor in whether or not someone converts. Barker notes that the most commonly proffered reason for rejecting the Unification Church was that certain guests did not believe the *Divine Principle* to be the truth, and the stumbling-block most often mentioned was the idea that Moon could be the Messiah.[171] While social and psychological influences are the greater determining factor in conversion,[172] MacLaren notes how plausibility may be generated on the basis of reasons for belief.[173] These need not be discounted as a mere *post hoc* rationalisation for existing beliefs that were predetermined by environmental factors. Instead, 'the believer may be thought of as an active agent in search of meaning, as well as, to some extent, a "product" of society. Believers are neither wholly free, nor wholly bound, within their personal and social worlds.'[174]

Lofland and Skonovd suggest that 'intellectual' conversions may be arrived at through attending lectures, reading, watching television and by way of other non-interactive methods, with little or no social pressure, and that this relatively rare type of conversion may be on the increase.[175] This might be due to the increasingly privatised nature of religion[176] or perhaps reflect the underlying self-growth philosophy of many individuals who experiment with alternative lifestyles.[177] It has become relatively easy for people privately to control their own decisions about religious beliefs, organisations and even ways of life quite apart from any physically embodied social contact, support, or inducement of an affect-laden sort.[178]

If this is so, which arguments are rationally convincing? Barker notes that there is no logically necessary connection between the nature of the process by

---

[169] Kenworthy 2003:138.

[170] Research in America has found that the 'hard' scientists – physicists, chemists, biologists and mathematicians – are substantially *more* religious than their counterparts in the social sciences and humanities (Iannaccone, Stark & Finke 1998). They suggest that views of religion as being irrational emerged from a Nineteenth Century scholarly tradition largely devoid of empirical support, tainted by prejudice, ignorance and anti-religious sentiment.

[171] Barker 1984:157.

[172] Kenworthy 2003.

[173] MacLaren 2003.

[174] MacLaren 2003:130.

[175] Lofland and Skonovd 1981.

[176] Luckmann 1967.

[177] Richardson 1985.

[178] Lofland and Skonovd 1981:377.

which people come to believe something and the credibility of the belief itself.[179] At one level, a group offering a logically *coherent* belief system can be sufficiently convincing, despite its being predicated on false premises. Many people believe on the basis of the most primitive and fragmentary logic. 'What matters is that individuals perceive there to be some compelling logic to the reasons presented to them, not that they are able to identify fallacies concealed in the argument'.[180] Alternatively, beliefs are not purely at the mercy of coherent but false arguments. The empirical world continually intrudes upon our beliefs, affirming some and casting doubt on others. Borhek and Curtis have observed that many beliefs are supported directly through personal experience in the world as it is, and the regularity of such experiences can explain belief. We believe that water is wet, that rocks are hard, and that night follows day because we are continually reassured by experience.[181] Negatively, false beliefs are likely to be under pressure from real events. I noted, above, the failed prophecies of a UFO doomsday cult and the cognitive dissonance felt by members.[182] Through a process of secondary elaboration, by reinterpreting the prophecies, these movements often continue. However, as Dixon puts it: 'Truth does not always win out, but it has a head start, as it were.'[183]

In sum, religious beliefs themselves may generate plausibility for the seeker rather than their being seen as merely a *post hoc* justification arrived at post conversion. The convert can be viewed as both an active searcher for meaning as well as to some extent a 'product' of society. Additionally, while reasons for belief do not have to be logically watertight to generate plausibility, 'truth is more likely to generate plausibility than falsehood, unless the false belief has little empirical relevance'.[184]

9. Cognitive Explanations and Alpha

Although this dimension was a relatively minor factor on Alpha,[185] there were several active searchers with genuine intellectual questions that they were hoping to have discussed on the course. What seemed important for the Alpha guests was that they *perceived* there to be some compelling logic to the beliefs presented to them, even if those beliefs were based upon fragmentary logic.

A number of guests referred to the importance that evidence and proof had for them:

---

[179] Barker 1984:137.
[180] MacLaren 2003:129.
[181] Borhek and Curtis 1975:112, 121.
[182] Festinger, Riecken and Schachter 1956.
[183] Dixon 1980:129.
[184] MacLaren 2003:130.
[185] See also Marsden 2006.

...there was lots of things that made me think this is real, it is happening and probably stronger than before because my faith before had always been, well, I need to believe but I've never had any proof that it's worth believing (St B G5).

Asking questions and people being able to answer them, like in a way that seemed true, so that I believe it. Like having an answer for everything really (St C G3).

The following guest was convinced by the 'facts' of Christianity and, similar to the intellectual conversion motif,[186] seemed to experience a moment of 'illumination':

...when people said, why is Christianity true and not the others? I couldn't see that at all until recently. And it was the book called *The Case for Christ*. I'm big on facts and when I read that, and it clearly laid out the facts: look, here's the history, we have very, very, very, overwhelming proof, much better than any proof than any history we have ever, that Jesus lived, he did these things. And it was just like, well, its true, deal with it [laughter]. So that was almost that defining moment. I was sitting there nodding, going yeah that's true, and then [I] eventually stopped and thought, wait a sec, that means something quite big. I was literally lying in bed, I can remember the exact point, reading this book, and I suddenly thought, well, if I believe that. And then I went from there (St D G5).

For this guest, it did not matter that there clearly are other historical events better able to be verified, not to mention Lessing 'ugly broad ditch',[187] the apologetic that he read was convincing to him.

While some guests may have been convinced by beliefs based upon fragmentary logic, others seemed convinced in the absence of argument, or rather based upon trust in an authority figure (Gumbel) who provided a 'semblance of rational justification'.[188] For example, in the training video, 'Leading small groups', Gumbel describes an occasion when a guest had a question concerning other religions:

I remember in one small group that I was in, there was a guy called Stephen, who was a 26-year-old lawyer, very bright guy. And at 9:43[pm], two minutes before the group was due to end, Stephen said, 'Well, what about those people who've never heard about Jesus? What happens to them?' So we said, 'Well, Stephen, that's a great question, but we've only got two minutes! So why don't we postpone that to next week.' And I said 'Stephen, well, why don't you come to the bookshop. I'd love to give you something to read before next week.' So I turned him to the section [in *Searching Issues*], 'What about other religions? and to the subsection which is headed 'What about those who've never heard about Jesus?'

---

[186] Lofland and Skonovd 1981.

[187] That is, the 'accidental truths of history can never become the proof of necessary truths of reason' (cited in McGrath 2006:296).

[188] MacLaren 2004:98.

And he looked at it like this and he said, 'Do you mean someone else has asked this question before?' That was all he needed to know. He never asked it again.

As Barker has observed, there was no logically necessary connection between the process of conversion and the credibility of the beliefs themselves.[189] An interesting comparison here is the response, in the remarks reported below of the open de-churched guests, to Gumbel's argument for the reliability of the Bible:

> I think it was quite convincing, what they were saying about Jesus and the Bible. You'd have to say well, yes, he must have existed. The Bible, there's so much evidence for the Bible and what it says for being highly likely to be true...I think they provided more fact and evidence... (St B G3).

> ...my argument was, hang on, this is a document which is 2,000 years old; it wasn't put together until 300 years after Jesus died; Jesus spoke in Aramaic, it was recorded in Greek and it was translated from the Greek into English. So it's not the word of God: it's the transcribed, translated, updated [laughter] abridged, whatever you like, word of God...they didn't seem to either want to understand that argument or they couldn't deal with it. So I think that was one of the main problems with the course...I think it was naïve as much as simplistic at times. It just seemed to be ignoring the last 200 years of theology (St D G1).

Here we have contrasting responses to the same argument. The former guest perceived there to be some compelling logic to the reasons given for the reliability of the Bible, whereas the latter guest, a theology student, thought that Gumbel's explanation was predicated on false premises and that he had identified fallacies in the argument. The apologetic task is clearly complex and does not convince everyone. As Dulles notes, it depends on the antecedent desires and expectations of particular human beings with their various hopes and fears, convictions and doubts.[190] However, while the former guest was convinced by the evidence for the reliability of the Bible, he chose to repress other questions that conflicted with his scientific background:

> I still have problems. If I put my biologist hat on, I'd have to say, the virgin birth and resurrection can't happen. But I don't say that because there's lots of things we don't understand. So I don't think too deeply about those, perhaps I should. I'm focusing more on the spiritual element (St B G3).

In Chapter 5, I described some of the difficulties that surfaced as a result of Alpha's multiple aims – that is, mission and spiritual formation. In contrast to Gumbel's theory, that guests end up answering their own questions,[191] many of

---

[189] Barker 1984:137.

[190] Dulles 1994.

[191] Gumbel 2006.

the open de-churched guests ended the course with questions that remained undiscussed:

> ...because there is no proof of things, its really hard for me to understand why they have faith in the first place. So I still have the standpoint of, maybe it came to you at a point when you were low and you're really clinging on to something that's not there. And they didn't really answer that question. It raised questions throughout that weren't answered, if you see what I mean. I can't really see where they are coming from because I don't have the same sort of faith, and it's a bit kind of, the blind faith, 'I know, regardless, that God is there and that he will protect me', I think is a bit, you're living in a fantasy world (St D G4).

One guest at St E (G3) had been on a pro-active long term spiritual quest. On the first week on Alpha he described how, coming from a scientific background, his question was not so much on who was Jesus, as on whether there was a God. This guest ended the course with a fundamental question, whether God exists, which was not adequately discussed. I asked him about this in the interview:

> I still haven't buttoned that one out yet...I suppose I grew up being told there was a God and so to try and to think that there isn't one, I almost can't really, because it's so engrained in me. But my logical mind tells me it's more likely the universe is just an energy that's been evolved in different ways and it doesn't need an intelligent creator, that's just a figment of humankind's imagination...I do believe in God, but my head is telling me that's probably not the right thing. So there's a bit of a struggle going on (St E G3).

As noted in Chapter 5, this guest expressed frustration over the lack of opportunity to ask questions not related to those on the Alpha agenda. This seemed partly due to the leaders being unable to cope with such questions.

The subject of evolution was unsatisfactorily handled for several guests. The conflict between an Alpha leader and a guest at St A2 was highlighted in Chapter 5 (§4.4.2). Another guest (St D G12), a natural science student, described how she could not give up belief in evolution. However, the Christians in her small group, including the leader, said that there was very little evidence for evolution and that they did not believe in the theory. She retorted that at least there was some evidence for evolution compared with belief in God, for which there was none. The response of the team members in these small groups contrasts to the advice given by AI, and how the subject was treated in *Searching Issues*,[192] where Gumbel remained agnostic concerning evolution. Another guest described how he was unable to reconcile his belief in evolution with Christian faith, and where, for example, dinosaurs featured in the creation narrative. Yet he did not feel that there was space on Alpha to ask

---

[192] Gumbel 2001f:90-93.

this sort of question:

> The trouble with Alpha, I felt it wasn't very structured in a sense to allow people to ask their own questions...[I]f no one's got any questions then it really falls down. 'Cause I can remember when there were some times when we all just sat in silence...they were showing a certain way rather than trying to explore the different things (St D G10).

Many guests continued attending Alpha despite the lack of opportunity to address specific questions they had. The *affective reasons* for continuing were powerful enough to override any cognitive dissonance.

10. Summary

In this chapter I first challenged the understanding of conversion as confined to crisis experiences. Evidence shows that conversion is not limited to radical personal change but could be less dramatic. Part of the difficulty has been due to a fascination with the more glamorous and exotic conversions to NRM. This book has helped to redress this bias within the sociology of conversion by assessing conversion within a mainstream religious group. Recent studies in the sociology of conversion have provided a helpful correction, recognising that it is simplistic to reduce conversion, for example, to the resolution of a crisis, to social tension or anomie, relationship deprivation, or a deep sense of cultural rootlessness and meaninglessness. Motives for converting are multiple, complex and malleable.[193]

Rambo's five conversion types were related to conversion on Alpha. While there were three affiliation conversions, the majority (seventeen) were intensification conversions, where faith that was formerly present in the form of a seed blossomed into full flower. This result related to the majority of guests who attended Alpha, that is, the open de-churched. Important to note for these conversions is that five were the result of a wider process of re-initiation in which Alpha played just one part, and another five were regular churchgoers whose faith was intensified during the course.

Rambo's process theory was then used to describe Alpha's role in conversion. The primary dimension functioning on Alpha was interaction. Before guests joined the course, more often than not, they had experienced some sort of crisis; some began a spiritual quest; then there was an encounter, usually through friends or church. Having joined Alpha, they became part of a small group where the interaction that took place was intensified. Four guests made a particular commitment; the rest (80 per cent) described a more gradual process. Lastly, the consequences dimension and the general lack of post-Alpha follow up was noted.

---

[193] Rambo 1993:140.

In the rest of the chapter, I used MacLaren's thesis as a theoretical framework in helping to decipher conversion on Alpha. He describes conversion through the matrix of three interweaving explanations: social–psychological, structural and cognitive. The social–psychological explanations were explained primarily as need-based: identity, belonging, compensation and certainty. On my research, the most prominent factors were the need both for belonging and compensation. The need for compensation was an important dynamic for seven people on Alpha. Interesting to note here is that three of those people had a non-churched background and were thus 'affiliation' conversions. Four described distorted parenting patterns, and as a result formed a strong emotional tie to the Alpha group. It was the Christian community experienced on Alpha, and/or belief in God, that compensated for insecure attachments to parents during childhood. By far the most prominent characteristic for the social–psychological explanations for conversion was the need for community. Notable for this group was that, bar one, members were all from the open de-churched category. Alpha thus functioned as a process of reinitiation, to 'refresh', or 'reawaken' a dormant faith. *The* key factor for this group was the strong affective[194] bonds that developed over the course of three months in the Alpha small group. These groups offered a sense of belonging, which provided the necessary bridge to the Christian community. Guests emphasised the friendliness that they met with when they first joined the course, and described how they felt a sense of belonging and support from the Alpha group. I raised the question of whether Alpha groups use 'love bombing' techniques. I concluded that while there were elements of it on some Alpha courses, it was relatively low in intensity, and there was a lack of *intentional* manipulation in aiming to construct group identity over and against non-members.

Structural explanations for conversion were then outlined. In a world of competing plausibility structures, Alpha functioned as a distinctive alternative plausibility shelter. Alpha performed the two functions of a plausibility structure: cohesion and exclusion. Cohesion was facilitated through strong affective relationships, talks by a charismatic figure and intense group interaction. The three processes of exclusion, or encapsulation, were significant on the course: social encapsulation on the weekly Alpha sessions and during the Alpha weekend or day away, which is where physical encapsulation was also experienced. Ideological encapsulation was achieved through the Alpha talks and small group discussion. The pressure to conform was most intense on

---

[194] I have frequently used the term 'affective' because of its central importance for conversion. It refers to things that are significant, but are of an essentially emotional nature. For example, at the beginning of his *Treatise on Religious Affections*, Jonathan Edwards (1959) wrote, 'True religion, in great part, consists in Holy Affections'. Schleiermacher (1928:§15) also described how 'Christian doctrines are accounts of the Christian religious affections set forth in speech'.

the Alpha weekend, as Gumbel himself admitted.

The Alpha talks and the small group discussion were the most prominent channels of legitimations. Gumbel constructs a (particular) Christian world-view through the use of high profile personalities, as well as quoting multiple Christian biblical scholars, writers, scientists and lawyers. Although Gumbel uses both hermeneutic and nihilation legitimations in his talks during the first two weeks of the course, the main discrepant views to Christian faith are left to the small group leaders to deal with. It was here where the employment of legitimations broke down. Lastly, it was noted that the maintenance processes at work post-Alpha were exceptionally weak. Continued socialisation and conversation, the two most important processes for the maintenance of plausibility, were almost non-existent. I therefore concluded that, for five of the six courses that I researched, AI failed in its aim of constructing a two-year programme of adult Christian education.

Lastly, cognitive explanations for conversion were related to Alpha. Several guests pointed to the 'evidence' and 'facts' presented for Christian belief on Alpha. Also noted was that no logically necessary connection existed between the process of conversion and the credibility of the beliefs themselves. What one person found convincing, another did not. One of the main difficulties experienced by the guests was due to Alpha's multiple aims of attempting mission and spiritual formation. Gumbel's optimistic view that guests end up answering their own questions was not realised. Many of the open de-churched guests ended the course with cognitive dissonance, with questions that remained undiscussed, and finding the strong views of the team members problematic.

In this chapter, I have attempted to give some explanation of conversion on Alpha, using sociological theories of conversion. As to the 'reality' and longevity of the conversions, only time will tell. And while the various 'explanations' for conversion can be helpful in uncovering some of the predispositions of people, their motivations and various processes involved, it is impossible to describe the essentially mysterious nature of conversion, as Rambo concludes:

> Conversion is paradoxical. It is elusive. It is inclusive. It destroys and it saves. Conversion is sudden and it is gradual. It is created totally by the action of God, and it is created totally by the action of humans. Conversion is personal and communal, private and public. It is both passive and active. It is a retreat from the world. It is a resolution of conflict and an empowerment to go into the world and to confront, if not create, conflict. Conversion is an event and a process. It is an ending and a beginning. It is final and open-ended. Conversion leaves us devastated – and transformed.[195]

---

[195] Rambo 1993:176.

Chapter 7

A Theological and Liturgical Critique of Alpha

The previous two chapters have assessed the empirical data. The actual experience of Alpha participants in relation to the official version has been compared and contrasted and, using the framework of the sociology of conversion, its primary aim of conversion has been appraised. However, a purely sociological analysis is insufficient in which to decipher Alpha. Accordingly, the third and final aim of this book, the evaluation of Alpha's theological foundations, will be examined.

Jeremy Begbie has described how theology and the Charismatic Movement have not always been happy partners. He suggests that this uneasy relationship is perhaps due to the deep strain existing within Western Christianity between spiritual experience and reflective tradition.[1] To recapitulate on comments that I made in Chapter 4, I write as an Anglican priest. As an insider, I recognise that HTB has made a valuable contribution to the life of the Church. Yet my role in this research is not, as Bennett describes it, a championing 'subcultural spokesperson', but rather that of a critical analyst.[2]

In this chapter, I shall draw on some of the themes that have arisen throughout this book and give a theological assessment of Alpha from the perspective of what has been termed 'Deep Church',[3] which is the historic faith as reflected in 'the adherence to the apostolic faith of the New Testament, as it was received, expounded and explicated in the patristic tradition of the early Christian centuries',[4] and as the 'rule of faith',[5] the common source of

---

[1] Begbie 1991:233. For a defence of Charismatic theology see Mark Cartledge 2004. The Eastern Orthodox Church, according to Kallistos Ware, avoids such division: '...just as mysticism divorced from theology becomes subjective and heretical, so theology, when it is not mystical, degenerates into an arid scholasticism...Theology, mysticism, spirituality, moral rules, worship, art; these things must not be kept in separate compartments' (Ware 1997:207).

[2] Cited in Hodkinson 2005.

[3] See Walker and Bretherton 2007.

[4] Walker in Stackhouse 2004:xiii.

[5] The canon of St. Vincent of Lérins describes this well: '...in the Catholic Church itself, all possible care must be taken, that we hold that faith which has been believed everywhere, always, by all' (*Commonitory*, Ch.2 in Schaff and Wace 1995:132). For a nuancing of this canon see O'Collins 1981:211-15. See also Walker 2007:64 and 72-74.

Catholicism, Eastern Orthodoxy and Protestantism.[6] I believe that the Alpha course could be enriched and deepened by drawing from this tradition, which in part it claims to do, drawing on C. S. Lewis's 'mere Christianity'. As I shall discuss below, there is a contingency about any evaluation of Alpha, including my assessment. However, this does not render the critique invalid. Throughout this chapter, I shall draw upon my empirical data (Chapters 5 and 6) to illustrate the paucity of serious engagement with the Christian tradition.

1. Link with Traditional Liturgical Practices of Initiation

In this section, I shall evaluate Alpha's attempt at combining mission and spiritual formation, and compare it with traditional liturgical practices and rites within the Church. It is possible to discern hints of how initiation developed within the New Testament, which itself covers three generations. For example, Jesus's commissioning passage in Matthew 28.16-20 probably reflects later development in the life of the primitive Church and the catechetical and liturgical practice of Matthew's own community.[7] What is clear in Matthew's account is that *making disciples* is the overarching commission with baptism and teaching as part of the overall process. Aidan Kavanagh suggests a fourfold pattern of the basic initiatory structure in the early NT church.[8] First, the proclamation of the gospel always preceded baptism. Second, those who responded turned in faith to Christ. This conversion could sometimes be accompanied by an overt outpouring of the Spirit even prior to baptism. Third, the gospel proclaimed and believed usually resulted in baptism. Fourth, the events that followed water baptism, the clearest record being Acts 2.42: 'They devoted themselves to the apostles' teaching and fellowship, to the breaking of bread and the prayers.'

However, attempting to force a settled *liturgical order* (for example, baptism followed by the gift of the Spirit) on the original chaotic events in Acts is fraught with difficulty. For example, there was a distinction between, on the one hand, the very first Christians, who were Jews or god-fearers, and who had the moral training of their Hebrew background. They were baptised immediately (Acts 2.37-41). On the other hand, for pagans with no such training in character and values, and no understanding of God's work in history

---

[6] Rather than viewing Deep Church as a set of core beliefs, Bretherton (2007) argues that it is preferable to understand it as a sort of immune system, which has developed and grown over time as it has faced both internal and external challenges.

[7] Johnson 1999:2. For example, Matthew's formulaic-sounding language of 'Father, Son and Holy Spirit' and the special missionary focus on 'all nations' is difficult to reconcile with the historical Jesus himself.

[8] Kavanagh 1978:20-23; cf. Webber 2003:18-20. For the theology of conversion, see Chester 2005; Conn 1978, 1986; Curran 1978; Finn 1997; France 1993; Gaventa 1986; Gelpi 1998; Gillespie 1991; Häring 1978; Kreider 1999, 2001; McKnight 2002; Newbigin 1969; Peace 1999, 2004; Rahner 1978.

with Israel, the Church soon developed an extensive form of discipleship and spiritual formation.[9] A settled order for Christian initiation took place over the next two centuries.

Johnson highlights the ecumenical consensus on the normativity of the classic ritual sequence of baptism, 'confirmation' or some kind of rite giving symbolic–sacramental expression to the sealing gift of the Holy Spirit, and Eucharist as constituting, in that order, the fullness of Christian initiation itself.[10] Within this framework, there was always considerable variety in different geographical areas of the early church, with significant improvisation and adaptation being exercised, each with a particular theological emphasis.[11] For example, while the early Syrian initiation pattern was associated with Christ's baptism (Christological), with the font viewed as a 'womb', the baptismal tradition in North Africa and Rome became one of sharing in Christ's death and resurrection (soteriological) with the font seen as a 'tomb'.[12]

The four phases of the catechumenate in the West[13] were largely developed from Hippolytus's *Apostolic Tradition*, written around 215 CE.[14] While there are doubts about the authorship and dating of the *Apostolic Tradition*, this does not retract from the importance that the work had for the development of the catechumenate. Bradshaw describes how after the conversion of Constantine in AD 313, the situation of the Church changed dramatically. Rather than being a tolerated sect, it became the established religion of the Empire, with Christian faith becoming not only respectable but advantageous.[15] In contrast to primitive Christianity in which baptism functioned as a ritual expression of a genuine conversion experience, the forth century baptismal process became much more dramatic in character so as to convey a profound experience to the candidates in the hope of bringing about their conversion.[16] Kreider writes, 'The difference

---

[9] Webber 2001:64; Kreider 1999:21.

[10] Johnson 1999:361; see also *Baptism, Eucharist, and Ministry*, WCC 1982; Wainwright 1997; *Common Worship: Initiation Services* 1998; Gelpi 1998; Kreider 2007:191.

[11] Bradshaw 1996; Finn 1997; Johnson 1999.

[12] Bradshaw 1996:12-21; Johnson 1999:382.

[13] The Eastern Church had a shorter and less structured or formalised catechumenate (Johnson 1999:87).

[14] A great deal is known about the fourth century practice and rites from the 'mystagogic catechesis' or homilies given by the bishops to the newly baptised. These sermons can be found in Yarnold's, *The Awe Inspiring Rites of Initiation* (1977). Augustine is the only Church Father from whom there survives instruction from each phase of the catechumenate. For a description, see Harmless, *Augustine and the Catechumenate* (Collegeville: Liturgical Press, 1995).

[15] Bradshaw 2001:3-4. Compulsion eventually followed in AD 529 with an edict of Justinian, which made conversion – including baptism of all infants – compulsory (Kreider 1999).

[16] Bradshaw 1996:22.

Christendom made was that conversion, which had made Christians into distinctive people – resident aliens – now was something that made people ordinary, not resident aliens but simply resident.'[17] Post-Constantine, the catechumenate eventually became abbreviated and made primarily theological rather than radically practical.[18] Conversion became largely unwilling, incomplete and included a significant degree of paganisation.[19] By the sixth century conversion had become more perfunctory,[20] giving rise to the (Western) monastic tradition, which was an attempt to retain the values that characterised the early church.[21]

The idea of a catechumenate has seen a revival recently, having been reformulated in the Rite of Christian Initiation for Adults (RCIA) in the Roman Catholic Church,[22] the Anglican Church[23] and even among some Evangelicals.[24] The chart below[25] outlines the four stages of initiation in the early church. Each period of formation had a rite of passage that marked the transition to the next period of growth:

Phase 1	Pre-catechumenate or evangelism
Rite of passage	Rite of welcome (enrolment)
Phase 2	Catechesis or pre-baptismal teaching and discipleship
Rite of passage	Election and public scrutiny
Phase 3	Sacramental initiation
Rite of passage	Baptism, confirmation and first communion
Phase 4	Mystagogy ('explanation of the mysteries') or post-baptismal nurturing of the *faithful* into full membership

Of central importance was sacramental initiation, which was the focus of the

---

[17] Kreider 1999:90.

[18] Ferguson 2001.

[19] MacMullen 1997, 2001.

[20] Kreider 1999.

[21] Bhaldraithe 2001.

[22] See *The Conversion Experience* (Gelpi 1998).

[23] See the House of Bishop's report *On the Way* (1995) and *Faith on the Way* (Ball and Grundy 2000).

[24] See *The Logic of Evangelism* (Abraham 1989); *Journey to Jesus* and *Ancient–Future Evangelism* (Webber 2001; 2003); and 'Early Church Catechesis and New Christians' Classes in Contemporary Evangelicalism' (Arnold 2004).

[25] This chart is a synthesis of Yarnold (1977) and Webber's (2003) outline of the catechumenate.

whole process, and within the context of the Church. Indeed, the metaphor of the Church as a mother, in whom new Christians are born and nourished, comes from Tertullian, Clement of Alexandria, Cyprian of Carthage and Justin Martyr.[26] As Cyprian's oft-quoted phrase emphasises: 'He cannot have God for his father, who has not the Church for his mother'.[27] The overall purpose of the catechumenate was that of formation in Christian living, of forming disciples of Christ, rather than just training in doctrinal content.[28]

I shall outline these four phases below and then make use of them comparatively to evaluate Alpha. In describing the catechumenate, it is important to avoid a romanticised view, as does Eusebuis in *Ecclesiastical History*, where the pristine church later becomes compromised.[29] On the one hand, the contemporary situation is not identical to the early church milieu, and thus I am not suggesting an unreflective return to the catechumenate after the manner of the *Apostolic Tradition*. Rather, there are valuable principles in the early church's process of mission–initiation that can address an increasingly pagan Western culture where there is a decreasing Christian narrative to draw upon.[30] On the other hand, it is important for both Church and individual that Christian mission, initiation and formation take place within a clear yet flexible framework. This means retaining the ecumenically agreed sequence of baptism, 'confirmation',[31] and Eucharist as constituting the fullness of Christian initiation.

1.1. Pre-Catechumenate

First, there was a time for inquiry into the Christian faith that could be seen as evangelism or the pre-catechumenate. No formal process of evangelism was outlined in the New Testament or early church.[32] However, there are some themes that indicate what it was that made Christianity so attractive that others wanted to join 'the way'. What is significant is the practice of the Apostles to establish small communities whose common life signified, what Hardy calls, 'true sociality in the pagan world'.[33] Their unity of true belief and true practice, expressed in many ways, accounts for the astonishing growth of Christianity in early times.[34] Hardy quotes Clement in noting how the practice of the early Christians made them notable and persuasive: 'let us confess him in our deeds,

---

[26] Webber 2001.

[27] *On the Unity of the Catholic Church*, 6, in Stevenson 1987:230.

[28] Johnson 1999:87; Kreider 2007:176.

[29] Cooper 2001.

[30] See Abraham 1989; Brierley 2000; MacLaren 2004; Savage et al. 2006.

[31] Or a rite giving symbolic–sacramental expression to the sealing gift of the Holy Spirit.

[32] Kreider 1999:21.

[33] Hardy 2001:30.

[34] Hardy 2001:30.

by loving one another, by not committing adultery, nor speaking one against another, not being jealous, but by being self-controlled, merciful, good'.[35] Kreider also highlights the importance of belief and behaviour, but also stresses that it was the sense of *belonging* that made Christians so attractive and explains why the Church grew, rather than their public witness, which was simply too dangerous (contra Green).[36]

1.2. Catechumenate

When the seeker was ready, he or she was admitted to the second phase of initiation, the catechumenate itself. Yarnold outlines the four elements[37] in the rite of welcome, or *enrolment*: a signing of the cross was made on the candidates forehead, showing that they belonged to Christ; salt was given, possibly to symbolise being the salt of the earth or to remind the convert of purification and wisdom; hand laying, the traditional sign of the dedication of an offering to God and a gesture of blessing; and exorcism.[38] Following this, the candidate was called a catechumen (a person under instruction). Hippolytus prescribed three years of catechumenate;[39] during that time catechumens belonged to the family of the Church but not fully. They had joined but were not yet baptised, and they did not take part in the Eucharist. Catechumens attended the liturgy of the word and heard the sermon, along with the faithful, with Jews and even pagans who were curious to hear about Christian teachings. Candidates were expected to begin living in a manner befitting a Christian – a manner that would be gradually moulded by the teaching, moral support, prayer, example and ritual patterns of the Christian community itself.[40] The only subjects off limits were baptism and the Eucharist, which is why special sermons were preached on the sacraments after Pascha.[41] During the three years, catechumens would have heard the texts of sacred scripture read and

---

[35] 2 Clement 308.4.

[36] Kreider 1999:12; Green 1970. From a social science perspective, Stark (1996) affirms that the church spread because it became known for its compassion. During some devastating epidemics in the second to fourth century, Christians cared for the sick, often contracting the disease themselves and dying from it. This is in contrast to the pagans who pushed sufferers away and fled. See also Sanders 2000.

[37] Yarnold 1971:7.

[38] In the early Church pagans were thought to be possessed by the devil (Yarnold 1977:7). Brown (1996:27) suggests that salvation was primarily understood as salvation from idolatry and from the power of the demons. MacMullen (1984:27) suggests that exorcism was 'the chief instrument of conversion'.

[39] It could also take less than three years, depending on the earnestness and perseverance of the catechumen. Syria and Egypt had a relatively short catechumenal period of possibly 'three weeks' and 'forty days' respectively (Johnson 1999:59).

[40] Kavanagh 1978:55.

[41] Senn 1997:148.

commented upon as well as the passing on and explaining of the central doctrines of the faith.[42] Yet while the catechumenate included catechesis, it was not merely an academic affair. It assumed a liturgical setting and included prayers and exorcisms.[43]

1.3. Sacramental Initiation

At the beginning of Lent those catechumens who wished to be baptised went to the bishop, together with their sponsors, to 'give in their names', or request baptism.[44] This 'election and public scrutiny' included a rigorous questioning of catechumens to see if they were worthy of baptism, and which included the testimony of parents and neighbours. The *Apostolic Tradition* (Ch.20) specifies:

> ...[L]et their lives be examined whether they lived piously as catechumens, whether they honoured the widows, whether they visited the sick, whether they have fulfilled every good work. If those who bring them [sponsors] bear witness to them that they have done thus, then let them hear the gospel.

Again, the importance of lifestyle and the spiritual formation of the catechumen were stressed, rather than simply relying on how much intellectual knowledge had been acquired. As well as being a time of discipline, the process that took place during Lent also included scriptural, doctrinal and moral instruction.[45] The content of this incorporated the ceremony of baptism itself, as well as the Creed and the Lord's Prayer. The bishop or a deputy taught the Creed phrase by phrase, a process called the 'Handing over of the Creed' (*Traditio Symboli*). Later, the candidate was required to return and repeat it in a ceremony called the 'Giving back of the Creed' (*Redditio Symboli*).[46] This time of preparation culminated at Easter in the baptism itself. Yarnold describes the ceremony. After almost daily fasts and instruction, repeated exorcisms and recurrent prayers,

> [F]inally on Holy Saturday night he takes part in prolonged prayers, he hears the voice coming out of the darkness commanding him to renounce the devil to his face, to turn to Christ and swear allegiance; he remains only half-comprehending as he finds himself stripped, anointed, pushed down into the water; he is greeted with joy, dressed in white, led into the Church, shown for his first time the secret

---

[42] Arnold 2004:34.

[43] Kavanagh 1978:57.

[44] Yarnold 1977:7.

[45] See Ferguson (2001:242-56) for a description of the biblical and doctrinal instruction given by Cyril of Jerusalem and Ambrose during lent.

[46] The sponsors helped them to learn these prayers (Senn 1997:149; Yarnold 1977:12).

rites of the Mass; receives the sacred meal of bread and wine – often without a word of explanation.[47]

The whole procedure was calculated to stir up emotions of spiritual exaltation and awe and to help make baptism a life-long and profound conversion. The goal of Christian initiation was the Eucharist. Holy Communion was, and has remained, 'closed' – at least to the extent that no unbaptised person could partake of it.[48]

1.4. Mystagogy

The fourth and last part of the initiation process was mystagogy, or post-baptismal teaching, which took place during the seven weeks of Easter.[49] During the Octave of Easter the neophytes attended church every day, wearing their white garments. It was only *after* the sacraments of baptism and Eucharist had been experienced that they were deemed ready to receive instruction about them.[50] As the bishop delivered these mystagogical homilies the 'faithful' were allowed to ask questions.[51] There was also an encouragement to move forward to perform works of charity. This period ended around Pentecost Sunday with some form of celebration for the neophytes.[52]

In summary, the four stages of initiation, while holding theological and cultural variation, included a remarkably common shape, from becoming a catechumen through to the first Eucharist. To repeat my earlier comment, it is important that Christian formation takes place within a clear and flexible framework, including the ecumenically recognised initiation process of baptism, 'confirmation' (or equivalent) and the Eucharist.

2. Alpha and the Catechumenate

How does Alpha relate to the traditional liturgical pattern of initiation? As I have suggested elsewhere,[53] Alpha shares many of the catechumenate ingredients:[54] *welcoming* people as they are, *accompanied journey*, *faith sharing*, usually through story and dialogue, and *community*, expressed through the involvement of congregation, sponsor and group leaders. The meal on Alpha, for example, resonates with the pre-catechumenate in which nothing, not even baptism, was required as preparatory steps. This 'table

---

[47] Yarnold 1977:55.
[48] Senn 1997:152.
[49] Webber 2003:46.
[50] Kavanagh 1978:142-43.
[51] Senn 1997:153.
[52] Kavanagh 1978:44.
[53] Heard 2007.
[54] See the report *On the Way* 1995:35.

companionship', with its prophetic enactment and embodiment of the messianic banquet (Isaiah 25), remained a primary characteristic of the early church (Luke 24; Acts 2.42, 46; 1 Cor. 10-11; *Didache* 9, 10, 14). As Johnson notes, conversion itself was a consequence of, not a pre-condition for, such meal sharing.[55] Gumbel suggests that the meal has a sacramental dimension to it.[56] Even if the similarities on Alpha have been fortuitous rather than planned, HTB have created a course which includes much from the catechumenate. AI has also been exceedingly generous in responding to requests from other churches and developing the course so as to make it more widely available. Through the Alpha format of meal, talk and small group discussion, the course has revolutionised the way many churches conduct evangelism.

Yet, there remains a crucial question about Alpha: where does it fit within the catechumenate framework? For people joining the course, despite AI's primary *intention* of being a pre-catechumenate, my research suggests that what it is *actually* doing, at this present stage in its history, is something more akin to mystagogy.[57] As noted in Chapter 5, 86 per cent of the guests who joined Alpha were either regular churchgoers or of the open de-churched. In my research, the latter group had all been christened, most had grown up with some church involvement, but at some stage had left. Whether this pattern of affiliation changes over the next ten or twenty years, with Alpha perhaps starting to attract large numbers of the non-churched, only time will tell.[58] Nevertheless, attracting predominantly churchgoers and the open de-churched need not be viewed negatively. In the context of what Brueggemann has described as 'gospel amnesia',[59] Alpha is performing an important role in reviving the faith of Christians, re-initiating those who have dropped out of church for whatever reason, and welcoming back prodigals. Brueggemann sees the evangelising of 'insiders' as being the primary agenda in evangelism for the western church.[60] The same concern was behind Pope John Paul II's repeated call for a 'new evangelisation'.[61] Further, Alpha has given a forum, often lacking in churches, for regular churchgoers to be able to ask questions and express doubt.

So, based upon the majority of guests who join, Alpha is aligned with mystagogy. My assessment of Alpha's content (see Chapter 2) revealed that the course is primarily undertaking the sort of catechesis that fits the

---

[55] Johnson 1999:5-6.

[56] Gumbel 2004.

[57] A French monsignor, Pierre d'Ornellas, also views Alpha as being like mystagogy (interview with Alpha Adviser, Florence de Leyritz, on 16 December 2004).

[58] The *Mission-Shaped Church* report (Cray 2004:107) notes that 'working with the non-churched means starting much further back and expecting to have to work for far longer in building aspects of community before seeing results in terms of any spiritual interest'.

[59] Brueggemann 1993:90-93.

[60] Brueggemann 1993:73; see also Abraham 1989:113-14; Stackhouse 2004.

[61] See *Ecclesia in Europa*, *Redemptoris Missio*, www.vatican.va, accessed 22 December 2006.

catechumenate stage. Apart from the first three weeks, where there is an evangelistic push for conversion, the rest of the course is followed by talks more congruent with spiritual formation: prayer, Bible, guidance, evangelism, charisms.[62] Yet Alpha's expectations and ethos for those who attend the course is quite different from the catechumenate. Whereas the catechumenate seeks to mature those who have already converted and aims at personal transformation and an intellectual grounding in both the Bible and the Christian tradition as a whole,[63] Alpha's ethos (at least in theory) of being non-pressurised and with low commitment expectations, fits its primary aim of being pre-catechumenate. There is thus an inherent conflict between Alpha's aims, its ethos and its content. Alpha's pre-catechumenate aspiration is unusual in that it forms an attempt to formalise this process of evangelism. And in contrast to the RCIA and the Anglican catechumenate, which is flexible and adapts its pre-catechumenate instruction according to the personal needs of each candidate, Alpha has a clearly set syllabus.

Alpha faces another difficulty due to its multiple aims of mission and spiritual formation. As discussed in Chapter 5, the mixed grouping and content meant that a clash of agenda occurred in Alpha groups between non-churchgoers and Christians seeking a refresher course.[64] The former felt totally outnumbered by Christians, and as a result were inhibited when it came to asking questions. This was the primary cause of discerption. Other guests were dissatisfied with the discussion time: questions were 'swept under the carpet' (St A1 G4); questions about evolution triggered difficulties that had previously been unproblematic because of the leaders' conservative views (St A1; St D); guests were 'given trite answers' (St B G3); others lacked the opportunity to ask questions (St E G3). Gumbel avoids the most difficult questions in his talks, the logic being that they are not 'attacking strokes'. Gumbel's tendency is to police his talks assiduously, only allowing objections when convinced they can be of service. As a result, guests and leaders tended to flounder. For example, no one knew how to manage questions regarding trinitarian grammar, homosexuality, God's existence and so on.

The other difficulty with a mixed group is how to deal with the Eucharist.[65]

---

[62] Brookes (2007:79) thus suggests that Alpha is a sort of 'kerygmatic catechesis' (cf. Knights and Murray 2002:147).

[63] Gelpi 1998:136-47.

[64] This is not just a problem for churches running Alpha. Some Anglican Churches running a catechumenate found that many enquirers were already baptised, raising the possibility of ignoring their baptism in order to fit them into the rites (*On the Way* 1995:35; Johnson 1999:349). Churches running a catechumenate resolved this issue by having two groups, so as to enable them to pursue their own separate agendas (*On the Way* 1995:129).

[65] On this, see Bates 2005. Rather than condemning *or* condoning the practice of communicating the unbaptised, he views it as an evangelistic opportunity, but acknowledges such practice as an exception rather than the norm.

Whether to offer the Eucharist to the unbaptised is a contentious issue. Put briefly, the Eucharist is the sacrament of nourishment of our continuing relationship with Christ, just as baptism marks its beginning. Offering the Eucharist to the unbaptised results in 'diluting' or even altering the very nature of the sacrament itself, not to mention ignoring centuries of church tradition.[66] Mike Riddell views the 'fencing of the table' as working against mission and cites John Wesley, who saw the Eucharist as a 'converting ordinance'. He argues that, ironically, while Christ's act of self-giving for the world demonstrates the inclusive nature of gospel grace, the Eucharist has traditionally been exclusive, alienating non-churchgoers.[67] However, it needs to be kept in mind that in Wesley's day, the overwhelming number of people in Britain were baptised as infants, so to speak of the Eucharist as a 'converting ordinance' means in all likelihood the awakening of faith in the *already baptised*. HTB's Alpha course includes an informal Communion at its weekend away. This underscores Alpha's historical roots as a discipleship course. Yet if Alpha is now aiming at the (unbaptised) non-churched, the placement of the Eucharist before baptism and confirmation, is highly irregular and a confusion of genres.

2.1 Sacramental Initiation

As we have seen, Alpha has various components of the pre-catechumenate, the catechumenate and mystagogy. What Gumbel omits from Alpha, *and* his two-year syllabus, is the third element of the catechumenate: sacramental initiation. As noted in Chapter 2 (§2.1.8), Gumbel justifies this by arguing that because Alpha is an ecumenical course, and thus only presents the 'basics' of the Christian faith, it shies away from teaching about the sacraments. This neglect is a general feature and criticism of Evangelicalism, although it has often been overplayed.[68] Anthony Lane[69] has noted the lack of any clear inclusion of baptism in initiation in the evangelism of the past fifty years or so, addressing as it did a mostly nominal Christian audience. For example, Norman Warren argued, in *Journey to Life*, that baptism and confirmation counted for nothing unless one had faith and repented. Evangelicals have believed that only through conversion, only by grace through *faith*, does a person become a Christian. Evangelicalism, Hindmarsh notes, was a protest against the idea that adhering

---

[66] See, for example, *The Didache* (9:10 in Ehrman 2003) and Justin Martyr's *First Apology* (Ch. 66 in Roberts and Donaldson 1976–83).

[67] Riddell 1999.

[68] Cocksworth (1993) points out that throughout its history there have been sacramental Evangelicals.

[69] Anthony Lane, 'British Evangelical Identity' conference at King's College London, 30 July 2004.

to Christian civil society as a nominal Christian was sufficient for salvation.[70] While infant baptism, Christian nurture, catechesis and worship might be valuable in preparation, *no one* is a Christian until they have personally encountered God in Jesus Christ, personally repented and accepted God's gift of salvation through faith in Christ.[71] The emphasis on 'believers' baptism'[72] meant that the stress was placed upon repentance and faith, and it tended to have an individualistic and cerebral bias. Barth, for example, saw faith as primarily having a cognitive character, a *knowing*.[73] He viewed baptism as being a mere dispensable sign. The outward sign of the water could disappear and leave the inward reality unaffected.[74] Christopher Cocksworth highlights theological issues that militate against the expression of an Evangelical form of sacramental faith:

> These stem from the Reformation break with a theology which incarnated Christ in the life and liturgy of the Church, in favour of a theology of direct spiritual interaction between the individual and God in Christ...Therefore, the real challenge to Evangelical Protestants is to identify the *real value* of the Eucharist over and against that of hearing and believing the Word.[75]

There is very little mention (one paragraph) of baptism on either Alpha or the four follow-on courses written by Nicky Gumbel. A critical question here is, 'What part of the Christian faith is seen as an intrinsic and necessary part of evangelism?' It might be understandable that baptism is not highlighted on the Alpha course itself, just as it was not a part of the catechumenate proper. But the lack of teaching on baptism, confirmation or Eucharist within Gumbel's two-year programme of initiation emphasises the fact that HTB has created an unsacramental form of Christian initiation. For the majority of Roman Catholics, Orthodox and Anglicans, it is inconceivable for a two-year programme of evangelism and discipleship not to stress the intrinsic link between baptism and evangelism, or to see baptism, confirmation (or equivalent) and the Eucharist as the goal of the initiation process. As

---

[70] Hindmarsh 2002; see also Cocksworth 1993:46; Walls 2002:211-14.

[71] See Bebbington (1989:9-10) for the tension between baptismal regeneration, as taught in the BCP, and conversion among Evangelical–Anglicans.

[72] See Beasley-Murrey, *Baptism in the New Testament* (1963), REO White, *The Biblical Doctrine of Initiation* (1960), Karl Barth, *Church Dogmatics* (1981:IV/4) and Moltmann, *The Church in the Power of the Spirit* (1977).

[73] Barth 1981:IV/1, 751f.

[74] Barth 1981:758-62 and 776; see also Moltmann 1977:226ff; Stott 1982:325.

[75] Cocksworth 1993. O'Donovan (1986:130) traces the problem to the weak link between word and action in the medieval sacrament: 'the word of the baptismal formula (or the words of institution for the Eucharist) served only to *define* the sacramental action and not to provide a proclamation to which faith could attach itself' (also see Jüngel 1999:44).

Macquarrie asks, 'Is this not a kind of docetism, a denial that human beings are embodied creatures whose being is a being-in-the-world?'[76] Evangelicals themselves have critiqued the tradition's (recent) neglect of sacramental theology.[77] Such disembodied spirituality is a denial of the incarnation and of God's repeated demonstrations that creation can host the divine.[78]

Alpha's theology and spirituality is materially impoverished in contrast to the material richness and depth of the catechumenate. The three-year process was a highly tactile affair encompassing repeated hand-layings, feeding with salt, milk and honey mixed, signings with the cross on the forehead, anointings with oil and of clothing in new garments.[79] It was, in one word, incarnational. Alpha stands in stark contrast to this. Its aim, in Sandy Millar's words, of 'stripping the gospel down to its bare essentials'[80] in order to make it accessible to the non-churched includes the use of simplified language, a simplified theology and a removal of ritual and symbols.[81]

In short, while Gumbel claims that Alpha is only part one of a two-year programme with the aim of bringing participants to 'spiritual maturity',[82] my empirical data revealed that it fails to do so in two main ways: it misses out and misorders key elements of the initiation process.[83] It therefore fails its own best intentions in its attempt to combine mission and spiritual formation. In contrast, the catechumenal process provides a deeper, fuller and more enduring and sustaining way of holding together evangelism and spiritual formation.

Of the four basic texts for Anglican initiation[84] – the Lord's Prayer, the Apostles' Creed, the Summary of the Law and the Beatitudes – Alpha and its follow-on courses misses out the Creed.[85] And compared with the modern catechumenate[86] there are other important areas that get scant attention: Creation; the Old Testament; historical Jesus; the Ascension; eschatology;

---

[76] Macquarrie 1997:71-72.

[77] On this see Cocksworth 1993, 2007; Colwell 2005; Dearborn 2003; Stackhouse 2004.

[78] Dearborn 2003:39; see also Cocksworth 2007:145; Lee 1986.

[79] Kavanagh 1978:65.

[80] Cited in Gumbel 2001g:22.

[81] Cf. Duffy 1992; Lyon 2000:148; Earey and Headley 2002; Kreider 2007. While this might not be self-evidently necessary, if the church is genuinely committed to making disciples, an embodied spirituality is vital for the retention and maturing of converts.

[82] Gumbel 2003a:10.

[83] Of course, elements that are missed out of the Alpha programme, like sacramental initiation, are included within HTB's ecclesial setting. However, such elements were stripped away from Alpha when it evolved into a rationalised, standardised and efficient commodity.

[84] See *On the Way* (1995) and *Common Worship: Initiation Services* (1998:187).

[85] The Lord's Prayer and the Summary of the Law are briefly covered on Alpha, while the Beatitudes are in *Challenging Lifestyle* (Gumbel 2001), although very few churches conduct any of Gumbel's follow-on courses.

[86] See Ball and Grundy 2000; cf. Kreider 2007.

public worship, including the shape of the Eucharist and other services; Church as one, holy, catholic and apostolic; Church ministry, including the place of bishops, priests and deacons (or equivalent); authority, including ordained and laity and how it is exercised; ethics; and interfaith dialogue. Some of these issues have been addressed in Mike Lloyd's recent book *Café Theology*, published by AI.[87] However, as yet, this has not become a part of Alpha's two-year programme of education.[88]

Alpha shares with many Evangelicals a suspicion of set prayers, avoidance of traditional liturgy or creeds, and, unlike the catechumenate, there is no connection with the church's yearly cycle and liturgical calendar, which could actually provide greater breadth and balance to one's journey of faith.[89] As such, on Alpha and its follow-on courses, there is a lack of *celebrations* or milestones within the ongoing worship of the Church, to affirm a person's journey of faith. In the catechumenate, these celebrations are not confined purely to those going through the initiation process. These 'rites on the way' are ecclesial events, providing an opportunity for all the baptised to continually explore as a community the riches of baptism and to re-examine and renew their own discipleship.[90] Having a communal dimension is an essential part of initiation.[91] The de-churched, those whose faith has come alive later in life, should be encouraged to make some public form of declaration of that faith. For example, for those already baptised as infants, a rite of re-affirmation of one's baptismal commitment can be significant.[92]

One of the consequences of a frail ecclesiology is a downgrading of the importance of the institutional life of the Church. As the Anglican doctrinal report, *We Believe in the Holy Spirit*, observes:

> Openness to change, vitality, warmth and surprise all need to be balanced by continuity, regularity, stability and rationality. In other words, structure and form

---

[87] Lloyd 2005.

[88] Another positive sign of greater theological depth is the HTB sponsored St Paul's School of Theology (see www.htb.org.uk/sptc).

[89] In *Natural Symbols*, anthropologist Mary Douglas (2003) describes the loss of ritual which has led to the private internalising of religious experience. This trend includes, 'a denunciation not only of irrelevant rituals, but of ritualism as such; exaltation of the inner experience and denigration of its standardised expressions; preference for intuitive and instant forms of knowledge; rejection of mediating institutions, rejection of any tendency to allow habit to provide the basis of a new symbolic system' (Douglas 2003:21).

[90] *Common Worship* 1998; Johnson 1999:348, 372.

[91] Carey 1986:17.

[92] See *Common Worship: Initiation Services* 1998.

are as important as the living content; both should be understood as the work of the one and the same Spirit.[93]

Ritual and rites of passage hold a very important part of initiation and, as Abraham argues, when baptism is ignored, as it largely has been within Evangelical revivalist campaigns, substitutes have been invented or borrowed to take its place.[94] This is seen in Charles Finney's 'new measure' where the 'anxious seat' acts as a public manifestation of becoming a Christian.[95] Finney's weak and pragmatic conception of baptism is extremely significant. By replacing baptism, 'evangelists have lost the richness of grace provided by the sacraments of the church'.[96] As noted in Chapter 2 (§2.1.8), although Alpha shies away from sacramental teaching, an experience of the Holy Spirit on the Alpha Weekend acts as a sort of surrogate form of initiation. Yet it is the stress on immediacy that has brought a weakening of convictions about sacramental grace and has led to 'a general amnesia concerning the central drama of the gospel'.[97] While Alpha and its follow-on courses create the appropriate theological and experiential context for the inclusion of sacramental initiation, it instead provides a non-sacramental alternative.[98] Gunton critiques this sort of 'laser beam' theology that offers an immediate experience of the divine based upon pure feeling.[99] Yet the stress on a purely 'inner work' is a form of gnosticism.[100] Wright argues, critiquing John Stott's comment in Nottingham, that it is not enough to be 'Bible people' and 'Gospel people'; Evangelicals must also be 'Church people'.[101] Justification, discussed below, is to be understood in the context of the historical people of God and cannot be separated from the covenant signs of baptism and the Eucharist.[102]

2.2 Conversionism

The last area in this section that I wish to highlight is that of the narrow focus that Evangelical conversion has taken in contrast to the catechumenate, where

---

[93] Report 1991b:55.

[94] Abraham 1989:130-31.

[95] Finney c1835.

[96] Abraham 1989:131; see also Finn 1997; Webber 2003:49-53.

[97] Stackhouse 2004:125.

[98] Peter Versteeg comments that the rejection of religion in Charismatic spirituality 'leads to a religiosity in which the emotional life of individuals is sacralised' (cited in Kay 2007:169-70).

[99] Gunton 1992:78. For example, Olson (2003:167) points out that at the heart of Evangelical spirituality is 'the personal relationship of immediacy between the repentant sinner's soul and the merciful God of forgiveness, comfort and strength'.

[100] Lee 1986.

[101] Wright 1980:34.

[102] See also Küng 1964:245; Häring 1978:218; Smail 1998:166.

there is an integral link between evangelism and discipleship. One of the four attributes Bebbington assigns to evangelicals is conversionism,[103] and it only takes a cursory review of *Alpha News* to see how significant it is for the course. Despite numerous calls from within the Anglican Church to recognise the changing mission context within the UK, it has mostly been Evangelicals, and courses such as Alpha, that have acted to any great extent on these challenges. The difficulty is when evangelism takes precedence over all else that the church does. As Abraham notes, 'it ignores the primary horizon of the kingdom of God within which evangelism, social action, pastoral care and all else that the church does and must ultimately be set'.[104] And if Alpha is to be run as recommended, three times a year, for most churches this leaves little time or energy for anything else. It also means that with such a focus on evangelism, many converts have not owned the intellectual claims of the Christian faith nor been supported in their spiritual and moral formation.[105] This is compounded by Evangelicals' suspicion of liturgy. As noted above (§1.4), the catechumenate included a 'handing over of the Creed', which the candidate, with the help of the sponsor, had to learn and then repeat in a ceremony called the 'giving back of the Creed'. At St A1 (Week 10), the speaker quoted part of the creed, 'We believe in one holy catholic and apostolic Church' and asked, 'Has anyone heard this before?' The two helpers and one Anglican guest raised their hand, but it is noteworthy that both the leaders (L1 and L2), who had been Christian for three years, and Alpha convert (H1), who had been a Christian for over one year, did not recognise this at all. This obviously reflects St A's non-traditional liturgical services.

One of the more serious failings of the Alpha programme was the discrepancy between Gumbel's vision of Alpha being part one of a two-year process of initiation, and with what was happening 'on the ground'. The overwhelming situation for guests post-Alpha contradicted this. And as noted in Chapter 6, in a modern, pluralist, mobile and individualistic society, plausibility needs to be continually maintained through conversation. To repeat Rambo's comment: 'Conversion is precarious; it must be defended, nurtured, supported and affirmed. It needs community, confirmation and concurrence'.[106] It seems as though AI lacks the patience or know-how for the lengthy and demanding process of catechesis and spiritual formation. This is where the Emmaus Course, which is essentially a modern catechumenate, has the edge over Alpha.[107]

Alpha and its follow-on courses would certainly gain in breadth and depth

---

[103] Bebbington 1989. The other three attributes are biblicism, activism and crucicentrism.

[104] Abraham 1989:86.

[105] Cf. Warren 1995:23.

[106] Rambo 1993:167.

[107] See Cottrell et al. 1996.

by listening to the experiences and insights that the revival of the catechumenate has brought.

3. Alpha's Theology and Spirituality

In this section I shall pick up on some of the salient theological themes that have arisen in this book. First of all, I shall assess Alpha's ecclesiology; then Gumbel's claim that the course includes the basics upon which all Christians agree; next, Alpha's soteriology and the doctrine of assurance; then, worship on Alpha will be discussed, and lastly various approaches to contextualisation.

3.1 Ecclesiology

Gumbel describes Alpha as something of an opportunity to look at the basics of the Christian faith. However, when attempting an ecumenically accepted course, questions are bound to arise over content. What elements of the Christian faith are viewed as the basics depends on one's Christian tradition, and it is at the level of ecclesiology where the heart of the criticism of Alpha lies. There is no ecclesially objective standpoint: Alpha's 'basics', and those who criticise them, must always be seen as something derived from a particular viewpoint. Liberal churchmen accuse it of a lack of any real social mandate and for its prescriptive theology; Catholics and mainline Protestant churches are dissatisfied with its lack of sacramental theology; conservative Evangelicals are unhappy with the lack of emphasis on sin and repentance; and while most of the above groups are concerned with an over-emphasis on the Holy Spirit, the Pentecostals have asked for *more* emphasis, especially on glossolalia. So far, the Orthodox Church has kept a cool distance.[108] So, there is a contingency about any evaluation of Alpha. For example, as noted in Chapter 3 (§2), Brian's critique is based upon a liberal Anglican perspective, and he judges Alpha based upon this 'normative' position. However, that does not render the ecclesiology at work on Alpha as representing something illegitimate. The problem is not so much that Alpha does not have an ecclesiology; it is just that Gumbel is not explicit about its (low church) ecclesiology.[109] As Wilson asserts: 'Evangelicals have an implicit, uncriticised ecclesiology smuggled into our life through marketing strategies, programmes and practices. Our ecclesiology in these instances is utilitarian.'[110]

---

[108] Metropolitan Philaret, Patriarch of Belarus, spoke at HTB of Alpha being 'important' (*Alpha News* November–February 2005/6). An Orthodox monastery in Russia has also begun running Alpha.

[109] See Olson's (2003) attempt to make Evangelical ecclesiology explicit. This includes the importance of a commitment to orthodoxy and orthopathy, voluntarism, non-hierarchical church polity and autonomy of local congregations.

[110] Wilson 2002:192.

Wilson is correct in highlighting Evangelicals' pragmatic utilitarian 'ecclesiology'. HTB has imbibed some of the elements of the Church Growth Movement,[111] with its pragmatist 'microwave solution' to numerical growth, including use of the Homogeneous Unit Principle.[112] As described in Chapter 1, the mechanistic 'ecclesiology' that underlies this movement views the congregation rather like a machine implementing reliable formulas for gaining converts. As a machine, the congregation, by grasping these 'formulas' and adjusting practices accordingly, will grow.[113] Hence, all that a church needs to do in order to grow is to conduct Alpha according to the prescribed recipe. Of course, Gumbel views Alpha's success through its being undergirded, or fuelled, by prayer,[114] although such language also suggests a utilitarian perception of prayer.

The concept of the Alpha recipe has an analogous relationship with Kenneth Copeland and Kenneth Hagin's idea of positive and negative confession.[115] Making a 'positive confession' has the power to cause things to happen. An example of negative confession might be a person going to see a doctor when feeling ill, rather than having faith. From the perspective of the Faith Teaching advocates, they had an ingenious device because it meant that their teaching was, in Popperian terms, unfalsifiable. In other words, when anything went wrong, it was not the Faith Teaching or the system that was at fault: it was because the followers did not follow the rules and make a positive confession. In his use of the Alpha recipe, Gumbel tends to use a similar technique. Whenever Alpha does not go well, it is never the fault of Gumbel or Alpha: it is because the instructions were not followed properly. Ireland notes this:

> [Gumbel and Millar were] rather defensive: they had an answer prepared for every point and did not give any ground – either no change was necessary, or they had already made slight amendments here and there, or *the problem identified was the fault of the user*…They were very keen to encourage and support us in making Alpha work at local level, but the core product was clearly non-negotiable. I left with the feeling that my research would have little appreciable impact on their thinking or on the future shape of Alpha.[116]

---

[111] McGavran 1955, 1970; Winter and Hawthorne 1992.

[112] For some of the issues raised over this principle, see Cray (2004:108-109). For a critique, see Abraham (1989) and Newbigin (1995:Ch.9).

[113] Hopewell 1988:23-26.

[114] Gumbel 2004.

[115] I owe this insight to Andrew Walker (personal interview 24 May 2006). For a critique of the faith teaching, see Dan McConnell's *A Different Gospel* (Peabody, MA.: Hendrickson, 1995).

[116] Ireland 2000:38, emphasis added. Meadow's (2007:408) locates the problem in our technological culture which holds to the illusion that the missionary traditions of a church like HTB, which have formed over a long and arduous history, 'can be reduced

Further, AI's obsession with numbers, its rationalising principles of efficiency and predictability, and the mechanics of continually running Alpha three times per year brings with it a serious danger of lapsing into an instrumentalism.[117] For example, what happens to Alpha guests who do not convert by the end of the course? Are they discarded when the church continues its rolling programme of another Alpha course? The Alpha administrators at St C had no official follow up for the two non-churched guests (G1, G3), one of whom had converted on the course, and they had 'forgotten' to follow up one de-churched guest whose faith was 'refreshed' (G3). And at another course (St D), the church neither contacted guests after Alpha, nor invited them at the end of the course to join the church's weekly student group. Those who were not regular churchgoers were left in limbo despite expressing an interest in continuing their spiritual journeys. This indicates that the churches primarily focus is on conversion rather than to a commitment to discipleship or to deepening and strengthening conversion.

AI staff members have also experienced the results of Alpha's depersonalising machine, too busy with the running of its programmes. Two senior staff members at HTB described the instrumentalist way they were treated while working for Alpha. One of them referred to the similarities in working for Alpha with previous experience in the business world where people were 'useable' for the greater task: 'I had fulfilled my function and was of no further use'.[118] The other staff member expressed similar hurt and also noticed how, 'Every Alpha Administrator [at HTB] had ended the job burnt out'.[119] And this is in a church with extensive personnel, financial and business resources. This seems to be one of the consequences of following Gumbel's instructions 'to run *at least* three [Alpha] courses a year'.[120] Further, most churches lack the human resources of HTB, and as a result find difficulty in recruiting appropriate small group leaders. Hunt also discovered the disenchantment of Alpha leaders who became exhausted after running Alpha for some time. He writes: 'The implications for Alpha is that a rationalised and standardised product reduces the course workers to minute parts of the great machinery of HTB – where potentially people become unemotional cogs.'[121]

This ecclesiology has serious problems. As Viv Thomas writes, 'People are not pieces of technology to be slotted into an organisational machine; they are reflections of God himself.'[122] Part of the problem lies in the managerialisation

---

to a set of universal laws and principles which, if reemployed exactly, will reproduce the same effect anywhere'.

[117] Cf. Abraham 1989:77 and the Church Growth Movement.

[118] Informal interview on 3 September 2004.

[119] Informal interview on 4 September 2004.

[120] Gumbel 2001g:66, emphasis in original.

[121] Hunt 2004:156.

[122] Thomas 2002:124.

of the church with 'leaders', rather than pastors or priests, who are caught up in the running of an efficient and 'successful' organisation. Croft traces the roots of this to the Church Growth Movement and especially Wimber's influence in the UK. Using insights from secular management theory, leaders become more of a Chief Executive Officer and less of a pastor.[123] Ironically, the obsession with numbers and growth is counterproductive. Stackhouse notes the 'faddism' of the pragmatic search for the appropriate key to unlock the harvest, which has led to an unchecked activism in which issues of spiritual formation are subsumed by categories of functionality.[124] He suggests that sustainable holy living demands 'organic, not mechanic, images of growth...Ironically, we discover growth occurs not by adopting the latest cure-all from somewhere around the world, but by relinquishing the numbers game altogether and attending to the larger frame of God in Christ ruling and saving'.[125]

In sum, *pace* Wilson, Evangelical 'ecclesiology', or way of ordering itself, is profoundly utilitarian. However, there is a more significant way of understanding Evangelicalism. It can be defined not so much as an *ecclesiology* but rather as an international transdenominational *piety*; a movement rather than an ecclesiology, which is why it can accommodate itself to virtually any form of church order – including that of Roman Catholicism.[126] So, while HTB itself is an Anglican Church, Alpha has a Pietist ecclesiology based upon an *ecclesiola in ecclesia*, small churches of regenerate believers, within the 'mixed church'.[127] As the vicar at St E described: 'we do have, primarily through Alpha, a church growing within a church' (St E LA1). French Alpha Adviser, Florence de Leyritz, also noted this difficulty in French Catholic contexts. She suggested that 'Alpha is like a bomb within a church' in the way that it touches all other aspects of church life.[128]

Any visible forms of church, the ordering of ministry and governance of the church, and its mode and administration of the sacraments, are viewed as adiaphora, irrelevant 'externals' secondary to what really constitutes the *esse* of the church: regeneration of the Holy Spirit. Thus the church is not constituted

---

[123] Croft 1999:Ch.2. For a discussion of leadership within a trinitarian matrix, see Thomas (2002).

[124] Stackhouse 2004:29.

[125] Stackhouse 2003a:248-49. Tomlin (2002:102) thus suggests that it is better to put the question of church *health* before church *growth*. See also Booker's (2003:Ch.9) discussion of 'natural church development'.

[126] Hindmarsh 2003; McGrath 1993:13. Walker (1983:105) makes a similar point about Pentecostalism, describing it as an experience rather than an institution. McGrath (1993) argues that Anglicanism offers a vision of the church which Evangelicals can and should embrace.

[127] Hindmarsh (2003) locates the origins of this in Philip Jakob Spener's (1635-1707) Pietism. As such, Alpha stands aligned with the Moravians and the Methodists who sought to renew mainline churches.

[128] Interview on 16 December 2004.

by ecclesiastical authority but by a mystical (invisible) church with an elective affinity of a spiritual sort.[129] Lee contends that this is yet another sign of gnosticism.[130] Yet if one rejects visible order, at some stage the vacuum will be filled with some other form of visible organisation and become vulnerable to a popular cult of personality and rhetorical persuasion.[131] While Gumbel describes the church as the body of Christ, there is no acknowledgement of the difficulty of locating the 'head', or where the source of authority lies. In terms of Dulles's five models of church, Alpha's ecclesiology fit 'mystical communion' and 'herald'.[132] Dulles's point, of course, was that *all* of these models had to be held together. The church is too complex to be reduced to one model. Two out of five means that Alpha's ecclesiology remains deficient. Further, settling for a vision of an 'invisible' church results in a docetic, idealised and primarily eschatological reality, which means that there is no great duty to seek visible unity. As Buchanan argues, if our 'oneness in Christ' is solely 'invisible' or eschatological, we are in breach of the Gospel, which stands as a corrective to any forming of a 'church' which is monocultural or monochrome, tribal or ethnic, national or denominational (John 17.20-23).[133] Galatians (3:28) paints a particular picture of the Church:

> There is no longer Jew or Greek, there is no longer slave or free, there is no longer male and female; for all of you are one in Christ Jesus.

With all of the complexities, messiness and power struggles such a vision of a church carries, as the church in Corinth reveals, such an ecclesiology stands as a critique to the Homogeneous Unit Principle, despite its pragmatic appeal as being the most 'effective'. The use of such principles merely mirrors contemporary culture and is a symptom of illness of which the church must be healed.[134] In his description of a eucharistic community in terms of local gatherings of those united simply by geography, Zizioulas writes:

---

[129] The irony of evangelical ecclesiology, Hindmarsh (2003:34) comments, 'is that while celebrating the spiritual union of all the truly regenerate, the movement itself was dogged by separatism'.

[130] Lee 1986. Farrow (1999) notes that it is through ecclesiology that Irenaeus constructs his whole anti-gnostic edifice. The church is an ontologically unique community, not a collection of spiritual individuals (Farrow 1999:70). Lee (1986:Ch.11) argues that the 'degnosticising' of Protestantism includes the preaching of grace, the 'freedom of authority', acceptance of the lifelong pilgrimage, being born again into the Church, an affirmation of ordinary Christianity and restoration of ritual.

[131] Hindmarsh 2003:35-36.

[132] Dulles 1988. The other three models are 'institution', 'sacrament' and 'servant'.

[133] Buchanan 1998:97-98.

[134] Volf 1998:18.

...groups or assemblies formed on the basis of a particular culture, class, profession or age should learn to regard themselves *not* as Churches, and be taught to seek the experience of the *Church* only in gatherings where *all* ages, sexes, professions, cultures etc. meet, for this is what the Gospel promises us to be the Kingdom of God: a place where all the natural and cultural divisions are transcended.[135]

3.1.1 AUTHORITY

Returning to the question of authority, if there is no ecclesially neutral perspective, who decides what are the basics of the Christian faith? Where, or with whom, does authority lie? For the Roman Catholic Church, this is relatively straightforward. One knows who the Pope is and where he is. The difficulty with the Evangelical tradition is that there are multiple 'popes' and it is not always entirely clear who they are! As noted in Chapter 3, Brian raises the question of authority and Alpha's 'basics'.[136] He argues that Nicky Gumbel is essentially Alpha's pope and that it is he who decides what the basics are, viz. an Evangelical–Charismatic, ethically conservative form of Christian faith. Criticism will be courteously listened to but, as Ward,[137] Percy[138] and Ireland[139] discovered, disregarded. But is there any reason why Alpha should be apologetic about producing a course that reflects its Evangelical–Charismatic theology? None at all, apart from the fact, argues Brian, that HTB portrays Alpha as being neutral in relation to all Christian traditions.[140] One particularly astute guest (St D G1) commented on this:

> It was definitely an introduction to a particular kind of Christianity and that for me was the most difficult thing. Christianity can be an awful lot broader than this...I was aware that this was very much organised by one church originally and it all seems to rotate around this quite charismatic figure...I think for it to hide its roots to the extent it did was misleading.

What is Alpha to do with the conflicting criticism that comes from all angles? First of all, it is not entirely fair to accuse Alpha of not listening to previous criticisms. David Payne, former Alpha for Catholics Adviser, described how Gumbel went out of his way in order to try to understand the difficulties that the course raised for Catholics.[141] Gumbel's friendship with Raniero Cantalamessa, preacher to the papal household, is well known. Second, it could

---

[135] Zizioulas 1985:255, emphasis in original.

[136] Brian (2002:31-44) relates this question to the post-modern concern about hidden issues of power. He views his Foucauldian task as to lay bear the carriers of power; to criticise the workings of institutions which appear to be both neutral and independent.

[137] Ward 1998.

[138] Percy 1997a.

[139] Ireland 2000; 2003.

[140] Brian 2003.

[141] Interview on 23 August 2004.

legitimately be argued, why should HTB listen to criticism from other churches at all? The course was devised by HTB for its particular context. It is only because of the interest and demand from other churches that HTB has made Alpha available more widely. HTB members have been extraordinarily generous in doing this, pouring in their time, energy and a huge amount of finance. If those from other traditions have difficulties with the course, they have the freedom to develop their own. And yet, from Alpha's passive beginnings, AI has become highly proactive in attempting to be not only an evangelism course – but *the* evangelism course. And this, I would suggest, requires dialogue and adaptation, of inculturation (see §4 below).

3.2 Soteriology

Since the primary aim of Alpha is conversion, I shall comment on its soteriology, a subject I highlighted in Chapter 2.[142] While 'becoming a Christian' on Alpha involves the matrix of repentance, faith, receiving the Holy Spirit and baptism, the main stress of initiation is on an experience, a charismatic encounter with the Holy Spirit, which then brings assurance of salvation. Part of the difficulty in locating Alpha's soteriology is because its explicit (substitutionary) atonement theology contrasts with its theoretical emphasis on process, although the normative experience in AI discourse is the crisis model. As such, it is subject to some of the difficulties inherent in this tradition.

Penal substitution has been critiqued by various theologians.[143] Mennonite, Weaver, argues that it places violence within the ontology of the Godhead and focuses on Jesus's death while neglecting what Jesus said and did throughout his life;[144] liberation theologians have critiqued it for spiritualising salvation;[145] and feminist theologians challenge the traditional image of sacrifice because it is in danger of being invoked to exploit and oppress the vulnerable.[146]

As discussed in Chapter 2 (§ 2.1.3), the doctrine has been critiqued from within Evangelicalism. Hans Boersma argues:

...the Calvinist tradition's understanding of penal substitution fell prey to juridicising, individualising and de-historicising tendencies that led to a view of

---

[142] For an outline of thirteen soteriological models, see McIntyre 1992. See also Ford 1999; Gunton 1988; White 1991.

[143] For a classic account of penal substitution see Hodge 1960.

[144] Weaver 2001.

[145] Bacote 2002; Bonino 1975; Conn 1978; Gutiérrez 1974; Wallis 1986.

[146] See *Contemporary Doctrine Classics* 2005:291-92 and 366-67. For a defence of the doctrine, see Holmes 2005. Holmes' main reason for defending this doctrine, as just one metaphor among many, is because it takes the reality of sin seriously. See also Grudem 1994:Ch.27; Jeffery, Ovey and Sach 2007; Stott 1996.

the cross dominated by a strict economy of exchange that obscured the hospitality of the cross.[147]

As a result, the atonement has been reduced to law court scenes and notions of personal forgiveness that limits the divine–human relationship to judicial categories.[148] Fiddes also critiques penal substitution, arguing that legal illustrations lose the personal nature of forgiveness and depends upon a strong individualisation of Father and Son as independent subjects.[149] On Alpha, Gumbel uses a law court analogy[150] and describes how the judge, a former friend of the criminal, offers to pay the cost of the sentence by writing out a cheque. Gumbel returns to this analogy at the end of his talk with an actual cheque written out:

> I have here a cheque, and in effect this is what God offers to every single one of us. It's forgiveness, freedom, cleansing, reconciliation, eternal life. That's what I've written under the 'pay' bit! And then by the pound sign I've just put 'All the riches of heaven'. It's signed 'The Lord Jesus Christ', because it was Jesus who made this possible. And I put today's date, because it's today that he makes the offer. The place here, I've left blank, so that you can put *your* name there, because it's to *you* that God makes this offer.

The judicial emphasis here is quite clear as is the individualising nature of such atonement theology.[151] Indeed, the close alignment between Evangelicalism and the Enlightenment can be seen in its taking the modern concept of the person as an autonomous individual; an atomistic attitude whereby everyone defines his or her purposes in individual terms but which ultimately fragments human life.[152] This is in contrast to earlier non-Western concepts of the person seen in terms of the place in the community.[153] By taking the Western modern concept of the individual, Evangelicalism has thus emphasised individual conversion and commitment, after which the individual might then join a church. As a result, religion is engaged in by individuals,[154] with little notion of the catholicity of the faith.[155] What is most important is wholehearted personal commitment. As Charles Taylor outlines, one of the central points common to all Reformers was their rejection of the notion of ecclesial mediation of divine

---

[147] Boersma 2004:19.

[148] Boersma 2004:164.

[149] Fiddes 1989; see also Travis's (1994) carefully nuanced analysis of *hilasterion*.

[150] Gumbel 2001e:47-48.

[151] Individualising of sin is not just a problem for Evangelicals. Baum (1978:286) points to the doctrine of original sin and the Catholic Church's confessional as being excessively individualistic.

[152] Taylor 1992.

[153] Bebbington 1989.

[154] Bellah 1985.

[155] Carey 1986:10; Hindmarsh 2002:65.

grace. This flowed from the most fundamental principle of the Reformers, that salvation was exclusively the work of God. The emphasis was on a man or woman's inability to do anything to earn salvation. Even faith is a gift of God. However, such faith required 'an outright rejection of the Catholic understanding of the sacred, and hence also of the Church and its mediating role'.[156] Along with the Mass went the whole notion of the sacred in medieval Catholicism: of special places, times or actions where the power of God is more intensely present and can be approached by humans. Protestant churches swept away pilgrimages, veneration of relics, visits to holy places, and a vast panorama of traditional Catholic rituals and pieties.[157] Gone were the bright colours of Catholic churches; Reformed churches white-washed their walls, which 'spoke to the worshipper of the light of reason'[158] and focused on the contemplation of the *Word*. Thus, for the Reformers, salvation was no longer mediated by the church, its clergy, or its saints. And where a mediated salvation is no longer possible, the personal commitment of the believer becomes all important. One no longer belonged to the saved by one's connection to a wider order sustaining a sacramental life, but by one's wholehearted personal adhesion. For Catholicism, Taylor writes:

> I am a passenger in the ecclesial ship on its journey to God. But for Protestantism, there can be no passengers. This is because there is no ship in the Catholic sense, no common movement carrying humans to salvation. Each believer rows his or her own boat.[159]

The Evangelical call for a wholehearted 'personal conversion' makes it difficult to understand the church in a genuinely corporate way, other than as a cumulative reality made up of many individual Christians. Although Schleiermacher's distinction that Protestantism 'makes the individual's relation to the Church dependent on his relation to Christ', while Catholicism 'makes the individual's relation to Christ dependent of his relation to the Church'[160] rather dichotomises the relationship,[161] he does make an important point. Evangelical ecclesiology tends to be fiercely individualistic, with 'each

---

[156] Taylor 1992:217. O'Donovan (1986) describes the difficulty that the Reformers had with the medieval doctrine of sacraments, which was in the attribution of faith to *sacramental* grace, rather than to the proclamation of the gospel. 'Faith comes by hearing, and hearing by the word of Christ' (Rom. 10.17).

[157] Taylor 1992:217; see also Duffy 1992.

[158] Cocksworth 1993:61.

[159] Taylor 1992:217.

[160] Schleiermacher 1928:§24.

[161] Cocksworth (2007:134) highlights the 'perichoretic quality' in Gospel, Church and Spirit, each implying the other.

individual standing by himself'.[162] Such individualism contributes further, argues Beaton, to the fragmentation within post-modern culture, with its emphasis on the local, contextual and particular.[163] Yet the personal narrative is but one element of the overarching narrative of God's people, into which an individual has been incorporated.[164] As Walls points out, in the context of the expansion of the early church, 'the influence of Jesus not only produces group responses; it works by means of groups, and is expressed in groups'.[165]

The third element of Boersma's critique of penal substitution, along with the juridicising and individualising tendencies, is a de-historicising. History gets sidelined in favour of a philosophical heritage from Plato, Augustine and Descartes, the outcome of which is an 'overvaluing of abstract logical connections between ideas and an undervaluing of everything else'.[166] N. T. Wright points out the similarities between Evangelicals and Bultmann, with the latter's 'emphasis on faith as experience unconnected with history, his existentialist call for decision, his view of justification as the establishment of a personal relationship with God, his wedge between justification and the historical people of God'.[167] Gumbel's above quote (p.212) certainly has a Bultmannian feel to it. The process involved on Alpha tends to mean giving guests the opportunity to have this existential, personal crisis experience. Yet the stress on crisis fails to do justice to the complex, varied and messy nature of spiritual formation.[168] Taking the doctrine of justification out of the context of the covenant and the historical people of God, Wright argues, is the reason why Evangelicals have a frail ecclesiology, an inward spirituality with a suspicion of outward performances, churchgoing and sacraments.[169]

Penal substitution necessarily carries a strong emphasis on the cross, what Bebbington calls crucicentrism,[170] in which the 'person' and 'work' of Christ become increasingly separated from each other, with Christology being made subservient to soteriology.[171] The missiological implications of overcoming poverty and tackling unfair socio-economic problems and working for political change tend to be ignored, or viewed as an added extra, the main task being to secure the individual's eternal salvation. Indeed, the stress on Jesus as 'personal saviour' is linked to the defence of the political status quo; it thus has significant political consequences despite the Evangelical's plea that their

---

[162] Schleiermacher 1928:§24; see also Tillich 1964:232. For an attempt at an Evangelical ecclesiology see Miroslav Volf (1998) and John Stackhouse (2003b).
[163] Beaton 2003:218; see also Gunton 1993.
[164] Beaton 2003:221.
[165] Walls 2002:10.
[166] Gunton 1988:17.
[167] Wright 1980:33.
[168] See Stackhouse 2004:83-90.
[169] Wright 1980:33.
[170] Bebbington 1989:14-17.
[171] Bosch 2003:394.

message is non-political.[172] In contrast, by stressing a salvation *for* the world and *within* history, liberation theology has brought a critique of such an over-spiritualised soteriology.[173] Gustavo Gutiérrez challenges the spiritualisation of conversion:

> Our conversion process is affected by the socio-economic, political, cultural and human environment in which it occurs. Without a change in these structures, there is no authentic conversion...Only thus, and not through purely interior and spiritual attitudes, will the 'new man' arise from the ashes of the 'old'.[174]

In contrast to a transactional view of the atonement, with its main emphasis on individual guilt, forgiveness, holiness, and little sense of corporate or institutional guilt,[175] Irenaeus's theology of recapitulation stresses Christ as being the representative of all humanity.[176] Boersma instead refers to 'penal representation' rather than penal substitution, and places it within an Irenaean framework.[177] In other words, there is a substitutionary dimension to Christ's death, but not in the sense of a straightforward exchange between Christ and certain individuals, but rather of someone representing all others.[178] The starting point is thus not the penal aspect of the atonement but the hospitable eschatology that is realised in principle in Jesus's resurrection, a hospitality which the Church in turn is called upon to display. This recapitulation thus indicates an identity between Christ and the Church. Emphasising the process and eschatological nature of *theosis*, Orthodox theologian Kallistos Ware prefers to describe salvation not as a single event, as a 'successful termination...[or as] I am saved', but rather, 'I am being saved'.[179] It is a soteriology more in line with Roman Catholic[180] and Anglican understanding,[181] with (infant) baptism as the beginning of a lifelong movement or journey to

---

[172] Baum 1978:290.

[173] This narrow soteriology is another feature of gnosticism. Withdrawal from engagement with the world, and, conversely worldliness, are both repugnant to a eucharistic world-view (Farrow 1999:72-73).

[174] Gutiérrez 1974:205. See Pannenberg's (1985) critique of the particularly Marxist framework of liberation theology.

[175] A theme that gets scant attention in charismatic worship (Begbie 1991:235).

[176] Boersma 2004:167.

[177] This is similar to N. T. Wright's (1988) 'reconstitution'.

[178] Boersma 2004:177; cf. Kelly 1958:173-74; Pelikan 1971:141-55.

[179] Ware 1996:6-7 and 14.

[180] 'The faith required for Baptism is not a perfect and mature faith, but a beginning that is called to develop...Preparation for Baptism leads only to the threshold of new life' (Catechism 1253, 1254, see www.vatican.va/archive/catechism).

[181] See *Common Worship: Initiation Services* (1998). As Bradshaw (2001:161) notes, *Common Worship* recognises that 'a person's spiritual journey does not always fall into one pattern', and places baptism as the theological centre-piece around which other rites are clustered.

discipleship, incorporation into Christ and his Church, and into the participation of his mission to the world. Baptism then becomes a prelude to faith, having an inescapable proleptic character because it is tied to the future of one's life for its completion. This means that churches must be as concerned with postbaptismal *mystagogy* as they are with the prebaptismal catechumenate.[182] As discussed above (§2), based upon guests who attend Alpha, rather than the course's soteriology, this is essentially what Alpha is doing. It is helping primarily the churched and open de-churched to re-own their faith, albeit within a Charismatic–Evangelical framework.

3.3 Arminianism[183]

Following on from Gumbel's crisis soteriology, the doctrine of assurance has had a considerable influence on the theology and spirituality of Alpha. Such assurance is vital for the effective proclamation of the gospel. It was this doctrine that inspired the dynamism of the Evangelical movement, the roots of which, as noted in Chapter 2, comes from Enlightenment empiricist philosophy.[184] As noted in Chapter 2, at the introductory evening on Alpha, Gumbel uses the analogy of a television set, drawing a contrast between a set without an aerial (life before becoming a Christian) and one with an aerial (life as a Christian), where the picture becomes clear. The whole of Week 3 on Alpha is dedicated to assurance: how can I be *sure* of my faith. The experiential element of the doctrine is tempered by Gumbel's reference to the 'objective word of God' and the 'work of Jesus'. However, according to the majority of the testimonies in the Alpha resources, the primary reference to assurance is the experience gained on the Alpha weekend. This doctrine was given even stronger emphasis among the churches I researched. The speaker at St B stated:

> You'll know that you know. It's like falling in love (St B Week 3).

The boldest affirmation came at St D. The curate speaker placed great stress on having absolute certainty, and being sure of one's faith:

> We can be absolutely sure of our faith...*there should be no doubt.* Absolutely certain. The Bible says, 'that you may know...' (St D Week 4, emphasis added).

The HTB speaker at St D's weekend also described how things become clear

---

[182] Johnson 1999:379.

[183] Arminianism is an unusual development because, apart from Methodism, most Evangelicals in Britain were Calvinist (see Bebbington 1989). Yet, according to Bebbington (1989:7 and 45), *assurance* was a doctrine that even Calvinists were attached to, although, believing in the perseverance of the saints, they necessarily held that the Christian is sure not only of his present state but of his future share in glory too.

[184] Bebbington 1989:42.

when one becomes a Christian.

> Before we are Christians, it is like we have a veil over our head, a lack of clarity. [The speaker then referred to Gumbel's television–aerial analogy.] This gives a proper picture; the sound is perfect. There is sharpness and clarity in all we do as Christians. The veil is taken away when we turn to God (St D Alpha weekend).

There are some difficulties with the doctrine of assurance. Firstly, it stresses closure, a termination, rather than a journey that is open-ended.[185] As such there is little space here for doubters or for those on a spiritual journey whose faith is, as *Common Worship* puts it, 'limited and unarticulated'.[186] Viv Thomas writes:

> The potential for splitting the self is clearly a possibility, with all of the resulting personal trauma and creation of organisational fantasy. If you do not have a strong inward assurance of salvation it is possible to create a fake so that social inclusion will be maintained.[187]

Further, how does one understand the Spirit's work in 'low' feeling stages, particularly where the Spirit is associated with the 'feeling of assurance'. What about the possibility of genuinely Christ-like dereliction?[188] As described in Chapter 6, contemporary people inhabit an extremely complex situation with increased competition between a plurality of plausibility structures. The television analogy that Gumbel describes, of 'clear and distinct pictures',[189] which brings assurance and certainty, contrasts with the bewildering array of competing signals. Such over-realised eschatology also contrasts with the picture painted by St Paul (1 Cor. 13.12), which highlights a more modest Christian epistemology. In Alpha's stress on assurance, of *knowing*, we see the tendency common among Evangelicals towards over-stressing the cataphatic, with a neglect of the apophatic.[190] The result is an inability to incorporate awe, majesty and mystery.[191]

---

[185] Mercer (1995) points out that expecting *closure* is problematic for a postmodern because it suggests something other than journey.

[186] Common Worship 1998:200.

[187] Thomas 2002:222.

[188] *We Believe in the Holy Spirit* Report 1991a:31.

[189] Gumbel 2001e:15.

[190] Cataphatic spirituality refers to the positive, affirmative and revelatory nature of theology expressed through creation, redemption, Bible and Creed. Apophatic spirituality emphasises the mysterious and essentially unknowable nature of God (see Davies and Turner 2002; for a recent discussion of 'Christian agnosticism' see Vernon 2006).

[191] Martin 1981:52-55; Thomas 2002:235.

3.4 Liturgia *and Alpha*

HTB is consumed with a passion to make the gospel known to seekers. Therefore, always thinking of the non-churched, their weekly services follow a simple Vineyard liturgy: sung worship, teaching and 'prayer ministry'. Alpha guests are slowly exposed to this style of worship as the course progresses, with the time for sung worship gradually becoming longer, and the style and songs increasingly reflecting the influence of John Wimber. The main characteristic of charismatic worship is intimacy. It is, Walker points out, 'open to the epicletic incoming and indwelling of the Holy Spirit with its concomitant sense of the presence of God'.[192] As Ward writes, '...as the Mass is for Catholics and sermon is for Protestants, so the singing of songs for charismatics'.[193] James Steven describes the cultural backdrop to charismatic worship as being that of

> popular culture developed from the 1960s counter-culture with its emphasis on individual participation and expressiveness, impatience with formality and institutional life and willingness to experiment with new forms of community life.[194]

However, such emphasis on the individual and his or her emotions can be traced much further back, with strong affinities to the Romantic Movement[195] and its reaction to the Enlightenment ideal of disengaged, instrumental reason.[196] This (emotionally) felt presence of God[197] contrasts with the cerebral Evangelicalism of those such as John Stott.

Charismatic worship is existential rather than didactic.[198] The style of such worship involves a flow of uninterrupted worship songs, each taking one more step towards intimacy with God. This is in contrast to the teaching function of hymns in Protestant traditions. By the Alpha weekend, at least in theory, guests are singing songs such as 'Everyday', where the worshipper, as Ward puts it, 'focuses the eyes of their heart towards the object of their love',[199] and, 'Your love is amazing, steady and unchanging...I can feel this love song rising up in me'. Such songs are similar to secular romantic love ballads, which Percy suggests, include a grammar of paternalism and passionate (or quasi-erotic) intimacy.[200] As noted in Chapter 3, critics of Alpha view this element of the

---

[192] Cited in Steven 2002:xiv.

[193] Ward 2005:199.

[194] Steven 2002:170.

[195] Fiddes 1989:9; Bebbington 1989:Ch.7.

[196] Taylor 1992:368-69.

[197] Goldingay 1996.

[198] Stackhouse 2004:55.

[199] Ward 2005.

[200] Percy 1997b. Of course, the same could be said of Teresa of Avila's mystical experiences.

course as a sort of 'charismatic imperialism'.[201] Others have questioned the therapeutic and individualistic nature of such worship.[202] The inclusion of sung worship had a mixed response from guests depending on their religious background (see Chapter 5 §4.2). Some testified to their faith coming alive through such worship while others felt alienated by it. Indeed, for non-churchgoers, it is difficult to sing many of these songs with honesty and integrity.

What about the theology of charismatic worship? Steven's research into charismatic worship includes a theological critique, which also relates to worship on Alpha. He found an implicit orthodox understanding of trinitarian worship, an 'instinctive trinitarianism', with praise and prayer offered 'in the Spirit' to each of the three persons of the Trinity. However, he found an inadequate theology conveyed by the more charismatic elements – the sung worship and 'prayer ministry' – that can be traced back to a failure to locate this worship in the Spirit *through* the Son, to the Father.[203] This included an overemphasis on the triumphant ascended Christ, with a neglect of the incarnate Christ; 'a failure to do justice to Christ's continuing priesthood in his risen humanity'.[204] As a result, the exalted Christ is called upon as the dispenser of spiritual presence or power so that the centre of gravity in the worship is located in the worshippers as opposed to locating worship 'in, with and through the priestly Christ in his offering to the Father'.[205]

Along with the Church Growth Movement and Wimber's pragmatic ecclesiology, which has influenced HTB, a mechanistic pneumatology has also been introduced to HTB and the Alpha course. On Alpha, the Holy Spirit, far from being sovereign, and, unlike references to the wind/spirit (*pneuma*) blowing where it chooses (John 3.8), the Spirit seems to be 'on tap' and 'goes where it is sent'.[206] As Gumbel comments, 'When we ask [the Holy Spirit], he comes'.[207] This has the tendency of undermining the Spirit's freedom and divine hypostasis.[208] Steven writes:

---

[201] Brian 2003; Hunt 2004:54.

[202] Percy 1997a, 2005; Smail 2003:60; Steven 2002:203-207.

[203] Steven 2002; see also Cocksworth 1997.

[204] Steven 2002:191; cf. Smail 1988:206. For example, 'Majesty', 'Open the eyes of my heart Lord...to see You high and lifted up'. These were all sung on Alpha.

[205] Steven 2002:192. Songs exemplifying this perspective on Alpha included, 'Spirit of the living God fall afresh on me', 'Come Lord Jesus (Great is the darkness)', 'Your love is amazing', 'Jesus be the centre/ Be my source be my light, Jesus'.

[206] Smail 1988:134.

[207] Gumbel 2003b.

[208] Smail 1988.

It is also ironic that a movement that was initially fuelled by a protest on behalf of the freedom on the Spirit should be showing tendencies of imprisoning the Spirit within a depersonalised, functional and performative role.[209]

It was such theology that was behind one worship leader's exclamation on an Alpha weekend (St C) as he introduced another song, 'This one should bring out the Holy Spirit!'

On the one hand, Alpha, together with charismatics generally, have brought a refreshing focus on the dynamic and experiential element of being a Christian, together with a genuinely optimistic hope that God's hand is at work in the world today. This contrasts with what is often a sober institutional Church.[210] On the other hand, the difficulty comes with subtle group pressures towards expressing constant joy coupled with a strong emphasis on intimacy. Such worship can all too easily neglect those present who may be in physical pain, grieving, clinically depressed or simply spiritually numb. The detrimental affect of such theology was noted by one grieving guest (St E G1).

Tom Smail's primary critique of charismatic worship has been to remind the movement of the need for a theology of suffering and a pastoral sensitivity to the unhealed. He writes:

> The defects spring from a *theologia gloriae* that does not wrestle with a *theologia cruces*, and can engender a worship style that concentrates too one-sidedly on the triumphs of Easter and Pentecost and does not sufficiently take into account that they can be reached only by way of the cross.[211]

Almost entirely lacking in charismatic worship are songs that reflect the interim, including the 'delayed gratification' that is fundamental in the experience of salvation. With its simple (and uninventive) four and eight-bar choruses, charismatic songs are a capitulation to the contemporary craving for immediate gratification, and a loss of the 'not yet' dimension of Christian life.[212] Begbie highlights the stress laid on the extension of resolution and consequent 'deferred gratification' in musical structure in Western tonal music, especially since the eighteenth century. He writes:

> ...there is a patience proper to Christian faith in which *something new* is *learned* of incalculable *value*, which cannot be learned in any other way. Music introduces us to just this kind of dynamic, this enriching meantime, in which we are made to cultivate a kind of patience which subverts the belief that delay must inevitably be void or harmful ('negatively problematic').[213]

---

[209] Steven 2002:202.

[210] *We Believe in the Holy Spirit* 1991a:54.

[211] Smail 1995:111.

[212] Begbie 1991:238.

[213] Begbie 2000:205, emphasis in original.

This reflects the provisionality or incompleteness of the Christian life (Rom. 8; 1 Cor. 13.12), and of the importance of persevering in the face of opposition (Heb. 11).[214]

Walker's remark that charismatic worship eventually becomes routinised over time is confirmed by the observations of Tom Smail, James Steven and Pete Ward that charismatic worship is carefully constructed.[215] The worship tends to start with up-tempo songs and then move to appreciably slower songs with ballad melodies. Smail describes how, 'Certain songs sung in a certain sequence can be guaranteed to produce singing in tongues that will be followed by one of the five predictable "prophecies" that we have all heard before.'[216] The careful crafting of charismatic worship may lead us to ask to what extent it has become a form of rite in itself. It is surely naïve to suggest, 'We don't do liturgy'. Rejection of traditional liturgy tends to be replaced with an implicit liturgy, which inevitably becomes just as structured as the explicit type. In setting out not to be liturgical, to what extent has charismatic worship become precisely this? Rather than viewing freedom and liturgy as being mutually exclusive, at some stage within Alpha's two-year programme of initiation, there needs to be some introduction to the liturgical tradition of the Church. The inclusion of seasonality, of different dimensions to the Christian life that includes penitential as well as celebration seasons, would no doubt enrich the course. In a critique of the minimalist worship at Willow Creek Community Church, Abraham observes: 'Surely we can find a way where, with adequate catechesis and formation, even the seeker can come to revel in the common life of the Church's liturgy.'[217] With people coming from further back – with no Christian narrative to build upon and from situations that can only be described as pagan – this process will be lengthy. Such a position forces a rethinking of what it is to be a mission-shaped church and how the gospel might be inculturated (see §4 below). While there is a logic, whether one agrees with it or not, behind Gumbel's desire to strip the Christian faith down to 'the essentials' to make it accessible, by leaving people at that point deprives them of some of the treasures of the Christian tradition.

We live in a world that is increasingly open to a spirituality that includes symbol and ritual, lights and colours, smells and food.[218] As Drane notes, all those spiritual paths that are emerging in the West as serious alternatives to mainline Christian belief incorporate significant elements of the mystical, the numinous, the unpredictable and the non-rational (which is not the same as the irrational). Arguably, the more rationalised everyday life becomes, the more

---

[214] Farrow 1999.

[215] Walker 1995; Smail 1995; Steven 2002; Ward 2005.

[216] Smail 1995:115.

[217] Abraham 2003:91; see also Cocksworth 2007:142-43.

[218] Walker 1996:199.

important it is for our lives to be focused on something mysterious.[219] To suggest that the Alpha Weekend is the spiritual post-modern element of the course is a moot point. The Emmaus course has the advantage of employing a more interactive and reflective method.[220] Or take the Essence course, which includes a learning style that is more experimental and involves activities such as relaxation exercises on the floor, making bracelets, smashing pots and modelling in dough.[221] As Booker and Ireland insist, by being more open-ended and allowing people to raise their own questions, Essence offers 'a more experiential approach that takes people's previous searches for spirituality and yet leads them on towards a clearly and distinctively Christian understanding of God'.[222]

Drawing upon my empirical data, this section has assessed some of the more contentious theological issues. Part of the difficulty in Alpha's attempt to 'roll out' the course ecumenically has been a profound lack of reflexivity as to its theological moorings. Gumbel's claim, that the course includes the basics upon which all Christians agree, is clearly inaccurate. It is thus hardly surprising that many churches have felt unease about adopting Alpha in its entirety, especially with the constraints that accompany a copyright statement. Prohibiting adaptation carries greater difficulties when attempting cross-cultural mission, and it is to a missiological theme, namely, contextualisation, with which we shall conclude.

4. Contextualisation[223]

In my outline of Alpha (Chapter 2), I contextually and theologically situated the course, noting the various influences. These included its Reformed–Evangelical and middle-class heritage, a Western Enlightenment rationalist apologetic, the influence of the Church Growth Movement, and a charismatic theology and spirituality that is particularly indebted to John Wimber. This challenges Gumbel's description that Alpha constitutes a sort of pure gospel package taken straight from the NT. In Chapter 3, I highlighted Ward's assessment that Alpha fits with today's consumerist mindset and can be seen as a significant contextualisation of the methods of evangelism.

There are various 'levels' of contextualisation: *translation, adaptation* and

---

[219] Drane 2000:45.

[220] Cottrell et al. 1996.

[221] Frost 2002.

[222] Booker and Ireland 2003:177.

[223] The term 'contextualisation' was first coined in the 1970s, in the Theological Education Fund, and was related to the task of the education and formation of people for ministry in the church (Bosch 2003:420).

inculturation.[224] It is important to note that these categories must not be viewed in an absolute sense.

4.1 Translation

The translation approach is similar to the 'dynamic-equivalence' method of Bible translation, where the Christian faith is capable of 'translation' into other cultures without injury to its essential content.[225] The basic Christian revelation is the kernel and the cultural settings it has been encased in is the husk.[226] In other words, the Christian message is freed from cultural accretions (its husk), thus providing the revelation data (the kernel), for translation into a new situation. The translation approach can be useful in the early stages of a Christian community's development because of the pastoral urgency of the rendering of significant texts into local languages. However, there are problems with this approach. First, it has a positivist understanding of culture. Cultural analysis is undertaken not on the terms of the local culture but only to find parallels, direct equivalents, with the 'sending' culture. Are there really such parallels?[227] Such an approach 'tends to encourage a one-way contextualisation process, which is problematic in terms of the power dynamic created as well as the authenticity of the contextualisation'.[228] Further, it assumes an understanding that the gospel is acultural, and that evangelism takes place in a culturally disembodied form.[229] Culture is viewed as an extrinsic, separable phenomenon, a 'husk' enclosing a 'kernel', or a 'theological soul in a cultural body'.[230] However, religion is by definition a cultural system and is integrally linked to culture. Roman Catholic missiologist, Aylward Shorter, writes:

---

[224] Luzbetak 1988; Schreiter 1986. I shall only focus on translation and inculturation. *Adaptation* incorporates varying degrees of contextualisation, some closer to the translation and others more akin to inculturation (see Schreiter 1986).

[225] For a positive assessment of translation, see Lamin Sanneh, *Translating the Message* (2004), and Andrew Walls, *The Cross-Cultural Process in Christian History* (2002). The former suggests that the missionary adoption of the vernacular included a radical indigenisation. This de-absolutises any attempt of conceiving one cultural form as *the* expression of the Christian faith. However, such an approach challenges the 'kernel and husk' translation paradigm and, with his discussion of reciprocity, has greater resonance with inculturation (see §4.2 below).

[226] Schreiter 1986:7.

[227] Schreiter 1986:7-8.

[228] Rogers 2000.

[229] Bosch (2003:421) traces this to a Greek metaphysic in which ideas are considered prior and more important than 'application'. It is an approach which received a new lease of life with the advent of the Enlightenment, in Kant's paradigm where, for example, 'pure reason' was superior to 'practical reason'.

[230] Cooper 2001:360.

We do not live in a world of essences, nor do magisterial faith statements arise in some privileged supracultural sphere; rather the Gospel travels throughout history from one inculturated form to another.[231]

Hiebert describes the period between 1800 to 1950 as the 'era of noncontextualisation' for Protestant missions in which it was thought that a singular Western culture simply had to be indigenised without surrendering any of its essence.[232] As Schreiter asserts: 'Without a more fundamental encounter with the new culture, that faith can never become incarnate. It remains an alien voice within the culture.'[233] Such a fundamental encounter takes more time.

With its standardised and controlled product, Alpha has many similarities to the pre-1950s colonial approach to mission. While publishers and users of Alpha are allowed to translate the course into different contexts and languages, such things must only be done without surrendering its core essence.[234] As Alpha's copyright statement puts it, to 'ensure the uniformity and integrity of the Alpha course...the essential character of the course must be retained'.[235] Of course, having been turned into a franchise, Alpha had to standardise its product and keep control so as to retain its brand integrity. This is essential if a uniform course is to be made available throughout the world. Pragmatically this makes complete sense in that it resonates with a consumerist culture that feels safe in purchasing branded products. However, it incurs the problems associated with the translation model of contextualisation. Bosch calls such an approach the 'absolutism of contextualism'. He writes:

> Contextualism thus means universalising one's own theological position, making it applicable to everybody and demanding that others submit to it.[236]

Neither the Church nor theology have ever been acultural. And this is one of the difficulties for Alpha: its attempt to be ecclesiologically free. Or rather, its naïve assumption that it is presenting the pure supracultural New Testament faith. As such it results in a docetic over-idealised spiritualisation; a 'one size fits all'[237] evangelism course. Perhaps underpinning this is Gumbel's perception

---

[231] Shorter 1994:91; see also Bosch 2003; Pelikan 1971:8.

[232] Cited in Bosch 2003:427.

[233] Schreiter 1986:8.

[234] As noted in Chapter 2, since the late 1990s, AI has allowed variations to the course, including Alpha for Youth, Students, Prisons, Seniors, Forces and Workplace. However, no substantive changes are made to the core product. Rizter (1996:149-50) refers to the diversification of product lines as 'sneakerisation' and sees this complexification as the direction that McDonaldization is heading in the future.

[235] Gumbel 2001g:208. On Alpha's copyright, see Drane 2007:376 and Meadows 2007:416.

[236] Bosch 2003:428.

[237] Ritzer 1996.

that the needs of people the world over 'are the same...' and that 'the Christian answer...is the same'.[238] This homogeneous tendency markets the same package, the same spirituality, and the same questions, regardless of local context. Meadows agrees, asserting:

> ...the root of our confusion lies in the moment when the machinery of our technological culture seized a locally developed programme of catechesis and commodified it into a globally marketed package for evangelism and disciple-making.[239]

One Alpha administrator (St C LA1) felt that Alpha was far too middle-class for the housing estate in which the church was trying to work. For example, the administrator explained that Gumbel's jokes about mistakes that GSCE students had made during exams (Introductory session) 'wouldn't have made sense because they wouldn't have known the answers...most of them can hardly read and write!' Even the word 'course' is foreign to them. In a context where mothers experienced domestic violence, had children from different fathers, Alpha, LA1 was beginning to conclude, was not the appropriate tool. If running Alpha was problematic for those in the UK from a different cultural and social context to that at HTB, what might this say about using the course in non-Western cultures? It is naïve to assume that African, Asian or Latin cultures have the same questions as those of Western Christianity.

4.2 Inculturation

In contrast to the translation model of contextualisation, the most costly and difficult process is that of *inculturation*[240] which involves a greater focus on the cultural context where the Christian faith is to take root and expression. The importance of a dialectical process of reciprocal and respectful listening, of journeying together, is stressed. The emphasis is on a holistic and community-centred, or local, approach rather than on a pre-packaged product. As Pope Paul VI put it, it is about transposing the gospel into a language that is 'anthropological and cultural', rather than 'semantic or literary', and to evangelise cultures 'not in a purely decorative way, as it were, by applying a thin veneer, but in a vital way, in depth and right to their very roots'.[241] The Roman Catholic missionary to the Masai tribe, Vincent Donovan, writes: 'Evangelisation is a process of bringing the gospel to people where they are,

---

[238] Gumbel 2007:436.

[239] Meadows 2007:407.

[240] Schreiter (1986:13) uses the term 'ethnographic approach' to describe this.

[241] *Evangelii Nuntiandi*, 63 and 20 (www.vatican.va/holy_father/paul_vi/apost_exhortations/documents/hf_p-vi_exh_19751208_evangelii-nuntiandi_en.html, accessed 1 January 2006).

not where you would like them to be.'[242] On his return to the United Sates, Donovan found American youth 'one of the most exotic tribes of all'. They had their own dress, music, rituals, language and values, all remarkably similar from New York to California. A university student advised Donovan:

> In working with young people in America, do not try to call them back to where they were, and do not try to call them to where you are, as beautiful as that place might seem to you. You must have the courage to go with them to a place that neither you nor they have ever been before'.[243]

Conversion ought not to involve simply the transfer of individuals from their native culture to the culture of the church, but rather the conversion of their culture which, in a reciprocal dynamic, enriches the cultural life of the church.[244]

There are also difficulties for inculturation, one being the possibility of relativism.[245] While recognising the contextual nature of all theology, there is the creedal trinitarian faith, the 'universal and context-transcending dimensions of theology',[246] that needs to be respected and preserved to remain authentically Christian.[247] Bretherton notes that within the Christian tradition, there is a necessary tension, a continuity and discontinuity, between '*homeostasis* (the ability to maintain an equilibrium and to re-arrange itself so as to keep things steady) with *morphogenesis* (the ability of to grow, change shape, and adapt

---

[242] Donovan 1993:vi.

[243] Donovan 1993:vii. Yet even Donovan's remarkable work did not survive when he left East Africa (Shorter 1994:108).

[244] Cray 2004:87.

[245] Another problem with inculturation is the possibility of syncretism. Yet this is present to a greater or lesser degree in every form of Christianity from NT times. Inculturation implies a continual struggle with syncretism, with the elements of culture which are incompatible with the Gospel. In fact de-syncretisation enters into the definition of inculturation itself. Yet what is clear is that fear of syncretism should not be invoked as a reason for postponing inculturation (Shorter 1994:152).

[246] Bosch 2003:427.

[247] The tendency has been for churches with an explicit institutional basis to dominate and crush the local, from which inculturation originates. For example, despite the Vatican II emphasis on inculturation, it has more often collapsed back into translation when put into practice. Shorter (1994:90) notes that (the then Cardinal) Ratzinger was known for his nervousness about inculturation, following Pius XII and the pre-conciliar Church, which favoured the idea of a monolithic hybrid Christian culture, in which the cultural matrix was Western. There is a sharp contrast between the official affirmations and the Magisterium's return to centralisation and authoritarianism (Shorter 1994:90). Yet the imperialism of a single Western Christian culture in the Church contradicts its vocation of catholicity.

without breaking apart)'.[248] Like an immune system, staying healthy involves a balance between the two so as to enable both maintenance and growth. Bretherton's understanding of hospitality, in contrast to tolerance, creates such a possibility.[249] He locates the theological roots of this in eschatology and ecclesiology, drawing on the Great Banquet (Luke 14) and the encounter between Peter and Cornelius (Acts 10) and Christian tradition. Hospitality offers a way of welcoming the stranger that is transformative of relationships. For those who might attend a modern catechumenate, the tradition-specific practice of hospitality creates space for conversation and takes proper account of difference. It is simultaneously centrifugal and centripetal: the church, Bretherton writes, 'neither separates itself from the world nor becomes assimilated to the world'.[250] The Church's task, then, is to be a martyr, a witness to the Christian faith and to invite its neighbours to participate. There is also a dialogical dimension to this:

> At times this invitation will involve the church changing its pattern of life together as it discerns in the life of its neighbours patterns of thought and action that bear more truthful witness to Jesus Christ.[251]

In summary, the Christian faith is never transmitted in a culture-free or culture-neutral cocoon: it needs to find its own place in the heart of each culture. In other words, it needs to be incarnated. A standardised pre-packaged 'solution' tends to encourage an unreflective and uncritical approach to contextualisation that fails to provide the appropriate space for inculturation and a fundamental engagement with the local context. Such inculturation is untidy and messy, it is difficult in practice and takes much skill and commitment.[252] Hence, Alpha's translation approach represents an enormous attraction for church leaders unskilled in evangelism. However, as Ireland discovered, locally written courses often had a greater impact than both Alpha and Emmaus because they could be better tailored to the local context.[253]

5. Summary

There are inherent tensions and even confusion between the use of Alpha as a (discipleship) course for Christians, or for those returning to the faith, and its use as an (evangelism) course for non-Christians. In comparison with the early church's catechumenate, Alpha's multiple aims of mission and spiritual

---

[248] Bretherton 2007:51. See Andrew Walls (2002) for how this process took shape in the early church.
[249] Bretherton 2006.
[250] Bretherton 2006:135.
[251] Bretherton 2006:151.
[252] Rogers 2000.
[253] Ireland 2000; 2003.

formation is a confusion of genres, with neither of them done adequately. It fails to do so in two main ways: it misses out and mis-orders key elements of the catechumenal initiation process. The confusion of genres reflects Alpha's history as originally being designed for new Christians and then adapted for the non-churched. Perhaps this makes the course more flexible but it certainly creates difficulty in how certain elements of the course are received – notably, the Eucharist on the Alpha Weekend. It also complicates how to follow up participants and in ensuring ongoing formation. For the non-Christian guest who converts on Alpha, this must surely lead to sacramental initiation. The mixed grouping on Alpha means that its initiation structure tends to be rather untidy and unfocused. As it currently stands, Alpha and its follow-on courses do not provide a sufficient model for initiating people into the Christian faith, nor does it fulfil all that Jesus asked in the baptising and making of disciples (Matt. 28:19-20). Churches running Alpha have different ecclesiologies but serious thought needs to be given to these issues and what else is needed for integrating people into the full richness of church life.

Alpha has faced diverse criticism in its attempt to 'roll out' the course ecumenically. I have outlined what I perceive to be the salient difficulties with Alpha's theology and spirituality. This included its ecclesiology: part of the problem here is that Gumbel is not explicit about Alpha's (low church) ecclesiology. Its 'ecclesiology', influenced by the Church Growth Movement, is mechanistic, utilitarian and pragmatic. This resulted in feelings of alienation and disillusionment among a number of Alpha guests, team members and AI staff. I have suggested that Alpha, with Evangelicalism, is better understood as a piety rather than as an ecclesiology. Alpha faces challenges from various critics over the source of its authority and thus of its theology and spirituality. It is as a result of dissatisfaction that multiple process evangelism courses have been written.

I then turned to Alpha's soteriology and used Boersma's critique of penal substitution theories to highlight some of the problems inherent in the Reformed tradition in which Alpha is situated. Problems include an individualistic, existential and spiritualised view of conversion, a frail ecclesiology with little notion of catholicity of the faith and a suspicion of the Church as a mediator of, for example, sacramental grace. While the notion of process is theoretically legitimated by Gumbel, the soteriology and the normative experience in AI discourse is one of crisis conversion. I then assessed Gumbel's expectation of assurance and some of the difficulties inherent in this doctrine. *Liturgia* and Alpha was then described, and the influence of Charismatic Renewal. While such worship has brought life and energy to a sober institutional church, it suffers from a mechanistic pneumatology which undermines the Spirit's freedom and divine hypostasis, and the lack of a theology of suffering, incarnation and of the Christian life lived in the interim. I suggested that a return to the liturgical tradition of the Church catholic would alleviate these difficulties and perhaps provide greater balance to Alpha and its follow-on courses.

Finally, I highlighted varying approaches to contextualisation, noting that Alpha was similar to the pre-1950s colonial approach to mission. Alpha naïvely assumes that it is presenting the pure supracultural New Testament faith. And combined with its copyright restriction, inculturation, where the Christian faith is more profoundly rooted in a local context, becomes hindered.

Conclusion

Within the context of a declining UK church attendance, and in reaction to the de-institutionalisation of religion in Europe, the Alpha course, with a theology 'dripping with reactionary supernaturalism'[1] has arisen and flourished. Emphasising small face-to-face groups and an experiential and affective type of religious faith, Alpha is one of the 'new forms of Christianity'.[2]

To recapitulate, this book has asserted three main aims. First, to compare and contrast the official version of Alpha, as set out by AI, with what happens 'on the ground'. The second objective has been to research conversion on Alpha, which is one of the primary aims of the course.[3] The last was to theologically and liturgically assess Alpha.

At the outset, I outlined both the history of HTB and Alpha, and attempted to situate the course contextually and theologically. Gumbel claims that Alpha represents basic Christianity upon which all Christians agree, and thus stands within the Evangelical tradition that views itself 'as the custodian of pure New Testament faith'.[4] To maintain this assertion Gumbel is forced to trace Alpha's theological roots through a very thin line. Only a narrow range of historical sources and theologians are recognised as being antecedent to the theology of the course. By appealing to these sources Gumbel employs a powerful legitimating device. As demonstrated in Chapters 1 and 2, Alpha is firmly situated within the Reformed, Charismatic–Evangelical tradition, with influences that include John Wimber, the Church Growth Movement and the Toronto Blessing. With its charismatic dimension, Alpha was particularly suited to the 4,000 to 5,500 churches affected by the 'blessing', and the energy thereby released, combined with the high profile that HTB gained from its involvement, led many churches to adopt Alpha. AI's attempt to roll out the course as a franchise – to be used across the denominational, cultural, socio-economic and intellectual spectrum – has met with diverse criticism, resulting in a plethora of alternative courses (see Appendix 2). However, the entrepreneurial spirit and business acumen of Ken Costa and Tricia Neill, combined with the charismatic leadership of Nicky Gumbel and the financial backing of HTB, has led to immense worldwide growth for Alpha.

The style of evangelism on Alpha contrasts with the previous two hundred years or so of mass evangelism. Alpha places evangelism within the local church, primarily conducted by the laity; it recognises that communicating the

---

[1] Berger 1999:4.
[2] MacLaren 2004:iix.
[3] See Gumbel 2001g:110.
[4] Cocksworth 1993:3.

Christian faith includes a process, a resocialisation, and that people need time to assimilate what they hear and discuss. The primary aim of the course is to convert guests, and it includes four pushes for 'closure'. However, Gumbel recognises that the longer term aim of 'spiritual maturity' or discipleship would inevitably take more than ten weeks. Hence Alpha represents only part one of a two-year process. Gumbel has thus attempted to create a programme that combines mission and spiritual formation. The question that arose for my empirical work was to assess whether it adequately did both, or either.

The empirical chapters (5 and 6) investigated the first two aims of the book. Having expected a high level of deviancy 'on the ground', I was surprised to find conformity in terms of Alpha's basic methodology. All of the courses I researched included the main elements of Alpha: meal, worship, talk, small group discussion and the weekend/day away. Such conformity conflicted with stories of 'hacking Alpha' about which I had previously heard. The extent of these less 'franchised' Alpha courses requires further research.

While the vast majority (90 per cent) of people attending Alpha were either churched or had some church background, it was suggested that Gumbel was correct in his conviction that non-churchgoers start to attend Alpha when churches persist with the course. However, most non-churchgoing guests were from the open de-churched category – that is, they had been christened, had some experience of church, but at some stage had left. Significantly under-represented were the non-churched and the closed de-churched. This raises the question of whether Alpha should start further back,[5] despite Gumbel's reluctance about the fewer numbers of guests this has previously attracted.[6]

Most guests (92 per cent) joined Alpha through the influence of Christian friends, church or church leaders, with Alpha's marketing strategies often helping with recruitment. Yet despite considerable effort, four courses had continuing difficulty in recruiting guests. My research revealed a defection rate of 30 per cent. This was a result of various factors: Alpha's theology, pressure exerted by leaders, and the somewhat overwhelming and stifling presence of Christians on the course. The latter two reasons were at variance with AI's explanations (see Chapter 5 §3.4).

The most unpredictable part of Alpha was the small group discussion, and it was in this area that the greatest problems occurred. I suggested that one of the reasons for this was Gumbel's deferral of the more difficult questions to the small group, with leaders lacking formal theological training. Further, Gumbel's vision of guests answering their own questions foundered when these more complex issues were tackled. On the whole, leaders were unable to assimilate the participatory style of leadership that Gumbel outlines (see Chapter 2 §2.4). Small group leadership requires sensitive interpersonal skills that are not easily acquired in two or three Alpha training sessions.

---

[5] See also Cray 2004:107; Hunt 2004:253-54; Murray 2004:160-63; Brookes 2007:74.
[6] Gumbel 2006.

On the Alpha weekend/day away, I discovered a marked contrast between HTB's weekend (which St D joined) and those of other courses, which lacked the life-changing experiences that AI's publicity suggested might occur. I concluded that the dramatic accounts at HTB's weekend resulted from various factors: the high degree of expectancy in the build up to the weekend, the reception of a large audience to platform cues and crowd happenings where the power of suggestion is strong,[7] the gradual increase in intensity during worship and the pressure to conform to group norms, which is invariably heightened in emotion-producing situations. In short, the Alpha weekend at HTB is perhaps a combined manifestation of the Divine, the social and the psychologically-induced.[8]

The second aim of the book was assessed in Chapter 6. By focusing upon conversion within a mainstream religious group this research has helped to redress the imbalance within the sociology of conversion with its fascination with the more exotic conversions to New Religious Movements. Rambo's five conversion types were related to conversion on Alpha. Most guests did not convert. This included at least fifteen that left the course, and eight churchgoing guests. While there were three affiliation conversions, the majority (seventeen) were intensification conversions, where faith that was formerly present in the form of a seed blossomed into full flower. The primary dimension of Rambo's process theory functioning on Alpha was *interaction*. Most guests had experienced some sort of *crisis* prior to the course; some began a spiritual *quest*; then there was an *encounter*. Having joined Alpha, they became part of a small group where the *interaction* that took place was intensified. Four guests made a particular *commitment*; the majority (80 per cent) described a gradual process. The 'reality' and longevity of these conversions requires further research.

Duncan Maclaren's thesis was then used as a theoretical framework in helping to decipher conversion on Alpha. The social–psychological explanations were explained primarily as need-based: identity, belonging, compensation and certainty. The relative lack of the factors of identity and certainty might partly be due to the age of the guests whom I researched, which averaged thirty-six.[9] Research on Alpha for Youth courses would provide a potentially interesting analysis for this dimension. The need for compensation was an important dynamic for seven people on Alpha with several guests describing distorted parenting patterns, and as a result formed a strong emotional tie to the Alpha group. The most prominent characteristic was the need for community. Affectional bonds with the Alpha team members was vital for the conversion process, and a course spread over three months allowed

---

[7] Walker 1995.

[8] Cf. Scotland 2000a:249.

[9] As noted in Chapter 6, the need for certainty represents an immature quest for a totalising explanation of everything, often prominent among adolescents.

these bonds a sufficient time to develop. These groups offered a sense of belonging, thus providing the necessary bridge to the Christian community.

Structural explanations for conversion were then outlined. In a world of competing plausibility structures, Alpha functioned as a distinctive alternative 'plausibility shelter'. Alpha performed the two functions of a plausibility structure: cohesion and exclusion. Cohesion was facilitated through strong affective relationships, talks by a charismatic figure and intense group interaction. All three processes of encapsulation (social, ideological, physical) were significant on the course. However, the maintenance processes at work post-Alpha were exceptionally weak. Continued socialisation and conversation, the two most important elements for the maintenance of plausibility, were almost non-existent.

The least significant factor for conversion on Alpha was cognitive explanations. Again, Gumbel's optimistic view that guests end up answering their own questions was not realised. It is in the small groups where the employment of legitimations broke down. Many guests completed the course with cognitive dissonance, with questions that remained undiscussed, and with team members causing additional confusion because of their views.

Lastly, I provided a theological assessment of Alpha from the perspective of Deep Church. I suggested that the Alpha course could be enriched and deepened by drawing from the deep wells of the patristic tradition of the early Christian centuries. While Alpha shares many of the catechumenate ingredients – *welcoming* people as they are, *accompanied journey*, *faith sharing*, and *community* – there is a lack of *celebrations* within the ongoing worship of the Church.[10] A major area of tension on the course lay in Alpha's broad aim of attempting to combine mission *and* spiritual formation. This multi-pronged focus meant that Alpha guests came from a wide range of backgrounds with differing, and sometimes conflicting, motivations for joining. While Alpha is officially only part one of a two-year programme with the aim of bringing participants to 'spiritual maturity',[11] my empirical data revealed that it failed to do so in two main ways: it missed out and mis-ordered key elements of the catechumenal initiation process. It therefore failed its own best intentions in its attempt to combine mission and spiritual formation.

As noted above, despite a number of guests expressing an interest in continuing their spiritual journeys, specific post-Alpha follow up was practically non-existent in relation to five of the six courses. For these, Gumbel's aim of 'spiritual maturity' was unsuccessful.

Further, the lack of teaching on baptism, confirmation (or equivalent) or Eucharist within Gumbel's two-year programme of initiation emphasises the fact that HTB has created an unsacramental form of Christian initiation. By contrast, the catechumenal process provides a deeper, fuller and more enduring

---

[10] Although at HTB a chosen few have the opportunity of giving a 'testimony'.
[11] Gumbel 2003a:10.

and sustaining way of holding together evangelism and spiritual formation. I concluded that Alpha and its follow-on courses could not stand alone as a holistic model for initiating people into the Christian faith and thus ecclesial life; nor did they fulfil all that Jesus asked in baptising and making disciples (Matt. 28:19-20). In short, Alpha falls between two stools of mission and spiritual formation and consequently ends up being deficient in both.

The Future of Alpha

Weber describes the process of 'routinisation' that occurs for every religious institution where the original 'charisma' runs down.[12] Scotland notes that the temptation is then to 'clone success' and to construct a complete package – doctrine, worship, vision and ministry.[13] The problem here is the potential for decline, a process which has been charted by Vance Havner, formerly of Wheaton College: 'It begins with a man; soon there emerges a movement; then a machine takes over; and finally there remains only a monument'.[14] Whether or not Alpha continues to grow depends upon its willingness to embrace risk, creativity and innovation by way of attempting a thorough revision of the course, and whether it is willing both to widen its horizons to encompass the whole of the Christian faith[15] and allow greater flexibility for local adaptation. As Gerlach and Hine remind us: '...in times of rapid social change, survival lies not in stability but in flexibility, not in devotion to the past but in commitment to the future'.[16]

Despite its numerous deficiencies, the Alpha course has transformed the style of evangelism, particularly for Evangelicals, compared with the revivalism of yesteryear. Many people have testified to experiencing the love of God or a faith coming alive through attending such a course. Clearly, the Holy Trinity's way of being, as the history of the pilgrim Church demonstrates, is to work through finite, sinful and fallible 'earthen vessels'. It remains for AI to be faithful to its Reformed heritage, with its transforming principle, *ecclesia reformata semper reformanda.*

---

[12] Weber 1964; see also Barker 1989; John Finney 2000.
[13] Scotland 2000c.
[14] Cited in Scotland 2000c:148-49.
[15] Finney 2000:8.
[16] Gerlach and Hine 1970:218.

APPENDICES

Appendix 1 – Alpha Research

Bockmuehl, Markus (1998). '"Dotty" Christianity – Assessing Percy on Alpha.' *Reviews in Religion and Theology* 1: 10-12.

Booker, Mike and Ireland, Mark (2003). *Evangelism – Which Way Now?* London: Church House Publishing.

Brian, Stephen (2003). *The Alpha Course: An Analysis of its Claim to Offer an Educational Course on the Meaning of Life.* PhD thesis, University of Surrey.

Brierley, Peter (2001). 'Church growth in the 1990s.' *Quadrant* May.

— (2003). *Leadership, vision and growing churches.* London: Christian Research.

— (2006). 'Alpha UK and worldwide.' *Quadrant* March.

Brierley, Peter and Wraight, Heather (1997). *UK Christian Handbook.* London: Christian Research.

Brookes, Andrew (ed.) (2007). *The Alpha Phenomenon: Theology, Praxis and Challenges for Mission and Church Today.* London: Churches Together in Britain and Ireland.

Curran, Kathryn L. (2002). *Finding God Behind Bars: An Exploratory Study of the Relevance of Prison Conversions to Criminology.* PhD thesis, University of Cambridge.

Evangelical Alliance (1998). *The Inaugural Annual Report of the EA/EMA Commission on Strategic Evangelism in the UK.* London: Evangelical Alliance.

Freebury, Charles (2001). *A Comparative Evaluation of the Alpha and Emmaus Course.* MA dissertation, University of Sheffield at Cliff College.

— (2004). Alpha or Emmaus? Assessing today's top evangelistic courses. Sheffield.

Hand, Chris (1998). *Falling Short? The Alpha Course Examined.* Epsom, Surrey: Day One Publications.

Hunt, Stephen (2001). *Anyone for Alpha? Evangelism in a post-Christian society.* London: Darton, Longman & Todd.

— (2003). 'The Alpha Programme: Some Tentative Observations of State of the Art Evangelism in the UK.' *Journal of Contemporary Religion* 18/1 (1 January): 77-93.

— (2004). *The Alpha Enterprise: Evangelism in a Post-Christian Era.* Aldershot: Ashgate.

Ireland, Mark (2000). *A study of the effectiveness of process evangelism courses in the Diocese of Lichfield with special reference to Alpha.* MA dissertation, University of Sheffield at Cliff College.

Lewis, Mike (2001). *Why not the Dove? (A study of the teaching and practice of the Holy Spirit as it was experienced in the Alpha Course in the Dove Valley Circuit 1997–2000).* MA dissertation, University of Sheffield at Cliff College.

McDonald, Elizabeth (1996). *Alpha: New Life or New Lifestyle? A biblical assessment of the Alpha Course.* Cambridge: St Matthew Publishing.

McDonald, Elizabeth and Peterson, Dusty (2001). *Alpha – the Unofficial Guide.* Cambridge: St Matthew.

Percy, Martyn (1997). 'Join-the-dots Christianity – Assessing Alpha.' *Reviews in Religion and Theology* 3: 14-18.

Race, John (2004). *A theological reflection on the Alpha course, including its application in prisons (England and Wales) and among ex-offenders (through Alpha for Prisons and Caring for Ex-Offenders).* MTh thesis, University of Oxford.

Rooms, Nigel (2005). '"Nice Process, Shame about the Content": The Alpha Course in Three Different Cultural Contexts.' *Journal of Adult Theological Education* 2/2 (Oct): 129-41.

Ward, Pete (1998). 'Alpha – The McDonaldization of Religion?' *Anvil* 15/4: 279-86.

Warren, Robert and Jackson, Bob (2001). *There Are Answers.* Abingdon: Springboard.

Watling, Tony (2005). '"Experiencing" Alpha: Finding and Embodying the Spirit and Being Transformed – Empowerment and Control in a ("Charismatic") Christian World-view.' *Journal of Contemporary Religion* 20/1 (January): 91-108.

Woodward, Matthew (2004). *An evaluation of the Alpha course as a tool for educating a parish.* MA thesis, Anglia Polytechnic University.

Appendix 2 – Process Evangelism Courses

Credo	Urwin, Lindsay (London: Church Union, 1996)
Christianity Explored	Tice, Rice (Carlisle: Paternoster Lifestyle, 2001)
Emmaus: the way of faith	Cottrell, Steven et al. (London: CHP/The National Society, 2001)
The Essence Course	Frost, Rob (Eastbourne: Kingsway, 2002)
Foundations 21	Bradley, Tony (Oxford, The Bible Reading Fellowship) Web: www.foundations21.org.uk
Foundations of Faith	Broadhurst, John (London: Church Union, 2003)
The Life Course	St Mary's Bryanston Square, London Web: www.stmaryslondon.com
Living the Questions	Procter-Murphy, Jeff and Felten, David (eds) Web: www.livingthequestions.com
Start!	CPAS, Athena Drive, Tachbrook Park, Warwick CV34 6NG Web: www.cpas.co.uk.

The Way: An Introduction to Orthodox Christianity
The Way, Institute for Orthodox Christian Studies, Wesley House, Jesus Lane, Cambridge CB5 8EJ
Web: www.iocs.cam.ac.uk/theway.html

The Y Course	Meadows Peter et al. (Bletchley: Word, 1999)

Appendix 3 – Interview Questions

Alpha Leaders

- Are there any questions you have before we start?
- Gender
- Age
- Ethnicity
- Highest educational qualification
- Occupation /job

Alpha Specific Questions

- How did you get to know about Alpha?
- How do you feel the course went?
- What did you think about the Alpha Weekend/Day Away?
- Positive aspects of Alpha?
- Negative aspects of Alpha?
- Have you arranged anything in the way of post-Alpha follow up?
- How do you feel my participation affected the Alpha course?
- Finally, is there anything that you would like to add?

Alpha Guests

- Are there any questions you have before we start?
- Gender
- Age
- Ethnicity
- Occupation
- Highest educational qualification
- Occupation /job
- How long have you lived here?

Background Information

- Siblings and birth order
- Parents' occupation
- Parents' religion
- Did you regularly attend church growing up? (baptised/confirmed?)
- What were your feelings about religion?

- What was your image of God growing up?
- How did you get along with your parents?
- How would you summarise your childhood? For example, were you depressed? disillusioned? happy?
- Did you make many friends?

Alpha Specific Questions

- In the year before you started Alpha, how were you feeling generally towards life?
- How did you get to know about Alpha?
- Why did you join Alpha?
- Having joined Alpha, what were your impressions?
- What do you think about the level of discussion? Too simple or too intellectually demanding?
- Have you become a Christian as a result of taking the Alpha course? If so, can you describe what happened?
- Has Alpha changed your view of Christianity?
- Has Alpha influenced your spiritual life?
- What do you feel are the positive aspects of Alpha
- What do you feel are the negative aspects of Alpha
- Did you feel pressurised or uncomfortable at any stage during the course?
- Finally, is there anything that you would like to add?

Bibliography

Abel, Theodore (1948–9). 'The Operation Called Verstehen.' *American Journal of Sociology* 54/3: 211-18.

Abraham, William (1989). *The Logic of Evangelism* London: Hodder & Stoughton.

— (2002). *Canon and Criterion in Christian Theology.* Oxford: Oxford University Press.

— (2003). *The Logic of Renewal.* London: SPCK.

Adler, P. A. and Adler, P. (1997). 'Parent as Researcher: The Politics of Researching in the Personal Life.' In R. Hertz (ed.), *Reflexivity and Voice.* London: Sage, 21-44.

Agar, Michael H. (1996). *The Professional Stranger: An Informal Introduction to Ethnography.* 2nd ed. London: Academic Press.

Aguilar, J. L. (1981). 'Insider Research: An Ethnography of a Debate.' In D. A. Messerschmidt (ed.), *Anthropologists at Home in North America: Methods and Issues in the Study of One's Own Society.* Cambridge: Cambridge University Press, 15-26.

Allen, Davina (2004). 'Ethnomethodological Insights into Insider–Outsider Relationships in Nursing Ethnographies of Healthcare Settings.' *Nursing Inquiry* 11/1: 14-24.

Allison, J. (1967). 'Adaptive Regression and Intense Religious Experiences.' *Journal of Nervous and Mental Disease* 145: 452-63.

Altheide, D. L. and Johnson, J. M. (1994). 'Criteria For Assessing Interpretative Validity in Qualitative Research.' In N. K. Denzin and Y. S. Lincoln (eds.), *Handbook of Qualitative Research.* London: Sage, 485-99.

Anthony, Dick and Robbins, Thomas (2003). 'Conversion and "Brainwashing" in New Religious Movements.' In J. Lewis (ed.), *The Oxford Handbook of New Religious Movements.* Oxford: Oxford University Press, 243-97.

Argyle, Michael (1983). *The Psychology of Interpersonal Behaviour.* 4th ed. Harmondsworth, Middlesex: Penguin Books.

Arnold, Clinton (2004). 'Early Church Catechesis and New Christians' Classes in Contemporary Evangelicalism.' *Journal of the Evangelical Theological Society* 47/1 (March): 39-54.

Asch, S. E. (1956). 'Studies of Independence and Conformity: A Minority of One Against a Unanimous Majority.' *Psychological Monographs* 70 (9, Whole no. 416).

Aune, Kristin J. (2004). *Postfeminist Evangelicals: The Construction of Gender in the New Frontiers International Churches.* PhD thesis, King's College, London.

Avis, Paul (2002). *Anglicanism and the Christian Church.* Revised ed. London: T & T Clark.

Awamleh, Raed and Gardner, William L. (1999). 'Perceptions of Leader Charisma and Effectiveness: The Effects of Vision Content, Delivery, and Organizational Performance.' *The Leadership Quarterly* 10/3: 345-73.

Bacote, Vincent (2002). 'What is This Life For? Expanding Our View of Salvation.' In J. G. Stackhouse (ed.), *What Does it Mean to be Saved?* Grand Rapids, Mich.: Baker Academic, 95-114.

Ball, Peter and Grundy, Malcolm (2000). *Faith on the Way: A Practical Guide to the Adult Catechumenate*. London: Mowbray.

Ball, Stephen (1990). 'Self-Doubt and Soft Data.' *Qualitative Studies in Education* 3/2: 157-71.

Barbour, Ian G. (1976). *Myths, Models and Paradigms*. San Francisco: Harper & Row.

Barker, Eileen (1984). *The Making of a Moonie: Choice or Brainwashing?* Oxford: Blackwell.

— (1989). *New Religious Movements*. London: Her Majesty's Stationery Office.

Barth, Karl (1981). *The Christian Life: Church Dogmatics IV*. Trans. G. W. Bromiley. Edinburgh: T & T Clark.

Bartholomew, Craig and Moritz, Thorsten (eds) (2000). *Christ and Consumerism*. Carlisle: Paternoster.

Bartholomew, Richard (2006). 'Publishing, Celebrity, and the Globalisation of Conservative Protestantism.' *Journal of Contemporary Religion* 21/1: 1-13.

Bass, Bernard M. and Steidlmeier, Paul (1999). 'Ethics, Character, and Authentic Transformational Leadership Behavior.' *The Leadership Quarterly* 10/2: 181-217.

Bassey, Michael (1984). 'Pedagogic Research: On the Relative Merits of Search for Generalisations and Study of Single Events.' In J. Bell, et al. (eds), *Conducting Small-scale Investigations in Educational Management*. London: Open University, 103-22.

Bates, J. Barrington (2005). 'Giving What Is Sacred to Dogs? Welcoming All to the Eucharistic Feast.' *Journal of Anglican Studies* 3/1 (June 1, 2005): 53-74.

Batson, Daniel and Ventis, Larry (1982). *The Religious Experience: A Social-Psychological Perspective*. Oxford: Oxford University Press.

Baum, Gregory (1978). 'Critical Theology.' In W. Conn (ed.), *Conversion: Perspectives on Personal and Social Transformation*. New York: Alba House, 281-95.

Baumeister, Roy F. and Leary, Mark R. (1995). 'The Need to Belong: Desire for Interpersonal Attachments as a Fundamental Human Motivation.' *Psychological Bulletin* 117/3 (May): 497-529.

Beasley-Murray, G. R. (1963). *Baptism in the New Testament*. London: Macmillan.

Beaton, Richard (2003). 'Reimagining the Church.' In J. Stackhouse (ed.), *Evangelical Ecclesiology: Reality or Illusion?* Grand Rapids, Mich.: Baker Academic, 217-23.

Bebbington, David (1989). *Evangelicalism in Modern Britain: A History from the 1730s to the 1980s*. London: Routledge.

— (2005). *The Dominance of Evangelicalism: The Age of Spurgeon and Moody*. Downers Grove, IL: IVP.

Beckford, James (1978). 'Accounting for Conversion.' *British Journal of Sociology* 29: 249-62.

Begbie, Jeremy (1991). 'The Spirituality of Renewal Music.' *Anvil* 8/3: 227-39.

— (2000). *Theology, Music and Time*. Cambridge: Cambridge University Press.

Beit-Hallahmi, Benjamin and Argyle, Michael (1997). *The Psychology of Religious Behaviour, Belief and Experience* London: Routledge.

Bellah, Robert N. (ed.) (1985). *Habits of the Heart: Individualism and Commitment in American Life*. Berkeley: University of California Press.

Berger, Peter (1967). *The Sacred Canopy: Elements of a Sociological Theory of Religion*. Garden City, N.Y.: Doubleday.

— (1970). *A Rumour of Angels: Modern Society and the Rediscovery of the Supernatural*. London: Allen Lane. Original publication 1969.

— (1980). *The Heretical Imperative: Contemporary Possibilities of Religious Affirmation.* London: Collins. Original publication 1979.

— (1998). 'Protestantism and the Quest of Certainty.' *Christian Century*, 26 Aug – 2 September, 782-96.

— (ed.) (1999). *The Desecularization of the World: Resurgent Religion and World Politics.* Washington, D.C.: Ethics and Public Policy Center.

— (2000). 'Epistemological Modesty: An Interview with Peter Berger.' *Christian Century*, 29 October, 972-78.

— (2001). 'Postscript.' In L. Woodhead, et al. (eds), *Peter Berger and the Study of Religion.* London: Routledge, 189-98.

Berger, Peter and Luckmann, Thomas (1991). *The Social Construction of Reality: A Treatise in the Sociology of Knowledge.* London: Penguin Press. Original publication 1966.

Bernstein, Richard J. (1983). *Beyond Objectivism and Relativism.* Oxford: Blackwell.

Bhaldraithe, Eoin de (2001). 'Early Christian Features Preserved in Western Monasticism.' In A. Kreider (ed.), *The Origins of Christendom in the West.* Edinburgh: T & T Clark, 153-78.

Bhaskar, Roy (1989). *Reclaiming Reality: A Critical Introduction to Contemporary Philosophy.* London: Verso.

Bibby, Reginald W. (1997). 'Going, Going, Gone: The Impact of Geographical Mobility on Religious Movement.' *Review of Religious Research* 38: 289-307.

Bion, W. R. (1961). *Experiences in Groups.* London: Tavistock.

Blumer, Herbert (1969). *Symbolic Interactionism: Perspective and Method.* Englewood Cliffs, N.J: Prentice-Hall.

Bockmuehl, Markus (1998). '"Dotty" Christianity – Assessing Percy on Alpha.' *Reviews in Religion and Theology* 1: 10-12.

Boersma, Hans (2004). *Violence, Hospitality, and the Cross: Reappropriating the Atonement Tradition.* Grand Rapids, Mich: Baker Academic.

Bonino, Jose Miguez (1975). *Revolutionary Theology Comes of Age.* London: SPCK.

Booker, Mike and Ireland, Mark (2003). *Evangelism – Which Way Now?* London: Church House Publishing.

Borg, Marcus J. (1994). *Jesus in Contemporary Scholarship.* Harrisburg, Penn.: Trinity Press.

Borhek, James T. and Curtis, Richard F. (1975). *A Sociology of Belief.* New York: Richard Farnsworth.

Bosch, David J. (2003). *Transforming Mission: Paradigm Shifts in the Theology of Mission.* Maryknoll, N.Y.: Orbis. Original publication 1991.

Bradshaw, Paul (1996). *Early Christian Worship.* London: SPCK.

— (ed.) (2001). *Companion to Common Worship.* London: SPCK.

Bretherton, Luke (2006). *Hospitality and Holiness: Christian Witness Amid Moral Diversity.* Aldershot: Ashgate.

— (2007). 'Introduction: Why Deep Church?' In A. Walker and L. Bretherton (eds), *Remembering Our Future: Explorations in Deep Church.* Milton Keynes: Paternoster Press, xv-xx.

Brian, Stephen (2003). *The Alpha Course: An Analysis of its Claim to Offer an Educational Course on the Meaning of Life.* PhD thesis, University of Surrey.

Brierley, Peter (2000). *The Tide is Running Out: What the English Church Attendance Survey Reveals.* London: Christian Research.

— (2001). 'Church Growth in the 1990s.' *Quadrant* May.

— (2003). *Leadership, Vision and Growing Churches*. London: Christian Research.

— (2006). 'Alpha UK and Worldwide.' *Quadrant* March.

Brierley, Peter and Wraight, Heather (1997). *UK Christian Handbook*. London: Christian Research.

Brookes, Andrew (ed.) (2007). *The Alpha Phenomenon: Theology, Praxis and Challenges for Mission and Church Today*. London: Churches Together in Britain and Ireland.

Brown, Callum (1982). 'A Revisionist Approach to Religious Change.' In S. Bruce (ed.), *Religion and Modernisation: Sociologists and Historians Debate the Secularisation Thesis*. Oxford: Clarendon, 31-58.

Brown, Peter (1996). *The Rise of Western Christendom: Triumph and Diversity, AD 200–1000*. Oxford: Blackwell.

Bruce, S. (1996). *Religion in the Modern World*. Oxford: Oxford University Press.

— (2003). 'The Demise of Christianity in Britain.' In G. Davie, et al. (eds), *Predicting Religion: Christian, Secular, and Alternative Futures*. Aldershot, Hants: Ashgate, 53-63.

Brueggemann, Walter (1993). *Biblical Perspectives on Evangelism: Living in a Three-Storied Universe*. Nashville: Abingdon Press.

Bryman, Alan (2004). *Social Research Methods*. Oxford: Oxford University Press.

Buchanan, Colin. (1998). *Is the Church of England Biblical?: An Anglican Ecclesiology*. London: Darton Longman & Todd.

Burgess, Robert G. (1991). *In The Field: An Introduction to Field Research*. London: Routledge.

Burns, James MacGregor (1978). *Leadership*. London: Harper and Row.

Calley, Malcolm J. C. (1965). *God's People: West Indian Pentecostal Sects in England*. London: Oxford University Press.

Cameron, Helen (2003). 'The Decline of the Church in England as a Local Membership Organisation: Predicting the Nature of Civil Society in 2050.' In G. Davie, et al. (eds), *Predicting Religion: Christian, Secular, and Alternative futures*. Aldershot, Hants: Ashgate, 109-119.

Carey, George (1986). 'A Biblical Perspective.' In M. Hill (ed.), *Entering the Kingdom: A Fresh Look at Conversion*. Kent: MARC Europe.

Carrier, H. (1966). *The Sociology of Religious Belonging*. London: Darton, Longmann and Todd.

Cartwright, Dorwin (1951). 'Achieving Change in People: Some Applications of Group Dynamics Theory.' *Human Relations* 4/4 (November 1, 1951): 381-92.

Casanova, José (1994). *Public Religions in the Modern World*. London: University of Chicago Press.

— (2003). 'Beyond European and American Exceptionalism: towards a Global Perspective.' In G. Davie, et al. (eds), *Predicting Religion: Christian, Secular, and Alternative Futures*. Aldershot, Hants: Ashgate, 17-29.

Chalke, Steve and Mann, Alan (2003). *The Lost Message of Jesus*. Grand Rapids, Mich.: Zondervan.

Charon, Joel M. (2001). *Symbolic Interactionism: An Introduction, an Interpretation, an Integration*. 7th ed. London: Prentice-Hall International.

Chester, Stephen (2005). *Conversion at Corinth: Perspectives on Conversion in Paul's Theology and the Corinthian Church*. London: T & T Clark. Original publication

2003.

Clarke, John (1995). *Evangelism That Really Works*. London: SPCK.

Clines, David J. A. (1997). *Bible and the Modern World*. Sheffield: Sheffield Academic Press.

Cocksworth, Christopher (1993). *Evangelical Eucharistic Thought in the Church of England*. Cambridge: Cambridge University Press.

— (1997). *Holy, Holy, Holy: Worshipping the Trinitarian God*. London: Darton, Longman & Todd.

— (2007). 'Holding Together: Catholic Evangelical Worship in the Spirit.' In A. Walker and L. Bretherton (eds), *Remembering Our Future: Explorations in Deep Church*. Milton Keynes: Paternoster Press, 131-49.

Colwell, John. (2005). *Promise and Presence: An Exploration of Sacramental Theology*. Milton Keynes: Paternoster Press.

Conger, Jay A. (1999). 'Charismatic and Transformational Leadership in Organizations: An Insider's Perspective on these Developing Streams of Research.' *The Leadership Quarterly* 10/2: 145-79.

Conn, Walter (ed.) (1978). *Conversion: Perspectives on Personal and Social Transformation*. Alba House: New York.

— (1986). *Christian Conversion: A Developmental Interpretation of Autonomy and Surrender*. New York: Paulist Press.

Cooper, Kate (2001). 'Epilogue: Approaching Christendom.' In A. Kreider (ed.), *The Origins of Christendom in the West*. Edinburgh: T & T Clark, 359-64.

Cottrell et al., Stephen. (1996). *Emmaus: The Way of Faith*. London: National Society/Church Publishing House.

Covey, Stephen R. (1989). *The Seven Habits of Highly Effective People: Restoring the Character Ethic*. New York: Simon & Schuster.

Cowan, Stephen B. (ed.) (2000). *Five Views on Apologetics*. Grand Rapids, Mich.: Zondervan.

Cray, Graham (ed.) (2004). *Mission-Shaped Church*. London: Church House Publishing.

Croft, Steven (1999). *Ministry in Three Dimensions: Ordination and Leadership in the Local Church*. London: Darton, Longman and Todd.

Curran, Charles E. (1978). 'Conversion: The Central Moral Message of Jesus.' In W. Conn (ed.), *Conversion: Perspectives on Personal and Social Transformation*. New York: Alba House, 225-45.

Curran, Kathryn L. (2002). *Finding God Behind Bars: An Exploratory Study of the Relevance of Prison Conversions to Criminology*. PhD thesis, University of Cambridge.

Davidman, Lynn and Greil, Arthur L. (1993). 'Gender and the Experience of Conversion: The Case of "Returnees" to Modern Orthodox Judaism.' *Sociology of Religion* 54: 83-100.

Davie, Grace (1994). *Religion in Britain Since 1945: Believing Without Belonging*. Oxford: Blackwell.

— (1999). 'Europe: The Exception that Proves the Rule?' In P. Berger (ed.), *The Desecularization of the World: Resurgent Religion and World Politics*. Grand Rapids, Mich.: Eerdmans, 65-84.

Davie, Grace, Heelas, Paul and Woodhead, Linda (eds) (2003). *Predicting Religion: Christian, Secular, and Alternative Futures*. Aldershot, Hants: Ashgate.

Davies, Charlotte Aull (1999). *Reflexive Ethnography: A Guide to Researching Selves and Others*. London: Routledge.

Davies, Oliver and Turner, Denys (2002). *Silence and the Word: Negative Theology and Incarnation*. Cambridge: Cambridge University Press.

Dearborn, Kerry (2003). 'Recovering a Trinitarian and Sacramental Ecclesiology.' In J. John Stackhouse (ed.), *Evangelical Ecclesiology: Reality or Illusion?* Grand Rapids, Mich.: Baker Academic, 39-73.

Denzin, Norman K. (1998). *Handbook of Qualitative Research*. London: Sage.

Dixon, Keith (1980). *The Sociology of Belief: Fallacy and Foundation*. London: Routledge and Kegan Paul.

Dodd, C. H. (1961). *The Parables of the Kingdom*. Revised ed. London: Nisbet. Original publication 1935.

Donovan, Vincent J. (1993). *Christianity Rediscovered: An Epistle from the Masai*. 2nd ed. London: SCM Press. Original publication 1978.

Doughty, W. L. (1955). *John Wesley: Preacher*. London: Epworth Press.

Douglas, Mary (2003). *Natural Symbols*. London: Routledge. Original publication 1970.

Drane, John (2000). *The McDonaldization of the Church: Spirituality, Creativity, and the Future of the Church*. London: Darton Longman & Todd.

— (2007). 'Alpha and Evangelism in Modern and Post-Modern Settings.' In A. Brookes (ed.), *The Alpha Phenomenon*. London: Churches Together in Britain and Ireland, 370-84.

Duffy, Eamon (1992). *The Stripping of the Altars: Traditional Religion in England, c.1400–c.1580*. London: Yale University Press.

Dulles, Avery (1988). *Models of the Church*. 2nd ed. Dublin: Gill and Macmillan.

— (1994). *The Assurance of Things Hoped For: A Theology of Christian Faith*. Oxford: Oxford University Press.

— (ed.) (1999). *A History of Apologetics*. 2nd ed. San Francisco: Ignatius Press.

Earey, Mark and Headley, Carolyn (2002). *Mission and Liturgical Worship*. Cambridge: Grove Books.

Ehrman, Bart D. (ed.) (2003). *The Apostolic Fathers*. Cambridge, Mass.: Harvard University Press.

Elkin, Frederick (1963). *The Child and Society: The Process of Socialization*. New York: Random House.

Fane, Rosalind S. (1999). 'Is Self-Assigned Religious Affiliation Socially Significant?' In L. J. Francis (ed.), *Sociology, Theology and the Curriculum*. London: Cassell, 113-24.

Farnsley, Arthur (2004). 'The Rise of Congregational Studies in the USA.' In M. Guest, et al. (eds), *Congregational Studies in the UK: Christianity in a Post-Christian Context*. Aldershot: Ashgate, 25-38.

Farrow, Douglas (1999). *Ascension and Ecclesia: On the Significance of the Doctrine of the Ascension for Ecclesiology and Christian Cosmology*. Edinburgh: T & T Clark.

Ferguson, Everett (2001). 'Catechesis and Initiation.' In A. Kreider (ed.), *The Origins of Christendom in the West*. Edinburgh: T & T Clark, 229-68.

Festinger, Leon. (1953). 'An Analysis of Compliant Behaviour.' In M. Sherif and M. O. Wilson (eds), *Group Relations at the Crossroads*. New York: Harper and Row.

— (1968). 'Informal Social Communication.' In D. Cartwright and A. Zander (eds), *Group Dynamics: Research and Theory*. 3rd ed. London: Tavistock, 182-91.

Festinger, Leon, Riecken, Henry W. and Schachter, Stanley (1956). *When Prophecy Fails*. Minneapolis: University of Minnesota Press.

Fiddes, Paul (1984). 'The Theology of the Charismatic Movement.' In D. Martin and P. Mullen (eds), *Strange Gifts? A Guide to Charismatic Renewal*. Oxford: Blackwells, 19-40.

— (1989). *Past Event and Present Salvation: The Christian Idea of Atonement*. London: Darton, Longman and Todd.

Fine, Gary Alan (1993). 'The Sad Demise, Mysterious Disappearance, and Glorious Triumph of Symbolic Interactionism.' *Annual Review of Sociology* 19: 61-87.

Finn, Thomas (1997). *From Death to Rebirth: Ritual and Conversion in Antiquity*. New York: Paulist Press.

Finney, Charles (c1835). *Revivals of Religion*. Old Tappan, N. J.: Fleming H. Revell.

Finney, John (1992). *Finding Faith Today: How Does it Happen?* Swindon: Bible Society.

— (2000). *Fading Splendour? A new Model of Renewal*. London: Darton, Longman and Todd.

Fish, Stanley (1980). *Is There a Text in This Class?: The Authority of Interpretive Communities*. Cambridge, Mass.: Harvard University Press.

Flax, Jane (1987). 'Postmodernism and Gender Relations in Feminist Theory.' *Signs* 12/4 (Summer): 621-43.

Forbes, Cheryl (1986). *The Religion of Power*. Bromley: MARC Europe.

Ford, David.(1999). *Self and Salvation: Being Transformed*. Cambridge: Cambridge University Press.

Fowler, James W. (1981). *Stages of Faith: The Psychology of Human Development and the Quest for Meaning*. London: Harper & Row.

— (1984). *Becoming Adult, Becoming Christian: Adult Development and Christian Faith*. San Francisco: Harper & Row.

France, R. T. (1993). 'Conversion in the Bible.' *The Evangelical Quarterly* 65.4, 291-310.

Francis, Leslie J. and Robbins, Mandy (2004). 'Belonging Without Believing: A Study in the Social Significance of Anglican Identity and Implicit Religion Among 13–15 Year-Old Males.' *Implicit Religion* 7/1: 37-54.

Freebury, Charles (2001). *A Comparative Evaluation of the Alpha and Emmaus Course*. MA dissertation, University of Sheffield at Cliff College.

— (2004). *Alpha or Emmaus? Assessing Today's Top Evangelistic Courses*. Sheffield.

Frost, Rob (2002). *The Essence Course*. Eastbourne: Kingsway.

Gadamer, Hans-Georg (1994). *Truth and Method*. 2nd revised ed. Trans. J. Weinsheimer and D. G. Marshall. London: Sheed and Ward.

Gaffin, R. G. (1991). 'Kingdom of God.' In S. B. Ferguson and D. F. Wright (eds), *New Dictionary of Theology*. Leicester: IVP, 367-69.

Gaventa, Beverly (1986). *From Darkness to Light*. Philadelphia: Fortress Press.

Geertz, Clifford (1973). *The Interpretation of Cultures: Selected Essays*. New York: Basic Books.

— (1973). 'Thick Description: Toward an Interpretive Theory of Culture.' In C. Geertz *The Interpretation of Cultures*. New York: Basic Books, 3-30.

Geivett, R. Douglas and Sweetman, Brendan (eds) (1992). *Contemporary Perspectives on Religious Epistemology*. Oxford: Oxford University Press.

Gelpi, Donald (1998). *The Conversion Experience: A Reflective Process for RCIA Participants and Others*. New York: Paulist Press.

Gerlach, Luther and Hine, Virginia (1970). *People, Power, and Change: Movements of*

Social Transformation. Indianapolis: Bobbs-Merrill.

Gillespie, V. Bailey (1991). *The Dynamics of Religious Conversion*. Birmingham, Ala: Religious Education Press.

Gillett, David (1993). *Trust and Obey: Explorations in Evangelical Spirituality*. London: Darton, Longmann and Todd.

Gillham, Bill (2000). *Case Study Research Methods*. London: Continuum.

Glaser, Barney G. and Strauss, Anselm L. (1968). *The Discovery of Grounded Theory: Strategies for Qualitative Research*. London: Weidenfeld and Nicolson. Original publication 1967.

Goffman, Erving (1990). *The Presentation of Self in Everyday Life*. London: Penguin. Original publication c1959.

Gold, R. L. (1958). 'Roles in Sociological Fieldwork.' *Social Forces* 36: 217-23.

Goldingay, John (1996). 'Charismatic Spirituality.' *Theology* 97: 178-87.

Goodhew, David (2003). 'The Rise of the Cambridge Inter-Collegiate Christian Union, 1910–1971.' *Journal of Ecclesiastical History* 54/1, 62-88.

Granqvist, Pehr and Kirkpatrick, Lee A. (2004). 'Religious Conversion and Perceived Childhood Attachment: A Meta-Analysis.' *International Journal for the Psychology of Religion* 14/4: 223-50.

Green, Michael (1970). *Evangelism in the Local Church*. Guildford: Eagle.

Greil, Arthur L. (1977). 'Conversion to the Perspective and Conversion to Perspectives of Social and Religious Movements.' *Sociological Analysis* 38/2: 115-25.

Greil, Arthur L. and Rudy, David R. (1984). 'Social Cocoons: Encapsulation and Identity Transformation.' *Sociological Inquiry* 54: 260-78.

Grudem, Wayne (1994). *Systematic Theology*. Leicester: IVP.

Guba, E. and Lincoln, Y. (1994). 'Competing Paradigms in Qualitative Research.' In N. K. Denzin and Y. S. Lincoln (eds), *Handbook of Qualitative Research*. London: Sage, 105-18.

Guest, Mathew, Tusting, Karin and Woodhead, Linda (eds) (2004). *Congregational Studies in the UK: Christianity in a Post-Christian Context*. Aldershot: Ashgate.

Gumbel, Nicky (1995). 'The Spirit and Evangelism.' In W. Boulton (ed.), *The Impact of Toronto*. Crowborough: Monarch, 80-85

— (2001a). *Challenging Lifestyle*. Eastbourne: Kingsway. Original publication 1996.

— (2001b). *A Heart of Revival*. Eastbourne: Kingsway. Original publication 1997.

— (2001c). *A Life Worth Living*. Eastbourne: Kingsway. Original publication 1994.

— (2001d). 'Principles of Alpha' talk, *Alpha Conference*, HTB, London, 2 July.

— (2001e). *Questions of Life*. Eastbourne: Kingsway. Original publication 1993.

— (2001f). *Searching Issues*. Eastbourne: Kingsway. Original publication 1994.

— (2001g). *Telling Others*. Eastbourne: Kingsway. Original publication 1994.

— (2003a). *Alpha Team Training Manual*. Revised ed. London: Alpha International.

— (2003b). 'Ministry on Alpha' talk, HTB, London, 10 June.

— (2003c). 'Response to Mark Ireland's Dissertation by Nicky Gumbel and Sandy Millar', *Evangelism.uk.net*, 20 November.

— (2004). 'Practicalities of Alpha' talk, *Alpha Conference*, HTB, London.

— (2005). 'UK Strategy Day' talk, HTB, London, 24 February.

— (2006). 'Introduction to Alpha' talk, *College Lecture*, Ridley Hall, 23 February.

— (2007). 'Initial responses and reactions from Nicky Gumbel.' In A. Brookes (ed.), *The Alpha Phenomenon*. London: Churches Together in Britain and Ireland, 429-37.

Gunton, Colin (1988). *The Actuality of the Atonement*. Edinburgh: T & T Clark.

— (1992a). *Christ and Creation*. Carlisle: Paternoster.

— (1992b). 'Universal and Particular in Atonement Theology.' *Religious Studies* 28/4, 453-66.

— (1993). *The One, the Three and the Many: God, Creation and the Culture of Modernity*. Cambridge University Press.

— (2002). *The Christian Faith*. Oxford: Blackwell.

Gutiérrez, Gustavo (1974). *A Theology of Liberation: History, Politics and Salvation*. Trans. S. C. Inda and J. Eagleson. London: SCM Press.

Hammersley, Martyn and Atkinson, Paul (1995). *Ethnography: Principles in Practice*. 2nd ed. London: Routledge.

Hand, Chris (1998). *Falling Short? The Alpha Course Examined*. Epsom, Surrey: Day One Publications.

Harding, Susan F. (1987). 'Frontiers of Christian Evangelism.' *American Ethnologist* 14/1 (Feb): 167-81.

Hardy, Daniel (2001). *Finding the Church*. London: SCM Press.

Häring, Bernhard (1978). 'The Characteristics of Conversion.' In W. E. Conn (ed.), *Conversion: Perspectives on Personal and Social Transformation*. New York: Alba House, 213-23.

Hart, Trevor (1997). 'Redemption and Fall.' In C. Gunton (ed.), *The Cambridge Companion to Christian Doctrine*. Cambridge: Cambridge University Press, 189-206.

Hassan, Steven (1988). *Combating Cult Mind Control*. Wellingborough: Aquarian.

Hastings, Adrian (2001). *A History of English Christianity 1920–2000*. 4th ed. London: SCM Press.

Healy, Nicholas (2000). *Church, World and the Christian Life: Practical-Prophetic Ecclesiology*. Cambridge: Cambridge University Press.

Heard, James (2007). 'Worship, Sacramental Liturgy and Initiation Rites within Evangelism and Alpha.' In A. Brookes (ed.), *The Alpha Phenomenon*. London: Churches Together in Britain and Ireland, 340-51.

Heinrich, M. (1977). 'Change of Heart: A Test of Some Widely Held Theories of Religious Conversion.' *American Sociological Review* 83: 653-80.

Hick, John (1993). *The Metaphor of God Incarnate*. London: SCM Press.

Hilborn, David (1997). *Picking up the Pieces: Can Evangelicals Adapt to Contemporary Culture?* London: Hodder & Stoughton.

— (ed.) (2001). *'Toronto' in Perspective: Papers on the New Charismatic Wave of the Mid-1990s*. Carlisle: Paternoster.

Hindmarsh, Bruce (2002). 'Let Us See Thy Great Salvation: What Did it Mean to be Saved for the Early Evangelicals?' In J. G. Stackhouse (ed.), *What Does it Mean to be Saved?* Grand Rapids, Mich.: Baker Academic, 43-66.

— (2003). 'Is Evangelical Ecclesiology an Oxymoron? A Historical Perspective.' In J. Stackhouse (ed.), *Evangelical Ecclesiology: Reality or Illusion?* Grand Rapids, Mich.: Baker Academic, 15-37.

Hirsch, E. D. (1967). *Validity in Interpretation*. London: Yale University Press.

Hocken, Peter (1997). *Streams of Renewal: The Origins and Early Development of the Charismatic Movement in Great Britain*. Revised ed. Carlisle: Paternoster. Original publication 1986.

— (2004). 'The Impact of the Charismatic Movement on the Roman Catholic Church.' *Journal of Beliefs and Values* 25/2: 205-16.

Hodge, Charles (1960). *Systematic Theology*. London: James Clarke.

Hodkinson, Paul (2005). '"Insider Research" in the Study of Youth Cultures.' *Journal of Youth Studies* 8/2 (June): 131-49.

Holmes, Steve (2005). 'Can Punishment Bring Peace? Penal substitution Revisited.' *Scottish Journal of Theology* 58: 104-23.

Hopewell, James F. (ed.) (1988). *Congregation: Stories and Structures*. Edited by B. G. Wheeler. London: SCM Press.

Houston, James (1996). 'Towards a Biblical Spirituality.' In E. Dyck (ed.), *The Act of Bible Reading*. Carlisle: Paternoster Press, 148-72.

Howes, Graham (2001). 'The Sociologist as Stylist: David Martin and Pentecostalism.' In A. Walker and M. Percy (eds), *Restoring the Image: Essays on Religion and Society in Honour of David Martin*. Sheffield: Sheffield Academic Press, 98-108.

Hunt, Stephen (2001). *Anyone for Alpha? Evangelism in a Post-Christian Society*. London: Darton, Longman & Todd.

— (2004). *The Alpha Enterprise: Evangelism in a Post-Christian Era*. Aldershot: Ashgate.

— (2005). 'Alpha and the Gay Issue: A Lesson in Homophobia?' *Journal of Beliefs and Values* 26: 261-71.

Hunter, Todd (2004). 'Todd Hunter New Alpha President', in Vol. 2006, http://www.quicktopic.com/26/H/ErRnwYKRwKk.

Huyssteen, Wentzal van (1989). *Theology and the Justification of Faith*. Grand Rapids, Mich.: Eerdmans.

Ireland, Mark (2000). *A Study of the Effectiveness of Process Evangelism Courses in the Diocese of Lichfield With Special Reference to Alpha*. MA dissertation, University of Sheffield at Cliff College.

Jackson, Bob (2002). *Hope for the Church: Contemporary Strategies for Growth*. London: Church House.

James, William (1902). *The Varieties of Religious Experience: A Study in Human Nature*. 1st reprinted, with revisions ed. London: Longmans, Green and Co.

Jamieson, Alan. (2002). *A Churchless Faith: Faith Journeys Beyond the Churches*. London: SPCK.

Janis, Irving L. (1982). *Group Think*. 2nd ed. Boston: Houghton Miffling Company.

Jeffery, Steve, Ovey, Mike and Sach, Andrew (2007). *Pierced for Our Transgressions: Rediscovering the Glory of Penal Substitution*. Leicester: IVP.

Johnson, Maxwell (1999). *The Rites of Christian Initiation*. Minnesota: Liturgical Press.

Jones, E. (1964). *Ingratiation*. New York: Appleton-Century-Crofts.

Jorgensen, Danny L. (1989). *Participant Observation: A Methodology for Human Studies*. London: Sage.

Jüngel, Eberhard (1999). 'On the Doctrine of Justification.' *International Journal of Systematic Theology* 1/1 (March 1999): 24-52.

Kahn, Peter J. and Greene, A. L. (2004). '"Seeing Conversion Whole": Testing a Model of Religious Conversion.' *Pastoral Psychology* 52/3 (January): 233-58.

Kaufman, G. D. (1981). *The Theological Imagination: Constructing the Concept of God*. Philadelphia: Westminster.

Kavanagh, Aidan (1978). *The Shape of Baptism: The Rite of Christian Initiation*. New York: Pueblo Publishing Company.

Kay, William (2007). *Apostolic Networks in Britain: New Ways of Being Church*. Carlisle: Paternoster.

Kay, William K. and Dyer, Anne E. (eds) (2004). *Pentecostal and Charismatic Studies: A Reader*. London: SCM Press.

Kelly, J. N. D. (1958). *Early Christian Doctrines*. London: Adam & Charles Black.

Kelsey, David (1975). *The Uses of Scripture in Recent Theology*. London: SCM Press.

Kenworthy, Jared (2003). 'Explaining the Belief in God for Self, In-Group, and Out-Group Targets.' *Journal for the Scientific Study of Religion* 42/1: 137-46.

Kilbourne, B. and Richardson, J. T. (1989). 'Paradigm Conflict, Types of Conversion, and Conversion Theories.' *Sociological Analysis* 50: 1-21.

Kim, Seyoon (1982). *The Origin of Paul's Gospel*. Grand Rapids: Eerdmans.

Kirkpatrick, L. (1997). 'A Longitudinal Study of Changes in Religious Belief and Behaviour as a Function of Individual Differences in Adult Attachment Style.' *Journal for the Scientific Study of Religion* 36: 207-17.

Kirkpatrick, L. and Shaver, P. (1990). 'Attachment Theory and Religion.' *Journal for the Scientific Study of Religion* 29: 315-34.

Klien, William, Blomberg, Craig and Hubbard, Robert (1993). *Introduction to Biblical Interpretation*. London: Word.

Knights, Philip and Murray, Andrea (2002). *Evangelisation in England and Wales: A Report to the Catholic Bishops*. London: Catholic Communications Service.

Köse, Ali (1999). 'The Journey from the Secular to the Sacred: Experiences of Native British Converts to Islam.' *Social Compass* 46/3 (September 1, 1999): 301-12.

Kreider, Alan (1999). *The Change of Conversion and the Origin of Christendom*. Harrisburg: Trinity.

— (ed.) (2001). *The Origins of Christendom in the West*. Edinburgh: T & T Clark.

— (2007). 'Baptism and Catechesis as Spiritual Formation.' In A. Walker and L. Bretherton (eds), *Remembering Our Future: Explorations in Deep Church*. Milton Keynes: Paternoster Press, 170-206.

Küng, Hans (1964). *Justification: The Doctrine of Karl Barth and a Catholic Reflection*. London: Burns & Oates.

Kvale, Steinar (1996). *InterViews: An Introduction to Qualitative Research Interviewing*. London: Sage.

Ladd, George Eldon (1980). *The Presence of the Future: The Eschatology of Biblical Realism*. 2nd ed. London: SPCK. Original publication 1974.

Lee, Philip J. (1986). *Against the Protestant Gnostics*. Oxford: Oxford University Press.

Lewin, K., Lippitt, R. and White, R. K. (1939). 'Patterns of Aggressive Behavior in Experimentally Created Social Climates.' *Journal of Social Psychology* 10: 271-301.

Lewin, Kurt (1947). 'Frontiers in Group Dynamics: Concept, Method and Reality in Social Science: Social Equilibria and Social Change.' *Human Relations* 1/1 (June 1, 1947): 5-41.

— (1958). 'Group Decision and Social Change.' In E. E. Maecoby, et al. (eds), *Readings in Social Psychology*. New York: Henry Holt & Company, 197-211.

Lewis, Mike (2001). *Why Not The Dove? (A Study of the Teaching and Practice of the Holy Spirit as it was Experienced in the Alpha Course in the Dove Valley Circuit 1997–2000)*. MA dissertation, University of Sheffield at Cliff College.

Lings, George and Perkins, Paul (2002). *Dynasty or Diversity? The HTB Family of Churches*. Encounters on the Edge. Edited by G. Lings. Sheffield: Church Army.

Lloyd, Mike. (2005). *Café Theology*. London: Alpha International.

Lofland, John (1966). *Doomsday Cult: A Study of Conversion, Prosyletisation and Maintenance of Faith*. Englewood Cliffs, N.J.: Prentice Hall.

— (1977). 'Becoming a World-Saver.' *American Behavioural Scientist* 20/6: 805-18.
— (1978). 'Becoming a World-Saver Revisited.' In J. T. Richardson (ed.), *Conversion Careers*. Beverly Hills, Calif: Sage, 1-23.
Lofland, John and Skonovd, Norman (1981). 'Conversion Motifs.' *Journal for the Scientific Study of Religion* 20 (371-85).
Lofland, John and Stark, Rodney (1965). 'Becoming a World-Saver: A Theory of Conversion to a Deviant Perspective.' *American Sociological Review* 30/6 (Dec): 862-75.
Louth, Andrew (2005). 'Deification.' In P. Sheldrake (ed.), *The New SCM Dictionary of Christian Spirituality*. London: SCM, 229-30.
Luckmann, Thomas (1967). *The Invisible Religion: The Problem of Religion in Modern Society*. New York: Macmillan.
Luzbetak, Louis J. (1988). *The Church and Cultures: New Perspectives in Missiological Anthropology*. Maryknoll, N.Y.: Orbis Books.
Lyon, David (1994). *Postmodernity*. Buckingham: Open University Press.
— (2000). *Jesus in Disneyland*. Malden, MA: Blackwell.
Lyotard, Jean-Francois (1984). *The Postmodern Condition: A Report on Knowledge*. Trans. G. Bennington and B. Massumi. Manchester: Manchester University Press. Original publication 1979.
MacIntyre, Alasdair (2004). *After Virtue*. 2nd ed. London: Gerald Duckworth. Original publication 1981.
MacKinnon, Catharine (1982). 'Feminism, Marxism, Method, and the State: An Agenda for Theory.' *Signs* 7: 515-44.
MacLaren, Duncan (2003). *Precarious Visions: A Sociological Critique of European Scenarios of Desecularisation*. PhD thesis, King's College, London.
— (2004). *Mission Implausible: Restoring Credibility to the Church*. Carlisle: Paternoster.
MacMullen, Ramsay (1984). *Christianizing the Roman Empire (AD 100–400)*. New Haven: Yale University Press.
— (1997). *Christianity and Paganism in the Fourth to Eighth Centuries*. New Haven: Yale University Press.
— (2001). 'Christianity Shaped Through it Mission.' In A. Kreider (ed.), *The Origins of Christendom in the West*. Edinburgh: T & T Clark, 97-117.
Macquarrie, John (1997). *A Guide to the Sacraments*. London: SCM Press.
Maines, D. R. (1977). 'Social Organization and Social Structure in Symbolic Interactionist Thought.' *Annual Review of Sociology* 3/1: 235-59.
Martin, David (1969). *The Religious and the Secular: Studies in Secularisation*. London: Routledge and Kegan Paul.
— (1981). 'Disorientation to Mainstream Religion: The Context of Reorientations in New Religious Movements.' In B. Wilson (ed.), *The Social Impact of New Religious Movements*. Barrytown, N.Y.: Unification Theological Seminary.
— (1984). 'The Political Oeconomy of the Holy Ghost.' In D. Martin and P. Mullen (eds), *Strange Gifts? A Guide to Charismatic Renewal*. Oxfore: Blackwells, 54-71.
— (1997). *Reflections on Sociology and Theology*. Oxford: Clarendon Press.
May, Tim (1997). *Social Research: Issues, Methods and Process*. 2nd ed. Buckingham: Open University Press.
Mayo, Bob, Savage, Sara and Collins, Sylvia (2004). *Ambiguous Evangelism*. London: SPCK.

McDonald, Elizabeth (1996). *Alpha: New Life or New Lifestyle? A Biblical Assessment of the Alpha Course*. Cambridge: St Matthew Publishing.

McDonald, Elizabeth and Peterson, Dusty (2001). *Alpha – The Unofficial Guide*. Cambridge: St Matthew.

McGavran, Donald A. (1955). *The Bridges of God: A Study in the Strategy of Missions*. London: World Dominion Press.

— (1970). *Understanding Church Growth*. Grand Rapids, Mich.: Eerdmans.

McGrath, Alister (1993). 'Evangelical Anglicanism: A Contradiction in Terms?' In R. T. France and A. E. McGrath (eds), *Evangelical Anglicans: Their Role and Influence in the Church Today*. London: SPCK, 10-21.

— (2006). *The Christian Theology Reader*. 3rd ed. Oxford: Blackwell.

McIntyre, John (1992). *The Shape of Soteriology: Studies in the Doctrine of the Death of Christ*. Edinburgh: T & T Clark.

McKnight, Scott (2002). *Turning to Jesus: The Sociology of Conversion in the Gospels*. Louisville, Ken.: Westminster John Knox Press.

McLoughlin, William G. (1958). *Modern Revivalism: Charles Grandison Finney to Billy Graham*. New York: Ronald Press.

Meadows, Philip (2007). 'Alpha as a Technological Phenomenon: Do Churches Need Technicians or Mentors for Mission?' In A. Brookes (ed.), *The Alpha Phenomenon*. London: Churches Together in Britain and Ireland, 398-418.

Meltzer, B.N., Petras, J.W. and Reynolds, L.T. (1975). *Symbolic Interactionism: Genesis, Varieties and Criticism*. Boston: Routledge & Kegan Paul.

Menzies, R.P. (1994). *Empowered for Witness*. Sheffield: Sheffield Academic Press.

Mercer, Nick (1995). 'Postmodernity and Rationality: The Final Credits or Just a Commercial Break?' In A. Billington, et al. (eds), *Mission and Meaning: Essays Presented to Peter Cotterell*. Carlisle: Paternoster, 319-338.

Millar, Sandy (2005). *All I Want is You*. London: Alpha International.

Mintz, Sidney W. and Bois, Christine M. Du (2002). 'The Anthropology of Food and Eating.' *Annual Review of Anthropology* 31: 99-119.

Moltmann, Jurgen (1977). *The Church in the Power of the Spirit: A Contribution to Messianic Ecclesiology*. Trans. M. Kohl. London: SCM Press.

Morgenthaler, Sally (1995). *Worship Evangelism*. Grand Rapids, Mich.: Zondervan.

Murray, Stuart. (2004). *Church after Christendom*. Carlisle: Paternoster.

Nandhakumar, Joe and Jones, Matthew (1997). 'Too Close for Comfort? Distance and Engagement in Interpretive Information Systems Research.' *Information Systems Journal* 7: 109-31.

Napier, Rodney W. and Gershenfeld, Matti K. (1985). *Groups: Theory and Experience*. 3rd ed. Boston: Houghton Mifflin Company.

Neill, Tricia (2006). *From Vision to Action*. London: Alpha International.

Newbigin, Lesslie (1953). *The Household of God: Lectures on the Nature of the Church*. London: SCM Press.

— (1969). 'Conversion.' In S. Neill and G. H. Anderson (eds), *Concise Dictionary of the Christian World Mission*. London: SCM Press, 147-48.

— (1995). *The Open Secret*. London: SPCK.

— (2000). *The Gospel in a Pluralist Society*. London: SPCK. Original publication 1989.

Noakes, Ronald (1984). 'The Instinct of the Herd.' In D. Martin and P. Mullen (eds), *Strange Gifts? A Guide to Charismatic Renewal*. Oxford: Blackwells.

Nock, A. D. (1933). *Conversion: The Old and the New in Religion from Alexander the*

Great to Augustine of Hippo. Oxford: Oxford University Press.

Noll, Mark A. (1994). *The Scandal of the Evangelical Mind*. Grand Rapids, Mich.: Eerdmans.

O'Collins, Gerald (1981). *Fundamental Theology*. London: Darton, Longman & Todd.

O'Donovan, Oliver (1986). *On the Thirty-Nine Articles*. Exeter: Paternoster Press.

O'Halloran, S. (2003). 'Participant Observation of Alcoholics Anonymous: Contrasting Roles of the Ethnographer and Ethnomethodologist.' *The Qualitative Report* 8/1 (10 January 2006), 81-99.

Odgers, James (2004). *Simplicity, Love and Justice*. London: Alpha International.

Olson, Roger E. (2003). 'Free Church Ecclesiology and Evangelical Spirituality.' In J. Stackhouse (ed.), *Evangelical Ecclesiology: Reality or Illusion?* Grand Rapids, Mich.: Baker Academic, 161-78.

Packer, J. I. (1973). *Knowing God*. London: Hodder and Stoughton.

— (ed.) (1986). *Here We Stand: Justification by Faith Today*. London: Hodder and Stoughton.

Pannenberg, Wolfhart (1985). *Anthropology in Theological Perspective*. Trans. M. J. O'Connell. T & T Clark.

Peace, Richard (1999). *Conversion in the New Testament: Paul and the Twelve*. Cambridge: Eerdmans.

— (2004). 'Conflicting Understanding of Christian Conversion: A Missiological Challenge.' *International Bulletin of Missionary Research* 28/1 (January), 8-14.

Pelikan, Jaroslav (1971). *The Emergence of the Catholic Tradition (100–600)*. Vol.1 The Christian Tradition, Chicago: University of Chicago Press.

Percy, Martyn (1996). *Words, Wonders and Power: Understanding Contemporary Christian Fundamentalism and Revivalism*. London: SPCK.

— (1997a). 'Join-the-dots Christianity – Assessing Alpha.' *Reviews in Religion and Theology* 3: 14-18.

— (1997b). 'Sweet Rapture: Subliminal Eroticism in Contemporary Charismatic Worship.' *Theology and Sexuality* 6: 71-106.

— (ed.) (2000). *Previous Convictions: Conversion in the Real World*. London: SPCK.

— (2001). *The Salt of the Earth*. London: Sheffield Academic Press.

— (2003). 'A Place at High Table? Assessing the Future of Charismatic Christianity.' In G. Davie, et al. (eds), *Predicting Religion: Christian, Secular, and Alternative Futures*. Aldershot, Hants: Ashgate, 95-108.

— (2005). 'Romancing Jesus: An Anatomy of Renewal', Gresham College, http://www.gresham.ac.uk, 10 May.

Peterson, Eugene H. (2006). *Eat This Book: A Conversation in the Art of Spiritual Reading*. Grand Rapids, Mich.: Eerdmans.

Phillips, D. Z. (1998). *Faith After Foundationalism*. London: Routledge.

Pickett, Joseph P. (ed.) (2000). *The American Heritage Dictionary of the English Language*. 4th ed. Boston: Houghton Mifflin Company.

Plantinga, Alvin (1993). *Warrant and Proper Function*. Oxford: Oxford University Press.

— (2000). *Warranted Christian Belief*. Oxford: Oxford University Press.

Plummer, Ken (ed.) (1991). *Symbolic Interactionism*. Aldershot: Elgar.

Polanyi, Michael (1962). *Personal Knowledge. Towards a Post-Critical Philosophy*. 2nd edition ed. London: Routledge.

Pollock, John (1997). *D. L. Moody*. Fearn: Baker Books.

Porter, Matthew (2003). *David Watson: Evangelism, Renewal, Reconciliation.* Vol. R12. Cambridge: Grove Books.

Porter, Stanley E. and Richter, Philip J. (eds). (1995). *The Toronto Blessing – Or Is It?* London: Darton, Longman and Todd.

Race, John (2004). *A Theological Reflection on the Alpha course, Including its Application in Prisons (England and Wales) and Among Ex-Offenders (Through Alpha for Prisons and Caring for Ex-Offenders).* MTh thesis, University of Oxford.

Rahner, Karl (1978). 'Conversion.' In W. E. Conn (ed.), *Conversion: Perspectives on Personal and Social Transformation.* Alba House: New York, 203-11.

Rambo, Lewis (1993). *Understanding Religious Conversion.* New Haven: Yale University Press.

— (1999). 'Theories of Conversion: Understanding and Interpreting Religious Change.' *Social Compass* 46/3: 259-71.

Ratzinger, Joseph (1992). *Letter to the Bishops of the Catholic Church on Some Aspects of the Church Understood as Communion.* Rome: Congregation for the Doctrine of the Faith.

Reason, Peter (ed.) (1988). *Human Inquiry in Action: Developments in New Paradigm Research.* London: Sage.

Richardson, James (1985). 'The Active vs. Passive Convert: Paradigm Conflict in Conversion/Recruitment Research.' *Journal for the Scientific Study of Religion* 24/2: 163-79.

— (1993). 'A Social Psychological Critique of "Brainwashing" Claims About Recruitment to New Religions.' In D. Bromley and J. Hadden (eds), *The Handbook of Sects and Cults in America, Religion and the Social Order.* Greenwich, CT: JAI Press, 75-98.

Richter, Philip J. (1995). 'God is Not a Gentleman!' In S. E. Porter and P. J. Richter (eds), *The Toronto Blessing – Or Is It?* London: Darton, Longman and Todd, 5-37.

Richter, Philip J. and Francis, Leslie J. (1998). *Gone But Not Forgotten: Church Leaving and Returning.* London: Darton, Longman & Todd.

Riddell, Mike (1999). 'Bread and Wine, Beer and Pies.' In P. Ward (ed.), *Mass Culture: Eucharist and Mission in a Post-modern World.* Oxford: The Bible Reading Fellowship.

Ritzer, George (1996). *The McDonaldization of Society: An Investigation into the Changing Character of Contemporary Social Life.* London: Pine Forge.

Roberts, Alexander and Donaldson, James (eds) (1976–83). *The Ante-Nicene Fathers with Justin Martyr and Irenaeus: Translations of the Writings of the Fathers Down to AD 325.* Grand Rapids, Mich.: Eerdmans.

Robinson, John A. T. (1963). *Honest to God.* London: SCM.

Robson, Colin (1993). *Real World Research.* Oxford: Blackwell.

Rogers, Andrew P. (2000). *A Critical Examination of African Hermeneutics in Relationship to Euro-American Hermeneutical Paradigms.* MA thesis, London School of Theology.

Rosen, Harold (1974). 'Language and Class: A Critical Look at the Theories of Basil Bernstein.' *The Urban Review* 7/2 (April), 97-114.

Rubin, Herbert J. and Rubin, Irene S. (1995). *Qualitative Interviewing: The Art of Hearing Data.* London: Sage.

Rudy, David (1986). *Becoming Alcoholic: Alcoholics Anonymous and the Reality of Alcoholism.* Illinois: Southern Illinois University Press.

Sanders, E. P. (1977). *Paul and Palestinian Judaism*. Philadelphia: Fortress.

Sanders, Jack T. (2000). *Charisma, Converts, Competitors: Societal Factors in the Success of Early Christianity* London: SCM Press.

Sanneh, Lamin (2004). *Translating the Message: The Missionary Impact of Culture*. New York: Orbis. Original publication 1989.

Sapsford, Roger and Jupp, Victor (eds) (1996). *Data Collection and Analysis*. London: Sage.

Saunders, Teddy and Sansom, Hugh (1992). *David Watson: A Biography*. London Hodder and Stoughton.

Savage, Sara (2000). 'A Psychology of Conversion – From All Angles.' In M. Percy (ed.), *Previous Convictions: Conversion in the Real World*. London: SPCK, 1-19.

Savage, Sara, Collins-Mayo, Sylvia, Mayo, Bob and Cray, Graham (2006). *Making Sense of Generation Y: The World View of 15 to 25-year-olds*. London: Church House Publishing.

Schachter, Stanley (1968). 'Deviation, Rejection and Communication.' In D. Cartwright and A. Zander (eds), *Group Dynamics: Research and Theory*. 3rd ed. London: Tavistock, 165-81.

Schaff, Philip (1995, c1888). *Homilies on the First Epistle of John Soliloquies*. Peabody, Mass: Hendrickson.

Schaff, Philip and Wace, Henry (eds) (1995). *Sulpitius Severus, Vincent of Lerins, John Cassian*. Peabody, Mass.: Hendrickson.

Schleiermacher, Friedrich (1928). *The Christian Faith*. Edinburgh: Clark.

Schreiter, Robert J. (1986). *Constructing Local Theologies*. Maryknoll, N.Y.: Orbis Books.

Schutz, Alfred (1962-1966). *Collected Papers*. The Hague: M. Nijhoff.

— (1967b). *The Phenomenology of the Social World*. Trans. G. W. a. F. Lehnert. Evanston: Northwestern University Press.

Schweitzer, Albert (1954). *The Quest of the Historical Jesus: A Critical Study of its Progress from Reimarus to Wrede*. 3rd ed. Trans. W. Montgomery. London: A & C Black. Original publication 1911.

Scotland, Nigel (2000a). *Charismatics and the New Millennium*. Guildford: Eagle.

— (2000b). *Sectarian Religion in Contemporary Britain*. Carlisle: Paternoster.

— (2000c). 'Shopping for a Church: Consumerism and the Churches.' In C. Bartholomew and T. Moritz (eds), *Christ and Consumerism*. Carlisle: Paternoster, 135-51.

Senn, Frank C. (1997). *Christian Liturgy: Catholic and Evangelical*. Minneapolis: Fortress Press.

Shaw, M. E. (1961). 'Group Dynamics.' *Annual Review of Psychology* 12/1: 129-56.

Shinn, Larry D. (1992). 'Cult Conversions and the Courts: Some Ethical Issues in Academic Expert Testimony.' *Sociological Analysis* 53/3 (Fall): 273-85.

Shorter, Aylward (1994). *Evangelization and Culture*. London: Geoffrey Chapman.

Smail, Tom (1988). *The Giving Gift*. London: Hodder & Stoughton.

— (1998). *Once and For All: A Confession of the Cross*. London: Darton, Longman and Todd.

— (2003). 'The Ethics of Exile and the Rhythm of Resurrection.' In A. Walker and K. J. Aune (eds), *On Revival: A Critical Examination*. Cumbria: Paternoster, 57-68.

Smail, Tom, Walker, Andrew and Wright, Nigel (1995). *Charismatic Renewal: The Search for a Theology*. London: SPCK.

Smart, Barry (1993). *Postmodernity*. London: Routledge.
Smith, John (1978). 'The Concept of Conversion.' In W. Conn (ed.), *Conversion: Perspectives on Personal and Social Transformation*. New York: Alba House, 51-61.
Snow, David and Machalek, Richard (1983). 'The Convert as a Social Type.' In R. Collins (ed.), *Sociological Theory*. San Francisco: Jossey-Bass, 259-89.
— (1984). 'The Sociology of Conversion.' *Annual Review of Sociology* 10: 167-90.
Spradley, James P. (1980). *Participant Observation*. London Holt, Rinehart and Winston.
Stackhouse, Ian (2003a). 'Revivalism, Faddism and the Gospel.' In A. Walker and K. J. Aune (eds), *On Revival: A Critical Examination*. Cumbria: Paternoster, 239-51.
— (2004). *The Gospel-Driven Church: Retrieving Classical Ministry for Contemporary Revivalism*. Bletchley: Paternoster.
Stackhouse, John (ed.) (2003b). *Evangelical Ecclesiology: Reality or Illusion?* Grand Rapids, Mich.: Baker Academic.
Stark, R. and Bainbridge, W. S. (1987). *A Theory of Religion*. New York: Peter Lang.
Stark, Rodney (1965). 'Psychopathology and Religious Commitment.' *Review of Religious Research* 12: 165-76.
— (1996). *The Rise of Christianity*. Princeton: Princeton University Press.
Stark, Rodney and Bainbridge, William. (1980). 'Networks of Faith: Interpersonal Bonds and Recruitment to Cults and Sects.' *American Journal of Sociology* 85/6 (May): 1376-95.
Stendahl, Krister (1977). *Paul Among Jews and Gentiles*. London: SCM Press.
Steven, James H. S. (2002). *Worship in the Spirit: Charismatic Worship in the Church of England*. Carlisle: Paternoster.
Stevenson, J. (ed.) (1987). *A New Eusebius: Documents Illustrating the History of the Church to AD 337*. Revised by W. H. C. Frend. London: SPCK. Original publication, 1957.
Stibbe, Mark (1995). *Times of Refreshing: A Practical Theology of Revival for Today*. London: Marshall Pickering.
Storkey, Alan (2000). 'Postmodernism is Consumption.' In C. Bartholomew and T. Moritz (eds), *Christ and Consumerism*. Carlisle: Paternoster, 100-17.
Stott, John. (1982). *I Believe in Preaching*. London: Hodder & Stoughton.
— (1996). *The Cross of Christ*. Reprinted ed. Leicester: IVP. Original publication 1986.
Straus, Roger A. (1979). 'Religious Conversion as a Personal and Collective Accomplishment.' *Sociological Analysis* 40 (Summer): 158-65.
Strauss, Anselm L. and Corbin, Juliet (1998). *Basics of Qualitative Research: Techniques and Procedures for Developing Grounded Theory*. London: Sage.
Stringer, Martin D. (1999). *On the Perception of Worship: The Ethnography of Worship in Four Christian Congregations in Manchester*. Birmingham: University of Birmingham Press.
Suchman, Mark (1992). 'Analyzing the Determinants of Everyday Conversion.' *Sociological Analysis* 53/S: S15-S33.
Taylor, Charles (1992). *Sources of the Self*. Cambridge: Cambridge University Press.
Thiemann, Ronald F. (1985). *Revelation and Theology*. Notre Dame, Indiana: University of Notre Dame Press.
Thiselton, Anthony C. (1992). *New Horizons in Hermeneutics*. London: HarperCollins.
Thomas, Viv (2002). *Leading with Trinity: An Exploration of Evangelical Christian Leaders' Decision-Making in the Light of Polycentric-Symmetrical Trinitarian Life*.

PhD thesis, University of London.

Tice, Rico and Cooper, B. (2001). *Christianity Explored*. Carlisle: Paternoster.

Tillich, Paul (1964). *Systematic Theology Vol III*. Herts: James Nisbet.

Tomlin, Graham (2002). *The Provocative Church*. London: SPCK.

Tourish, Dennis and Pinnington, Ashly (2002). 'Transformational Leadership, Corporate Cultism and the Spirituality Paradigm: An Unholy Trinity in the Workplace?' *Human Relations* 55/2 (1 February): 147-72.

Travis, Stephen H. (1994). 'Christ as Bearer of Divine Judgment in Paul's Thought About the Atonement.' In J. Green and M. Turner (eds), *Jesus of Nazareth Lord and Christ*. Carlisle: Paternoster Press, 332-38.

Tuckman, Bruce W. (1965). 'Developmental Sequence in Small Groups.' *Psychological Bulletin* 63/6: 384-99.

Tuckman, Bruce W. and Jensen, Mary A. (1977). 'Stages of Small Group Development Revised.' *Group and Organisational Studies* 1: 419-27.

Turner, Max (1996a). *The Holy Spirit and Spiritual Gifts: Then and Now*. Carlisle: Paternoster Press.

— (1996b). *Power From on High, The Spirit in Israel's Restoration and Witness in Luke-Acts*. Sheffield: Sheffield Academic Press.

Ullman, Chana (1982). 'Cognitive and Emotional Antecedents of Religious Conversion.' *Journal of Personality and Social Psychology* 43/1 (July): 183-92.

Urquhart, Colin (1974). *When the Spirit Comes*. London: Hodder & Stoughton.

Van Vugt, Mark, Jepson, Sarah F., Hart, Claire M. and De Cremer, David. (2004). 'Autocratic Leadership in Social Dilemmas: A Threat to Group Stability.' *Journal of Experimental Social Psychology* 40/1: 1-13.

Vanhoozer, Kevin J. (1998). *Is There a Meaning in This Text?* Grand Rapids, Mich.: Apollos.

Vernon, Mark (2006). *Science, Religion and the Meaning of Life*. Basingstoke, Hamps.: Palgrave Macmillan.

Volf, Miroslav. (1998). *After Our Likeness: The Church as the Image of the Trinity*. Grand Rapids: Eerdmans.

Wagner, C. Peter (1992). 'On the Cutting Edge of Mission Strategy.' In R. D. Winter and S. C. Hawthorne (eds), *Perspectives on the World Christian Movement*. Revised ed. Pasadena, Cal.: William Carey Library, D45-59.

Wainwright, Geoffrey (1997). *Worship With One Accord: Where Liturgy and Ecumenism Embrace*. Oxford: Oxford University Press.

Walker, Andrew (1983). 'Pentecostal Power: The "Charismatic Renewal Movement" and the Politics of Pentecostal Experience.' In E. Barker (ed.), *Of God's and Men*. Macon, Ga.: Mercer University Press, 89-108.

— (1987). *Enemy Territory: The Christian Struggle for the Modern World*. London: Hodder & Stoughton.

— (1989). *Restoring the Kingdom: The Radical Christianity of the House Church Movement*. London: Hodder and Stoughton.

— (1992). 'Sectarian Reactions: Pluralism and the Privatization of Religion.' In H. Willmer (ed.), *20/20 Visions: The Future of Christianity in Britain*. London: SPCK, 46-64.

— (1996). *Telling the Story*. London: SPCK.

— (2007). 'Deep Church as Paradosis: On Relating Scripture and Tradition.' In A. Walker and L. Bretherton (eds), *Remembering Our Future: Explorations in Deep*

Church. Milton Keynes: Paternoster Press, 59-80.

Walker, Andrew and Atherton, James S. (1971). 'An Easter Pentecostal Convention: A Successful Management of a Time of Blessing.' *Sociological Review* 19/3 (August): 367-87.

Walker, Andrew and Bretherton, Luke (eds) (2007). *Remembering Our Future: Explorations in Deep Church*. Milton Keynes: Paternoster Press.

Wallis, Jim (1986). *The Call to Conversion*. Herts: Lion Publishing.

Walls, Andrew (2002). *The Cross-Cultural Process in Christian History*. Edinburgh: T & T Clark.

Ward, Pete (1998). 'Alpha – The McDonaldization of Religion?' *Anvil* 15/4: 279-86.

— (2005). *Selling Worship: How What we Sing has Changed the Church*. Bletchley: Paternoster Press.

Ware, Kallistos (1996). *How Are We Saved?: The Understanding of Salvation in the Orthodox Tradition*. Minneapolis, Minn.: Light & Life.

— (1997). *The Orthodox Church*. New ed. London: Penguin. Original publication 1963.

Warner, Rob (2003). 'Ecstatic Spirituality and Entrepreneurial Revivalism: Reflections on the "Toronto Blessing".' In A. Walker and K. J. Aune (eds), *On Revival: A Critical Examination*. Cumbria: Paternoster, 221-38.

Warner, Robert (2006). *Fissured Resurgence: Developments in English Pan-Evangelicalism, 1966–2001*. PhD thesis, King's College, London.

Warren, Robert and Jackson, Bob (2001). *There Are Answers*. Abingdon: Springboard.

Watling, Tony (2005). '"Experiencing" Alpha: Finding and Embodying the Spirit and Being Transformed – Empowerment and Control in a ("Charismatic") Christian Worldview.' *Journal of Contemporary Religion* 20/1 (January): 91-108.

Watson, David and Jenkins, Simon (1983). *Jesus Then and Now*. Tring: Lion in association with Lella Productions.

Watts, Fraser, Nye, Rebecca and Savage, Sara (2002). *Psychology for Christian Ministry*. London: Routledge.

Weaver, J. Denny (2001). *The Nonviolent Atonement*. Grand Rapids, Mich.: Eerdmans.

Webber, Robert (2001). *Journey to Jesus: The Worship, Evangelism and Nurture Mission of the Church*. Nashville: Abingdon Press.

— (2003). *Ancient–Future Evangelism: Making Your Church a Faith-Forming Community*. Grand Rapids, Mich.: Baker Books.

Weber, Max (1964). *The Theory of Social and Economic Organisation*. Trans. A. M. Henderson and T. Parsons. London: Free Press. Original publication 1947.

Weiss, Johannes (1971). *Jesus' Proclamation of the Kingdom of God*. Trans. R. H. Hiers and D. L. Holland. London: S.C.M. Press. Original publication 1892.

White, Ralph and Lippitt, Ronald (1968). 'Leader Behaviour and Member Reaction in Three "Social Climates".' In D. Cartwright and A. Zander (eds), *Group Dynamics: Research and Theory*. 3rd ed. London: Tavistock, 318-35.

White, Reginald Ernest Oscar (1960). *The Biblical Doctrine of Initiation*. London: Hodder & Stoughton.

White, Vernon (1991). *Atonement and Incarnation*. Cambridge: Cambridge University Press.

Whyte, William Foote (1981). *Street Corner Society: The Social Structure of an Italian Slum*. 3rd ed. London: University of Chicago Press.

Williams, Malcolm (2000a). 'Interpretivism and Generalisation.' *Sociology* 34/2: 209-24.

Williams, Rowan (2000b). *On Christian Theology*. Oxford: Blackwell.

Wilson, Bryan (1970). *Religious Sects: A Sociological Study*. London: Weidenfeld and Nicolson.

— (1973). *Magic and the Millennium: A Sociological Study of Religious Movements of Protest Among Tribal and Third-World Peoples*. London: Heinemann.

— (1982). *Religion in Sociological Perspectives*. Oxford: Oxford University Press.

— (2003). 'Prediction and Prophecy in the Future of Religion.' In G. Davie, et al. (eds), *Predicting Religion: Christian, Secular, and Alternative Futures*. Aldershot, Hants: Ashgate, 64-73.

Wilson, Jonathan R. (2002). 'Clarifying Vision, Empowering Witness.' In J. Stackhouse (ed.), *What Does it Mean to be Saved?: Broadening Evangelical Horizons of Salvation*. Grand Rapids, Mich.: Baker Academic, 185-94.

Wimber, John (2001). *Power Evangelism*. London: Hodder & Stoughton. Original publication 1985.

Winter, Ralph D. and Hawthorne, Steven C. (eds). (1992). *Perspectives on the World Christian Movement*. Revised ed. Pasadena, Cal.: William Carey Library.

Wolcott, Harry F. (1999). *Ethnography: A Way of Seeing*. London: AltaMira.

Woodhead, Linda (ed.) (2001). *Peter Berger and the Study of Religion*. London: Routledge.

Wright, Andrew. (1998). *Discerning the Spirit: A Survey and Critique of Contemporary Spiritual Education in England and Wales*. Culham: Culham College Institute.

— (2004). *Religion, Education, and Post-Modernity*. London: Routledge/Falmer.

Wright, N. T. (1980). 'Justification: The Biblical Basis and its Relevance for Contemporary Evangelicalism.' In G. Reid (ed.), *The Great Acquittal: Justification by Faith and Current Christian Thought*. London: Collins, 13-37.

— (1988). 'Jesus.' In D. F. Wright, et al. (eds), *New Dictionary of Theology*. Leicester: IVP, 348-51.

— (1996). *Jesus and the Victory of God*. London: SPCK.

— (2000). *The Challenge of Jesus*. London: SPCK.

— (2003). *The Resurrection of the Son of God*. London: SPCK.

Wright, Nigel (1995). 'The Rise of the Prophetic.' In T. Smail, et al. (eds), *Charismatic Renewal: The Search for a Theology*. London: SPCK.

Yarnold, Edward (1977). *The Awe Inspiring Rites of Initiation*. Slough: St Paul's Publication.

Yukl, Gary (1999). 'An Evaluation of Conceptual Weaknesses in Transformational and Charismatic Leadership Theories.' *The Leadership Quarterly* 10/2: 285-305.

Zerubaevel, Eviatar (1997). *Social Mindscapes: An Invitation to Cognitive Sociology*. London: Harvard University Press.

Zimbardo, Philip G., Ebbesen, Ebbe B. and Maslach, Christina (1977). *Influencing Attitudes and Changing Behaviour: An Introduction to Method, Theory, and Applications of Social Control and Personal Power*. 2nd ed. London: Addison-Wesley.

Zizioulas, John D. (1985). *Being as Communion: Studies in Personhood and the Church*. Crestwood, N.Y.: St. Vladimir's Seminary Press.

Church Reports

(1991). *We Believe in the Holy Spirit*. London: Church House Publishing.

(1995). *On the Way: Towards an Integrated Approach to Christian Initiation*. London: Church House Publishing.

(1998a). *Common Worship: Initiation Services*. London: Church House Publishing.

(1998b). *The Nature and Purpose of the Church: A Stage on the Way to a Common Statement*. Faith and Order Paper 181. World Council of Churches.

(2005). *Contemporary Doctrine Classics from the Church of England*. London: Church House Publishing.

Pope Paul VI (1971). *General Directory for Catechesis*. Vatican: Documents of the Magisterium.

WCC. (1982). *Baptism, Eucharist, and Ministry*. Geneva: World Council of Churches.

Periodicals/Newspapers

Alpha News (2006). Vol. 40. London: Alpha International.

Alpha Annual Review (2007). London: Alpha International.

Alpha News (2008). Vol. 45. London: Alpha International.

Alpha News (2009). Vol. 46. London: Alpha International.

Appleyard, Brian (2001). 'Answering the Call of God and Gucci', *Sunday Times* (29 July).

Arguile, Roger (2002). 'Needed: Proper Nourishment', *Church Times*, Vol. 7273 (19 July).

Atik, Nilufer (2001). 'Geri's Christianity Conversion', *Daily Mail* (24 November).

Gill, A. A. (2001). 'Would You Want to Tuck Him In?', *Sunday Times* (5 August).

Grzyb, Jo Ellen (2004). 'You and Yours', *BBC Radio 4* (15 January).

HTB Focus (1994). 'A Mighty Wind from Toronto – The Word "Revival" is on Everyone's Lips', Vol. 12 (June). London: HTB.

HTB Annual Review (2008). London: HTB.

Marsden, Michael (2006). 'Alpha Male: Michael Marsden Goes in Search of the Holy Spirit', *New Humanist*, (7 July).

Rose, Hilary (2004). 'Middle-Class Heaven?' *The Times Magazine* (3 July).

Ronson, Jon (2000). 'Catch Me If You Can', *The Guardian* (21 October).

Hymn Books

(1990). Mission Praise. London: Marshall Pickering.

(1998). Songs of Fellowship. Eastbourne: Kingsway Publications.

(2001). Survivor Songbook No.1. Eastbourne: Kingsway.

General Index